D1545654

Shadows

of

Revolution

Books by David A. Bell

Lawyers and Citizens: The Making of a Political Elite in Old Regime France, Oxford University Press, 1994.

The Cult of the Nation in France: Inventing Nationalism, 1680–1800, Harvard University Press, 2001.

The First Total War: Napoleon's Europe and the Birth of Warfare as We Know It, Houghton Mifflin, 2007.

Napoleon: A Concise Biography, Oxford University Press, 2015.

SHADOWS
OF
REVOLUTION

REFLECTIONS ON FRANCE,
PAST AND PRESENT

DAVID A. BELL

OXFORD
UNIVERSITY PRESS

OXFORD
UNIVERSITY PRESS

Oxford University Press is a department of the University of Oxford. It furthers
the University's objective of excellence in research, scholarship, and education
by publishing worldwide. Oxford is a registered trade mark of Oxford University
Press in the UK and certain other countries.

Published in the United States of America by Oxford University Press
198 Madison Avenue, New York, NY 10016, United States of America

Library of Congress Cataloging-in-Publication Data
Bell, David Avrom.
Shadows of revolution : reflections on France, past and present
/ David A. Bell.
pages cm
Includes bibliographical references and index.
ISBN 978-0-19-026268-6 (hardback : acid-free paper)
1. France—History. 2. France—Politics and government.
3. France—History—Revolution, 1789–1799—Influence.
4. National characteristics, French—History.
5. Politics and culture—France—History.
6. France—Social conditions.   I. Title.
DC38.B39 2016
944—dc23   2015011667

1 3 5 7 9 8 6 4 2
Printed in the United States of America
on acid-free paper

In memory of Paul Lemerle, and for his family

CONTENTS

———◦◦◦———

PART VII. PARALLELS: PAST AND PRESENT

SHADOWS

OF

REVOLUTION

The entrance to the École Normale Supérieure, Paris. On the round window are written the words: "By Decree of the Convention, 9 Brumaire, Year III." Photo by Patrick Luiz Sullivan de Oliveira.

INTRODUCTION: 45, RUE D'ULM

THE ESSAYS IN THIS BOOK were written over more than a quarter of a century. For the most part, I wrote them in response to a particular book or political event, rather than to be parts of a larger project. But at the same time, in each one I drew on an engagement with France and its history that has consumed me through all of my adult life, and in the course of which I have developed some fairly consistent ideas and points of view. The essays gave me the chance to refine and develop those ideas and points of view. I hope the reader will have no trouble recognizing what binds this book together, but in this Introduction I would like to offer some more explicit thoughts about the book's common themes and how I came to them.

I can date the beginnings of my serious engagement with French history very specifically: to September 1983, when I arrived in Paris to spend a year as a visiting student at the École Normale Supérieure. I was then twenty-one years old, fresh out of college, and excited and apprehensive in equal measure. I knew the École's impressive reputation as an institution of higher learning. Its alumni roll could be mistaken for a hall of fame of French thinkers, from Louis Pasteur and Émile Durkheim to Jean-Paul Sartre, Raymond Aron, Michel Foucault, Pierre Bourdieu, and Jacques Derrida. I felt comfortable in France, where I had spent two summers and made close friends. I had learned French well. Yet I had never set foot in the École's venerable buildings at 45, rue d'Ulm in the fifth arrondissement and had not met a single student or faculty member.

My initial impressions of the place did not do much to relieve my apprehension. The École bears very little resemblance to the American college campuses I had known, consisting as it does of a series of nondescript large buildings crammed together around a few narrow streets in the heart of the Left Bank. Its public spaces seemed mostly to consist of endless, gloomy corridors, with lights on timers that always seemed to switch off at the wrong moment, leaving me fumbling in the dark. The dorm rooms were tiny and shabby, the bathrooms equipped only with *toilettes turques*—flushable holes in the floor (renovations have since improved matters somewhat). In lieu of anything resembling a printed catalogue, course offerings were announced on small handwritten notices pinned to bulletin boards. The French students I met in my first few days seemed singularly uninterested in getting to know a well-meaning if somewhat clueless American visitor.

Yet over the following weeks and months, my mood improved. I found and bonded with other foreign students, and started to become friends with French students as well. A kindly history tutor, Philippe Boutry, helped me design a program of study for the year. My first visit to the street market in the nearby rue Mouffetard, where the smells wafting from the cheese shops left me pleasurably dizzy with hunger, convinced me that the École's location more than made up for its subpar amenities (over the next year I gained fifteen pounds and did not regret a single ounce of them). I bought a monthly Metro pass and zoomed around the city to my heart's content, feeling very Parisian.

I also started to feel a powerful new connection to the French past. I had come to the École to study history, and everywhere in Paris history seemed to press itself on me. In one of my courses, the instructor, Boutry himself, spent a lecture describing Paris's medieval fortifications, and then casually remarked to the students that we should go out the door, and turn right, left, then right again. After class I did so, and there, spilling onto the sidewalk of the rue Clovis, was a ruined section of the stone city wall built by King Philippe Auguste nearly eight centuries earlier. A few days later, a classmate took me down the old Roman road that was the rue Saint-Jacques to a sight most visitors to Paris never see: a real

Roman arena, the "Arènes de Lutèce," nearly two thousand years old. Another short expedition, just a couple of stops away on the Metro, led to the eeriest tourist attraction Paris has to offer: the catacombs. In a series of dark tunnels, far below the surface of the city, lie the bones of literally millions of Parisians, exhumed in the nineteenth century from older mass graves and carefully stacked in neat, macabre piles: femurs and ribs and vertebrae, and rows on rows of sightless staring skulls.

Two particular periods of the French past came to fascinate me. First, and foremost, there was the French Revolution. Its traces, too, were un-avoidable. Just down the street from the École stands the gloomy bulk of the Panthéon, a former church which the Revolution had converted into a shrine to the "great men of the fatherland." A couple of miles away, across the Seine, lay the Place de la Bastille, a vast, traffic-clogged square on the site of the great fortress whose fall to Parisian crowds marked the Revolution's first great triumph. Soon after I started at the École, French labor unions staged one of their regular massive rallies on the square, and I ran into a group of union members on a nearby street, singing loudly and off-key a song whose refrain ended with the words "à la Bastille," as if they were back in 1789. The great Right Bank axis that cut west across the city from the Bastille featured one Revolutionary site after another. There was the Palais Royal, where Camille Desmoulins had leapt onto a café table in July 1789 and rallied the crowds that would soon march to the Bastille. There was the Church of Saint-Roch, near where a young officer named Napoleon Bonaparte gained political favor in 1795 by suppressing royalist crowds with a deadly "whiff of grapeshot" (I was told, mistakenly as it turned out, that scars on the church wall came from the barrage). There was the Place de la Concorde, once called the Place de la Révolution, where on January 21, 1793, the heavy blade of the guillotine severed King Louis XVI's head from his body. Nor could the Revolution be escaped at the École itself. Painted in large gold letters above its main entrance is an inscription marking its founding: "By Decree of the Convention, 9 Brumaire, Year III." The Convention was the body that had ruled France during the most radical phase of the Revolution. The date came from the revolutionary calendar that started time anew from the birth of the French Republic. (It gave the months poetic names drawn from nature—"Brumaire" is the season of fog.) Both the Convention and the revolutionary calendar it had decreed vanished long ago, but you would not know it from the inscription—and that was the point (the École, traditionally a bastion of staunch republicanism, professes a loyalty to the revolutionary heritage).

The second period of French history that fascinated me was World War II and the collaborationist regime of Vichy. As a Jew, I could not forget that just forty years earlier, my coreligionists in France had been subject to harsh legal discrimination and public vilification, forced to wear the yellow star. Nearly a quarter of them had died in Nazi extermination camps. Worse, it had been a French government initially considered legitimate by a large majority of the French population that had, on its own initiative, implemented the anti-Semitic policies and rounded up Jews for deportation to an almost certain death. In stark contrast to the rest of the country's history, however, the Vichy years seemed to have left strangely few traces that I could see in Paris. There was as yet no Holocaust monument in the city. (The memorial to wartime deportations near Notre Dame made no specific reference to Jewish victims.) In the Jewish neighborhood of the Marais, where I often went with friends, a small plaque in front of a former Jewish school read: "165 Jewish children from this school, deported to Germany during the Second World War, were exterminated in the Nazi camps. Do not forget!" Nearly all the other public commemorations of the war years that I saw honored Parisians who had died in the August 1944 uprising against the Germans, as the Allied armies approached the city. I attended lectures at the Sorbonne by the eminent Napoleon specialist Jean Tulard, unaware that his father, André, had been the police official responsible for drawing up lists of Jews ahead of the infamous roundups of 1942.

During my year at the École, the Revolution took up much more of my time than Vichy. I focused on it in the courses I attended and read voraciously. I discovered Jules Michelet's gorgeously lyrical history of the events, and thrilled to his description of the Night of August 4, 1789, when the revolutionary National Assembly voted to abolish inherited privileges: "There vanished, that night, the immense and toilsome dream of a thousand years of the Middle Ages. The dawn that would soon break was the dawn of liberty." Each week, I walked over to the Boulevard Raspail, where, at the École des Hautes Études, the historian François Furet would elaborate on his controversial interpretation of the Revolution (on which I have much to say in the pages that follow). I read his book

Penser la Révolution française, covering the pages with enthusiastic scrawls as I struggled through his dense prose.

A highlight of the year came when Philippe Boutry invited me to take part in a collaborative research project on the Revolution, a project that sent me, for the first time, into the French archives. Although my assignment was simply to count the number of radical political "clubs" that had sprung up during the Revolution in the former department of the Seine, I spent many more hours simply reading through their records, not quite able to believe that I was holding two-hundred-year-old documents in my hands, composed by those actually involved. And as I read, there came a moment of particular delight. Five years earlier, during high school, I had spent several weeks living with a French family in the Parisian suburb of L'Isle Adam. They had taken me to one of the local churches, where a leaflet explained that its expensive gold decorations had been stripped away in 1793 to raise money for the French revolutionary armies. Now, in the archives, I came across the deliberations of the area's Jacobin Society and read the minutes of the decision to confiscate the decorations.

The reasons I was drawn to the Revolution were partly romantic ones. The events were astounding, inspiring, unbelievably dramatic, and sometimes fascinatingly horrific. So much happened in so short a time that the great writer Chateaubriand later claimed that many centuries had crammed themselves into a single quarter century. The personalities were no less absorbing: the tortured, repressed Maximilien Robespierre; the flamboyant, careless, but ultimately heroic Georges Danton; the fanatically determined Jean-Paul Marat. During my year at the École, the Polish director Andrzej Wajda released his film about the Revolution, *Danton*. In France itself he was widely attacked for reading the French past through the lens of the Polish present, likening the Reign of Terror to Communist totalitarianism, and Danton to Lech Wałęsa. But the lead performances, by Gérard Depardieu as Danton and Wojciech Pszoniak as Robespierre, were searing and unforgettable.

But along with the romantic reasons were intellectual ones, related to the controversies that the Revolution continued to inspire. These controversies spilled far outside the bounds of the academy. They resonated deeply in French public life, giving history a sense of vitality and importance that I had never felt while studying the subject in college. I knew, from college, that the Revolution had remained a key dividing line in French politics until as late as the 1930s, its heirs on the left facing off against its enemies on the right. Vichy had explicitly committed itself to extirpating the heritage of the Revolution, starting with the abolition of the Republic itself (replaced by the "French State" of Marshal Philippe Pétain). I had assumed, however, that with the discrediting of the traditional right, after Vichy, the Revolution had faded from public life. In fact, it was now making something of a public comeback, thanks above all to François Furet. In his books and essays he claimed, somewhat disingenuously, that the time for quarrels had passed. He even titled his most famous essay "The Revolution Is Over." Yet the same essay argued that the Revolution, almost from the start, followed a pathological course that made it impossible for France to develop a stable political culture. A "Jacobin" impulse toward collectivism and homogeneity continued to prevail long after the Jacobins themselves had disappeared, Furet maintained. Not surprisingly, his work attracted ferocious criticism, and more than once I would hear other lecturers on the Revolution denounce what I had heard him say in his seminar just the week before.

Furet was writing with an eye to contemporary French politics, a subject that had little attraction for me: it seemed an affair of incessant squabbling and regular paralysis (*plus ça change...*). But reading the historians' debates made it clear that the Revolution's importance extended far beyond contemporary French politics. More than any other single set of events, it served as the most important political laboratory the world had ever known—a laboratory in which, in the space of less than a decade, many of the modern world's key political ideas and practices first took shape. At the start of the year 1789, France had been an absolute monarchy, under a king who claimed the mantle of divine right, and who combined supreme executive, legislative, and judicial functions in his own person. Within two years, the Revolution transformed it into a constitutional monarchy. A year later, the king was gone, and the country had become a democratic republic in which every adult male had the right to vote. This republic—as it was called—itself quickly degenerated into an unstable ideological dictatorship, which was then overthrown in its turn, paving the way for a corrupt and limited democracy, subject to repeated coups d'état. And in the final coup, in 1799, Napoleon Bonaparte took power, establishing a military-backed authoritarian regime. In short, this decade in France produced a series of scripts that much of the world has been following, in one sense or another, ever since. Put another way, billions of people in the centuries since 1789, including many who never even heard of the French Revolution, have lived under its shadow.

This shadow has certainly never vanished from my life. As soon as I returned to the United States in the fall of 1984 I eagerly applied to graduate school in French history. And in the thirty years since, my professional life has centered on the Revolution. I wrote a Ph.D. dissertation—and first book—about how members of the legal profession fomented dissent against the French monarchy, thereby helping to bring the Revolution about. My second book looked at the birth of nationalism in France during the eighteenth century and revolutionary period. My third made the argument that the revolutionary and Napoleonic wars amounted to "the first total war," and arose out of a deep shift in the way Western societies understood war. I have also written a short study of Napoleon Bonaparte's "revolutionary life," and am now working on a book about charismatic authority in the age of revolutions.

My teaching, too, has revolved around the French Revolution and on the way it speaks to the present. Yet I have also never been able to stop thinking about Vichy and the long shadows it has cast. One reason was the occasional anti-Semitism I encountered in France—minor incidents, but still without parallel to anything I ever experienced in the United States, and inevitably triggering thoughts about the past. One day while in Paris to do dissertation research, I went for a run around the Luxembourg Gardens, wearing a T-shirt with Hebrew lettering. As I swung past the Law Faculty on the rue d'Assas, a hotbed of far right politics, a group of students saw me and started shouting "sale Juif!"— "dirty Jew." That same year, I went to see an elderly Frenchman in the hope he would allow me to study papers he possessed belonging to one of his ancestors, a prominent eighteenth-century barrister. When we met, he quizzed me about my ancestry, asking where my grandparents had come to America from. It was obvious what he wanted to know. "They were Polish Jews," I told him. He frowned, said a courteous good-bye, and the next day sent me a polite note regretting that he did not feel able to show me the papers. His ancestor, ironically, had been one of the great champions of religious freedom of the eighteenth century. A few years later, in a restaurant, the owner (a Greek immigrant) came over to the table, commented on my "Jewish looks" ("vous avez l'air israélite"), told me he loved National Front leader Jean-Marie Le Pen, and then went on an anti-Semitic tirade. My dining companion and I rushed out, deeply shaken. I spent the next day thinking that every passerby in the street was looking at me, thinking "Juif, Juif, Juif." These were the years when Le Pen was becoming infamous for his anti-Semitic comments, including calling the gas chambers a "detail" in the history of World War II. It was hard not to feel that the same bigotry that had produced Vichy had never quite disappeared from France.

I have struggled not to exaggerate these incidents and not to exaggerate Vichy's importance in the broader sweep of French history. When I lecture on French Jewry, I generally start by observing that France gave Jews full civil rights earlier than any other Western country. By the late nineteenth century, French Jews were encountering fewer obstacles to professional advancement—including in the universities—than Jews anywhere else in the world, including the United States. For all the distress the late nineteenth-century Dreyfus Affair caused French Jewry, the good side won. Jewish army captain Alfred Dreyfus, convicted on treason charges out of sheer anti-Semitic prejudice, eventually walked free, fully exonerated. The "anti-Dreyfusards" produced floods of hateful rhetoric, but committed relatively little physical violence against Jews. Even Vichy would never have taken place without the German occupation. Today, a new wave of anti-Semitism has swept over certain areas of France, pushing an increasing number of French Jews to emigrate. But it is an anti-Semitism mostly confined to poor Muslim communities and linked to the Israel-Palestinian troubles far more than to the history of France itself. France is not an anti-Semitic country. And yet, as with the Revolution, the shadows of Vichy still loom over France.

I have never made Vichy a subject of my scholarly research, but I continue to read about it obsessively, both in history and in fiction. I have also followed, with fascination, the long and painful process by which the French have come to terms with it, including the creation of monuments to the Holocaust, exhibitions devoted to Vichy and the fate of the French Jews, and the historic speech that President Jacques Chirac made in 1995, recognizing French responsibility for the deportation of Jews to the camps. Although the events of the war have now largely slipped below the horizon of living memory, the French public today has a far greater awareness of them than it did thirty years ago.

As the contents of this book will make clear, Vichy had many connections to the Revolution. Vichy's leaders called their program the "National Revolution" and saw their own regime as a political laboratory of sorts. The Revolution of 1789 obsessed them, as it had obsessed generations of French conservatives before them, and they tried assiduously to eliminate its traces from French life. Of course, they did not see their program as a literal restoration of the pre-1789 Old Regime, but they spoke of a return to what they saw as its spirit, hoping to turn France into an "organic" community, limited by race and organized along "corporatist" lines. In a different vein, historians have recently emphasized that far more extensive continuity existed between Vichy and the regimes that preceded and followed it than anyone at the time or immediately afterward wanted to admit. The scaffolding of the contemporary French state contains more than a little Vichy-era timber.

But Vichy was not just a political laboratory—it was also a moral drama of the first order. This drama did not owe its startlingly piercing nature to any unique criminality or murderousness on the part of Marshal Philippe Pétain's regime. Its crimes were dwarfed by those of Hitler's Germany, Stalin's USSR, Mao's China, or Pol Pot's Cambodia, and even today Vichy finds defenders in France. The French Jewish writer Éric Zemmour spurred one recent controversy in a best-selling book by repeating the old extreme right argument that Vichy deserved the *thanks* of French Jews for "saving" all but a quarter of them from Hitler. And not everyone thinks that resistance represented the right choice for the French under the Occupation. In the essay "Everyday Choices," I examine a book in which an eminent British historian characterizes armed resistance to the Germans as reckless and foolhardy, while writing with considerable sympathy of local officials who collaborated with the occupiers.

Vichy's moral drama arose in fact precisely from the *difficulty* of the moral choices that it presented to the French. Consider the contrast with Nazi Germany. There, to those with eyes to see, the evil of the regime became evident very early on, but at the same time, the regime's monstrous power made that evil horrifically difficult to resist. Choosing active resistance in most cases amounted to an act of suicide. In France, things were very different, especially in the first years of the Occupation. On the one hand, Marshal Pétain, leader of the Vichy state, was no Nazi, but one of France's most revered national heroes, even if he had embraced far-right causes in the 1930s. In the despairing days of the summer of 1940, with the French armed forces smashed and the Wehrmacht marching triumphantly down the Champs-Élysées, most of the French felt that they had little choice but to make the best of the defeat, and hailed Pétain for stepping in to serve as their self-proclaimed "shield." It was all too easy to make the case for carrying on with life as usual. On the other hand, even in the areas of France directly occupied by the Germans, participation in the Resistance, while hugely dangerous, did not amount to suicide. It is for these reasons, I think, that so many talented writers and filmmakers have set their works in Vichy (for instance, Nobel Prize–winner Patrick Modiano, American novelist Alan Furst, and directors François Truffaut and Louis Malle). This is why Vichy remains such a favorite subject for historians, who often cannot resist posing the question, "What would *you* have done?"

Of course, no historians, however complete their knowledge, however acute their judgment, can ever truly respond to this last question. People may, arguably, possess some sort of innate moral sense, but far too much still depends on education, experience, and circumstance for anyone to venture more than a guess about how they would have acted in the past. Yet these limits should not stop us from using our imaginations to identify with people in the past, and they should not stop us from passing judgment where passing judgment is called for. These are things I have tried to do in the essays that follow.

These essays range over many centuries of French history, but, given my particular interests, center on the Revolution and Vichy (they appear largely as originally published, but with some light editing to remove repetitions). Those in Part I address long time spans—what the French call the *longue durée*—paying particular attention to how the French themselves have conceived of their national story and the role played in it by Jews, women, and peasants. The second part turns to the Old Regime and the Enlightenment, looking particularly at how the French monarchy reached a point of collapse and the role played in this collapse by Enlightenment ideas. Part III turns to the Revolution itself,

addressing human rights, women, language, war, and the overall significance of the events.

Napoleon Bonaparte—always an irresistible subject for historians—
is sometimes treated as the Revolution's heir, sometimes as its grave-
digger, and sometimes as a combination of the two. But no one doubts
that the Revolution made him possible, and that under his rule, much
of the Revolution's intense political experimentation spread throughout
the European continent, most often, admittedly, at the point of a bay-
onet. Part IV looks at Napoleon, as a military leader, political leader,
writer, patron of the arts, and finally continuing symbol of the Revolution
in the nineteenth century, in France, and beyond.

The essays in the fifth part, on the nineteenth century, treat a variety
of themes, including the great writer Victor Hugo and his relation to
Napoleon. Several of these essays look in different ways at the development of the French ultra-Right and French anti-Semitism, and therefore
to the forces that ruled under Vichy. The sixth part then moves on
to Vichy itself, concentrating on particular individuals and the moral
choices they made.

The final part of the book consists of short essays that offer parallels
between the era of the French Revolution and our own time. Written
over a period of more than a quarter of a century, they speak to issues as
diverse as the collapse of the Soviet Union, the massive French riots of
2005, the Iraq War, and the Arab Spring. They explore the ways that political and cultural patterns that were first set in the age of revolutions,
and challenged so dangerously in the twentieth century, continue to resonate powerfully, not just in France but throughout the world. They
bring out more explicitly the connections between past and present that
I hope readers will also glimpse in the earlier essays. The patterns set so
long ago do not imprison us, but we cannot ignore them. We still live,
very much, under their shadows, as I realized so powerfully during the
year I lived at 45, rue d'Ulm.

The book ends with a short coda discussing some of the most important dilemmas France faces today.

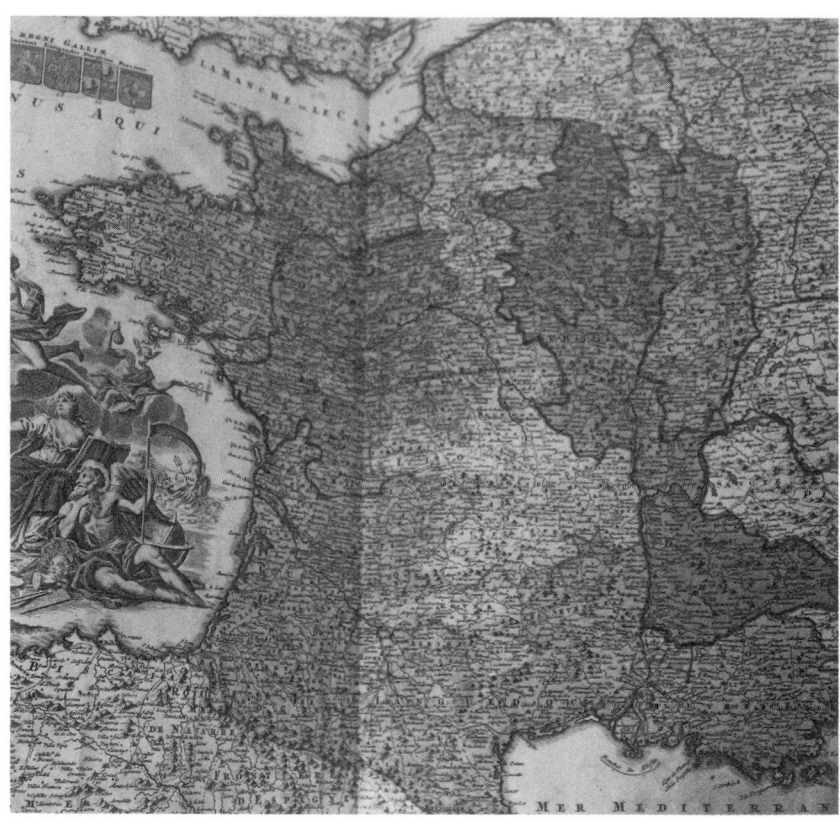

Map of France from the 1700 atlas by Alexis-Hubert Jaillot, showing the country's traditional provinces. Courtesy of Firestone Library, Princeton University.

Part I

THE "LONGUE DURÉE"

———————◁◇◇◁————————

Nations used to be thought of as individuals writ large. Historians wrote accounts of "national destiny" that spanned many centuries, spoke of a nation's birth and maturation (and possible degeneration), and generalized wildly about "national character." France's greatest Romantic historian, Jules Michelet (1798–1874) wrote such histories, and described his homeland as an object of powerful longing, a woman who disappointed again and again yet remained his beloved. "It is you that I beg for help, o my noble country," he wrote in his private journal, asking it to fill the void that "extinguished Christianity" had left in the world.

Today's historians mostly dismiss such attitudes as romantic illusions. They recognize that nations are immensely complex and mutable human and geographic assemblages that defy easily generalization. They treat works like Michelet's as stories that help to bind nations into "imagined communities" but at the same time exclude many events and people from these communities. As the nineteenth-century French thinker Ernest Renan famously remarked, nations are defined both by what they collectively remember and by what they collectively forget. Today, historians are more likely to generalize about these processes of remembering and forgetting than they are to generalize about nations themselves. They are more likely to challenge the primacy of national borders, and to stress the transnational, even global processes that flow in and around nations than they are to posit any sort of national "essence." Simple narratives of national history are mostly relegated to textbooks.

Nonetheless, more ambitious works do continue to appear that address long stretches of national history, and raise the question of how to characterize the continuities that emerge. The following four essays all deal with the *longue durée*—spans of many centuries. They take a somewhat jaundiced view of attempts to highlight a single national story, especially when the attempt emerges, improbably, from an explicitly postmodern analytical framework. They pay particular attention to the experiences of groups often marginalized in the national story—Jews and women, above all—but warn against trying to go too far in restoring the supposedly marginalized to the center.

I

Paris Blues: History and the French State

DURING THE YEAR I SPENT *at the École Normale in 1983–1984, friends there often told me that the French Ministry of Education had more people reporting to it than any other organization in Europe except for the Red Army. The quip (which, as far as I can tell, was true) highlighted the huge weight the state continues to have in French life in general, and in French education in particular. The vast majority of French educators at all levels are civil servants,* fonctionnaires. *The students at the École are themselves salaried* fonctionnaires *who owe the state a term of service after graduation (like cadets at American military academies). It is therefore often rather difficult for French historians (who include a very high proportion of* normaliens*) to imagine a country in which the state did not have such influence. Since the 1960s, various strands of postmodern thought have helped to make the best French historians strongly suspicious of "metanarratives" that ascribe sweeping meanings to historical change. But as the following essay suggests, when it comes to the history of France itself, the temptation to treat the*

Book under review: Pierre Nora, ed., *Realms of Memory: The Construction of the French Past*, vol. 1 (Columbia University Press, 1996). Essay originally published in *The New Republic*, September 1, 1997.

French state as a living actor of sorts that deliberately forged the nation can still be almost impossible to evade.

———————

The original French edition of Pierre Nora's *Realms of Memory*, which appeared in three installments during the presidency of François Mitterrand (1981–1995), was the intellectual equivalent of the period's monumental public architecture. With 150 separate articles spread over seven volumes, totaling close to six thousand pages, and weighing nearly twenty pounds, it was monumental in scale. Its prestigious list of contributors made it something of a monument to contemporary French historical studies. And its final installment, like I. M. Pei's pyramid, was something of a media sensation. *Les Lieux de mémoire*, or "the sites of memory," was the most prominent French intellectual accomplishment of the Mitterrand years, and perhaps the most important one.

And yet this work received little attention in America when it began to appear, and nothing to compare with the reception that greeted important works of French thought in earlier decades. Why? Certainly not for any obvious lack of quality. Like many of Mitterrand's monuments, *Les Lieux de mémoire* had its share of embarrassments, but the essays selected for inclusion in the first English translation (roughly one-third of the total) were the high-carat jewels of the project and some of the best French historical writing produced in the twentieth century. And, far from losing anything in translation, some of the essays gained considerably more lucidity than they had in the original French. (Arthur Goldhammer deserves a medal for putting into clear English the lucubrations of Marcel Gauchet, whose brilliance is matched only by his opacity.)

Perhaps the lack of attention was owed to the project's somewhat insular goal: to explore France's memory of itself. Yet there was a time, not too long ago, when France gazed fixedly at its own navel, and the rest of the world gazed with it. But for some time this has no longer been the case. And this fact testifies to what is, in a way, *Realms of Memory*'s real subject: the decline of France.

Pierre Nora did not present the project in this way. His beautiful introductory essay, "Between Memory and History," addressed not only things French but also the contemporary Western mania for commemoration of things past, in which every year brings more monuments and museums and well-celebrated anniversaries. (One year the Marshall Plan and Watergate, the next, the Berlin airlift and the Edict of Nantes...) Nora interpreted this mania as the by-product of a particular moment of historical transition. Modern societies, he argued, have lost the shared sense of tradition, the public memory that once bound past and present together through a living sinew of consciousness, so that centuries-old victories and defeats seemed as viscerally "real" as what had happened the previous day. Yet neither have modern societies developed a fully "historical" consciousness that treats all past events as wholly disconnected from the present.

Their citizens still long, nostalgically, for the comfort that the older sort of memory provided, and attempt as best they can to recreate it by investing specific sites (the *lieux* of the French title) with particular mnemonic significance. These sites of memory are not necessarily physical ones. They can be conceptual, even whimsically so. Along with the Louvre, the Eiffel Tower, the Panthéon, and other perforations of the Parisian skyline, Nora's original French sites of memory also included the colors of the French flag, the centenary of the French Revolution, the painter's landscape, the "genius of the French language," and even "visits to great writers."

The goal of *Realms of Memory* was not to consecrate these sites of memory by anointing them with its industrial-strength scholarship. If anything, Nora ostensibly aimed to subvert them, and the mania for commemoration in general, by exploring the fallible and capricious nature of collective memory itself. Nora advised his authors not simply to describe the sites, but to peel away the successive layers of meaning that had accumulated around them. Their task was to expose the supposedly unambiguous, eternal icons of Frenchness as the contested products of continuous cultural reinvention. The project's presiding deity was not a grand Romantic apologist for things French like Jules Michelet but rather the original master of "genealogy," Friedrich Nietzsche. Consider Krzysztof Pomian's essay on France's ancestral peoples, the Gauls and the Franks, which leads off the first volume of the translation. Instead of simply summarizing the current state of historical knowledge, Pomian showed skillfully how such historical knowledge twisted and changed over the centuries. Pomian was no relativist, denying all possibility of ascertaining historical truth. He wrote with real respect for factual evidence, and for the methodological advances of the nineteenth and twentieth centuries. Yet his essay also revealed how, for generation after generation, the antiquity of the French nation served as a tablet into which historians chiseled the obsessions of their day.

Thus royalist writers of the sixteenth century, desperate for French Catholics and Protestants to unite against the Habsburgs and the Vatican, tended to depict Franks and Gauls as allies against a predatory Roman Empire. Eighteenth-century aristocratic historians, by contrast, exalted the Franks—their own supposed forefathers—as proud warriors who had subdued brutish peasant Gauls and thereby won the right to dominate their commoner descendants for all eternity. Nineteenth-century bourgeois turned this story upside down, making the Gauls the ancestors of a heroic middle class that would eventually revolt against unjust noble (Frankish) privileges. Gallic antiquity remained political fodder as late as the 1940s, when Vichy propagandists argued that just as wise Gauls had once accepted the tutelage of the larger Roman Empire, so France should integrate itself willingly into the new Nazi Europe. Only in the last two generations have the French started to view their origins with more ironic detachment. Thus the cartoonists Goscinny and Uderzo could gleefully feed schoolbook pablum about "our ancestors the Gauls" into a blender of irony and absurdity until it yielded the late twentieth century's most familiar French (excuse me, Gaulish) figure, the comic strip hero Astérix.

Gérard de Puymège provided another fine example of Nora's method, in an essay on that archetypal French figure Nicolas Chauvin, the eponymous father of chauvinism. Dictionaries have long identified Chauvin as a real-life character, a superpatriotic old soldier in Napoleon's Grand Army, seventeen times wounded, who returned home after Waterloo to live out his days peacefully on his family farm. In an inspired piece of detective work, however, Puymège discovered that Chauvin never existed outside vaudeville theater, where a character of the name flourished in the 1820s and 1830s. Originally a bawdy young soldier obsessed with making love more than war, the character only slowly evolved into the crotchety veteran of legend. (The truth about Chauvin's origin makes the term "male chauvinist pig" more appropriate than Germaine Greer could have guessed when she coined it in 1970.) Only in 1840, apparently, did a functionary of the Ministry of War concoct a spurious biography for "Nicolas Chauvin" to fool a gullible man of letters.

After establishing this etymology, Puymège took a more serious tack, tracing the development of the mythical patriotic "farmer-soldier" that "Chauvin" embodied to caricatural excess, from its early nineteenth-century origins down to the present. In a nation in which the population remained heavily rural until World War II, it was this sort of quintessentially agricultural figure who most powerfully symbolized the French people as a whole; and as a result both left and right fought hard to appropriate him for their causes. (They also frequently paired him in their writings with an "inauthentically" French antihero: the Jewish cosmopolitan.) The farmer-soldier remained a familiar feature of French political culture until Vichy, which virtually deified him, and as a result the increasingly urban France of the postwar period repressed his memory along with that of Pétain.

To the extent that Pierre Nora simply wished to demonstrate the innovative critical method that Pomian, Puymège, and the other contributors employed, the focus on France itself in *Realms of Memory* was almost incidental. True, the French have devoted more time and energy to fashioning themselves as a nation than most other peoples, and have a peculiarly intense consciousness of their own history. Nora has even argued that, in France, the "practical ideologues" of national consciousness have traditionally been historians (in Germany, by contrast, philosophers filled the role). It is this claim that allowed him to raise what was essentially a work of historiography to the status of a new form of national history. (The key essays of *Les Lieux de mémoire* concerned individual historians and their works; Nora contributed not one but two on the emblematic Third Republic "educator of the nation," Ernest Lavisse.) Still, all nations have sites of memory, even if professional historians have not always contributed as much to their development. And so Nora's project has inspired imitations in Spain, the Low Countries, and central Europe, with Italy, Germany, and Israel possibly to follow. No one has yet proposed an American version, but the possible "sites" are endless, from Plymouth Rock to Ellis Island, the Alamo to Bunker Hill, Webster's dictionary to Walt Disney.

Yet something else was going on in *Realms of Memory*, something less critical and more devotional—and more specifically French. It was not evident in all the chapters. But while the authors never acknowledged the fact, they clearly found some *lieux* more memorable than others. It was one thing to write about matters such as the Gauls, or the convent of Port Royal (home of the Jansenist Catholic tradition and the subject of a fine essay by Catherine Maire) or even the court of Louis XIV (whose continued relevance to French politics is underlined by Jacques Revel). These *lieux* provoke few quarrels in France; few people have any personal stake in them. The same cannot be said, however, of the great institutions of French government and French culture: I refer to the *grandes écoles* (the elite centers of higher education), the Académie Française, the Louvre, the Republic itself.

These institutions shaped, rewarded, and in one way or another employed nearly all the contributors to *Realms of Memory*. Many of these men and women, it is worth noting, were not merely public intellectuals beyond the wildest dreams of Americans who aspire to this title; they could practically be called official intellectuals. Nora himself taught at the elite graduate school founded by Fernand Braudel, edited *Le Débat*, France's leading political magazine, and was one of the powers-that-be at Gallimard, the country's leading publishing house—a concentration of cultural power unthinkable on this side of the Atlantic. His brother Simon Nora used to direct the all-powerful National School of Administration, which produces nearly all of France's political leaders.

So it is perhaps not surprising that, when the essays in *Realms of Memory* touched on France's elite institutions, a striking change of tone took place. Irony softened into elegy, and genealogy into genuflection. Marc Fumaroli's long essay on the Académie Française, which was established in the seventeenth century to standardize and oversee the French language, exemplified this tendency. It was in many ways a fine piece of work. Fumaroli's prose was luscious, and his erudition enormous. His intuitions were consistently remarkable. Yet he did not exactly write on this subject with critical detachment. Fumaroli loved the Académie Française (which welcomed him into the ranks of its forty "immortals"). He saw it as the guarantor of a certain French idea of literature, in which fine writing not only has an explicitly public function, but actually furthers the cause of social unity.

The Académie, Fumaroli wrote, has always included not only writers of poetry and fiction but also critics, historians, statesmen, jurists, scientists.

The very act of gathering them together as guardians of the language serves notice that the different realms that they represent must converse with each other, and not become bastions of narrow, specialized knowledge. By the same token, the Académie also helps to protect French literature itself from turning inward, becoming "gnostic" and overspecialized and unintelligible to a broad public. Fumaroli went so far as to suggest that by providing a central point of unity for French culture, the Académie preserves something of the unifying spirit of the French monarchy, which founded it. As for the many critics who have lambasted the Académie over the centuries for its stuffiness, its conservatism, and its devotion to privilege, Fumaroli tended to dismiss them as narcissistic gripers unable to see over the walls of their own literary enclaves.

Fumaroli adored the institution, but he also mourned it. What role could it still play, he asked elegiacally, "in a world of specialists, where literature itself has become a specialty?" What future is there for the idea it embodies "in a world eroded by utilitarian language and a transnational subculture, in an age when every group, fleeing this gimcrack universality, is seeking a reality, perhaps wholly imaginary, in its own distinctive roots?" The idea of the place was a noble one, but the global age will not support such luxuries, and so a treasured part of the French soul is vanishing. Fumaroli's essay was, finally, as much a memorial as an analysis.

Nora himself shared Fumaroli's pessimism. The deep, molding influence that Fumaroli found in the Académie Française Nora generalized to the French state as a whole. As he put it, in an untranslated essay in the French edition: "Other countries may owe the sinews of their cohesion and the secret of their togetherness to economics, religion, language, social or ethnic community, or to culture itself. France has owed them to the voluntary and continuous action of the State."

But how can the state continue to wield such (implicitly benevolent) influence in a world in which France has grown so weak, the pressures for European union so strong, American cultural influence so pervasive, and the logic of global economic integration so implacable? The pathos of the situation for Nora was only magnified by his conception of historians such as himself as the midwives who helped the state give birth to the French nation. In an era when disillusioned and overworked history teachers in dilapidated *lycées* cannot hope to compete with rock music and the ubiquitous television, this aspect of French nationhood, too, is passing away.

It is no surprise, then, that Nora also affected an elegiac tone in his own contributions. "Our consciousness," he wrote in the first paragraph of the introduction, "is shaped by a sense that everything is over and done with, that something long since begun is now complete." Sites of memory are "compounded of life and death, of the temporal and the eternal." He invoked "our inexpungable, intimate attachment to...faded symbols of the past," and recalled "the mourning for lost love so well described by Proust: that moment when the obsessive grip of passion finally loosens." Proust, indeed, haunted much of *Realms of Memory*—how could he not haunt a French work on this of all subjects?—lending it an air of exquisite, muffled longing. Quite fittingly, one of the best essays in the entire work was Antoine Compagnon's incisive analysis of how Proust, the outcast, the Jew, the homosexual, was transmogrified over the course of the twentieth century into the very symbol of modern French literature.

This elegiac accent gave *Realms of Memory* a beauty that is rare among contemporary works of history. Yet it also somewhat undercut the work's ostentatiously postmodern purpose. Postmodern critics aim to expose the essential and eternal as constructed and ephemeral, as Pomian did in the case of the Gauls. They strive to show the seams in every supposedly seamless narrative. For Nora, however, the French state and its cultural institutions, despite all the tumult of France's political history, despite all the shifts back and forth between monarchy, republic, and empire, have an eternal, essential, unchanging quality, and are the heroes of the great epic of the nation. Nora has called France the "statocentric" nation par excellence. This begs the question of whether the "state" of the Middle Ages, of the French Revolution, and the present day can really be lumped together. Haven't the French continuously reinvented the state, too, along with the other aspects of their society and their culture?

Where the state is concerned, this perspective turned *Realms of Memory*'s punch into more of a caress. It also led the authors to underestimate elements of French nation-building that did not fit into their story. After the publication of the second installment of the work in 1986, the French historian Gérard Noiriel roundly chastised Nora for omitting almost all mention of immigration, when in fact France has rivaled the United States as an "immigrant nation" since the late nine-teenth century. (Today more than one French citizen out of four has at least one foreign-born grandparent.) But the Republic and its formi-dable pedagogical apparatus effectively repressed popular awareness of modern France's ethnic diversity, less for racist reasons than for the fear that an acknowledgment of diversity might damage a tenuous national unity predicated on a shared language and culture. And Nora never challenged this official version. Similarly, the American historian Steven Englund has shrewdly criticized Nora for his statocentrism, and for identifying the modern, post-1789 state wholly with the Republic, disre-garding the failed empires and monarchies that ruled France for well over half the nineteenth century. Rather astonishingly, for a work claiming to address the whole of French history, *Realms of Memory* con-tained few mentions of that vulgar but influential adventurer Bonaparte.

To his credit, Nora took some of these criticisms into account when preparing the third installment of *Les Lieux de mémoire*, which appeared in 1992. He even invited Noiriel to contribute an incisive essay called "Frenchmen and Foreigners." Still, the lapses of memory in *Realms of Memory* remained quite remarkable. The work still had little on Napoleon and not much more on the far left-wing movements that have had considerable impact on French history. (Nora did contribute a characteristically sharp piece on "Gaullists and Communists.") A plethora of essays dealt with the countryside, but except for the great monuments of central Paris, and a delightful contribution by Daniel Milo on street names, *Realms of Memory* had little to say about urban life. The mystique of the land, once symbolized by Puymège's farmer-soldiers, clearly survived rural depopulation. Religious minorities got their due, with Pierre Birnbaum providing an illuminating look at French Jewish history, but, with the exception of Noiriel's essay, racial minorities barely appeared. And one would have been hard-pressed to know from *Realms of Memory* (with the exception of a single essay on the Colonial Exhibition of 1931) that for most of the past five centuries France possessed an extensive overseas empire.

Most significantly, perhaps, the work bristled with essays on the many sorts of geographical divisions that the French have drawn on the map of their nation (Roger Chartier and Alain Corbin had exceptionally in-teresting things to say on the subject), but social divisions, and even the word "class," received far less attention. The way Nora and his American coeditor, Lawrence Kritzman, organized the essays in the abridged translation (following Nora's scheme for the third installment of the original) was particularly revealing on this score. They titled the first English volume "Conflicts and Divisions" (the next two were called "Traditions and Symbols"), and it had three parts: "Political Divisions"; "Minority Religions"; and "Divisions of Time and Space." Has France never suffered from social conflicts and divisions? Do they not matter? Readers of Hugo and Zola would find this hard to imagine, as would any student of the French Revolution. One hardly needs to be a Marxist to consider the subject worthy of investigation.

But this was a work about memory, and the essence of memory is selectivity. We cannot possibly give equal weight in our recollections to every facet of our past experiences. We pick and choose, we select and reject. And, of course, we repress. Certain memories threaten our sense of who we are too deeply to be acknowledged openly. And what is true for individuals is also true in a certain sense for communities and even for nations.

For modern France's Republican elite, which very much includes Nora and most of his colleagues in this enterprise, memories of social division and social conflict fall into this uncomfortable category. Since its first incarnation in 1792, the Republic has always promised unity and equality. Its most characteristic public institutions, the *grandes écoles*, admit students regardless of social background. What could be more egalitarian and meritocratic? Not only social conflict itself but even the open discussion of social divisions call into question the reality of this egalitarianism, and in this way challenge the Republic's legitimacy. The same, incidentally, is true for ethnic division and the open discussion of ethnicity, in light of the painful Algerian conflict that helped destroy the Fourth Republic in 1958, the ongoing strife over immigration, and the manifold problems of France's large Arab minority.

It would be foolish to reproach Nora and his authors too strongly for these silences, or to expect them to have written in a spirit of ironic detachment. The very fact that they still felt such a strong sense of identity—as French, as Republicans, as educators—made it impossible for them to do so. And the absences did not affect the superb quality of the individual essays, or the important contribution to historical science made by the work as a whole. Whatever its flaws, *Realms of Memory* was a magnificent achievement.

In the end, though, it is not only a work of history, it is also something of a historical document itself. It testifies to the ongoing crisis in French national identity, brought on by France's geopolitical marginalization, the forces of cultural and economic globalization, the pressure for European union, immigration, and all the other subjects that the French currently wring their hands over, with little to show for it but ineffectual laws restricting the public use of English. In the world of Maastricht, McDonald's, and Microsoft, the claims of the French Republic and its elite servants to represent—and to be able to reshape—the French nation ring increasingly hollow.

Nora and his authors perceived this change as something of a tragedy, and for them it certainly has been one. Whether it has been a tragedy for those outside the Parisian cultural mandarinate is a different question. The thick arteries of contemporary French culture might well benefit from a dose of diversity and decentralization. Still, it was the authors' tragic vision that gave *Realms of Memory* its force, just as it was the separation that they felt from an earlier France that gave them such trenchant ideas about its history. The irony is that the same developments that allowed them to write such a powerful work also ensured that the world gave it less consideration than it gave to many lesser pieces of Parisian wisdom in the past.

2

The Ordeal of Legitimacy: France and Its Jews

THE STORY OF PERSECUTED MINORITY groups can often illuminate a national history just as well as the history of its central institutions does, and nowhere is this statement more true than in the case of French Jews. True, as the following essay notes, the direct role that Jews have played in French history has often been exaggerated—sometimes by Jews themselves, more often by anti-Semites. But Jews have been in France throughout nearly all the long sweep of its history, and for much of that time, questions of if and how Jews could be French have served as another way to ask the question: what does it mean to be French? This essay suggested that rapid assimilation might soon relegate questions of French Jewish identity to the past. Since it was

---

Books under Review: *The Jews of France: A History from Antiquity to the Present*, by Esther Benbassa, translated by M. B. DeBevoise (Princeton University Press, 1999); *Jewish Destinies: Citizenship, State and Community in Modern France*, by Pierre Birnbaum, translated by Arthur Goldhammer (Hill and Wang, 2000); *Uneasy Asylum: France and the Jewish Refugee Crisis, 1933–1942*, by Vicki Caron (Stanford University Press, 1999); *The Jews of Modern France*, by Paula E. Hyman (University of California Press, 1998); *Nationalism, Anti-Semitism and Fascism in France*, by Michel Winock, translated by Jane Marie Todd (Stanford University Press, 1998). Essay originally published in *The New Republic*, February 28, 2000.

published, the rise of a new anti-Semitism amid young French Muslims has unfortunately led the old questions to be posed yet again, in a new key.

———

Has France been good for the Jews? The history of the last century or so makes it hard to say yes. The images are indelible: the falsely accused Jewish army officer Alfred Dreyfus being ritually stripped of his rank in the courtyard of the École Militaire, his insignia ripped off and his sword broken while crowds howled "Death to the Jews!" outside; Vichy French police, without direct orders from the Nazis, rounding up Jews, imprisoning them in an indoor bicycle racetrack, and then putting thousands on trains to Auschwitz; violent attacks on Jewish cemeteries, restaurants, and synagogues in the 1970s and 1980s; Jean-Marie Le Pen, leader of a political party that routinely polls over 15 percent of the French vote, making deliberately anti-Semitic statements.

Actually, the balance sheet is far more ambiguous. For all its history of anti-Semitism, France was also the first European country to grant the Jews full civil rights—not just in France itself but also in the vast territories conquered by Napoleon. Indeed, the Jews of nineteenth-century France enjoyed such a high level of success and acceptance—including access to elite universities and high government offices—that they set about refashioning the Jews of other countries in their own image, in a Jewish version of France's *mission civilisatrice*. As for the overall success of Jews in French society, recall only the names Emile Durkheim, Camille Pissarro, Leon Blum, Marc Bloch, Pierre Mendes-France, Claude Levi-Strauss, Raymond Aron, and Jacques Derrida, not to mention (stretching the definition of Jewishness) Sarah Bernhardt, Michel Debré, and Marcel Proust.

But the story does not end there, either. There is still a sense in which the history of French Jewry has been peculiarly, even uniquely, unsettling. More clearly than the history of any other Jewish community, it throws into sharp relief the fact that modern anti-Semitism cannot be comfortably dismissed as a primitive relic of ancient hatreds, or as an atavistic, irrational reaction against modern society. It derives from tensions that lie at the heart of the modern nation-state and of modern democracy. Pierre Birnbaum and Michel Winock are achingly aware of this point in their new books. Indeed, Birnbaum despairs at French Jews ever successfully negotiating the contradictions of modernity, and ends his book with a deeply bleak assessment of their present and future, asserting that on the "path that led them from Biblical times to the dawn of modern history," they are now heading the wrong way, and backward. His pessimism is ultimately unconvincing and reflects an ideal of assimilation that was always something of a myth; but the history of French Jewry makes it at least understandable.

Americans often have trouble grasping the issues that haunt Birnbaum, owing to the fortunate history of our own nation-state and democracy. All modern democratic nations have demanded a degree of conformity and homogeneity from their citizens: a commitment to common principles and, to some extent, participation in a common culture. But the vast majority of Americans descend from men and women who freely chose to come here, and so the United States has been able to afford an unusually large degree of cultural heterogeneity without its national unity coming into question. Americans may take loud pride in their ethnic origins without easily incurring charges of dual loyalties. The classic canard of modern anti-Semitism (it originated, incidentally, in France) is that the Jews are "a state within a state"; but which group, in the United States, is not a state within a state? The American revolutionaries helped matters further at the start by ruthlessly driving out the Loyalists, who might otherwise have constituted a permanent challenge to our national identity—a historical episode of which most Americans know little. Not surprisingly, the greatest challenges to American national identity have arisen in connection with the African American minority whose ancestors did not freely travel to these shores.

The situation of France has been dramatically different. Far from enjoying any degree of consensus about common principles, France has perceived itself, from 1789 until quite recently, as a nation rent in two, between supporters of the Catholic, traditional, Old Regime and advocates of the French Revolution. And unlike Britain, Spain, or indeed any other major European state, France has faced no serious threat of regional secession for centuries. (Except in Corsica, recent regional militantism has been largely an academic affair.) The threats to its national unity are not physical, in the sense of the country literally splitting in two; the threats are cultural and political.

As a result, not only the reactionary right in France but also the republican left have long been obsessed with cultural homogeneity to an extent that Americans tend to find bewildering. While it is a leading nation of immigration, France has no tradition of celebrating immigration, still less ethnic groups maintaining distinct identities. Indeed, as Birnbaum points out, the very word "ethnic," in the American sense, only entered the French language recently. The antipathies of both the reactionary right and the republican left have always focused principally on each other—yet both have also fixated on those members of the French community who have differed most obviously from the cultural norm and seemed most threatening to it. Which brings us back to the Jews.

For as long as Jews have lived in France, they have aroused a powerful mixture of fascination, fear, admiration, and disgust in their gentile neighbors. As Esther Benbassa recounts in her dry but impressively succinct and informative history, they arrived in the Roman province of Gaul in the first centuries of the Common Era, and soon found themselves trod underfoot by the ascendant Christian church. They could not hold public office or own Christian slaves and had to fend off accusations of treachery. Even under the favorably disposed Charlemagne, Jewish litigants needed two or three times as many witnesses as Christians when going to court.

It did not help that the Jewish community itself was almost continuously divided. In its earliest days, prominent exiles from Judea rubbed shoulders with Jews who had arrived from other parts of the diaspora, descended in many cases from non-Judean converts. In the High Middle Ages, northern French Jews loyal to the traditions of the eleventh-century French commentator Rashi and his heirs fought against currents in Provençal Jewry influenced by Greco-Arab philosophy and its great Jewish interlocutor, Maimonides. (In 1233, the feuding reached the point that the northerners denounced Maimonides's *Guide to the Perplexed* to Dominican monks, who burned the book in public.) Yet even a united Jewish community could not have prevented the persecutions of the times; and although French Jews largely escaped the horrific massacres carried out by Crusaders in Germany, a series of expulsions nonetheless brought their history to a temporary end by the late fourteenth century.

Eventually they came back. Marrano merchants from Portugal and Spain settled in Bordeaux and Bayonne, and by the middle of the seventeenth century they felt secure enough to drop the pretense of Catholicism, ceasing to notify local priests of their births, deaths, and marriages. Jews lived in towns under papal rule in Provence (the astrologer Nostradamus was descended from one such family) and in the newly annexed eastern territories of Alsace and Lorraine. But the age of discrimination was hardly over. When the Marranos finally received official toleration from the French Crown in 1723, it was only in return for a payment of 100,000 French pounds. The Alsatian city of Colmar levied a notorious tax on Jews and cattle entering its walls. In Provence, the Jews lived in ghettos and were forced to wear yellow hats. All French Jews remained ineligible for public office, though one did manage to buy a barony in Picardy, and with it the feudal right to name the local parish priest.

Such was the lot of Jews across Europe, and the temptation is great to write it off to the continent's backward and unenlightened condition. But the Jews did not always fare better in the writings of the apostles of toleration and modernity. Voltaire denounced the "raging fanaticism in their hearts" and slandered them in more than a quarter of the articles of his *Philosophical Dictionary*. Diderot impugned them as a "superstitious and ignorant people." Were these writers (and they were hardly alone) simply echoing a primitive, age-old anti-Semitism? The historian Ronald Schechter has convincingly argued that the Enlightenment's concern with the Jews derived rather from a generalized hostility toward organized religion, and from a suspicious amazement that the Jews had so long managed to remain a distinct and cohesive community, separate from their host nations.

Ironically, this cohesiveness made the Jews (despite their lack of a national territory) seem the very model of a nation at the moment when French nationalism itself was beginning to take shape. Thus Rousseau lavishly praised Moses for turning "a swarm of unhappy fugitives into a political body, a free people....He gave it this durable form....which five thousand years have not been able to destroy or even alter, and which even today retains all its strength." This image of the Jews has endured, but it has rarely been proposed in Rousseau's spirit of admiration. In 1905, for instance, the polemicist Urbain Gohier wrote that "although dispersed across the surface of the earth, the twelve million Jews compose the only homogeneous, and the most resolutely nationalist, nation." Gohier made the observation in *The Jewish Terror*, an extraordinarily vile book even by the standards of French anti-Semitism at the time of the Dreyfus Affair, which argued that the presence of a distinct Jewish community on French soil threatened French national identity. In the next sentence, Gohier lashed out at the Jews for their "extraordinary discipline in the acquisition of universal dominion."

Many other French voices have echoed these charges, and stories about the all-powerful Jewish Internationale can still be found in publications available at any Parisian kiosk, such as *Présent* and *Minute*. This sort of conspiracy theorizing is hardly unique to French anti-Semites. What is remarkable about modern French Jewish history, however, is that the specter of the Jews constituting a separate nation within the nation has been at the heart of nearly all political discussion of the Jews, not only on the ultra-Catholic Right, but on the ultrasecular Left as well; for philo-Semites as much as anti-Semites. The idea that the Jews might legitimately remain a separate community in certain respects, while still participating fully in the life of the nation, an idea elaborated in Germany as far back as the eighteenth century by Moses Mendelssohn and W. C. Dohm, and central to the history of American Jewry, has historically enjoyed almost no resonance in France.

At the time of the French Revolution, for instance, the leading advocate of Jewish emancipation, the Lorraine priest Henri Grégoire, called for the Jews to be "melted into the national mass"—to lose all their distinctiveness, including even their religious distinctiveness. For Grégoire, the solution to the "Jewish problem" lay, ultimately, in conversion. And when it came to the differences between the Jews and their neighbors, Grégoire himself could sound like the worst sort of anti-Semite, describing the Jews "pullulating" in "sad hovels from which foul odors continually emanate" (although he noted that this condition was due to anti-Semitism, and added that "in their place we would perhaps have been worse"). Not surprisingly, while French Jews have traditionally hailed Grégoire as an emancipator, today a large portion of them bridle at honoring him in any way, ironically putting themselves in the same camp as the ultra-Catholics who detest the priest for his Jacobinism and for his break with Rome.

When the revolutionary Constituent Assembly voted to give the Jews full civil rights at the end of the eighteenth century, it was explicitly on the condition that they renounce their distinctive privileges, laws, and customs. In 1789, the Comte de Clermont-Tonnerre declared in debate that "everything must be refused to the Jews as a Nation in the sense of a corporate body and everything granted to the Jews as individuals.... They must make up neither a political body nor an order within the State; they must individually be citizens." The Assembly first granted rights to the small, wealthy, and relatively assimilated Sephardic community in the southwest but waited another year and a half before extending the decree to the more numerous, Yiddish-speaking Ashkenazi Jews of Alsace and Lorraine, who lived principally as impoverished peddlers and moneylenders in villages that resembled the shtetls of central and eastern Europe. Meanwhile the arguments of the Comte de Mirabeau, an enthusiastic follower of Mendelssohn's position on Jewish emancipation, and one of the rare French advocates of genuine pluralism, found almost no audience.

Ever since, the French left and moderate center have repeatedly expressed their horror at the slightest hint of Jewish separatism. Before the Dreyfus Affair, this attitude easily slid into raw anti-Semitism, even on the part of Jean Jaurès, the icon of French socialism, who spoke of the Jewish "fever for profit." After Dreyfus, to be sure, anti-Semitism became politically incorrect on the left, but the change did nothing to diminish the fear of the "nation within the nation." In a particularly telling incident from 1907, French Socialists condemned the government for allowing children in the Marais district of Paris, then inhabited almost entirely by immigrant Jews, to attend neighborhood schools. These schools had exactly the same curriculum as every other public school in France and taught exclusively in French. And yet the Socialist daily *L'Humanité* warned that simply by virtue of being educated together, the Jewish children would "form a closed caste and later...a very distinct society scarcely penetrable by the customs of modern life.... How can we be surprised at racial hatred when...the administration itself favors the particularist development of these races instead of seeking to facilitate their fusion, even from childhood?"

As recently as twenty years ago, French Jews had another vivid and painful reminder of the mainstream French tendency to conflate the smallest manifestations of Jewish difference with separatism. In October 1980, terrorists exploded a bomb outside the synagogue in the rue Copernic in Paris, killing six people, including gentile passersby. Centrist Prime Minister Raymond Barre rushed to condemn the "odious act" but added that it was an act "which intended to strike Jews going to synagogue and which struck innocent Frenchmen crossing the rue Copernic." Barre was in no way an anti-Semite. In fact, he was one of the most decent and honorable of French politicians. And his general decency just made the remark all the more telling and awful: even Barre, in a moment of stress, instinctively distinguished between Jews going to synagogue and "innocent Frenchmen."

Of course, Barre's remarks hardly compare to the astonishingly virulent anti-Semitism of the prewar nationalist right. Whereas figures on the left and center have believed that Jewish assimilation is possible, and rarely condemned Judaism itself, the right-wing anti-Semites combined traditional bigotry with a fervent conviction that Jews could never truly become French. These anti-Semites loathed the assimilated Jews far more than the Orthodox immigrants who really did live in "closed societies"; in the paranoid fantasies of French reaction, the assimilated Jews were perpetrating a dangerous deception in disguising their true, malevolent natures. It is no coincidence that the two most hated Jews in French history have been examples of extreme assimilation: the right-wing army officer Alfred Dreyfus (who, it has been remarked, in other circumstances would have made a natural anti-Dreyfusard) and the secular socialist Leon Blum, who was prime minister under the Popular Front in the 1930s.

It was under the aggressively secular Third Republic (1870–1940) that the Catholic French right felt most beleaguered, and most despairing about French national identity; and it was largely for this reason that French anti-Semitism grew enormously potent during this period. As George Mosse once remarked, looking at pre–World War I France and Germany without benefit of hindsight, it was France that seemed more likely to produce National Socialism. Germany, after all, had no Dreyfus Affair. And it had no Édouard Drumont, the publicist and politician who has as good a claim as any to be called the father of modern anti-Semitism.

Drumont's anti-Semitism was so intensely pathological that when a flood drove him out of his Paris apartment in 1910, he racked his brains until he found a way of blaming the Jews: he attributed the rising river waters to deforestation financed by cousins of the Rothschilds. Yet his influence was immense. His book *La France juive*, published in 1886 by Flammarion (still a leading French publisher), went through 145 editions within a year and sold millions of copies. It was the mother of all conspiracy tracts. As Drumont wrote, "everything comes back to the Jew." To Drumont's followers, Dreyfus's supposed betrayal of France to the Germans, and later Blum's rise to the premiership, confirmed all their worst suspicions and gave to their already zealous convictions the intensity of a religious cult.

It is true, as Pierre Birnbaum observes, that Drumont's feverish language rarely translated into actual violence before 1940 (and even Vichy mostly left the dirty work of killing Jews to the Germans). More Italian immigrants than Jews died at the hands of street-level French bigots. Still, anti-Italian and even anti-Arab sentiment have never suffused French politics and culture as anti-Semitism did before and during World War II. Michel Winock illustrates this point in painful detail, in his discussion of Drumont and also in his fine essays on left-wing anti-Semitism, on Céline's obsession with the Jews, on the Catholic writer Georges Bernanos's lack of such an obsession (despite his veneration for Drumont), and on the way anti-Semitic publicists constructed an image of Joan of Arc as a sort of perfectly pure and perfectly French anti-Jew. Winock calls anti-Semitism "the most solid cement" of French nationalism in general. It is a statement that badly needs complication, since it does not really apply to the 1870s, or to the period of World War I, when the Germans aroused far more nationalist anger in France; but it does fit the 1890s, when the Dreyfus Affair occurred, and the 1930s, when anti-Semitic hatred found targets both in Blum and in the thousands of Jewish refugees from Germany and eastern Europe who sought asylum in France.

The poor treatment these refugees received has recently emerged as a significant topic for historians. Some have gone so far as to draw a straight line between French attitudes and policies toward Jewish refugees before 1940 and the fate of French Jews in general thereafter. They have thereby deepened the indictment, developed most fully by Robert Paxton and Michael Marrus in *Vichy France and the Jews* in 1981, that French authorities, weaned on homegrown anti-Semitism and tacitly supported by much of the population, participated willingly in the Holocaust. As Marshall Pétain's own chief of staff damningly remarked after the war: "Germany was not at the origin of the anti-Jewish legislation of Vichy. This legislation was, if I dare say it, spontaneous, native."

The indictment has so shaken French political culture in recent years that right-wing academics have blamed it for damaging French national identity, while the historian Henri Rousso has diagnosed postwar France as suffering from "the Vichy Syndrome." But did all roads really lead to Vichy? It is this question that makes Vicki Caron's detailed and quietly authoritative history of the refugee crisis so important. Caron in no way denies that Vichy had deep indigenous roots, and that its policies, particularly the establishment of its wretched internment camps, were built on foundations that were established in the previous decade. She brilliantly describes the absurd plight of the refugees who, trapped in a juridical no-man's-land, found themselves denounced first as Fifth Columnists acting on Hitler's orders and later as anti-German warmongers seeking to undermine France's wise policy of appeasement.

And yet Caron correctly insists on drawing a fundamental distinction between the imperfect democracy of the 1930s and the reactionary, collaborationist regime that followed, which came into being only thanks to the Nazis. Before 1940, as Caron shows, anti-Semitism met with loud and often successful opposition, and the refugees received a great deal of support from the government and public opinion alike, particularly under Blum's Popular Front. It was only when the Nazis gave power to Édouard Drumont's faithful readers that this support was wrenched away, paving the way for seventy-six thousand French Jews, two-thirds of them foreign-born, to perish. Caron's work should be a model for future historians. France's record with regard to the Jews is disturbing enough; historians do not need to distort it by presenting it as nothing but an arrow pointing straight to the wartime persecutions and deportations.

Still, it is hardly surprising that many French Jews, faced with suspicion of Jewish particularism across the political spectrum and with virulent right-wing anti-Semitism, have historically reacted by embracing a version of assimilation that stopped only at the church door. From the early nineteenth century until fairly recently, many even chose not to describe themselves as "Juifs," a word that to them evoked the "closed societies" of the past (and that gentiles used as a slur), preferring the supposedly more neutral term "Israélites." From Napoleon onward, leading French rabbis accommodated themselves to the demands of assimilation, citing the ancient rabbinical maxim *dina d'malkhuta dina*, or the law of the kingdom is the law, to justify such measures as French Jewish soldiers fighting on the Sabbath and eating nonkosher food. French Jews in the 1930s were so determined to appear as patriotic French citizens that they permitted the right-wing anti-Semitic Croix de Feu movement to parade through the Synagogue de la Victoire in Paris in ceremonies honoring the dead of World War I. And so strident were the voices denouncing Blum's premiership as a "foreign yoke" that Blum himself felt the need to declare, pathetically: "I was born in Paris...of French parents.... My four grandparents were all born in France.... As far as it is possible to trace the outlines of my modest family's history, my ancestry is purely French." (Even today, the French Jewish historian Benbassa feels obliged in her book to deny the reality of Judeo-Masonic conspiracies and to insist that Jews "represented no danger" to French workers. What does she think her French readers believe?)

For more than a century, these Jewish anxieties about acceptance have been further reinforced by something that all these books mention but only Paula Hyman appropriately emphasizes: the constant demographic renewal of French Jewry by means of immigration. At the time of the French Revolution, the Yiddish-speaking Jews of Alsace and Lorraine still seemed "foreign" even to their assimilated Sephardic brethren in Bordeaux and Bayonne. A hundred years later, they had largely abandoned Yiddish for French, moved to the cities, and joined the middle classes; but no sooner did their assimilation seem complete than waves of Jewish immigrants from eastern Europe began to arrive.

By 1872, a quarter of all Jews in Paris were foreign born, and by 1939 an absolute majority of France's three hundred thousand Jews belonged to the new groups. Since World War II the process has repeated itself, as Sephardic immigrants from France's former North African colonies have again doubled the French Jewish population. As a result, French Jewish history somewhat resembles a permanent performance of *Our Crowd*, with not all that much having changed since wealthy and assimilated Bordeaux Sephardim wrote to the revolutionary National Assembly to protest their fundamental differences from the alien Ashkenazi Alsatians. ("The Portuguese Jews, except for their religious belief, differ in no respect from the peoples among whom they live;... but a German Jew is German everywhere with regard to his customs.") Raymond Aron once quipped that he felt "less distant from an anti-Semitic Frenchman than from a South Moroccan Jew who speaks no language but Arabic and is barely removed from what looks to me like the Middle Ages."

And yet, given the persistence of French anti-Semitism, these attitudes were never really sustainable. As Birnbaum notes, Aron himself felt driven to express solidarity with his fellow Jews after hearing Charles de Gaulle, at the time of the Six Day War, denounce the Jewish people as "sure of themselves and domineering." Émile Durkheim, born David Durkheim and descended from a long line of rabbis, had a similar experience at the time of the Dreyfus Affair. And more recently, many further anti-Semitic incidents have forced yet another generation of assimilated Jews to confront their Jewish identity.

These recent incidents are on an entirely different scale from Vichy or the Dreyfus Affair, but they nonetheless seem to have marked a turning point in the history of French Jewry. Birnbaum claims that they have led to nothing less than the collapse of the traditional republican model of assimilation. Today, he writes, Jews and gentiles alike have again begun to treat French Jews less as individual citizens and more as a collective. Certainly the assimilationist term "Israélite" has fallen largely into disuse. One of France's Grand Rabbis, a North African Sephardi, has asserted a greater role for Jewish communal institutions, and even challenged the sacrosanct principle of secular education. And Jews have collectively played a major role in forcing the French to confront and atone for Vichy, culminating in President Jacques Chirac's public apology for the French state's "unforgivable crimes" in 1995.

Still, the collapse of the republican model has less to do with continuing anti-Semitism than with broader changes in French political culture as a whole. Since World War II, and the discrediting of the traditional right in the wake of the Liberation, the polarization of the French into warring political camps has vastly diminished. French unity has come to seem less fragile, and so cultural homogeneity has no longer seemed quite so urgent a task. Since the student revolts of 1968, the idea of a missionary state using the educational system to meld a diverse population of peasants, immigrants, and Jews into the "national mass" has rusted away. And along with McDonalds, American pop music, and the

Internet, late twentieth-century France also absorbed American notions of pluralism, multiculturalism, and identity politics.

Traditional French republicanism is dying. It is now the ideal of France as a mosaic of ethnic groups, so alien and repulsive to the old school, that enjoys increasingly wide support. What will these changes mean for French Jewry? A certain number of Jews prominent in the great, traditional institutions of the state and higher learning—the type that Birnbaum calls "les Juifs d'état," or "state Jews"—have angrily denounced the changes and clung for dear life to the sinking republican ideal. The intellectuals Chantal Benayoun and Dominique Schnapper (who is Raymond Aron's daughter) have gone so far as to call Jewish leaders "counterrevolutionaries" for advocating a greater public presence for the Jewish community. Other Jews have emerged as leading advocates of absolute secularism in the school system, defending the expulsion of students who openly manifest their religious beliefs, for instance by wearing a yarmulke or a Muslim headscarf.

Pierre Birnbaum takes much the same stance, but with greater sympathy for the arguments on the other side and more in sorrow than in anger. "There seems to have been an effort," he writes, "orchestrated from on high, to redefine French Jews as a community apart.... Jews now find themselves relegated to an imaginary community not by those who once reviled them but by those who were formerly their most zealous defenders." He counts up uses of the phrase "Jewish community," as if each one amounted to another block in a symbolic ghetto wall. "The increasing democratization and gradual Americanization of French society," he declaims, "may... have devastating implications for the destiny of French Jews.... Jews may come to occupy a less central place in the French imagination.... and will increasingly figure as one of many 'ethnic,' religious, linguistic or regional minorities."

Birnbaum hyperbolically concludes that French Jews are doing nothing less than retreating from modernity. His lamentation has a certain power, but when he follows his logic to such an extreme, he loses hold of reality. Is France really on the point of breaking into a collection of self-ghettoized minorities? In a huge irony, even as the ideal of a diverse and pluralistic France has been gaining acceptance, the reality of such a dispensation is fast disappearing: under the pressure of social and economic forces originating well outside their borders, the French are becoming more alike than ever before. The dramatic developments that we call "globalization" are melting the French into a single mass more effectively than the Republic could ever have done. Already, regional differences in language and custom, so visible a century ago, have almost disappeared, while one immigrant group after another, with the important exception of North African Arabs, has fulfilled the abbe Grégoire's hopes and been entirely assimilated. Identity politics, in France at least, is more a desperate reaction against this relentless homogenization than a resurgence of real, intractable, and threatening differences. It is useful in this context to recall the old characterization of modern Jews as "reverse Marranos": on the outside they protest their difference; on the inside they are the same as anyone else.

If France does end up "Americanized," surely the real danger faced by French Jews will not be "communitarization," as Birnbaum puts it, but rather the same danger faced by American Jews, namely disappearance. More than half of French Jews marry non-Jews, and the rise of Jewish identity politics lamented by Birnbaum has done nothing to reverse this trend. It is also hard to see why the place of the Jews in a more pluralistic France would be marginal. Hyman concludes, more convincingly, and in diametrical opposition to Birnbaum, that "as France becomes increasingly multicultural and multiethnic at the beginning of the twenty-first century, the history of French Jewry moves from the margins to the center." And isn't it the essence of pluralism to efface, or at the very least to blur, the distinction between the center and the margins?

Birnbaum believes the Jews were central to French life because they were central to French republicanism. In the final analysis, however, it is hard to resist the conclusion that this centrality has itself been something of a myth: a myth embraced by Jews and anti-Semites alike, and so all the more powerful—but a myth nonetheless. French Jews have been an extraordinarily successful, extraordinarily visible, and extraordinarily vilified minority; but they have been also a very small minority. They have never constituted much more than 1 percent of the population.

The Jews in France have never achieved anything close to the influence of the Jews in America. They have loomed larger in the French imagination than in French reality, and even in the French imagination, the fever rises only at certain times and in certain areas of the political spectrum. Today the Jews of France face a real danger, but it is not the danger that they will fall from a privileged place at the heart of French politics and culture into the narrow confines of a self-erected ghetto. It is the danger, shared by Jewish communities throughout the Western world, that with anti-Semitism at a historical nadir, and acceptance by the gentile world easier to come by and more sincere than ever, and material attractions all around, their very success will accomplish, in the most peaceful, banal, and harmless of ways, what Drumont and Vichy never could.

3

The Never-Ending "Herstory": History from Below, Women, and Gender

One of the groups most systematically excluded from the grand national histories of the nineteenth and early twentieth centuries was women. Not coincidentally, the rise of "women's history," followed by "gender history" and the notion of gender as a category of historical analysis, coincided with the retreat from such grand histories. But as a result, women and gender have been "written into history" even as the boundaries and shape of "history" itself have fluctuated wildly. In France, even this "writing in" has faced considerable resistance, including from some historians who have attacked an emphasis on gender as an unwanted import from America—what they referred to for a time as "le politically correct." As a result, much of the pioneering work in French gender history has been done by non-French historians, who have often placed it in a broader European context. The following essay considers an attempt to write the history of women in Europe as whole between 1500 and 1800. But the focus remains heavily on France, particularly in arguing for the ways in which a "gendered"—as opposed to a "women's

---

Book under Review: Olwen Hufton, *The Prospect Before Her: A History of Women in Western Europe, 1500–1800* (Knopf, 1996). Essay originally published in *The New Republic*, January 27, 1997.

history"—approach can illuminate the history of a subject like the French Revolution.

———

Consider a few scenes from the history of women in Europe:

- In the late seventeenth century, at Versailles, the young Duc of Saint-Simon asked an influential courtier for his fourteen-year-old daughter's hand in marriage. The courtier replied that the girl in question had already committed herself to the church. Not to worry, Saint-Simon countered brightly. Any of her six younger sisters would do. What he really wanted, he explained, was to marry the family.
- In 1721, in the Breton capital of Rennes, following a disastrous fire, the city fathers undertook to rebuild the city's drainage system. In one of the old drains, workers uncovered the skeletons of eighty newborn infants, apparent victims of infanticide at the hands of their mothers.
- In 1576, in England, the legal age of consent for females was lowered from twelve to ten.
- In early modern Ireland, it was an established practice for penniless sons of the minor gentry to abduct and to rape young heiresses. Having been deflowered, the women found their reputations hopelessly compromised and, in many cases, had no choice but to marry their rapists.
- In the early modern Netherlands and Britain, more than two hundred women were discovered to have passed themselves off for years as men. Some of them fought in the British and Dutch navies, where they became legendary for their bravery. Several more contracted marriage with other women. In a few rare cases, while disguised as men, they even committed bigamy.

These are just a few of the facts and stories, often horrifying, sometimes darkly comic, occasionally inspiring, that Olwen Hufton recounts in her sparkling history of the prospects awaiting women in western Europe between 1500 and 1800. It is a book that revels in the gritty details of forgotten lives. Ranging with enormous skill and knowledge from the glitter and pomp of Versailles to the shining stoops of Amsterdam's middle-class houses (and just who was washing them?) to the fetid urban slums and dark, wretched, dirt-floored farmhouses, often shared with farm animals, where most early modern Europeans were born and died, Hufton aims at nothing less than a total history of these women's experiences. To a remarkable degree, she succeeds. And yet in some important ways she fails, and in so doing reveals some of the limits of the sort of history that she writes.

Hufton's sort of history is not merely "women's history," it is also what is sometimes called "history from below." The latter method represents a turning away from the doings of the rich and powerful in order to bring the forgotten masses of the common people back into the light of historical analysis. In 1974, Hufton produced what is still one of the masterpieces of this historiography, *The Poor of Eighteenth-Century France*, which presented a sweeping and evocative picture of how most French men and women actually lived in the age of Diderot and Madame de Pompadour.

Always uncomfortably close to the knife-edge of subsistence, Hufton's humble subjects managed to make ends meet through what she called an "economy of makeshifts," supplementing the insufficient yields of their miserable plots of land by spinning wool, repairing tools, growing grapes wherever a vine could catch a ray of sun, and a hundred other such expedients. Every year, millions of them would take to the road as migrant laborers, tramping hundreds of miles in search of the odd penny (and just as important, leaving one less mouth to feed at home). And if an irrepressible tide of bad luck slopped over these meager defenses, they would slide from poverty into indigence and destitution, desperately resorting to theft, beggary, and prostitution to keep from starving (one in thirteen women in Paris in the eighteenth century earned money from prostitution), sometimes even committing infanticide, and finally succumbing by the tens of thousands in times of famine or plague.

Hufton also laid out lucidly the ways the poor struggled to avoid such a fate. The heroines of her history were the peasant girls who would set out, between puberty and their midtwenties, to accumulate a dowry sufficient to make a good match and to establish a household prosperous enough to survive bad times. Putting in endless hours of harsh, dreary labor as domestic servants, or risking early death from tuberculosis working in the damp textile factories of Lyons or Lille, balancing the terrible loneliness of their situations against the dangers of seduction and pregnancy, facing all manner of obstacles, they patiently accumulated their pitifully small stakes, one battered copper coin at a time. Some of them met their goal; more did not.

By turning from France to western Europe as a whole, from the eighteenth century to the entire period that historians call "early modern," and from the poor of both sexes to women of all classes, Hufton has now accumulated many other heroines. They are fully on display in her new book. There is the eighteenth-century Dutch midwife Catharina Schrader, who claimed in her memoirs to have assisted in four thousand deliveries over more than fifty years. "The widow of a surgeon, who may have endowed her with some anatomical knowledge above the run of midwives," Hufton writes, "she was inherently suspicious of medical men when it came to the delicate business of bringing babies into the world."

And there is the seventeenth-century Venetian nun Arcangela Tarabotti, who penned eloquent works in praise of women and who denounced, far more cogently than Diderot (who wrote a novel on the subject), the practice of putting girls in convents against their will. "Her vocabulary is that of the Enlightenment which has yet to take place. The convent is hell when free will is excluded." There are also the more familiar figures of the early feminists Mary Wollstonecraft and Olympe de Gouges, who in 1791 wrote a "Declaration of the Rights of Woman" to protest her exclusion from the Rights of Man. But still standing front and center is the humble peasant girl, whose difficult progress from child to servant, to wife, to mother, and finally, perhaps, to widow, forms the heart of the book's first 250 pages.

There are villains aplenty, too. "Edward Coke, the father of English liberties in his struggle against the absolutist tendencies of the Stuarts, tied his daughter to the bedpost and whipped her until she agreed to the match he had arranged for her," Hufton writes acidly, adding a little superfluously that "the marriage was a disaster." There are the textile owners who mercilessly exposed their mostly female labor forces to deadly working conditions, and the clerics and the philosophers who considered women nothing more than reproductive vessels, possessed of inferior powers of reasoning as well as uncontrollable lust.

There are the legislators who wrote women's supposed inferiority into law, and the writers who enshrined it in poetry and prose. There are the Irish abductors. Above all, there are the priests and ministers and judges who, between 1560 and 1660, condemned tens of thousands of women to death for witchcraft. While men as well as women were accused of that crime, the learned prosecutors singled out a particular social type for particular attention: elderly, isolated, poor, and often infirm women who survived only on the grudging charity of their neighbors. In their trials for witchcraft, Hufton writes, "the most tragic aspects of the female predicament were converted into a potential capital offense."

Hufton's genius as a historian is for selecting striking, visceral details that bring something of the smell and the feel of the early modern period out of the ground. Indeed, she has a particular fascination with dirt and the things that live there. She reports that one luckless farmer was found after his death to have harbored no fewer than thirty-nine separate species of worms in his digestive tract. She also relates that mothers considered the scaly infant skin ailment called cradle cap a natural protection for the developing skull, and allowed it to form a hard crust that remained on the child's head for years. "There was something of a cult of bodily filth," she explains. "It was believed that the body produced fluids that were needful to good health and which should not be washed away but merely sponged to remove odor. James I [of Great Britain] never washed more than his fingers." History from below, indeed.

It is when Hufton soars high above the level of the soil and attempts to survey the broad landscape of her subject that her touch becomes a little less sure, her tone markedly more hesitant. A degree of hesitation is understandable, to be sure. How can one possibly generalize about women from Sicily to Scotland and Brittany to Bavaria, over a period that ranges from Luther to the French Revolution, and across every social class? Hufton's conclusion is remarkable mostly for its lack of large claims. It is that women's lives, like men's lives, changed relatively little during these three hundred years. For most women, the simple struggle for existence remained paramount, and meaningful choices about spouse, children, residence, career, and so on remained severely limited.

The most important changes between 1500 and 1800, in Hufton's account, derived from modifications in the structure of European religious life: witchcraft trials ended, in many countries convents were dissolved, charismatic sects that offered women spiritual outlets declined in importance, and religious observance became more tightly associated with "private" life—thus giving rise to the stereotype of women as particularly pious. Beyond this, a few women gained more liberty in regard to marriage, took part in a consumer revolution that allocated a special place to them as arbiters of fashion, and increasingly found work outside the home. Still, for the millions of peasant women engaged in backbreaking labor scratching subsistence out of the ground, these developments amounted to little more than distant whispers.

In this emphasis on the material constraints of life, and on the slow pace of change across the centuries, Hufton presents a very different view of the period than the view given by most of the leading women's historians working today. These historians tend to dwell less on obscure peasants and more on female writers and political figures, less on specific individuals and more on the way women and men generally were represented, mostly in the realms of literature, the arts, law, and politics. If Hufton deals with the history of women, they deal with the history of gender, by which is meant both the relationship between the sexes and the way this relationship figures in different areas of human endeavor. They tend to write cultural history rather than economic and social history, and to see the centuries Hufton covers as notable for complex patterns of cultural change, as traditional forms of patriarchy were broken down—often to be succeeded, they claim, by new and more rigorous forms of separation and discrimination.

The differences among the historians are in large part generational. Hufton, with her "history from below," belongs to a cohort of scholars trained in the heyday of the *Annales* school, when leading historians (particularly of France) concentrated on the slow patterns of climactic, demographic and economic change over the *longue durée*. It is wholly characteristic of this approach that Hufton turns only with a certain reluctance to women's participation in the realm of culture and "mentalities" after thoroughly immersing herself in the grit and grime of economic and social history. Inevitably, cultural themes get slighted. Writing by women receives a subtle, if overly compressed, thirty-nine pages, but the fascinating subject of actresses gets just two pages, and women painters (admittedly a rare species, but including such well-known figures as Vigee-Lebrun) are dismissed in a single paragraph.

Hufton also belongs to the first, pioneering, optimistic generation of feminist historians, linked to the women's liberation movement of the 1960s and 1970s, who saw their task as recovering the stories of those women left out of history as it had been written by men, and who believed that their work, through its capacity to inspire, could palpably further the cause of women's equality. The subsequent generation of women's historians are far more complex in their analyses, and far less certain about the potential of political action, given how deeply and intricately they perceive gender roles to be entwined with the social and cultural foundations of the modern world. Contrast Hufton's stories of inspiring heroines with Joan Wallach Scott's book *Only Paradoxes to Offer: French Feminists and the Rights of Man*. The very first page of Scott's book brings up "the downside of feminist experience: its intractable contradictions, the obsessive repetitions that seem to doom one generation to relive the dilemmas of its predecessors, and its inability to secure equal representation for women even when a long-sought goal such as the vote has been won." Through the prism of Scott's analysis, the writings of an early feminist such as Olympe de Gouges seem inspiring, but also deeply problematic.

Hufton has certainly read and absorbed the more recent "gender history" (her bibliography runs to forty-nine closely printed pages); but she remains distinctly suspicious of it. Again and again she warns against "overspeculation," against concentrating on the "theoretical or 'generic' woman and man" at the expense of "real women" and "the vast majority of people." Again and again she cites recent feminist studies, only to ask: "How do such representations relate to the lives of real men and women?" Against postmodern feminists who sometimes treat the very category of "woman" as a "social construction," she starkly invokes biological difference: "In the early modern period, biology has to count for something. No one, for example, could plough a five-inch furrow in a condition of advanced or even early pregnancy."

To some extent, it is hard not to sympathize with Hufton's point of view. These days, works of gender history, like most sorts of cultural history, often require the reader to press through a forbidding thicket of theory, only to reach a discussion that bases vast claims on the close reading of two or three texts. The language is frequently thick with jargon. Attention is lavished on textual and visual "representations," to which vast power and influence are attributed without much consideration of how widely they circulated, or how women and men of the time received them. After a large dose of this, Hufton's insistence on the lives of "real women" and her ability to conjure up the sights and smells of the past come as something of a relief.

Still, a more lucid style and a more vivid subject do not by themselves make one work of history superior to another. How illuminating is Hufton's approach, particularly in regard to the present-day situation of women, compared to that of the leading gender historians? A definitive answer to this question will have to await the publication of Hufton's second volume, which will cover the massive transformations in women's lives that have occurred since 1800. But consider one founding feature of political modernity that Hufton dwells on at length, on which she has carried out pioneering research: the French Revolution.

The women's historians of the 1960s and 1970s concentrated on putting women back into the story of the Revolution: the handful of women, such as de Gouges and Madame Roland, who established reputations for themselves at the time; the larger but still small number who joined revolutionary clubs and associations; and the considerably larger number who figured in the great revolutionary crowds that stormed the Bastille. Hufton herself did seminal work on that classic revolutionary figure the female bread rioter. Subsequently, though, attention has shifted to broader and more abstract questions of gender. Why did the revolutionary government never consider giving women the vote? (The question did arise, not only in the writings of early feminists but also in those of a major thinker such as Condorcet.) Why did the (male) revolutionaries first tolerate the creation of women's political societies and then, in 1793, abruptly close them down? Did these actions signify the sequestration of women in a purely domestic "private sphere"? More recently still, leading women's historians have made ambitious attempts to view the Revolution as a whole through the prism of gender. Lynn Hunt has offered a psychoanalytic interpretation of the event that makes the revolutionaries' hysterical treatment of the mother-figure of Marie-Antoinette (whose trial in 1793 focused as much on her supposed abuse of her son as on her alleged treason) just as important as their execution of the "father of his country," King Louis XVI. Joan Scott has asked what the exclusion of women from the suffrage says not only about the situation of women themselves, but about the contradictions of the liberal democracy that the Revolution helped to "engender."

These are the sorts of arguments that Hufton, without dismissing them entirely, tends to find unduly speculative and insufficiently supported by the evidence. It is true that literary and political texts studied by many gender historians tell us relatively little about the actual lives of the vast majority of women, and drawing large generalizations from them is indeed speculative. Yet these texts can sometimes furnish insights into the dynamics of political and cultural change that Hufton's subject matter cannot.

Consider a short book published in France in 1798, by a judge named Gilles Boucher-Laricharderie, on the subject of how the Revolution had wrought changes in the French national character. Rather than discussing the effects of liberty and equality, or the Terror, Boucher preferred to dilate on the changing roles of men and women. Before 1789, he wrote, queens and mistresses had dominated the royal court, and the rest of French society had slavishly followed their example: "In all conditions and all ranks, women were granted the same predominance they had usurped over kings and ministers. Thus the humiliating expression, nothing gets done without women, was in every mouth, and governed all behavior."

This state of affairs made France the laughingstock of Europe, but Boucher could take consolation from the fact that it no longer prevailed. "This strange domination," he wrote sententiously, "expired on July 14, 1789." Eight years later, he continued, the French had come to understand that women "deviate from their natural purpose when, as Rousseau energetically put it, they make men of themselves. Women should limit their learning and the use of their talents to whatever makes them good mothers and excellent wives. They should have no other dominion than that of grace and sweetness, for the very delicacy of their organs, which makes them so successful in the realm of charm, makes them incapable of grasping those grand insights that constitute the science of government."

Hufton spends relatively little time on texts of this sort, whose influence is uncertain and whose relationship to the lives of "real women" is dubious. To be sure, Boucher enormously exaggerated the power of women in France before the Revolution, as well as the extent of their retreat into a "dominion of grace and sweetness" thereafter. Hufton suggests that opinions like his represent little more than variations on the timeless theme of male misogyny. And yet Boucher's text is a remarkable one. It not only posited natural differences between men and women that rendered the latter biologically unfit for political life, it also put these differences at the heart of Boucher's conception of politics as a whole: a state could only function properly if women stayed in their own, proper, private sphere.

Moreover, Boucher expressed in particularly blunt and telling language a point of view shared by many others of the period, including Rousseau. Not everyone agreed with them. Condorcet famously asked "why individuals exposed to pregnancies and other passing indispositions should be unable to exercise rights which no one has dreamed of withholding from persons who have the gout all winter"? But why did Condorcet's egalitarian ideas (not to mention those of Olympe de Gouges) fall on such barren soil? Why did the drafters of the Napoleonic Code subsequently do so much to restrict women's legal rights? Indeed, why did women not receive the right to vote in France until 1944, and why do they still have such a feeble presence in French politics?

Attributing all this to misogyny is not sufficient. Such an explanation begs the questions of why certain people embraced misogyny and others resisted it, and why, at a moment when the French were throwing so many other ancient prejudices onto the bonfire, they maintained and even reinforced this one. That is why it is important to trace more exactly the nature and the operation of sexual ideologies through close readings of works such as Boucher's. These sources reveal how powerful men understood the world around them at the turn of the nineteenth century. The world may have resisted these men's attempts to muster it into a new order, but the attempts still remain crucial to our understanding of historical change.

Hufton would probably not deny this point. But for her it is precisely the world's resistances, the messy, complex, and half-regimented reality of history, that most profoundly matters. This is what she lavishes her attention on, what she describes with such intelligence and panache. *The Prospect Before Her* is a tour de force. It stands as a monument to history from below and to the first generation of women's history. But if we are to ask how our own world, and the present-day relations between the sexes in all their complexities and their contradictions, emerged out of the patriarchal peasant culture that Hufton describes, we have to look not only at the resistances, at the enormous inertia of traditional societies, but also at the attempts made to force them into new channels. And here Hufton's successors may prove better guides.

4

Bicycle History: The Supposed Lost Tribes of Rural France

Peasants do not exactly constitute a "marginal" or forgotten group in French history. Through the early nineteenth century they made up the vast majority of the population, and as late as World War II, nearly half of all French people still lived in the countryside, most of them working the land. Throughout this long period, peasants were mocked and reviled as often as they were idolized—think of Émile Zola's savage portrayal of French rural life in his novel The Earth *(La terre). More recently, however, France's relatively late urbanization and the pathos of rural villages standing empty and abandoned have prompted a nostalgia for peasant communities supposedly swept under by the relentless steamroller of modern capitalist development and by the modernizing French state. This nostalgia has had positive consequences, notably in drawing attention to the remarkable heterogeneity of France in past centuries. It is too easily forgotten, traveling in France today, that just 150 years ago, a large majority of the population did not speak anything like standard French at home and that from many points of view, places like Provence and Alsace could look like foreign countries to a Parisian. But at the same time, it has become too easy to see peasant communities as*

Book under Review: Graham Robb, *The Discovery of France: A Historical Geography, from the Revolution to the First World War* (Norton, 2008). Essay originally published in *The New Republic*, February 7, 2008.

forgotten by time, standing outside history until history came along and crushed them. This essay deals with an egregious example of this tendency, and uses it to argue, most immediately, for understanding French rural history as part and parcel of the larger social, cultural, and political changes the country has undergone. More broadly, the essay points to how badly popular histories can go wrong and why academic history remains necessary.

For a book of "historical geography," Graham Robb's *The Discovery of France* has received remarkable attention and acclaim: long and appreciative reviews in British and American newspapers, the title of "notable book of the year" from the *New York Times*, rapturous applause in the *New York Review of Books*, and so forth. The reason is not hard to see. Graham Robb is an engaging and gifted writer, known for his enjoyable and instructive biographies of Hugo and Rimbaud. Moreover, *The Discovery of France* is the sort of history that seems almost to have disappeared from the world of professional academic historians: written in a light and pleasant style, crammed with colorful and unexpected details, it offers what seem like tantalizing glimpses into a vanished, forgotten past.

All the more pity that it is actually a distressingly bad book. Robb has set out to uncover the true story of France's cultural diversity, and to show how cartographers, surveyors, travelers, and officials of the French state started to come to terms with this diversity between 1789 and 1914. But he falls headlong into some of the biggest traps that await overly enthusiastic historians. He presumes without justification that source material drawn helter-skelter from widely differing regions and periods belongs to a single story—a melodramatic saga of a "lost world." He therefore elides crucial regional and chronological distinctions, while ignoring some rather large and important phenomena—the Counter-Reformation, absolutism, proto-industrialization—that fail to fit his thesis. And he accepts deeply tendentious accounts of French life, marred by ideology or romance, as if they were transparent descriptions of it. As a result, when he claims to be mapping historical terra incognita, he is often doing little more than recycling nineteenth-century myths. And he fails to put any of what he is doing in a larger historical or geographical context, again and again greeting with delighted surprise what are in fact well-known elements of European social and cultural history.

What makes matters worse is that these mistakes were so unnecessary. Over the past century, some of the greatest names in European and American scholarship—Fernand Braudel, Emmanuel Le Roy Ladurie, Natalie Zemon Davis, Laurence Wylie, Alain Corbin, Eugen Weber, and many others—have produced shelves' worth of books on virtually every subject Robb touches on. Robb cites some of this work in a scattershot way, but he has learned little from it, and he acknowledges hardly any of it. Indeed, he goes so far as to write in his introduction that "for some time, it had been obvious that the France whose literature and history I taught and studied was just a fraction of the vast land I had seen"—a statement that, if true, means that he either failed to read or failed to understand most of the secondary works in his own bibliography.

He wanted to write a book, Robb says, "in which the inhabitants were not airlifted from the land for statistical processing, in which 'France' and 'the French' would mean something more than Paris and a few powerful individuals." It is a fine objective, but dozens of books in his own bibliography—by Braudel, Corbin, Weber, Pierre Goubert, Robert Darnton, and many others—have done precisely this. Robb does seem to have paid close attention to one of them, Weber's path-breaking study *Peasants into Frenchmen: The Modernization of Rural France*, which appeared in 1976, for he repeats a good many of its arguments about how a culturally isolated countryside became truly integrated into the nation only in the late nineteenth century. But he ignores nearly all of the vigorous debates Weber provoked (I participated in some of them), which ended up overturning or modifying many of his initial conclusions. And so Robb ends up trying to resuscitate a vision of pre-modern French rural life that serious scholarship has by now thoroughly discredited, while missing the ways this scholarship has rendered the subject not just far more complex but also far more interesting than its Romantic eulogists ever suspected. *The Discovery of France* is a case study in why academic history, for all its flaws, still matters.

Am I being too harsh? Robb's book, after all, is not an academic monograph. Indeed, he presents it as a sort of whimsical, historically informed guidebook that will help travelers discover France on their own. He calls it the fruit not only of "four years in the library" but also of "fourteen thousand miles in the saddle," traveling the length and breadth of the country on a bicycle. His title refers not just to efforts by historical geographers to map and to describe the country between 1789 and 1914 but also to his own physical and intellectual journey. And the book is certainly lively. Yet Robb's readers have the right to expect not just an engaging account of the French past but a well-informed and accurate one, particularly given his insistent claims to be overturning conventional wisdom and revealing hidden secrets about history. Robb presents his own research as a sort of Romantic quest that allowed him to recover truths that the dusty scholars missed or forgot. It is a charming (and ancient) conceit. The trouble is that when it comes to a subject as large and complex as the one he has taken on, it is nearly impossible for knight-errant research of this sort to come to any truly important or original conclusions, no matter how many years in the library and miles in the saddle the researcher puts in. If you don't rely on and engage with the collective accomplishments of serious scholarship, you are going to get the story wrong. Not every way of discovering France is equally good.

The problems arise above all in the first part of the book, in which Robb gives his overview of what he calls the "undiscovered continent" of premodern France—a continent "that had yet to be fully colonized." He casts the story as one of a vast and colorful diversity, which he contrasts to the monotone sameness that casual readers and travelers supposedly encounter in the France of our own day. Like Eugen Weber, he explains that customs, dress, and even language once varied from region to region, and sometimes from village to village. He vividly describes lost "tribes," such as the "Colliberts," who lived in the marshes of the Atlantic coast, rarely setting foot on dry land; and the "Cagots," who constituted a virtual caste of untouchables in the southwest; and the "Polletais" fisherfolk of Dieppe, who "spoke a dialect that was barely recognizable as a form of French."

Yet Robb fails to take this diversity seriously. For, unlike Weber, he soon starts dealing in generalizations that cover the entire country and several centuries of history. Robb actually knows quite well that this sort of approach is roundly ahistorical: in his first chapter, he writes reprovingly of existing scholarship that the people "who made up the 'rural' three-quarters of the population received historical rather than anthropological attention only when they began to think of themselves as French." (I would like to see Robb make this charge stick against any real scholar of the subject of the past forty years.) But he then proceeds to practice precisely what he preaches against, repeatedly implying that all parts of premodern French rural society lived according to essentially the same unchanging rhythms, until the advent of a modern state and economy wrenched them into history some time after 1800.

Here are some examples of the way Robb proceeds. When talking about premodern Catholicism, he offers the blanket assertion that "Jesus Christ was a relatively minor figure" and characterizes popular religious practice as everywhere dominated by pre-Christian and quasi-Christian beliefs: "a world of saints and fairies." He claims that French peasants—all of them, presumably—took "season-long siestas" in the winter, spending much of their time asleep, like hibernating animals. He insists that only the inhabitants of the Parisian basin thought of themselves as "French," and adds: "There was no deep-rooted sense of national identity."

In fact, each of these large generalizations collapses as soon as one looks more closely at the actual history. Calling premodern Catholicism heavily pagan ignores the Counter-Reformation, which not only did a great deal to formulate the dubious thesis of "pagan survivals" in the first place (so as to justify a massive enterprise of evangelization to overcome them) but also introduced hugely significant changes into the practice of rural religion, bringing much but not all of rural France surprisingly close to what would now seem conventional forms of Catholic observance. This transformation has been the subject of long and careful examination and debate by historians such as Jean Delumeau and Dominique Julia and religious sociologists such as Gabriel Lebras (all of whom Robb fails to cite on the subject). As for the winter "hibernation," it not only plays down the considerable work French peasants did in the winter repairing tools, making clothes, tending to animals, and traveling outside their villages as hired laborers; more important, it also ignores the crucial phenomenon of proto-industrialization. As historians such as Liana Vardi have shown, in some areas of northern France already in the eighteenth century a majority of rural households had abandoned subsistence farming to become weavers, producing textiles on a fairly large scale as part of extensive commercial networks based in the cities.

Robb's big assertions about national identity do not jibe with the fact that even in the middle of the eighteenth century, French military victories were cheered across the country, including in many rural areas. Or with the fact that millions of rural French people proudly asserted their identity as "French citizens" in the festivals of the French Revolution. Robb does not consider the possibility that these men and women might have stressed their regional identity when dealing with Parisians but their French identity when dealing with foreigners, as the historian Peter Sahlins showed in his book *Boundaries: The Making of France and Spain in the Pyrenees* (also not cited by Robb). Sahlins's fascinating work, which would have both enriched and complicated Robb's story, suggested that a strong sense of national identity first emerged in the borderlands—for instance, as villages sought the support of the French state in property claims against neighbors living on the other side of international frontiers. Again and again, scholarship on the subject has uncovered dynamic and interesting historical patterns that Robb's overarching generalizations simply cannot encompass.

Robb runs into these problems not only because he ignores so much important historical writing on premodern France but also because of the way he reads his sources. Throughout his book, he adopts a frustrating and contradictory strategy of reading: he chides earlier observers for perpetuating stereotypes and myths about the peasantry but then turns around, when it suits his purpose, and cites some of the most myth-laden sources as empirical descriptions of reality. Thus he oddly asserts that "some towns and villages were flourishing democracies when France was still an absolute monarchy," a claim belied by any number of histories of French rural life. Robb bases his claim largely on an account of a Picard village called Salency, written by a Norman merchant who visited it not long before the French Revolution. Robb is apparently unaware that Salency had been a fashionable destination for proto-Romantic pilgrims ever since the novelist Félicité de Genlis "discovered" it in the 1760s and enthused about the pristine pastoral charm of its annual "rose festival." Salency's villagers benefited considerably from this attention, but before the Revolution they still lived under a heavy burden of feudal law, which among other things forbade them from marrying outside their parish and subjected them to the rule of their overlord and parish priest. The merchant knew all about Salency's cult status and was eager to add to its legend.

Throughout his book, Robb repeatedly quotes travelers' accounts, novels, polemical histories, and political petitions without asking certain elementary questions about them. How were their descriptions shaped by generic convention? How were they influenced by their author's politics or aesthetics? What were the circumstances of their composition? Not surprisingly for a biographer of Victor Hugo, Robb draws with particular delight on Romantic literature for source material. But of course the Romantics liked nothing better than to portray rural life as isolated from the pernicious effects of the city and commerce, dominated by the rhythms of the natural world, and maintaining a close connection to a wild, ancient prehistory. These preconceptions derived directly from their artistic and philosophical ideals and colored everything they wrote on the subject. Robb correctly chides some of his authors for their condescension toward the peasantry but otherwise he tends to read their characterization of rural life with a surprising lack of skepticism. And so he ends up perpetuating many myths that the Romantics devised.

Admittedly, it can be very difficult to grasp the complex realities of premodern French culture, and it is worth looking more closely at one particular chapter of *The Discovery of France* to see why. The fourth chapter is amusingly titled "O Óc Sí Bai Ya Win Oui Oyi Awè Jo Ja Oua"—all different ways of saying "yes" in different French dialects and local languages. The point is to illustrate the idea that premodern France was a crazy quilt of different tongues, from Basque and Breton to Occitan (the distinct Romance language that dominated southern France, of which Provençal is the best-known dialect) and dialects of French itself. As a result, a great degree of misunderstanding occurred, often with comic results.

This characterization of French linguistic history is largely correct in a basic sense—although it is also utterly familiar to scholars at least since the publication of Ferdinand Brunot's fundamental *Histoire de la langue française—des origines à 1900* in the early twentieth century. (Robb does not seem to know it, although nearly all his secondary sources on this subject draw their evidence largely from it.) Yet the characterization is also woefully incomplete because of two further points, which historians and sociolinguists have often made but Robb largely misses. The first of these, as the existing scholarship amply recognizes, is that different local languages and dialects had greatly different histories and roles in French society. The German of Strasbourg and the Flemish of

Dunkirk were closely related to literary and administrative languages spoken just across the border and prevailed in towns and cities as well as the countryside. Occitan existed as a literary and administrative language until the progress of royal absolutism pushed it aside in favor of French. Breton and Basque did not exist as commonly written languages until modern times and were not much spoken by local social elites after the Middle Ages. Some non-French languages, in other words, were exclusively oral, limited to peasants, and easily looked down on as *patois* (the derogatory word comes from *patte*, an animal's paw, suggesting a whiff of the barnyard). Others, above all Alsatian German, managed to compete with French in many realms.

Second, the best-known sources have a strong tendency to exaggerate the extent of premodern linguistic diversity and mutual incomprehension. Most important here is the man Robb seizes on as the central figure in his discussion: the radical priest Henri Grégoire, best known for his efforts in favor of Jewish emancipation, who in 1790 sent a questionnaire on local languages to correspondents throughout France and received a fascinating set of responses. (Most of them were published in the 1880s and have received intensive study.) In 1794, at the instigation of the revolutionary government, Grégoire then composed a legislative report calling for the "eradication of *patois*" and the establishment of standard French as the country's sole language. In his report Grégoire stated categorically that only three million of France's nearly twenty-eight million people spoke proper French, while listing no fewer than thirty *patois* that supposedly competed with it. This evidence seems to corroborate Robb's thesis perfectly.

But here's the rub: Grégoire's work was anything but a neutral description of linguistic reality. A less well-known legislative report on language from the same year found serious linguistic difficulties only in four small peripheral regions: Brittany, the Basque country, Alsace, and Corsica. Its author, a Jacobin named Bertrand Barère, himself came from an Occitan-speaking area, but he did not regard the Occitan-French divide as an important one. The reason for the difference is that Grégoire had much higher standards than Barère for what it meant to "speak" a language. As a radical priest, he wanted to accomplish the political equivalent of a religious conversion with the peasantry, something that demanded a very high level of mutual comprehension. From this perspective, it was indeed true that very few people in France spoke sufficiently good French. But the historical evidence suggests that most speakers of Romance dialects could conduct basic market transactions in French, obey basic French military orders, understand the gist of French sermons or court proceedings, and so forth. Even in Celtic Brittany, French was widely understood, although barriers to comprehension were much higher.

In sum, claims to vast degrees of linguistic difference have to be taken with a great deal of salt. But Robb gives credence not only to Grégoire but also to later groups that had an even more obvious interest in exaggerating France's language problems, notably educational officials seeking to justify vast projects of language instruction and regionalist militants seeking to justify political autonomy on the basis of linguistic difference. The scholarly advances in this field have depended in part on relatively technical work in sociolinguistics, but it has been clearly summarized by historians, whom Robb could easily have consulted had he not been so enchanted by his own Romantic vision.

In the second part of his book, Robb recounts how educated, largely urban elites discovered his "undiscovered continent" between 1789 and 1914. They did so, he stresses, largely to pave it over, reducing its colorful and deeply human diversity to a bland and uniform sameness. "Pave over" should be taken rather literally, for Robb places a great deal of emphasis on transportation and is fascinated by the speed at which news and people traveled. At the time of the French Revolution, he notes, even high-speed messengers averaged only seven miles per hour over long distances. Road construction allowed for some improvement (it actually started well before the Revolution), but only the railroads brought real change. In 1828, France had fourteen miles of railroad track; sixty years later it had twenty-two thousand. And as the railroads connected previously isolated areas to major cities, an aggressively centralizing state began sending its "colonial" forces into the interior. "The Third Republic," Robb writes, sought to "erase local cultures," notably by "[massing] its pedagogical army on the wild frontier of language."

It is an attractive story (and a close cousin to the one Eugen Weber told thirty years ago). But once again, it is more than a little incomplete and misleading. As Tocqueville recognized a long time ago, the central state had a significant presence in rural France well before the nineteenth century. Meanwhile, even without railroads, a surprisingly large number of French people routinely traveled great distances long before the nineteenth century. Millions of often-desperate French men and women took to the roads each year in the 1700s, walking tens or hundreds of miles to find work. Shepherds took flocks across international borders. And as for artisans and servants, their established migration routes led not only to major cities, but even across the Atlantic, to French Canada and the Caribbean. Elsewhere Robb repeats the familiar claim that Third Republic schoolteachers harshly punished children for speaking *patois* in the classroom. Yet the historian Jean-Francois Chanet has shown that such stories have been exaggerated. Moreover, some parents *wanted* their children punished for speaking *patois* because they recognized the enormous social advantages that came with fluency in the national language.

Once again, one can only wish that Robb had engaged more seriously with the dusty old library. Olwen Hufton's magnificent study of the eighteenth-century poor contains the sort of stunning original material that begs for a writer of Robb's talent to convey to a larger public. Her vision of millions of men and women struggling to get by through an "economy of makeshifts," many of them tramping at their tragically slow pace through the French countryside, often reduced to petty theft or prostitution to survive, is as colorful and as powerful as Robb's vision of millions of men and women living their entire lives in virtual isolation, rarely encountering strangers or leaving the valleys of their birth. But Hufton's tale has the advantage of being supported by the evidence.

The Discovery of France has charmed many people because it is not, in truth, a discovery at all. For all its claims to novelty, its Romantic vision of a lost world is a very familiar and oddly comforting one. We like to see the past as a wild, colorful English garden that contrasts sharply with our own electrically lit, tightly scheduled lives. We like to imagine a world that may have been brutal and unfair, but was also close to nature and full of mystery and color and life—a world of saints and fairies, populated by idiosyncratic isolated "tribes" like the Colliberts and the Polletais. Above all, it is delightful to think that we can get tastes and glimpses of this world by pedaling through charming stretches of the French countryside, with someone like Graham Robb as our entertaining guide. If only it were so. But the work done by scholars since the

Romantic era has shown that the French past was really a very different sort of place—strange and mysterious and beguiling, but not in the way the Romantics imagined. And we can hope to grasp its reality only through hard digging in the archives and the libraries and the toil of historical analysis. A bicycle will not take us there.

The "salon" of Madame de Geoffrin, one of the most important gathering places for *philosophes* and members of French high society in the heyday of the Enlightenment. © RMN-Grand Palais / Art Resource, NY.

Part II

FROM THE OLD REGIME TO

THE REVOLUTION

———————⊃●○●⊂———————

FOR A PERIOD SO OFTEN called the "Age of Reason," the years from the late seventeenth century to 1789 have inspired a remarkable degree of mythmaking. But, then, humans tend to mythologize their origins, and modern intellectuals are no exception. As long as so many of these intellectuals locate the origins of their modern world in early modern Paris, we can expect their accounts of this time and place to come heavily freighted—not with deliberate fictions, but with narratives, concepts and conclusions that say as much or more about these intellectuals themselves as about their ostensible subjects. For some of them, the story is one of liberation—a glorious struggle for self-evident truths against obscurantist religion and despotic monarchs. For others, it is one of enslavement, of a sinister "Enlightenment Project" imprisoning helpless "subjects" in shackles that are all the more constraining for being invisible, and supposedly rational. There are stories about the rise of individualism—sometimes bourgeois, sometimes not. There are stories about the fall of an older, more graceful civilization—sometimes aristocratic, sometimes not. And at the end of most of these stories stands the French Revolution, whose character (whether seen as liberatory or horrific or something else) is held to confirm the points made about what preceded.

Not all the essays in this part deal with myth-inflected accounts of the period. The first essay discusses that bizarre baroque assemblage, the early modern French state, and one of the first great conscious attempts to modernize and rationalize it. The third and fourth look in detail at members of the eighteenth-century French Republic of Letters, including one who remains utterly obscure and two whose fame has never dimmed. The fifth notes that the supposed "Age of Reason" was also, very much, an age of Celebrity. But the other essays, more critically, take on three of the great enduring myths about the period: about the fall of a chivalrous aristocracy, about the rise of an individualist bourgeoisie, and about the Enlightenment as a conscious, unproblematic struggle for freedom.

I

The Colbert Report: Information Management, Bourbon-Style

THE NATURE OF THE STATE under which the French Enlightenment took shape has been almost as hotly debated as the Enlightenment itself. Contemporaries often compared it to a mansion built at different times, in wildly different architectural styles, of which half the wings had fallen into ruin. They labeled this assemblage "feudalism." Many of them also discerned, at the center of the state, a dangerous ambition by France's kings to gain tyrannical authority and bring "oriental despotism" to the country. Alexis de Tocqueville, a century later, believed that something rather different had taken place: a pathological drive for centralization, authoritarian in character, but also modernizing and rational, and producing a form of social equality. More recent historians have questioned whether any such deliberate process took place. They have again emphasized the enormous complexity and confusion of the state, and the endless negotiation and compromise that accompanied the actual business of French government. Their work has been persuasive. But it should not distract us from the fact that at the heart of the labyrinth, some farsighted figures were nonetheless elaborating

---

Book under Review: Jacob Soll, *The Information Master: Jean-Baptiste Colbert's Secret State Intelligence System* (University of Michigan Press, 2009). Essay originally published in *The New Republic*, October 7, 2009.

nfluential plans for reconstruction. Here is one of them, the subject of Jacob Soll's fine study.

———

That resonant piece of verbal shorthand, TMI—or Too Much Information—would make a fine epigraph for our age. Anyone with an Internet connection today has access to exponentially greater quantities of writing, images, sound, and video than anyone on earth could have imagined just twenty years ago. Small wonder that we have become obsessed with the idea of "information" as an abstract substance independent of its content—something that we accumulate, measure, and "process," rather than ponder and understand. And small wonder that the management and control of information, whether by its "producers," by governments, or by corporations such as Google, has emerged as an increasingly important political concern, and as a subject of scholarship.

This scholarship, in the field of history, has recently taken an intriguingly paradoxical turn. While the extreme availability of information today should presumably have highlighted its relative paucity in earlier periods, historians—most notably Ann Blair—have in fact extended the concept of "information overload" all the way back to the sixteenth century, arguing that while we now associate the phenomenon with the Internet, the printing press had a comparable effect. Until its invention, most literate people had access to relatively little written material. They could manage to read literally everything they could get their hands on. After Gutenberg, however, books multiplied rapidly, and soon many libraries became too large for their owners to read more than a small percentage of the available texts. It became necessary to devise strategies for dealing with the excess. Scholars invented systems of note-taking, methods of summarizing and skimming, and principles of triage. As Francis Bacon famously remarked: "Some books are to be tasted, others to be swallowed, and some few to be chewed and digested: that is, some books are to be read only in parts; others to be read, but not curiously; and some few to be read wholly, with diligence and attention." That is, among other things, a comment about coping.

We cope in the same way; and anyone who identifies Wikipedia with the end of civilization should be reassured to learn that early modern Europeans already possessed an impressive arsenal of intellectual crutches and shortcuts, some of them quite dubious. By the seventeenth century there already existed a large genre of reference works, compendia, and reading guides, so as to lead the uninitiated through the increasingly dense thickets of learning, sometimes at breakneck speed. Some readers made use of little else, with classical compendia particularly prized for the quick simulacra of learning they provided. As Jonathan Swift advised young critics, "Get scraps of Horace from your friends, / And have them at your fingers' ends." More serious scholars put together their own guides and reference works. Blair has shown that many of the greatest Renaissance thinkers had no compunction about attacking their books with scissors, cutting and pasting what they considered the crucial passages into commonplace books or card files for easy reference. By illuminating all these systems, methods, and reference works, Blair and her fellow scholars are giving us a new vision of Renaissance learning, grounded not simply in our own reading of the texts, but in an attempt to grasp what people at the time actually knew, and how they knew it.

Printed books and periodicals were not the only form of writing to proliferate wildly in early modern Europe. So did reports, memoranda, briefs, circulars, directives, and all the masses of paper that form the crinkly carapaces of modern governments. By the time of the French Revolution, it had become almost impossible for officials to imagine how earlier ages survived without them. "The ministry is a world of paper," wrote Saint-Just at the height of the Terror. "I don't know how Rome and Egypt governed without this resource." Saint-Just also identified the problems that arose as a result: "Government is impossible with too many words...the demon of writing makes war on us, and government stops." In short, early modern government needed information management just as much as early modern scholarship did.

The development of state information management might seem a dull subject. Ledgers, account books, and filing systems generally do not make for heroic drama or grand epic. Yet in the hands of Jacob Soll these mundane objects become strangely mesmerizing. A gifted intellectual historian known for a fine book on seventeenth-century French humanism and politics, Soll here shifts his attention to the core of the early modern state, and the attempt by the French monarchy under Louis XIV to establish a new sort of political preeminence over its large, diverse, and notoriously fractious nation: what historians today call the project of absolutism. In this process, Soll argues convincingly, officials began consciously to treat the generation, the control, and the management of information as a central instrument of power.

It helps that Soll's story has a genuinely fascinating protagonist. He is Jean-Baptiste Colbert, Louis XIV's chief minister. A ruthless and brilliant parvenu who rose to the commanding heights of French society and became the chief promoter of the economic policies known as mercantilism, Colbert is a well-known historical figure. But Soll reveals a new side of him, casting him as a sort of magnificent obsessive—a practical-minded Casaubon who pursued, throughout his life, an impossible dream of universal knowledge. Colbert, as Soll shows, took inspiration from the humanist scholars who longed to create a usable universal library, but he sought to direct his own information management system toward the single goal of strengthening the French monarchy. He would not collect information in general, but information of use in governing. And instead of making it available to all interested readers, he would hoard it as a valuable commodity, deploying it publicly only when it served the purpose of the state.

In designing this system, Soll argues, Colbert brought together two very different European traditions: not just the forms of information management developed in the humanist Republic of Letters, but also the reporting and accounting systems developed by Europe's great merchant houses. Here one great inspiration came from the Fugger family of Augsburg and its vast sixteenth-century trading empire, which depended on regular news reports from a far-flung network of correspondents (in a very real sense, the first "reporters"), and on sophisticated filing and accounting methods to manage them. Colbert himself came from a mercantile background in eastern France, and had an education appropriate to the milieu, with more attention to calculation and the mysteries of double-entry bookkeeping than to the subtleties of Latin verse.

In his early years, this mercantile background brought Colbert a great deal of scorn, both from the grand aristocrats who dominated the French state and the humanist scholars who advised them. They mocked his vulgar manners, his bourgeois dress (especially his "merchant's collar"), and his literary ignorance. But to Cardinal Mazarin, Richelieu's successor as France's chief minister in the war-torn 1640s, Colbert's talents for managing money spoke more eloquently than the scholars' talent for glossing Tacitus: thanks to him, Mazarin's personal fortune swelled to tens of millions of French pounds, an astonishing sum for the period.

While treating Colbert as a sort of glorified servant, Mazarin none-theless made him his principal accountant and trusted adviser, and then, most crucially, his librarian. The cardinal possessed the largest and best-kept library in France, which would become the core of the royal library, and thus the direct ancestor of today's Bibliothèque Nationale. Colbert grasped that the position gave him privileged access to precisely the sort of information Mazarin most needed in order to protect and strengthen the prerogatives of the monarchy against increasingly sharp challenges from at home and abroad.

To understand Colbert's strategies for collecting and managing in-formation, it is necessary to understand something about the baroque disaster area that was the early modern French state. Soll rightly calls it "staggeringly arcane—a feudal web of laws and taxes." Since the Middle Ages, the French monarchy had allowed layer after layer of institutions, laws, and practices to accumulate, often in competition with each other, and each possessing its own royally guaranteed privileges and responsi-bilities. The resulting confusion was a dream for lawyers and a nightmare for almost everyone else. France's provinces had one set of boundar-ies when it came to the authority of royal governors, another when it came to legal jurisdictions, another when it came to royal tax collect-ing, and still others for excise taxes, internal tariffs, and Catholic dio-ceses. Enlightenment commentators repeatedly likened the structure to a huge half-ruined mansion, and dreamed of blowing it up and starting again from scratch. (It is small wonder that the first great proj-ect of the French revolutionary state was the literal demolition of that hated symbol of royal power, the Bastille.) But the kings of the Old Regime, however "absolute" their supposed authority, could not simply call in the wrecking ball, because their regime, always skating the edge of bankruptcy, depended on the revenue gleaned from the complex and confusing web of privileges that ambitious subjects remained ever willing to pay for.

In this context, the single most valuable sort of information for the government concerned precedents. What share of its tax revenues did a particular town owe to the central state? How much had it actually turned over in the past? Who had the right to name its aldermen? How much could be charged for the privilege? What right did its courts have to interpret or obstruct royal legislation? What had taken place in previous disputes? If the Crown controlled the sources of information on such questions, it could resolve disputes in its own favor without incurring the charges of arbitrary rule and despotism that might destroy confidence in the system altogether.

Mazarin made good use of Colbert's talents in this area, and so did Mazarin's pupil King Louis XIV. When Mazarin died in 1661, the twenty-three-year-old Louis declared he would henceforth manage the government himself. But Colbert became chief minister in all but name and continued to build his state information system. Most immediately, he worked with the king to stifle challenges to royal authority from the obstreperous sovereign courts (*parlements*). And this was only the beginning. In the 1660s, he began to train, and send throughout the country, a cadre of "professional state observers" to put together what amounted to a political fact book of France: population numbers; information on land holdings, regulations, and laws; sketches of important personalities; data on economic activity. Soon Colbert expanded his ambitions to include neighboring countries as well. When he sent one observer—his son—to Italy in 1671, he gave him the following instructions. In each state, he said,

> look at... its situation, its military forces, the number of its peoples, the greatness of the state, the number and size of cities, towns, and villages, the quantity of the peoples that compose the whole; the form of State government, and if it is aristocratic... the names and status of noble families that have taken or will take part in governing the Republic; their different functions; their general and particular councils; who represents the State, in whom the sovereign power lies and who resolves peace and war, who makes laws; etc... the suffrages collected and the results taken and pronounced; the particular councils for the militia, the admiralty, justice, for the city and for the rest of the State; the laws and the customs under which they live; in what consist the militias meant to guard the main square.... Visit the public works, maritime and on ground, all the palaces, public houses, and generally all that is remarkable.

The letter itself proves that it is in no way anachronistic to apply terms like "information gathering" and "information management" to the seventeenth century.

The letter also gives evidence of Colbert's mania. He worked feverishly, always collecting, filing, and calculating. Soll calls him "a man apparently never happier than when filling out account ledgers." He reserved his anger above all for his son, whom he trained to take his place but who, predictably, could never live up to expectations. "I will visit every night my table and papers," the son promised Colbert obsequiously in 1671, "and I will expedite, before going to bed, that which I can, or I will put aside and send later, before marking, in my agenda that I will keep exactly on my table, the affairs that I will have sent out." But he repeatedly let down his demanding parent, who scolded him with cold fury in 1676: "You must still take care to look after your papers . . . [as] I asked you to do, and which I still do every day, for you, and which I now find rolled in a desk, in the worst state of filth, in spite of the fact that they contain the quintessence of the spirit of the most accomplished people in the kingdom." Outside the troubled bosom of his family, Colbert showed little emotion, earning the sobriquet of *le nord*—the north—from Madame de Sévigné.

Not surprisingly, Colbert's long-term goal proved impossible to realize. Soll defines it as the idea that "all knowledge, formal and practical, could be used together in one archival system to understand and master the material world." Colbert could no more complete this system than the Renaissance humanists could complete their ideal universal library.

Indeed, Louis XIV finally concluded that it was better not even to try, lest the attempt end up placing excessive power in hands other than his own. In 1683, after Colbert's sudden death (probably from a kidney stone), the king dismantled the system, and spread the responsibilities of information collecting and management among different ministries. Soll suggests, quite plausibly, that in doing so Louis "hobbled" the French state, making it even less possible to manage and setting it on the path to the mammoth bankruptcy and breakdown that, a century later, would usher in the French Revolution.

Yet Colbert did accomplish a great deal. He bought whole libraries and archives, and by the time of his death, the royal library had tripled in size, housing some thirty-six thousand books and 10,500 manuscripts.

His aides produced by far the most systematic and detailed descriptions of the country ever attempted, and for the first time in history the "nation" of France began to come into focus as a social unity that could be managed and transformed by political action. Colbert trained a cadre of talented officials to implement all these projects. He also enlisted some of the most gifted intellectuals of the day to help, including Charles Perrault, the famous author of fairy tales, and the academician Jean Chapelain. And he made excellent use of the information he harvested, particularly against the principal sources of domestic resistance to the king's absolutist project: the *parlements* and the Catholic Church. In 1682 he deployed his vast erudition to ensure wide support for measures subjecting the Church to an unprecedented degree of state control.

Colbert also worked to restrict the public flow of information, and here he set particularly long-lasting precedents. He made secrecy his byword and insisted that no one outside government had any right to a knowledge of its workings—particularly its financial workings. Soll depicts him at work ensuring that no Paris printer could learn Greek or Latin without official approval, so that potentially seditious classical scholarship would remain under close surveillance. He shows Colbert striving to suppress Richard Simon's pioneering critical treatment of the Old Testament—one of the first attempts to treat Scripture as a historical text—and promoting the idea that "history should serve only to conserve the splendor of the King's enterprises." While Louis XIV abandoned other elements of Colbert's information system, he happily retained all of these.

Soll tells this story in wonderfully lucid prose, and with a great gift for concision. Colbert emerges from his pages not only as the patron saint of modern bureaucrats, but as a forceful—if somewhat repellent—personality, and as another of the great early modern figures who sought to gain unprecedented knowledge of, and mastery over, the material world. What Galileo and Newton strove for in natural science, and Hobbes and Montesquieu in political science, Colbert, we now see, pursued in the less glorious but still vital realm of management and paperwork. In revealing this side of the minister, Soll has made a major contribution to our understanding of early modern history.

The principal criticism to be leveled at the book—a distinctly odd one for an academic monograph—is that there is not enough of it. Even

Soll's talent for concision does not save some chapters from feeling sparse, and Colbert's great enterprise devoid of a thicker and richer context. Soll does give tantalizing glimpses of this context. He knows the precedents for Colbert's projects well—especially those carried out by Italian and Spanish monarchs. He discusses them clearly, if briefly, and shows how Colbert's ambitions outstripped those of his predecessors. He also gives a brief, intriguing sense of how the story continued in the eighteenth century and afterward. But here, particularly, some important issues could have used fuller attention.

Following the French historian Roger Chartier, Soll suggests that the more the absolute monarchy became associated with secrecy, the more its opponents deployed the banner of "publicity" to resist it, seeking to promote both the free circulation of information and free debate about what that information meant. The antithesis of Colbert's philosophy of state secrecy came in the visions of a public sphere of free, rational, critical debate developed in the eighteenth century by writers such as Malesherbes, Condorcet, and Kant. As Soll astutely points out, this dialectical relationship between secrecy and publicity makes the state a much more important actor in the development of the early modern public sphere than most of its historians (who have principally studied the institutions of the sphere itself, such as salons and coffeehouses) have recognized.

Soll then gestures toward the modern consequences of the story. "Even for the most open of democracies," he writes, "the culture of state secrecy is necessary and potent, but at the same time, in its very essence, perverse and dangerous." True enough, but while such sentences conjure up images of a a sinister National Security Agency, the true modern heirs of Colbert's information system did not work for the American government but in Hitler's Chancellery, in Stalin's Kremlin, and in the East German Ministry of State Security, infamously known as the Stasi. It was in the bulging files the Stasi insanely tried to compile on each and every East German citizen, enlisting a substantial proportion of the population to spy on the rest (and each other), that Colbert's dream of encyclopedic information came closest to realization. Since the collapse of communism, the spirit of Colbertism lingers on in such places as Moscow, Beijing, and Tehran. And it is in such places that dissidents are now deploying the tools of the current information revolution, from e-mail to Facebook to Twitter, to establish a new public sphere in defiance of state secrecy.

What distinguishes democracy from authoritarian rule, on the level of information systems, is that in democracy such systems have the double purpose of informing the state about its citizens and its citizens about the state. What is at stake here is the principle of accountability. In absolutist France, the state's agents were ultimately accountable to no one but the king. Colbert's system, with its accompanying bureaucracy and paperwork, allowed the state to keep watch on civil society, but not the reverse. Democratic societies, however, demand this reversal. As the historian Ben Kafka has recently shown, French revolutionaries in 1789 made public accountability a key demand and wrote it into the Declaration of the Rights of Man and Citizen. From then on, Saint-Just's "demon of writing" would provide a public record of the state's doings and therefore help to protect citizens against the abuses of its agents. Modern bureaucracies remain riven by this tension between the two purposes of "public information."

More broadly, Soll does not engage explicitly enough with the large, fascinating question of how the control of information relates to the control of knowledge. He deals at great length with one of Colbert's minions, a certain Joseph-Nicolas Foucault, but another Foucault, the philosopher Michel, lurks ineluctably in the background of any book of this sort. Foucault's famous work on knowledge and power mostly investigated very different issues from the kind of information management ones Soll explores. Foucault showed the ways the naming of things, the categorization of knowledge, and the construction of "discourses" can radically shape the field of human action. In his later years, he brought this perspective to bear more closely on questions of governance, looking at how practices of categorization and discipline work through institutions to shape and control individual "subjects" (what he called "governmentality"). But his orientation toward philosophical problems rather than historical ones, and his tendency to see "discourses" and practices as all-encompassing and uniform, make it difficult for his work to explain actual processes of historical change. For this reason, careful historians still tend to shy away from invoking him too sweepingly.

Yet Soll's fine book makes it clear that Colbert's ministry represented not only a crucial stage in the development of state information management but also something new in the broader history of ideas. The mercantile perspective the minister brought to bear on statecraft and scholarship was, despite the mirage of universal knowledge it came bound up with, deeply utilitarian. When trying to understand and to evaluate the information that he so assiduously collected and organized, Colbert applied a single clear criterion: its practical use-value to the French state. In a world of statesmen and scholars obsessed with fame, glory, and eternal salvation, the introduction of such a perspective at the very summit of the state represented a significant change. Colbert may have been a quintessential figure of the Old Regime in his attachment to royal power and noble privilege, but in his utilitarian and empirically minded way of thinking he was nothing less than a precursor of the Enlightenment. Soll notes that the great *Encyclopedia* of Diderot and d'Alembert made reference to Colbert no less than 143 times.

The path from Colbert to the Enlightenment needs further investigation. So, for that matter, does the path to the Enlightenment from the scholarly forms of information management studied by historians such as Blair. How does our relationship to formal knowledge change when we do not read through a book from start to finish, submitting ourselves to its logic and authority—when we impose our own organizational scheme on it through sophisticated forms of note-taking and the use of reference guides? The suddenness and completeness of the shift from one form of reading to another should not be exaggerated, but the phenomenon still has clear importance to the development of what we call, however imperfectly, modernity. The still more radical challenge to reading posed by the electronic dissemination of texts likewise promises, in the long run, to have profound effects on our broader intellectual universe.

The great irony about Colbert is that the ways of knowing he championed would ultimately prove incompatible with the social and political values he defended. He himself, of course, did not see any contradiction between a utilitarian perspective and a system of absolute monarchy grounded in the divine right of kings, brutal religious intolerance, and social privilege; but later generations would see a flagrant contradiction and act decisively to resolve it. In this sense, the aristocrats and the scholars who saw Colbert as an alien, threatening presence in their midst had things exactly right. It is true, as Jacob Soll claims, that in the short term the French monarchy benefited from Colbert's ministrations, and might have benefited still more if his "system" had persisted after his death. From another perspective, however, he was less the state's servant than one of its gravediggers.

2

Twilight Approaches: Myths and Realities of the Literary Salons

THE FRENCH ARISTOCRATS WHO DISDAINED Colbert as a vulgar, upstart par-
venu liked to imagine themselves as the incarnation of more elevated quali-
ties: refinement, delicacy, wit, honor, splendor, civility, and courage. They
attempted to cultivate these qualities in their daily behavior, and the litera-
ture they sponsored and produced reflects this concern —often quite beauti-
fully. But however attractive the nobility's self-representation, it was never
more than one facet of a much more complex and conflicted social world that
depended, for its very existence, on the backbreaking labor of millions of
peasants. The collapse of this world at the time of the French Revolution was
itself an enormously complex affair. But the myths conjured up by the en-
chanting literature about both this world and its extinction have been re-
markably enduring, as this essay reveals.

There is a fable about the French past that goes as follows. Sometime in
the seventeenth century, the country's proud noble caste was humbled

Book under Review: Benedetta Craveri, *The Age of Conversation*, translated by Teresa Waugh (New York Review, 2006). Essay originally published in the *London Review of Books*, May 11, 2006.

and tamed by imperious ministers and kings. Where once it had swayed the destinies of Europe, it was now confined to the gilded cage of the royal court and the elegant salons of Paris. Others might have raged against this fate, but the French nobility adapted to it. Its members developed exquisite manners. They made beauty their grail and cultivated sophisticated, graceful pleasures. Guided by refined *salonnières*, they reveled in wit, savored the joys of idleness, and raised polished conversation to the level of fine art. Sometimes their delights devolved into debauch, but even the debauch retained a certain indefinable elegance. The nobles never forgot who they were. And when the supreme test came, in the French Revolution, they did their duty with a gallantry that shamed their coarse, plebeian tormentors. In the killing fields of the Vendée, noblemen and noblewomen alike rediscovered the heroism of their chivalric ancestors. In the Jacobin prisons, they retained their dignity and *savoir-vivre*. According to Hippolyte Taine, "women particularly went to the scaffold with the ease and serenity with which they attended a soirée."

This fable has had remarkable staying power, in popular history, fiction, and film—yet nearly everything about it is wrong. The French nobility was never a caste. It was a porous and untidy social category that incorporated hundreds of thousands of individuals, ranging from the grand aristocrats of Versailles to retired provincial aldermen. The French state sold off noble titles by the bushel to support its perennially woeful finances, with the result that by 1789 a large majority of titleholders could not trace their noble ancestry back beyond 1600. Only a small percentage of the nobility ever lived at Versailles, and a sizeable proportion of the men there did not pass their lives in idle court ritual, but remained devoted to the traditional calling of their class, the military. Despite a loss of independent political power, nobles continued to dominate the state apparatus. In the provinces, they managed their estates with an almost bourgeois dedication to profit and led the way in developing mining, metallurgy, and the beginnings of French industry. In the Revolution, most nobles did not stand and fight gallantly. They fled abroad, or kept their heads low, or became revolutionaries themselves. The Duc de Lauzun, renowned as the best-mannered aristocratic dandy of the eighteenth century, fought in the Vendée on the side of the Jacobins, helping to slaughter the region's Catholic, royalist rebels.

Graceful and refined conversation did take place in the Ancien Régime, and the ideal of graceful idleness held a powerful allure. So did the famous salons, often presided over by wealthy noblewomen, that brought together high-ranking aristocrats and fashionable writers and artists. But this institution also served some very serious social purposes, as Antoine Lilti shows in his new book *Le Monde des salons: Sociabilité et mondanité à Paris au XVIIIème siècle*. It was a site for the socialization of elites, for the negotiation of patronage relationships, for competition between different aristocratic cliques, for the establishment of the most severe sorts of social distinction. The degree of aesthetic refinement that prevailed there is easily exaggerated. Lilti also makes clear that the salons varied widely in their social composition, in the role women played, and in their relationship to literary life.

Benedetta Craveri's book on the salons, *The Age of Conversation*, first published in Italy in 2001, often resembles the fable more than the reality. To be sure, it is grounded in serious research. Craveri has read through the voluminous memoirs and correspondence about the salons, and the voluminous historical writing on the subject. She pays the American scholar Daniel Gordon, author of an important study of Enlightenment ideas of sociability, the compliment of following him so closely as to lapse, on occasion, into paraphrase. And yet, time and again, the entrancing fable dances away with her like a seducer at a ball.

For instance, she ends the book with a long passage from Hippolyte Taine that describes, in prose worthy of *The Scarlet Pimpernel*, imprisoned aristocrats defying their Jacobin jailers by paying social calls from cell to cell, composing madrigals, retaining utter self-control and carrying on with light, debonair conversation, even while awaiting the tumbrels that would take them to the guillotine. Is there any reason why we should trust this late nineteenth-century reactionary—an interesting thinker, but an exceptionally sloppy and tendentious historian? The republican historian Alphonse Aulard filled an entire short book enumerating the factual errors in Taine's history of the Revolution. Taine based the passage in question on noble memoirs and letters, and they are as self-serving and mythological as any sources of this kind. Did middle-class prisoners in the Luxembourg whimper in fear while the aristocrats held fast to their *savoir-vivre*? Or did some of the commoners face death stoically, perhaps even compose a madrigal or two, while some of the aristocrats cowered? Taine won't tell us, and neither will Craveri. Instead, she cites the passage as proof that in the Revolution "the privileged order revealed its true value and the strength of its civilisation."

The problem with this statement, and with Craveri's book, is not so much that France's privileged order depended for its existence on a vast structure of misery and exploitation, although of course it did, but that Craveri takes idealized, flattering descriptions of noble life, and rules for how to behave in salons, as accurate accounts of their historical reality. Although she introduces the book as "the story of an ideal," the distinction between ideal and real quickly blurs in her pages. In describing the first great salon of the early seventeenth century, that of Madame de Rambouillet in her famous "Blue Room," she repeatedly uses one particular adjective: "a utopian place," "this frankly utopian quality," "this utopian way of life," "the Blue Room's utopian world." Is she referring to the way the authors wanted to see the room, or to the way she believes it actually was? She never quite makes it clear. At another moment she quotes several descriptions of the room, including this: "The air is always scented...various magnificent baskets of flowers impart a continuous springtime to her chamber, and the room where one usually sees her is so agreeable and so well conceived that one imagines oneself in an enchanted place." But this particular passage comes from Mlle de Scudéry's novel *Le Grand Cyrus*, which may be "thinly veiled" fiction, but is still, decidedly, fiction. Craveri devotes all too little attention to the difficult questions of early modern French generic conventions, literary style, the meaning of patronage relations for literature, and the effect that authors intended to have through their writing.

In justifying her approach, Craveri writes that she sought a "narrative mode unburdened by academic language." She has succeeded, but academic language is not always pointless jargon. Some brief, clear analyses of literary conventions, of modes of representation, of social structure, even of (dread word) "discourse," might have given her book a degree of badly needed precision. And then there is the problem that, in practice, her "marrative mode" can stray perilously close to the style of Harlequin Romance. A noble home is "illuminated by a thousand candles, shimmering with crystal and silver, and teeming with the full flower of the French nobility"; Mlle d'Epernon had "a tender, chaste love" for the Chevalier de Fiesque, while "no one had a happier youth than Mlle de

Bourbon." Noblemen are generally "glorious," "bold," or "valorous." As for the unfortunate Mme de Montbazon, she "knew no law other than her own desire. She loved love, sex, money and power, which she high-handedly demanded, bowling men over with her sumptuous, sensual beauty." All that is lacking are tenderly heaving bosoms and a hero's stern, noble brow. (Teresa Waugh, the book's translator, is not to blame here—the prose is just as purple in the Italian original.)

Despite these problems, Craveri sketches vivid portraits of individual salons and *salonnières*. She starts with Madame de Rambouillet and the select company who gathered in her Blue Room, conversing on courtly love and courtly virtue, composing light verse in rounds, and partaking of deceptively casual conversation. It was in this setting that the basic roster of salon activities—meals, reading out loud, theatricals, music, dancing, and conversation—took definitive shape. Craveri describes how, with the mid-seventeenth-century rebellion known as the Fronde, this extended romantic idyll gave way to more insistent forms of aristocratic sociability, exemplified by Mme de Montbazon. She also writes about the salon hostesses and their retinues who subsequently gravitated toward the gloomy, austere Catholicism of the Jansenists. The brilliant, phobic Madame de Sablé (afraid of falling too deeply asleep, she had a servant sit by her side through the night, shaking her at regular intervals) set up a glittering salon in the grounds of the sober Jansenist convent at Port-Royal.

While Craveri stresses the continuities in salon life across the seventeenth and eighteenth centuries, she also shows how certain salons of the later period developed important new intellectual ambitions, attracting the likes of Montesquieu, Diderot, d'Alembert, d'Holbach, and Helvétius, and becoming central institutions of the French Enlightenment. Indeed, the style of salon conversation arguably shaped much of Enlightenment thought. "I have neither the time nor the taste for reading," Diderot once told a friend. "To read all alone with no one to talk to, no one to argue with, no one to shine in front of, to listen to or to listen to one, is impossible." The salon, not the study, was Diderot's true milieu, and the playful, speculative, deliberately unfinished quality of his writing owes everything to it. His most daring philosophical work, *D'Alembert's Dream*, took the form of a salon-style conversation, and introduced the salonnière Julie de Lespinasse as a character. Craveri doesn't mention the fact, but the great early condemnation of European imperialism and slavery called *History of the Two Indies*, on which Diderot collaborated, was compiled in large part during salon discussions.

Throughout her book, Craveri argues for the importance of the salons for women—or, at least, that small number of aristocratic women to whom they offered unprecedented influence and freedom. There was no other early modern country in which women took on the effective leadership of polite society so fully and also helped shape the direction of literary life. They exercised leadership because it was in the intimate, feminine spaces of salons that the high aristocracy sought refuge from the glare of the royal court, and solace for their loss of independent political power. They shaped literary life because they acted as arbiters of the spoken language. Despite their generally poor education (and notoriously awful spelling), the conversation of salonnières set the standard for polite, appropriate speech, and therefore directly influenced the literature that emerged from their homes, whether the playful poetry of Vincent Voiture, the tart maxims of La Rochefoucauld, or Diderot's philosophical speculations.

Beyond making these points, Craveri has an eye for some delightful stories. A nine-year-old Mlle Montmorency was chided by her tutor, Mme de Richelieu, for a small fault. "I could kill you," Richelieu exclaimed to her charge. "It would not be the first time that the Richelieus were executioners of the Montmorencys," the girl replied (too good to be true, perhaps, but first recorded in a private diary). Writing to an eleven-year-old princess, Voiture, the poet laureate of the Blue Room, fantasized about being tossed in a blanket, so high that all Europe appeared below him: "I saw the winds and the clouds passing under my feet; I discovered countries I had never seen and seas I had never imagined...I saw you crossing the Saône at Lyon...I could not easily discern who was with you, because I was upside down at the time." The fastidious Madame de Sablé objected to the sight of a nun's body awaiting burial at Port-Royal: "The day advances, twilight approaches," the convent's famous abbess, Angélique Arnaud, gently explained. Nonetheless, from then on the nuns kept corpses well away from their wealthy benefactress.

Craveri does particularly well with the character of Claudine Guérin de Tencin, one of the greatest, most colorful figures from the world of the salons. Born to a family of Grenoble magistrates in 1681, she entered a convent at her father's wish, but not before secretly visiting a notary to sign an affidavit stating her unwillingness to take the veil. After her father's death, she used it to sue, successfully, for a release from her vows, and moved to Paris. There, she wrote several fine novels and started a series of affairs with the most powerful men in the kingdom, using her influence over them to advance her brother's career in the Church (she did it so well he ended up a cardinal). She also founded the first great literary salon of the century, attracting Montesquieu, Fontenelle, Marivaux, and Bolingbroke, among others. After giving birth to an illegitimate child in 1717, she left him on the stairs of the Church of Saint-Jean-le-Rond in Paris, never to acknowledge his existence. The boy grew up to become the philosopher and mathematician Jean le Rond d'Alembert, coeditor with Diderot of the *Encyclopédie*, and a popular salon figure in his own right. Mme de Tencin's story is not unfamiliar, but Craveri tells it with great verve.

What larger meanings do these stories have? In recent years, the salons and their privileged denizens have featured with remarkable frequency in arguments about the origins of modern culture. It has been argued that they represented a new sort of space for free, critical discussion, prefiguring the modern, democratic public sphere. It has been claimed that they helped engender modern ideas of sociability and society. Like Craveri, several historians have emphasized the freedom and influence they offered to women, and even suggested that they spawned a sort of proto-feminism. Dena Goodman has contended that the gentle guidance given by salonnières to philosophical discussion itself constituted a critical contribution to Enlightenment thought. Lilti powerfully criticizes all this work (including Craveri's) for focusing arbitrarily on a small number of salons that actually formed part of a far larger web of aristocratic sociability, much of it dominated by men, and relatively indifferent to the joys of literary conversation. The very idea that there existed a distinct, female-dominated literary institution called the "salon," Lilti contends, is an invention of postrevolutionary aristocratic nostalgia for what Talleyrand termed the vanished "sweetness of life" in the Ancien Régime. The word "salon" itself was not used to describe gatherings like Madame de Rambouillet's until 1794.

Craveri, unfortunately, has surrendered far more deeply to the nostalgic myths than the other work Lilti criticizes. For, very much like the nineteenth-century memoirists and belletrists who first cultivated the fable of the salons, she has no desire to see them as modern in any significant way. For her, they represent precisely what a cold, grasping modernity has largely destroyed: a utopian realm of beauty, refinement, wit, cultivated leisure, and sexual equality. "How," she asks in her introduction, "can we compare the intimidating, prefabricated notion of 'free time' with a culture of leisure in which art, literature, music, dance, theatre and conversation all constituted a permanent training for the body and the mind?"

This is a perfectly defensible view (if rather distressingly indifferent to all those servants and serfs whose sweat made the "culture of leisure" possible), and one shared by many scholars. But in Craveri's hands, the sheer weight of nostalgic celebration, and the stubborn unwillingness to distinguish representation from reality, leave the critique of modern life largely unpersuasive. It is one thing to hold up our modern forms of social interaction against the actual practices of past societies and to find ourselves wanting. It is quite another to compare our present lives with past ideals, flattery, and myths. There is nothing wrong with writing history in an elegiac mode. But Craveri has written the elegy of a dream. It makes for charming reading, but not for convincing scholarship.

3

Profane Illuminations: The Enlightenment's Feuding Giants

HISTORIANS IN SEARCH OF THE ORIGINS of modernity naturally like to portray the French Enlightenment as a rupture in time. The great French scholar Paul Hazard located this rupture in the decades around 1700, claiming that, virtually in the blink of an eye, the French went from "thinking like Bossuet" (a great bishop and theologian of the age of Louis XIV) to "thinking like Voltaire." By this he meant, above all, that they embraced the cause of reason while questioning their Christian faith and the aristocratic values of the Ancien Régime. But as this essay underlines in considering two excellent biographies, even the Enlightenment's most famous philosophes, for all their originality, cannot be placed into such an attractively simple schema. Voltaire, for all his reputation as an iconoclastic advocate of religious toleration, had a distinctly Ancien Régime temperament and Ancien Régime ambitions. In many ways, he adored the values of aristocratic salons discussed in the previous essay and felt very much at home in them. Jean-Jacques Rousseau was by far the greater rebel. But Rousseau rebelled not just against

---

Books under Review: Roger Pearson, *Voltaire Almighty: A Life in Pursuit of Freedom* (Bloomsbury, 2005); Leo Damrosch, *Jean-Jacques Rousseau, Restless Genius* (Houghton Mifflin, 2005). "Profane Illuminations" by David A. Bell from the December 5, 2005, issue of *The Nation*. Copyright 2005–2006, *The Nation*.

the Ancien Régime, but also, just as important, against the Enlightenment itself.

In the early 1980s, while studying in Paris, I stumbled across the wonderful bookstore of the Libre Pensée (Free Thought) association. Tucked away in the narrow streets of the Fifth Arrondissement, near where Balzac set *Le Père Goriot*, it seemed a relic of the past: shabby, dim, and cluttered, with the gentle odor of old book leather hinting at hidden treasures on the shelves. And indeed, most of the books appeared, delightfully, to have come out of an alternate timeline in which the age of Voltaire had never ended. Thick volumes denounced the hidden conspiracies of the Jesuits and chronicled the crimes of the Inquisition. Pamphlets offered concise defenses of Deism. And a rickety postcard stand displayed, alongside the usual images of the Panthéon and the Seine, engravings of the execution of Jean Calas, an eighteenth-century victim of religious bigotry posthumously exonerated through the efforts of Voltaire. One half expected to see the philosophe himself browsing quietly at the next shelf.

Back then, La Libre Pensée seemed like nothing more than a pleasant curiosity. After all, the great battles of the Enlightenment had burned out long before. Religious intolerance and fanaticism were no longer matters of major concern. Indeed, for many of my French fellow students, the great enemy was the Enlightenment itself. Every week they would cram into a crowded lecture hall at the Collège de France to hear Michel Foucault, then in the last year of his life, explain how the eighteenth century saw the imprisoning of the Western world in a straitjacket of mental discipline. They struggled to grasp the quicksilver sentences in which Jacques Derrida deconstructed the criteria of rationality and truth that eighteenth-century philosophy had taken as axiomatic. They spoke derisively of an Enlightenment that had culminated not in modern democracy but in Auschwitz.

Today, things look rather different. Pace Foucault, enlightened psychiatrists and prison reformers do not seem particularly dangerous compared with suicide bombers and book burners. In the twenty-first century the Enlightenment appears anything but the triumphant imperial "project" denounced by vulgar postmodernists. Its heritage is fragile and endangered. Admittedly, its works remain in the "canon"—but perhaps only because they go largely unread in certain quarters. I sometimes wonder what would happen if, for instance, a public university system asked all entering students to read Voltaire's *Philosophical Dictionary*, with its deep, deliberate offensiveness toward Christianity. What if a major studio attempted to film his *Mahomet*, a play far more systematically disparaging of the Prophet than Rushdie's *Satanic Verses*?

If nothing else, though, our own century's retreat from the Enlightenment should help us appreciate that this great movement of ideas has been a fragile thing all along, and never more than in its supposed eighteenth-century heyday. Its swift apparent triumph in the American and French revolutions makes it easy to forget that its greatest authors constantly ran afoul of the authorities and took great personal risks throughout their careers. Both Voltaire and Jean-Jacques Rousseau, as these two excellent new biographies point out, had books officially shredded and burned in Paris—even if, in Voltaire's case, the responsible official surreptitiously substituted another volume at the last minute, so as to take the offending one home for himself. Roger Pearson reminds us that Voltaire served several stints in prison, lived much of his life in exile from his native France, and had to have the sheets of his first great work, the *Philosophical Letters*, smuggled into Paris in a furniture cart. Even his most famous patron, Prussia's Frederick the Great, once remarked of him: "I shall have need of him for another year at most, no longer. One squeezes the orange and throws away the peel." As for Rousseau, Leo Damrosch recalls that the threat of prosecution kept him constantly on the move among France, Switzerland, and Britain. "I never get a virtuous or useful idea," Rousseau wrote to his patron Malesherbes in 1765, "without seeing the gallows or the scaffold before me."

The remark may seem overly dramatic, even paranoid—and Rousseau very likely did suffer from clinical paranoia in his last years. But consider that in 1766, a twenty-one-year-old nobleman named Jean-François de La Barre was publicly tortured, decapitated, and burned in the northern French town of Abbeville for the "crime" of impiety—with the charge proved by nothing more than the fact that he owned a copy of Voltaire's *Philosophical Dictionary*. The executioner threw the book onto the funeral pyre next to his victim's head.

How, then, did the Enlightenment manage to survive at all, let alone flourish? To answer this question, historians generally try to locate figures like Voltaire and Rousseau within large-scale cultural shifts. They talk of the general weakening of religious orthodoxy, despite cases like de La Barre's, and the declining ability of the Christian churches to impose beliefs on the supposed faithful. They invoke the vertiginous expansion of the book market and the even more vertiginous rise of institutions—lending libraries, coffeehouses, newspapers, reading circles—that brought Enlightenment ideas to the attention of a new reading public. Between them, Voltaire and Rousseau largely invented the phenomenon of the intellectual celebrity, and their resulting popularity, of which even absolute monarchs took heed, gave them a form of protection that unknown figures like de La Barre tragically lacked.

Of course, both men also enjoyed a more traditional form of writers' insurance: aristocratic patronage. Rousseau may have written the century's most eloquent defenses of social equality, but he could never have done so without the money, shelter, and protection offered him by the Duke and Duchess of Luxembourg, the Prince de Conti, the Earl Marischal, the Marquis de Girardin, and many others. Had Voltaire not made close friends at school with the future Marquis d'Argenson and Duke de Richelieu, his youthful poem accusing France's ruling regent of incest might well have been his last (as it was, the regent had him banished from Paris for it). Historians of late have given particular prominence to female patrons who transformed intellectual conversation with Enlightenment authors into an art form. In the case of Voltaire's liaison with the Marquise du Châtelet, and Rousseau's with the Countess d'Houdetot, the relationship turned passionate and erotic, although in the latter case it remained unconsummated. (Both women, incidentally, also took as a lover the aristocratic poet Saint-Lambert; Châtelet died giving birth to his baby.)

Neither Pearson nor Damrosch, both literary critics by training, engages extensively with this historical background, and as a result their books give relatively little sense of the Enlightenment as a cultural phenomenon. While both provide exhaustive accounts of the aristocratic patrons, they spend much less time on their subjects' equally important relationships with the common reader. The books chronicle the personal dangers but largely ignore the broader intellectual reactions that the two men provoked, including a smoking lava flow of condemnation from the Christian churches. For that matter, neither Pearson nor Damrosch gives much attention to the Enlightenment as an intellectual movement or to his subject's relationships with other thinkers.

Rather, the books offer conventionally framed life stories of two figures who were intellectual colleagues, rivals, and ultimately bitter enemies. Pearson takes us through the familiar territory of François-Marie Arouet's 1694 birth in the home of a Paris notary (although his true father was probably a writer of popular songs), his brilliant school career and quick success as a playwright under the name Voltaire, and the early notoriety he earned for his daring *Philosophical Letters*, based on his observations of England. We follow him through his prolific love affairs, his even more prolific travels, his fantastically prolific publications, and his unbelievably prolific correspondence, as he transformed himself into the century's grand, totemic intellectual. Living just across the border in Switzerland, Voltaire waged crusade after crusade for freedom of thought, finally returned to Paris for a triumphant visit at age eighty-four, and then, with impeccably theatrical timing, died.

Damrosch begins in 1712 with Rousseau's birth to a Genevan watchmaker father and a mother who died from complications resulting from childbirth. We learn of his idiosyncratic early education, his running away from home before his sixteenth birthday, his subsequent picaresque wanderings, his tardy achievement of fame, and his writing of some of the most influential works of the century, including *The Discourse on Inequality*, *The Social Contract*, *La Nouvelle Héloïse*, *Emile*, and the *Confessions*. The book concludes with Rousseau's slide into increasing eccentricity and paranoia, his break with nearly all his former friends, and his death, on the gentle grounds of the château of Ermenonville, just five weeks after Voltaire's.

In the classic Anglo-American biographical manner, both books focus heavily on personality, personal relationships, and the physical settings. (Both therefore devote considerable space to the scenery of Switzerland, place of Rousseau's birth and Voltaire's exile.) Pearson gives a lavish account of the landscaping and renovations carried out at Voltaire's château in Ferney—even the heating and plumbing. ("The sanitary requirements of master, mistress and guests were met by the *chaise percée*...water was heated in a boiler and delivered through lead piping to a tin bath lined with marble.") Damrosch includes photographs of Rousseau's surviving abodes and describes the plaques and street signs that now adorn them. Both authors give lavish attention to clothes, notably the flow-ingly effeminate Armenian gown Rousseau had made for himself in the early 1760s, to the astonishment of his neighbors, and the velvet-and-ermine housecoat Voltaire wore to keep warm (it cost twice the average workman's yearly wages). Bodily complaints naturally receive detailed treatment as well, particularly since, like nearly everyone in the eight-eenth century who survived to middle age, both men suffered from painful chronic ailments. Voltaire had a notoriously weak digestive system, which he could only soothe by drinking ass's milk. Rousseau often found it almost impossible to urinate, relying on primitive cathe-ters that caused frequent infections and terrific discomfort.

Above all, of course, there is sex, in both cases titillatingly irregular, although for Rousseau largely in the head. ("D. H. Lawrence used to preach against sex in the head, but that is where Rousseau's sex life nearly always took place," Damrosch comments nicely.) Rousseau's urinary af-fliction obviously contributed to his inactivity on this front, but as Damrosch plausibly suggests, his obsession with his penis probably had psychosomatic origins. Nor did the affliction cause complete impair-ment. In 1766 the young James Boswell, of all people, seduced Rousseau's longtime companion, Thérèse Levasseur, meticulously recording that they made love thirteen times. "Don't imagine you are a better lover than Rousseau," she chided him, deflatingly. Thérèse, an engaging but barely literate laundress whom visitors routinely mistook for Rousseau's housekeeper, may have borne as many as five of his children. But in the behavior that has caused his admirers the most pain, the philosophe deposited each newborn child at a foundling home, where the dreadful conditions almost certainly killed them.

Curiously, for both men important chapters of their sexual lives in-volved incest. Rousseau, after running away from Geneva, found a home with the eccentric and beautiful Madame de Warens, whom he called "mother." Three years later the relationship, the most important of Rousseau's life, became amorous. As for Voltaire, after the death of his great love the Marquise du Châtelet, he set up house with his own niece, Madame Denis, and in 1753 made her pregnant, although she miscar-ried. ("Would her child have called its famous progenitor 'Great Uncle' or just plain 'Papa'?" Pearson asks irreverently.) Despite living in this exceptionally fragile glass house, it was Voltaire who revealed the fate of Rousseau's abandoned children in a vicious 1764 pamphlet.

Little of this material is unfamiliar to specialists. Pearson and Damrosch have both drawn principally on their subjects' published works and correspondence, the memoirs of acquaintances, and other established sources from the period. Nor does either author pretend to offer dramatically new interpretations. Damrosch, while making persuasively strong claims for Rousseau's radical originality, relies heavily on the earlier work of Jean Starobinski and Arthur Melzer. Pearson closely follows earlier studies as well, particularly by the French Voltaire scholar René Pomeau. Both books, in other words, amount to popular distillations more than original research.

But popularization was an honorable and important Enlightenment art. Voltaire collaborated with the Marquise du Châtelet on popular expositions of Newton's work, and both he and Rousseau engaged brilliantly with broad general audiences throughout their careers. As popularizations, both new biographies succeed marvelously. They provide full, vivid, dramatic, and well-informed portraits of their subjects. And by doing so, they remind us of something professional historians of the period all too often forget: if the Enlightenment did in fact survive and flourish, it did so not only because of sweepingly impersonal changes in structures of belief, the book market, and institutions of intellectual sociability but because of the actions of some remarkable individual thinkers.

Pearson and Damrosch have also managed to overcome obstacles that have defeated many previous biographers. True, neither Voltaire nor Rousseau presents the sort of problems found in a figure like Shakespeare, who died just eighty years before Voltaire's birth, yet on whom we have such little information that biographers must resort again and again to little more than hopeful speculation. The works and correspondence of Voltaire fill hundreds of large, dense volumes, and while Rousseau takes up less shelf space, among his works is the astonishing autobiographical *Confessions*. But the sheer volume of Voltaire's material quickly becomes overwhelming, and Rousseau's *Confessions* mislead as well as inform, reflect their author's creeping paranoia, and present the constant dilemma of what to make of episodes for which no independent corroboration exists. Pearson's and Damrosch's books weigh and distill this daunting source material as well as any concise biographies in English.

The books make clear that despite many surface parallels (the incest, the chronic afflictions, the persecution and exile, the aristocratic patrons),

Voltaire and Rousseau were not just remarkable but remarkably different: the Janus faces of the Enlightenment. Voltaire, despite his reputation, became a radical against his own inclinations. Throughout much of his career he longed for nothing more than to ascend the established cultural heights of the Ancien Régime, particularly membership in the Académie Française and the post of historiographer royal (he succeeded in both). He ruled his Swiss domain like a lord of the manor and, in classic aristocratic fashion, treated his life as one long elegant, utterly assured theatrical display. He disdained the poor; and despite his stinging critiques of war, he made a fortune investing in military contracting. His hatred of established religion bled into a vicious anti-Semitism that went far beyond the Orientalism-tinged anticlericalism of his play *Mahomet* (itself mostly meant as a covert attack on the Catholic Church and understood as such at the time). He was insufferably vain. "It is not enough for him to be the hero of the century," wrote his disciple La Harpe (in a passage quoted by Damrosch, not Pearson). "He wants to be the news of the day, for he knows that the news of the day often makes people forget the hero of the century."

Pearson acknowledges all these points—with the exception, perplexingly, of the anti-Semitism. And he admits that Voltaire was not really an original thinker. But he compellingly argues that the man's very lust for fame, tied to a basic sense of justice, led him into the fray, again and again, against intolerance and fanaticism, most notably in the campaign to exonerate Jean Calas. This lust also led him to employ his wonderfully powerful wit in an unending flow of essays, histories, and philosophical tales (especially *Candide*) that brought the Enlightenment credo of tolerance and rationality to an entire continent of readers.

Rousseau, though no amateur when it came to vanity, could not have been more different. Neither a brilliant student nor an artistic prodigy, he struggled for decades before making his reputation. Damrosch plausibly suggests that he suffered from dyslexia, which forced him to read very slowly but also, perhaps, with unusual concentration and intensity. Although capable of great charm, he usually felt ill at ease in social situations and ostentatiously scorned the sort of glittering positions Voltaire so avidly sought, for fear of ending up in a situation of dependence. Eventually he broke with society altogether and decided to live the life of a modern hermit (in truth, a rather coddled hermit). He gave sincerity the place of honor among the virtues and longed for what Jean Starobinski famously called "transparent" relations between people, unobscured by deceitful appearances. He praised simple sentiment above complex reasoning and called religion a matter of feeling, not intellection. From his condemnations of the hypocrisy and corruption of society stem two centuries of radical critique.

Many others had made such critiques before, in the religious language Rousseau could not help echoing. What gave his version such immense power and originality was the way he tied it to the modern concepts of social and personal development. Most of the philosophes, including Voltaire, saw both sorts of development as a simple matter of overcoming ignorance and barbarity. In this view, as both individuals and societies grow older, they learn manners and refinement, adopt more rational forms of behavior, and put behind them the willfulness, violence, and ignorance of earlier stages of growth. These stages themselves—infancy or "primitive" society—have little inherent interest. Rousseau, by contrast, articulated the quintessentially modern idea that these stages have a formative influence on what follows. As societies develop, so does mutual dependence, and with it exploitation, inequality, insincerity, and unhappiness. Meanwhile, as children develop into adults, significant influences and relationships determine enduring patterns of behavior. Of Rousseau's great works, *The Discourse on Inequality* and the *Confessions* provide classic diagnoses of social and personal development, and the origins of what we would now term collective and individual pathologies. *Émile* and *The Social Contract*, both published in 1762, offer conjectural blueprints on how to avoid these pathologies: how one might go about creating a just society, or raising an unalienated "natural" individual.

As a concrete example of the vast gulf between Voltaire and Rousseau on the subject of development, consider the ways the two dealt with what modern readers would consider the most painfully formative of youthful experiences: sexual molestation. Voltaire, we learn from Pearson, once casually remarked to the mother of Alexander Pope that "if he suffered such constant ill health . . . it was because he had been repeatedly sodomized at school." However, he otherwise said nothing about the experience and apparently did not consider it very significant. In the only autobiographical sketch he ever wrote, he dismissed the very idea of its significance: "Nothing is more insipid than the details of infancy and the time spent at school" (again, a statement quoted by Damrosch, not Pearson). By contrast, in a famous episode in the *Confessions*, Rousseau recounted how a fellow lodger at a Catholic hospice tried to seduce him, and he did not flinch from a single detail: the odor of chewing tobacco, the filthy groping hands, even the sudden spurt of something "sticky and whitish." Precisely through the vivid analysis of such "details of infancy," and the realization that they constitute foundation stones of the adult personality, the *Confessions* virtually created the genre of modern autobiography, and the narrative still stands as one of the greatest, most penetratingly introspective self-portraits ever written.

Not surprisingly, given these differences, the two men ended up loathing each other. Voltaire, characteristically, deprecated Rousseau with witty elegance: "That man is artificial from head to foot, in mind and in soul"; "He is like a child who thinks he has done something impressive when he blows soap bubbles or makes ripples by spitting into a well." Only when Voltaire got truly annoyed did he stoop to calling Rousseau a "Jeanfoutre" (Jean-fuck) and urging that he be hanged. Rousseau, meanwhile, quite typically expressed his own dissatisfaction in more psychological language: "I do not like you, sir. You have chosen to wrong me in the ways that would cause me the most grievous hurt, and I your disciple and enthusiastic admirer....I hate you as one who could more worthily have loved you, had you but wished it." It's worth noting that Voltaire loathed the novel, that most introspective of modern art forms, while Rousseau wrote the most popular novel of the century: *La nouvelle Héloïse.*

Pearson and Damrosch succeed so well in conveying these points because, like their subjects, they both understand the importance of style. Damrosch, who gives an excellent précis of Rousseau's ideas, settles mostly for a brisk, pleasantly dry tone. Still, he can turn wryly ironic on occasion—as when contrasting Rousseau's unceasing belief in his imminent demise (he was the century's champion hypochondriac) with the abundant evidence of his generally robust health (penis aside). Damrosch also has a brilliant eye for quotations, and he sprinkles them through the book to great effect. For instance, Rousseau's comment to Malesherbes on the gallows, or David Hume's marvelous verdict on Rousseau's increasing paranoia: "He is plainly mad, after having long been maddish." Or Rousseau himself, creepily expressing this madness: "The ceiling above me has eyes, the walls around me have ears. [I am] surrounded by spies and by malevolent, vigilant watchers."

Pearson, who has less to say about his subject's less original ideas, has greater stylistic ambitions. He shifts between cinematic evocations of the setting ("the clatter of wheel on cobble, the crack of whip and driver's curse, the hawker's cry and the policeman's halloo") and passages that echo Voltaire's style. The chapter titles come straight out of *Candide*, which Pearson has previously translated (e.g., "How the lawyers had themselves a lovely holocaust, and how two cuckolds turned a blind eye"). Sometimes Pearson strives too hard for effect, as with the stale trick of calling Voltaire by different names to underline his shifting identities: "Voltaire," "François," the family name "Arouet," even the toddler nickname "Zozo." Pearson speaks twice of Frederick the Great's "bitchiness," when once would have been too much. But when he hits his stride he can be magnificent, as in his description of how Voltaire read Rousseau's assertion that the splendor of dawn in the mountains demonstrates the existence of God. "Let's see if Rousseau was right," he announced to a sleepy houseguest in the middle of the night and bundled the man out the door for a two-hour journey to the top of a hill:

> The Jura mountains rose before them, the dark green tips of their trees etched against the pale blue light of morning, while below their feet a landscape of meadow and stream began to emerge from the crepuscular blur. And there, on the far horizon, among the pine-clad peaks, the sun rose in a vast semicircle of purple fire. Resplendent. Incontrovertible. Voltaire removed his hat and prostrated himself on the ground. Thus prone... he improvised a quasi-poetic chant of worship: "I believe. I believe in You. Almighty God, I believe." Whereupon he got to his feet, replaced his hat, and dusted the dirt from his elegant breeches... and added: "As for Monsieur, the son, and Madame, his mother, that is quite another matter."

The episode may never have taken place, but if it didn't, it should have.

Both books end, not surprisingly, in the same place: the Paris Panthéon, just a few blocks from La Libre Pensée, where the French revolutionaries transferred both Voltaire's and Rousseau's bodies, and where the two men now lie in an austere neoclassical crypt, just a few feet from each other. Damrosch comments on the irony of this juxtaposition (both men must be spinning madly in protest at the other's presence), but neither biographer discusses its broader, unintended symbolism. The revolutionaries, of course, in transferring the two bodies to this shrine of "the great men of the fatherland," meant simply to signify the triumph of the Enlightenment, which they associated with their own political movement. And the authors undoubtedly deserved their status as the Enlightenment's two principal French representatives: They came out of the same "enlightened" coterie of friends, contributed to the same "enlightened" projects, shared the same basic epistemological assumptions.

But in Jean-Jacques Rousseau the great critical glare of the Enlightenment, which Voltaire had fixed so scorchingly on prejudice and superstition and intolerance, was turned on itself. Critique became auto-critique, and crusade shifted into introspection. Not surprisingly, nearly all the early enemies of the Enlightenment ended up being influenced by Rousseau, often despite themselves: Romantic poets, embryonic socialists, even ultra-Catholic defenders of throne and altar (for did not the mountains at dawn proclaim the existence of God?). Even today, often without knowing it, the enemies of the Enlightenment echo him. The critique of Western civilization that Ian Buruma and Avishai Margalit call "Occidentalism," which they find shared by everyone from the Nazis to Al Qaeda, is to a great extent a perversion of Rousseauism. The notion of the Enlightenment as cold, mechanistic, materialistic, instrumental, overly rational, devoid of sentiment or sincerity or religious feeling: all this, we owe to him. The critique, sharp and stinging, has been there from the very start. Is it any wonder, then, that the Enlightenment has been such a fragile thing?

4

Enlightenment's Errand Boy: The Enlightenment and the Republic of Letters

ALTHOUGH VOLTAIRE, ROUSSEAU, AND THE OTHER LEADING philosophes continue to attract enormous attention, over the past generation scholars have argued that the social boundaries of the Enlightenment stretched far beyond this small group of thinkers. Some of the most innovative works have looked at obscure "Grub Street" pamphleteers, at journalists, at Freemasons, at members of learned academies, at contributors to essay contests sponsored by these academies, and at participants in salon and coffeehouse conversation. As a result, it is now possible to see the Enlightenment as a broad-based cultural movement (or movements, plural), which included women as well as men, and members of many different social classes. This scholarly shift, however, while profitable, has come at the risk of further blurring the already fiercely contested question of how to define the Enlightenment (or Enlightenments, plural). Perhaps, some scholars have even suggested, the term "Enlightenment" should be discarded. In this essay I argue against this idea and try to suggest some ways to redraw boundaries. I do so in considering a study of an eighteenth-century

---

Books under Review: L. W. B. Brockliss, *Calvet's Web: Enlightenment and the Republic of Letters in Eighteenth-Century France* (Oxford University Press, 2002); Colin Jones, *The Great Nation: France from Louis XV to Napoleon* (Allen Lane, 2002). Essay originally published in *The London Review of Books*, May 22, 2003.

scholar who was certainly connected to the Enlightenment, but not, I would argue, a participant in it in any meaningful way.

———

The French revolutionaries identified the Enlightenment as the work of a small, brave band of eighteenth-century philosophes, whom they rushed to entomb as heroes in the gloomy crypt of the Panthéon. In the corrupt and desolate wasteland of the Ancien Régime, the revolutionaries proclaimed, the philosophes had cast welcoming rays of light and reason, stirring the dull roots of popular discontent. On the other end of the political spectrum, angry defenders of religious and political orthodoxy accepted this image, but in photo-negative: for them, the wasteland was a happy garden; the rays of light were menacing shadows; and the angelic philosophes were demons, casting Europe into perdition. Thus the fiery gospel of the abbé Barruel and Joseph de Maistre, to which reactionary Catholics and many others held fast throughout the nineteenth century and much of the twentieth.

For two hundred years, these popular images of the Enlightenment have retained considerable force. Textbooks (including Colin Jones's superb new one) have repeated them to new generations of readers, while literary historians, such as Daniel Mornet, have taken them for granted and proceeded to tell the story of the Enlightenment's steady diffusion outward from its Parisian source. In the 1960s, Peter Gay gave them new power in his brilliant extended essay *The Enlightenment: An Interpretation*. Gay recognized the international dimensions of the Enlightenment, and included Scots, English, Germans, and Italians as well as French in what he called the "little flock of *philosophes*." He recast it as a dialectic in which "modern paganism" overcame Christianity and ushered in "the science of freedom." But at heart Gay's Enlightenment remained the exploit of a handful of brave eighteenth-century souls.

Yet there have always been challenges to this view. Some critics have tried to expand the Enlightenment's geographical and chronological boundaries. Others, more daringly, have denied its essential unity. J. G. A. Pocock, in his study of the intellectual worlds of Edward Gibbon, insisted on the existence of multiple Enlightenments, some of them remarkably conservative, religious, and devoted to erudition. The most radical critics of all have gone far in the other direction, subsuming the Enlightenment into even larger, sweeping historical shifts. Max Horkheimer and Theodor Adorno's notorious (and notoriously abstruse) *Dialectic of Enlightenment* traced "Enlightenment" thinking back to the age of Homer. Foucault recast eighteenth-century Europe as the scene of a dramatic break in Western habits of thought, and darkly associated it with new, menacingly ubiquitous patterns of discipline and repression. Subsequent authors have often mistaken these radical critiques for attacks on the Enlightenment of convention and proceeded to blame the Parisian *philosophes* for all the ills of modernity. This sort of thinking amounts to vulgar postmodernism, and enjoys an alarming degree of popularity on American and British university campuses.

L. W. B. Brockliss is no postmodernist, vulgar or otherwise, and his elegantly instructive study falls into older traditions of critique. Like the great historian Paul Hazard, Brockliss wants to push the boundaries of the Enlightenment beyond the "little flock of *philosophes*," and in particular to identify it with the intellectual phenomenon known as the "Republic of Letters"—an international network of correspondents born in the seventeenth century and committed to unfettered critical inquiry. Hazard made this argument by showing that the founders of the Republic anticipated the philosophes in many of their lines of thought. As Diderot himself later acknowledged, "we had contemporaries during the age of Louis XIV." (Jonathan Israel has restated this argument in a different form in *Radical Enlightenment*, focusing on the Netherlands and the circle of Spinoza.) Brockliss takes a different tack. He wants to show, first, that the Republic of Letters survived into the late eighteenth century, and second, that its membership shared the principal concerns and beliefs of the narrower group of philosophes. "The Enlightenment," he concludes, "should be subsumed within the Republic of Letters and the *philosophes* treated as the citizens of a singular mini-Republic within a broader federation." In fact, Brockliss would like to get rid of the term "Enlightenment" altogether.

It is a tempting suggestion, not least because of the way it would discomfit those who mutter so ominously about the "Enlightenment Project." To make his case, Brockliss, rather than writing yet another sweeping survey, has chosen the path of microhistory, looking at the career of a single republican of letters about whom remarkably abundant information has survived: an Avignon doctor called Esprit Calvet.

By illuminating the ideas of Calvet and his correspondents—"Calvet's web"—Brockliss hopes to "put some flesh" on a period of European intellectual history usually observed from its commanding Parisian heights.

Brockliss himself acknowledges that Calvet's flesh was not the sort that made anyone thrill at its touch, at the time or since. A doctor and teacher by profession, a collector and antiquarian by avocation, he lived a long, comfortable, and mostly very dull life in his pleasant, comfortable, and dull Provençal city (which remained a papal enclave until its annexation by France during the Revolution). A confirmed bachelor, he kept regular hours, eschewed games and exercise, and read virtually no contemporary literature. Brockliss calls Calvet a "prig," an "intellectual and moral snob," and a "social climber." At first sight, the most interesting thing about him was his apparently bizarre medical views. He treated patients with anal injections of sheep gut, warned that vaccination could cause cancer, and campaigned strenuously against the evils of coffee-drinking, which he held responsible for "emaciation, phthisis, sterility, impotence, paralysis and especially apoplexy and melancholy." But, alas, in an era when some popular physicians treated patients by immersing them in tubs of iron filings to repair their magnetic orientation, Calvet's medical opinions were actually quite conventional. His papers hint at illicit liaisons, and even an illegitimate child, but there is little indication that he placed much value on either sex or female companionship.

What Calvet did place value on was intellectual sociability, and it is here that his true interest lies. He had a close circle of friends in Avignon, with whom he gathered for serious conversation, and he maintained a regular correspondence with them and many others—in all no fewer than 350. Nearly all male, and drawn from the professions, the clergy, and the nobility, their seriousness and stuffiness mostly matched Calvet's own, and provided him with a cosy, convivial circle: the epistolary equivalent of a Victorian gentleman's club. In his voluminous letters, he repeatedly lamented the hours not spent in his friends' company owing to the regrettable necessity of earning a living. With these friends, he discussed his real passions: coins, Roman inscriptions, fossils, and books.

Although he gained considerable expertise in each of these fields, Calvet never established any sort of true scholarly reputation. His sole, short publication, in a long life of scholarly curiosity, concerned the

Roman guild of the Utricularii (river boatmen), whose activities he managed to illuminate through an analysis of a newly discovered inscription. If he stood out at all, it was in his dogged acquisitiveness. Over the course of his life he compiled one of the finest Roman coin collections in France, a library of more than five thousand volumes, and a smaller but still impressive number of fossils, some collected personally from Provençal hillsides. These became, after his death, the basis for the Musée Calvet, which exists in Avignon to this day.

Drawing on the material from the museum, the correspondence, and the records of Calvet's possessions, Brockliss has been able to draw up a remarkably full portrait of this mildly unattractive man. In fact, Brockliss takes us about as far into the head of an eighteenth-century French person as we are ever likely to get, even if in this particular case the trip is disappointingly uneventful. But what does it have to do with the Enlightenment?

According to Brockliss, a great deal. Conventional though Calvet may have been, his correspondence shows that he shared the outlook and principal goals of the philosophes. While he and his correspondents cared more immediately about antiquarianism and natural history, they nonetheless had a serious commitment to freedom of thought, religious toleration, and unrestrained critical inquiry. They took broadly utilitarian views of social questions and believed in the improvement of humanity. Moreover, their Republic of Letters itself stood as an exemplar of a key aspect of Enlightenment thinking: meritocracy. Within its ranks, Brockliss insists, bourgeois like Calvet could rub shoulders as equals with high-ranking nobles and earn marks of distinction through scholarly achievement alone. "They may not have imagined the new France, but they had experienced it avant la lettre." They were not egalitarians and had little but disdain for the common people and women— but then again, so did many of the philosophes. (Voltaire warned sternly of the dangers of overeducating peasants.)

Yet extrapolating from these similarities to the fundamental unity of the Enlightenment and the Republic of Letters depends, it seems to me, on a misconception of the former. Had someone forced the leading philosophes to sit down together and draft a sober statement of principles, the resulting document might not have looked that different from one composed by the members of Calvet's web. But the Paris Enlightenment was not an affair of sober statements of principle. (Nor could its members generally be persuaded to sit down with one another for more than a few minutes without squabbling.) It produced very few significant philosophical treatises, and of those, some of the most prominent were deliberately shocking assertions of atheism that even today would earn banishment from the shelves of school libraries in many American states and fatwas in much of the Islamic world, if one or the other set of fundamentalists ever bothered to read them.

The great works of the French Enlightenment came rather, for the most part, in the form of fiction (*Persian Letters, Candide, Julie*), travel literature (*The English Letters*), dramatic dialogues (*Rameau's Nephew*), child-rearing manuals (*Émile*), even pornography (such as Diderot's *The Indiscreet Jewels*, whose title characters are talking vaginas). And when cast in more traditional forms, they placed a premium on three things to which Esprit Calvet had a positive aversion: wit, brevity, and shock value. Colin Jones recalls one of Diderot's classic pieces of provocation: in the *Encyclopedia* he edited with d'Alembert, after a learned and sober article on cannibalism (*anthropophagie*) comes the sly note: "See also: Holy Communion."

These differences amounted to much more than simply a divergence in taste and style. Yes, both Calvet's web and the philosophes believed in freedom of expression, but why? To express what? For Calvet's circle, freedom of expression mostly meant allowing men like themselves to enquire eruditely into what they wished and to publish the results. The matters in question could certainly stretch beyond coins, fossils, and Roman inscriptions. The Republic of Letters first coalesced not around antiquarianism, but around the application of a critical gaze to traditional forms of superstition, prejudice, and intolerance, and around the subjection of even sacred texts to critical analysis. Yet it remained mostly a genteel affair and grew more genteel over time.

The Parisian philosophes, by contrast, felt they had a mission not merely to publish, but to publicize: to expose intolerance and injustice wherever they found it, and to the largest possible audience. They wanted not merely to express, but to enlighten. And even if Diderot and Voltaire knew how to bend their knees to kings and emperors on occasion, they both retained an impressive capacity for rudeness when the cause of enlightenment demanded it. The true God, Voltaire once wrote, "can surely neither be born of a virgin, nor die on the gallows, nor be eaten in a piece of dough, nor have inspired these books filled with contradictions, madness and horror." The Republic of Letters saw very few such utterances, even in its early, heroic days, when figures like Pierre Bayle ran real personal risks and published the daring newspaper *Nouvelles de la république des lettres*.

Is this contrast overdrawn? The French historian Daniel Roche has spent much of his productive career investigating the principal arena in which the Republic of Letters and the Enlightenment came together in France: the network of provincial academies where men like Calvet gathered to discuss ideas, hear lectures, take part in essay and poetry contests, and sponsor projects for all manner of "improvements" and charitable works. Roche makes clear that these academies were anything but revolutionary. They drew their membership from both the bourgeoisie and the privileged orders, and believed in prudent, consensual reform, not radical upheaval. Yet many of their members, unlike Calvet, had a real hunger for the new ideas emanating from Paris, as seen by the books they bought: Voltaire and the *Encyclopedia*, the atheist philosophy of Baron d'Holbach, the utopian fantasies of Louis-Sébastien Mercier. And, of course, it was the Academy of Dijon that launched the career of a previously obscure Genevan author and composer called Jean-Jacques Rousseau by awarding him their annual essay prize. There are probably provincial republicans of letters with whom Brockliss might have forged a stronger case for the unity of the Enlightenment and the Republic of Letters than Esprit Calvet.

Historians must use the sources available to them, however, and what Brockliss's sources suggest is the large degree of separation between the Enlightenment and the Republic of Letters. For all that Calvet shared many of the philosophes' ideas, he had little inclination for spreading them beyond his small circle of erudite correspondents, still less for engaging in deliberate and risky provocation. As Brockliss shows, he did drift away from the Catholic Church over the course of his life, as did many of his fellow Provençal bourgeois, but that was not the same thing as attacking the Christian God in the manner of Voltaire, or courting prosecution for publicizing clerical abuses. Not for Calvet the large-scale recasting of human knowledge pioneered in the *Encyclopedia*. Not for him Rousseau's cult of natural sentiment, still less Rousseau's democratic politics. And while Calvet and his noble friends may have treated each other as equals in some circumstances, in others he was more than happy to serve as their errand boy (in one case, Brockliss reports, hiring servants for a noble bishop). During the Revolution, when many readers of the philosophes leapt at the chance to put their ideas into practice, a stunned Calvet concentrated on surviving. And while he was briefly arrested under the Terror, lost a great deal of money, and had to serve several years as an army doctor, he lived to praise Bonaparte sycophantically as a "second Augustus."

So should we, then, dispense with the term "the Enlightenment"? Brockliss points out that eighteenth-century French people themselves did not describe their age in this way (although they did write endlessly about "spreading enlightenment"). The term "Republic of Letters," he writes, "would have made far more sense" to them. True enough; but we do not insist on writing Aztec history in terms that would have made sense to the Aztecs, or Mongol history in terms accessible to Genghis Khan. The historian's job is to interpret the past in terms that make sense to his or her own readers, and from this point of view, for all of Brockliss's erudition and careful analysis, Esprit Calvet's story does little to disprove the utility of the label.

Its utility is underscored by a reading of Colin Jones's new survey of eighteenth-century France. Although Jones and Brockliss have worked closely in the past, cowriting the standard history of eighteenth-century French medicine, Jones takes a very different view of the Enlightenment from his colleague. In many respects it is the traditional view, in that his focus is squarely on the philosophes, and he underlines the extraordinary ambitions and provocations that set them apart from their predecessors in the Republic of Letters. If he offers something new, it is in his post-Marxist linkage of the Enlightenment to changes in France's economy and social structure. Without in any way seeking to revive the "rising bourgeoisie" of Marxist legend, which a generation of revisionist work has consigned to the historical rubbish pile, Jones stresses a series of changes that left France increasingly prosperous and increasingly dependent on the production and sale of consumer goods (in his words, "the Great Chain of Buying and Selling"). Cash increasingly counted for more, and social rank for less. In this changed social universe, Jones traces the rise of an ethos of "civic professionalism" oriented around the themes of meritocratic promotion and public service, which both nurtured and was nurtured in turn by the philosophes.

Jones's book has been needed for some time. The last comprehensive history of eighteenth-century France in English, covering both the Ancien Régime and the Revolution, appeared more than forty years ago, since when historians have changed their views on many aspects of the period. They have highlighted the surprising vigor of the prerevolutionary economy and political culture, explored the experiences of women and minorities, and raised disturbing questions about the unstable and repressive nature of revolutionary politics as a whole. Jones covers all this material with aplomb and an easy wit, even if he sometimes strains rather too hard for the bon mot (he has Louis XV dodging a crowd "like a character from a Molière farce trying to dodge an enema," calls the Duchesse d'Orléans "a superannuated tomboy," and labels Diderot the "product manager" of the *Encyclopedia*). As one would expect from a medical historian, Jones is particularly good on death and lesser bodily complaints. His portrait of Louis XIV's deathbed scene is a tour de force, as is his horrifying description of the Marseille plague of 1720—the last significant outbreak of the Black Death on French soil. Along the way, he also provides such interesting details as the number of coffeepots in Paris in 1789 (one for every two households), the number of carts required by the Prince de Conti to lug home his stock market profits during the 1720 bubble (three), and the fact that Elisabeth Vigée-Lebrun caused a scandal in 1787 by painting herself with her mouth open, in defiance of artistic convention.

If the book has a weakness, it is that Jones has a hard time sustaining his interest in the more familiar aspects of the story. He deals brilliantly with the early eighteenth century, which has long suffered a dearth of serious historical attention, and with the subjects highlighted by recent research. But when he reaches the taking of the Bastille, he begs off with the excuse that the events feature in every "storybook history of France" and "need little retelling." My own experience teaching American undergraduates—including one who once referred to the French national holiday as "Saint Bastille's Day" and another who placed Lafayette at the Battle of the Somme—would suggest otherwise. The death of Robespierre, which Carlyle described so unforgettably ("'he had on the sky-blue coat he had got made for the Feast of the *Etre Suprême*'—O

Reader, can thy hard heart hold out against that?") gets similarly summary treatment from Jones, in contrast to his fine pages on Louis XIV.
Still, the book does capture the essential drama of this remarkable time
and place, and the way the cataclysm of 1789 overturned so many ancient beliefs, ancient institutions, and comfortable little worlds. "We
were walking on a carpet of flowers; we did not see the abyss beneath,"
the Comte de Ségur wrote in his memoirs. Esprit Calvet, although not
given to such rhetorical flights of fancy, would doubtless have agreed.

5

The Fault Is Not in Our "Stars," but in Ourselves: The Invention of Celebrity

THIS ESSAY, LIKE THE PREVIOUS ONE, ALSO LOOKS at the broader cultural setting in which the Enlightenment developed. More particularly, it looks at the phenomenon the historian Antoine Lilti calls "the invention of celebrity," and endorses Lilti's argument that the eighteenth-century "public sphere" cared about personality and scandal as much as or more than rational, enlightened discussion. Like the previous essay, it therefore points to the dangers of defining "the Enlightenment" too broadly and as a cultural phenomenon rather than as an intellectual movement. The essay also raises questions, however, about just how much eighteenth-century celebrity had in common with its twenty-first-century descendant—do Snooki and Brangelina really deserve to be in the same category as Marie-Antoinette?

In a recent undergraduate journalism project at Texas Tech University, hardly any of the students interviewed on camera knew which side had won the American Civil War, which country the United States had

Book under Review: Antoine Lilti, *Figures publiques: L'invention de la célébrité, 1750–1850* (Fayard, 2014). This article was originally published in *Books & Ideas*, January 8, 2015, www.booksandideas.net.

gained its independence from, or the name of the current vice president. The same students, however, had no trouble remembering Brad Pitt's current and former wives, or identifying the show on which the American reality television star "Snooki" appeared.

The spectacle is depressing. Yet before we start to lament the triumph of celebrity culture over even the most basic civic literacy, we might ask if things were truly better in the past. After reading Antoine Lilti's *Figures publiques*, it has become easier for me to imagine an English university student of the 1760s unable to identify the chancellor of the exchequer, or to know which king had united the thrones of England and Scotland a century and a half before, but who could discuss in detail the love life of David Garrick, the leading actor of the day.

One of the principal arguments Lilti makes in this sweeping, fluidly written, and thoroughly engaging work of history is to show that modern celebrity culture had its origins in the middle of the eighteenth century. The new forms of "publicity" that emerged at this time may have helped to promote rational public discussion and critique, as Jürgen Habermas famously argued fifty years ago. But they did just as much, if not more, to feed a public fixation on the personalities and private lives of a new class of individuals who, while not simply "famous for being famous" (in the phrase coined by Daniel Boorstin) were famous in new and unprecedented ways.

Lilti relies heavily on case studies, and in one sense the book amounts to a great parade of past celebrities. Some of them have mostly faded from popular memory, like the eighteenth-century castrato Farinelli, or the nineteenth-century Swedish singer Jenny Lind. But many others remain celebrities of a sort even today: Rousseau, Marie-Antoinette, Franklin, Washington, Bonaparte, Byron. One can only shudder at the sheer quantity of biographical material Lilti had to scale in the course of his research. Celebrity culture, with its generation and repetition of endless masses of trivial information, actively impedes its own analysis. But by taking carefully directed soundings in the ocean of his material, Lilti has successfully mapped out its key features, concentrating on Britain, France, and the early United States.

Readers of Lilti's first book, *Le monde des salons*, will not be surprised to find that this successor to Daniel Roche grounds his study in meticulous social history. A key chapter entitled "A First Media Revolution" explores how, in the mid-eighteenth century, ways of representing individuals in public media proliferated enormously. Newspapers, including scandal sheets interested principally in personalities, multiplied, and found large new audiences. Technical innovations allowed printed engravings to circulate in unprecedented numbers, with the result that by 1789, 60 percent of Parisian households possessed a print of some sort, most often a portrait. Wax museums opened, displaying life-size statues of celebrities, and ceramics manufacturers like Wedgwood successfully marketed colored figurines. Expanding book markets in the Western world favored the genres of the biography and the memoir, while scandalous exposés of "Private Lives" rivaled them for sales.

But it was not just the volume and variety of representations that differentiated "celebrity" from the older phenomena of fame, glory, renown, notoriety, and "reputation." Equally important was the new sort of relationship members of the public imagined between themselves and celebrities: an affective, intimate one. Readers and spectators longed for a glimpse of the unguarded, "real" people behind the public façade, thinking of them as friends they could talk about—and even talk to—in a familiar, informal manner. This aspect of celebrity culture will come as no surprise to anyone who has ever overheard a conversation about where Brad and Angelina should really have gone on their honeymoon, but Lilti convincingly traces its genealogy back to the eighteenth century, bolstering his general argument that we should see celebrity as "a characteristic trait of modern societies." Lilti casts this imagined intimacy as a reaction to the theatricality of the early modern "société du spectacle," which, whether at the court, theater, opera, urban fairs, or even artistic exhibitions, cast members of the public as mere passive spectators of highly stylized artistic productions and social rituals. Celebrities, unlike other famous figures, did not have spectators. They had "fans," an anachronistic word that Lilti deliberately uses to highlight their active participation in celebrity culture. (As leading examples of the revolutionary-era "fan," he cites Samuel Johnson's biographer James Boswell, and Napoleon's chronicler Emmanuel de Las Cases.)

Lilti's most brilliant chapter gives his story an additional, highly significant twist. Unlike the other chapters, "The Solitude of the Famous Man" analyzes a single public figure, Jean-Jacques Rousseau, and shows quite dazzlingly how the mechanisms of modern celebrity can also become mechanisms of tragedy. Rousseau, more than any other author of his day, deliberately invited the sort of intimate, prying attention that Lilti calls central to celebrity culture. Unlike most other leading authors of the French Enlightenment, Rousseau did not publish his books anonymously. Indeed, he not only claimed authorship, but insisted on the direct connection between his works and his own personality. He of course wrote the first great modern example of autobiography, the hugely intimate and revealing (if not always truthful) *Confessions*, and many other works that promised glimpses into the depths of his character. And his massively successful novel *Julie, or La nouvelle Héloïse*, elicited an intense public reaction centered as much on Rousseau the author as on his fictional characters. It is no accident that he became known to his adoring readers as "friend Jean-Jacques."

But Rousseau himself increasingly experienced this public adulation as a form of oppression. Far from enjoying his status as arguably the most popular author in European history, Rousseau felt that the public did not understand him and had developed a false representation of his authentic self. This sense of falsity, as well as the ceaseless personal demands Rousseau received, tortured him, and fed the paranoia that became painfully visible in the later books of the *Confessions* and in the strange, haunting work entitled *Rousseau Judge of Jean-Jacques*, in which he appeared to suspect even God of joining a conspiracy against him. Rousseau thus expressed, in piercingly radical form, a traumatic experience common to celebrities then and since. But unlike most other celebrities, he transformed his suffering into insight, imagining a new sort of genuinely authentic "self" independent of all social representations—one that has become central to modern conceptions of selfhood.

Celebrity also had political significance from the start. In England, the radical Whig campaigner for parliamentary reform and press freedom John Wilkes made use of precisely the mechanisms of celebrity that Lilti describes to advance his causes. As John Brewer observed many years ago, Wilkes's enthusiastic supporters wrote to him and about him in exactly the same sort of intimate, familiar terms that fans used with celebrity actors and writers. (Lilti could easily have written an entire chapter on Wilkes.) And in America and France, the revolutionary overthrow of traditional authority and the birth of new, tumultuous forms of electoral politics gave celebrity literal, not just figurative power. In a chapter on these revolutions, Lilti points to the paradox of movements carried out in the name of the general will and the common man invest-ing power in a handful of mostly elite representatives. He suggests that the mechanisms of celebrity that had developed in the literary sphere, which allowed ordinary readers and spectators to feel an imagined inti-mate connection with famous figures, provided representative democ-racy with a crucial form of legitimation. Referring to what the French today derisively term the "peopolisation" of politics, Lilti argues that "far from being a regrettable deviation that tarnishes the public weal, under the pernicious influence of the 'society of the spectacle,' it shows that the democratic public sphere and the public sphere of the media are bound indissolubly to one another." To be sure, the forms of political celebrity could vary enormously, as Lilti shows by using four very dif-ferent political figures to exemplify the revolutionary changes: Marie-Antoinette, the French orator Mirabeau, George Washington, and Napoleon Bonaparte.

Figures publiques ends on a somewhat ambivalent note. On the one hand, an informative chapter on "Romanticism and Celebrity" asserts that with the advent of mass culture in the second half of the nineteenth century, celebrity culture underwent fundamental changes. Yet the book's conclusion, in line with the logic of the earlier chapters, insists on the continuities between the eighteenth century and the present day. "Phenomena that we are used to seeing as the result of recent technolog-ical and cultural revolutions, indeed as lamentable symbols of our post-modern vacuity, in reality have roots that reach back deeply into the heart of modernity, to a period two centuries before the invention of television." These lines offer a striking challenge to those strains of contemporary cultural criticism that tend precisely to see celebrity worship as a recent pathology (one thinks, for instance, of Christopher Lasch's *Culture of Narcissism*), rather than as a constituent feature of modernity itself.

While *Figures publiques* makes an exceptionally important contribu-tion to our understanding of the century 1750–1850, this larger argu-ment about modernity invites debate. When Lilti discusses this early period, he gives due and fascinating attention to the role of entrepre-neurs in promoting celebrities. But when he turns to mass culture at the end of the book, he tends to stress the cultural and technological changes that brought it about (with particular attention to photography and cinema) rather than the economic ones. But what makes the celebrity culture of the present day so radically different from that of the eighteenth century is not just new technologies and new cultural norms, but the power exercised by large corporations that use highly sophisticated advertising and marketing techniques to create and control celebrity images in a way that the press barons of the eighteenth century could only dream of. In some cases, individual corporations (Fox, Comcast/NBC/Universal) control almost every aspect of the process, from the initial works or events that turn people into celebrities to the news reports about them, to the advertising that promotes them, and to the very wires over which the resulting "content" makes its way into consumers' homes.

I wonder if Lilti, even while criticizing Jürgen Habermas, might have developed his argument in a manner more structurally similar to the German philosopher's. Habermas (in his book *The Structural Transformation of the Public Sphere*) postulated that the eighteenth century saw the emergence of forms of "publicity" that allowed for genuinely rational, critical public debate. In the nineteenth and twentieth centuries, however, the economic transformation of mass communications and media undermined and corrupted these older practices. Similarly, Lilti's analysis suggests a possible contrast between two different forms of celebrity culture, with one serving as the basis for an immanent critique of the other. In the earlier one, celebrity culture, while often trivializing, and easily abused, nonetheless served important purposes. In particular, it created mechanisms by which ordinary citizens learned to feel sympathy and trust for elected representatives whom they did not know personally, and might not have voted for, thereby providing crucial popular legitimation for new and untried democratic systems. In our own day, however, the transformation of celebrity culture into part of a vast news and entertainment industry that operates according to its own profit-seeking logics has arguably corrupted and undermined this already highly imperfect process of legitimation.

The twentieth-century political uses of celebrity raise other questions about the long-term continuities. Arguably, the cults of personality in twentieth-century totalitarian systems also built on the mechanisms of celebrity that Lilti describes, but took them in new and sinister directions. Nazi propaganda, for instance, did not simply portray Adolf

Hitler as a superman, but also took care to show him in supposedly un-guarded moments chatting in a familiar manner with ordinary Germans. Where Lilti sees celebrity culture paradoxically helping to generate belief in an autonomous, authentic "self," the totalitarian systems deliberately exploited a sense of intimate, personal connection with a public figure so as to dissolve the "self" of the ordinary person into the mass.

Even in the period Lilti studies, what began as "political celebrity" could sometimes change into something very different. In his short, fas-cinating section on Napoleon Bonaparte, Lilti looks particularly at the years of exile and the quasi memoir composed by Napoleon's aide Las Cases, *The Memorial of Saint-Helena*. This book, Lilti writes lyrically, "allows us to hear, behind the organ music of the Napoleonic legend, the soft melody of celebrity." Las Cases brilliantly juxtaposed Napoleon's own reminiscences of glory with first-person, intimate accounts of his petty struggles with his British captors, to produce a work of enormous pathos that indeed deserves to stand in the first rank of celebrity litera-ture. But Napoleon also made use of Europe's emerging celebrity culture at the beginning of his career, when his propagandists cast him as the providential man of genius, sent to save the French nation, and simulta-neously as the accessible "little corporal" who could joke on familiar terms with his soldiers. Under the Empire, this political celebrity devel-oped into something approaching a cult of personality, especially in the army, with soldiers now expected to join together into a single, undiffer-entiated mass and to sacrifice their lives willingly for the emperor. Lilti generally avoids discussing the relationship between celebrity and the potent phenomenon of political charisma, and the way the transforma-tion of the one into the other potentially threatens the very existence of the system that the former can also help to legitimate.

Figures publiques will undoubtedly provoke many other questions, but that is precisely the mark of an important, wide-ranging book of this sort. Overall, Lilti's achievement is highly impressive. He provides a new perspective on the transformations of Western culture in the age of revolutions, and on the genesis of modern notions of selfhood and per-sonal authenticity. And he reminds us that even as we laugh at contem-porary celebrity culture, we need to take it seriously, and not merely as an excrescence or a pathology, but as a constituent element of political and cultural modernity.

6

Handsome, Charming...: Comedy, Social
Climbing, and the End of the Old Regime

*THIS ESSAY EXAMINES A FIGURE Antoine Lilti could easily have included in his
study of eighteenth-century celebrity: the controversial and endlessly fascinating playwright Beaumarchais, author of* The Marriage of Figaro. *It
shows how Beaumarchais, the subject of a new biography, used the mechanisms of celebrity in spectacular fashion to triumph over powerful enemies
and advance his career. But at the same time, it argues that Beaumarchais
used these new, modern mechanisms in the service of a very traditional form
of social advancement. Even more than Voltaire, this most eccentric of writers had Ancien Régime ambitions and an Ancien Régime temperament. He
flourished in the aristocratic circles and salons—and boudoirs—that prized
delicacy and wit. His plays seem, in retrospect, to ridicule the nobility in the
name of social equality, but in reality, the ridicule was more of a sly tweak.
Unfortunately, the myth that eighteenth-century France saw the rise of a
self-conscious, politically ambitious bourgeoisie bent on overthrowing the
nobility has proven remarkably resistant to empirical correction, and even*

Book under Review: Maurice Lever, *Beaumarchais, a Biography*, translated by Susan
Emanuel (Farrar, Straus, 2009). Essay originally published in *The London Review of
Books*, October 22, 2009.

today, historians and literary scholars continue to portray the would-be aristocrat Beaumarchais as a bourgeois combatant in the class struggle.

———

The eighteenth century was the great age of the European parvenu. Social hierarchies were rigid enough to make a sudden leap up the ladder not just unusual but shocking. Yet even before the French Revolution these hierarchies were coming under unprecedented pressure as a result of a surging commercial economy, Enlightenment philosophy, and absolute rulers who sought to twist traditional elites into new forms. Thus more people than ever before—women as well as men—had the chance to bound upward in a variety of colorful ways.

The single most impressive of these was probably Martha Skavronska, an illiterate Latvian of peasant background. For years she worked as a common servant, but her unusual beauty and even more unusual luck brought her to the attention of Peter the Great, who made her first his mistress, then his wife, and finally his successor. She became Tsarina Catherine I, and from 1725 to 1727 she reigned as absolute monarch over an empire that already stretched from the Baltic to the Pacific. Peter was responsible for several other cases of extraordinary social mobility, including that of a Sephardic cabin boy from Amsterdam called António de Vieira, whom he plucked from the crew of a Dutch merchant ship in 1697, brought back to Russia as a page, and eventually made a count and adjutant-general of police for his new capital of Saint Petersburg.

Among parvenus from other parts of Europe, few did better, at least for a time, than John Law, son of an Edinburgh banker, who gained an early reputation as a reckless gambler, but also as a brilliant thinker on economic matters. A companion from the gaming tables, the French Regent Philippe d'Orléans, brought him to Paris in 1715 to reform France's perennially disastrous finances. Law quickly became the second most important man in the country, and cobbled together a reform scheme that had all the solidity and common sense of an Icelandic hedge fund prospectus circa 2008; it ambitiously tethered government finances to a new stock market, along with a national bank and joint stock company that would help pay for it all by exploiting the supposedly fabulous wealth of France's new colony, Louisiana. But Louisiana was then rich in little but yellow fever, and the scheme quickly collapsed, forcing Law to flee the country. Italy, meanwhile, produced the extraordinary Lorenzo da Ponte. The son of a Jewish tanner from an Italian ghetto, he converted to Catholicism, became a priest, was defrocked, then rose to become Poet of the Theaters in Vienna and wrote the librettos for Mozart's great Italian operas. He later emigrated to America, where he spent some time working as a greengrocer before ending up as the first professor of Italian literature at Columbia University.

But it was France that came up with the word *parvenu* (first recorded in a dictionary in 1694), and bred the most impressive collection of the species, even before the Revolution abolished the nobility and brought a host of "obscure provincial advocates," as Burke called them, to the highest positions of power. Consider the case of Denis Diderot, born the son of a cutler in the small Burgundian town of Langres, who ended his days hobnobbing with some of France's greatest aristocrats and his patron Catherine the Great (not to be confused with her Latvian predecessor).

The purest example of the species, however, was undoubtedly Pierre-Augustin Caron, better known as Beaumarchais. Born the son of a bourgeois watchmaker in 1732, he became a familiar figure at the French court while still in his early twenties, after which his life consisted of an almost entirely uninterrupted series of scandals and lawsuits. He served as a secret French agent across Europe, notably helping to arrange clandestine shipments of weapons to the American revolutionaries before France had formally taken their side. He is best known for two witty plays that have long formed part of the French canon: *The Barber of Seville* and its sequel, *The Marriage of Figaro*, featuring the classic Spanish trickster of the titles. Beaumarchais has inspired scores of biographies, including Maurice Lever's exhaustive and exhausting three-volume work, which his widow, along with the translator Susan Emanuel, has now boiled down to a much more manageable size.

Beaumarchais was a manic character, of the sort who would now be diagnosed at a young age with attention deficit disorder or something similar, and placed on medication designed to ensure a long life of obscure mediocrity. When the first performance of *The Barber of Seville* unexpectedly bombed in 1775, he rewrote the play in less than forty-eight hours, and audiences hailed the second performance as a triumph. On one particular "mad day" in 1773 (*Figaro*'s full title is, fittingly, *La Folle Journée, ou le mariage de Figaro*), he was chased across Paris by a sword-wielding duke whose mistress he had seduced. The same evening, despite having just barely avoided an aristocratic skewering, with his face badly scratched and a large chunk of hair torn out, he nonetheless gave a reading of *The Barber of Seville*. Handsome, charming, and sexually ravenous, he accumulated an impressive number of mistresses (as well as three wives) in what was also the great century of the rake, but he often made a very bad impression on men. Benjamin Franklin called him an "ostentatious pimp," while Louis XVI simply thought him insane.

Indeed, he didn't just live life on the edge, but frequently hurtled over it. After his fight with the duke, the royal authorities sent him to the prison of Fort-l'Evêque. He spent time in jail in Vienna and London as well, and during the Revolution had a stay in the sinister Prison de l'Abbaye, where only a fortunately timed release saved him from the September Massacres of 1792. When not in prison, he was often in court, defending himself against charges that included fraud, forgery, and stealing government money, or suing others for money he claimed he was owed. A suit against the American government concerning business transacted in 1776 lasted, *Bleak House* fashion, until 1835, some thirty-six years after his death. Goethe found enough drama in Beaumarchais's life for not one but two minor plays.

Even before his death, Beaumarchais had gained a reputation for helping to bring down the Ancien Régime. It rests not on his frequent trouble with the law, but rather on a passage from *The Marriage of Figaro* in which Figaro addresses his haughty employer, the Count of Almaviva: "Just because you're a great lord, you think you're a great genius! Nobility, wealth, rank, office—it all makes a man so proud! And what did you do to deserve all this good fortune? You took the trouble to be born, and nothing else; otherwise you're just a rather ordinary man. But me? Damn it all. Lost in the crowd, I've needed more skill and ingenuity just to stay alive than they've shown in a hundred years of governing all of Spain!"

On this basis, Napoleon called *Figaro* the first cannon shot of the Revolution, while Danton claimed the play "killed the aristocracy." History textbooks long repeated the charge, casting the watchmaker's son as the herald of the revolutionary bourgeoisie. Lever, too, repeats it: "In the eighteenth century a bourgeois was no longer a person whose faults Molière could freely mock and ridicule; he belonged to a class moving upwards socially, a class of which Beaumarchais himself was the pure product."

Unfortunately, not only is this thesis wrong, it also deprives Beaumarchais of a great deal of his true historical interest. It has been decades since serious historians tried to write the history of eighteenth-century France as a tale of class conflict between a rising bourgeoisie and a declining aristocracy. It is now generally recognized that the boundary between nobles and wealthy commoners was hugely porous, and that the commoners were not in any real sense "capitalist." Both they and the nobles mostly placed their fortunes in the same safe forms of noncommercial investment (land, government office, and government annuities), and nothing was easier or more common for a wealthy man than to buy a title. While the nobility existed as a legal category of person, very few people had any sense of the "bourgeoisie" as a distinct social class, let alone one at odds with other classes.

Beaumarchais, far from challenging the nobility, wanted nothing more than to be accepted by it. He eagerly took up his posh-sounding name, although he had no legal right to it. (It came from a small piece of property his first wife inherited from her previous husband.) He successfully sought out a series of positions at court, including horologist to the king, harp master to the king's daughters, and best sounding of all, lieutenant-general of the hunt in the bailiwick and captaincy of the preserves of the Louvre. If he taunted the aristocracy on occasion, he did so in fulfilment of a very traditional sort of role. The historian Sarah Maza has described him as "court jester to the high and mighty." *The Marriage of Figaro*, supposedly so seditious, won approval from a royal censor, reached the stage thanks to the support of the king's youngest brother, and played to rapt, high-ranking audiences at the Comédie-Française. This was not exactly the profile of a piece of proto-Jacobin propaganda. For all Lever's confident pronouncements, *Figaro*'s premiere was in no sense "a decisive turning point in the visible decomposition of the old order and in the constitution, at first subterranean, of the new."

This mistaken perspective aside, Lever tells the story well for the most part, with copious detail and clear explanations of Beaumarchais's invariably convoluted quarrels and scandals. The book provides striking glimpses of the French court, the Comédie Française, and the world of eighteenth-century espionage. It does so, however, in an affected style, all too common to French biographies, and often reads like a pastiche of eighteenth-century French picaresque novels. The reader must put up with endless remarks of the kind "this devil of a man always surprises us," or "but he was not yet at the end of his woes!" Susan Emanuel doesn't help matters by sticking as closely as possible to the original French (e.g. "What would become of him if he was deprived of all that made life spicy?"). And her evident lack of familiarity with eighteenth-century France results in such mistakes as "provost of merchandise" for *prévôt des marchands* ("chief alderman" or "mayor"), "Santo Domingo" for "Saint-Domingue" (modern-day Haiti), and "memorandum" for *mémoire judiciaire* (a printed legal brief).

Those who want to read about Beaumarchais just to be entertained will do very well with Lever. But this remarkable parvenu deserves a different sort of biography as well, one that focuses less on his constant quarrels and more on what they signify in eighteenth-century culture as a whole. For despite his desperate desire to be accepted by traditional aristocrats as one of their own, Beaumarchais also relied on something else in aid of his advancement: modern celebrity. It took time for this novelty to develop. In the early days of his career, Beaumarchais looked to prominent patrons to help him climb the ladder, and succeeded in gaining the favor of the wealthy financier Joseph Pâris-Duverney, himself a parvenu of no mean accomplishment. But the relationship ended with Pâris-Duverney's death in 1770, and a legal challenge from the man's family thwarted Beaumarchais's expectation of a large legacy. With no other powerful patron in sight, he found a brilliant way to exploit his situation. During the trial over Pâris-Duverney's estate in the *parlement* (sovereign court) of Paris, he accused the lead magistrate in the case, Louis Goëzman, of extorting more than his fair share of the customary "presents" that all litigants traditionally gave to judges. With the help of sympathetic lawyers, he composed a series of *mémoires judiciaires* that, with tremendous wit, savaged Goëzman and his wife as crude, venal, grasping hypocrites. The *mémoires* capitalized both on the deep public hostility to the *parlement* (in 1770, Louis XV had forcibly replaced its popular and independent predecessor with a new panel directly responsible to the Crown) and on the fact that trial documents could circulate freely, without prepublication censorship. They became best sellers, humiliated the Goëzmans (who sued Beaumarchais for defamation), and overshadowed the case itself (which ended, after the usual twists and turns, largely in Beaumarchais's favor). They made Beaumarchais himself not simply a national figure, but one whose fame came from deliberately making a spectacle of his own life and character.

He was certainly not the first celebrity of this sort. Both Voltaire and Rousseau, in different ways, had preceded him. But ultimately they both put their celebrity in the service of an ideal of authorial independence encapsulated in the title of philosophe (even if both wrestled, in very different ways, with what independence truly meant in an aristocratic society). Beaumarchais, by contrast, did not belong among the philosophes, and had notably frosty relations with them. His briefs against Goëzman reveled in precisely the sort of precious wit and poise that characterized courtly conversation—and that the true radical writers of the late eighteenth century thoroughly detested. Fittingly, the king's mistress, Madame du Barry, staged a scene from the *mémoires* in her apartments at Versailles, and the king laughed so hard he had to leave the room.

The two *Figaro* plays, which confirmed Beaumarchais's reputation, exhibit the same sort of writing, along with the persistent, playful eroticism typical of courtly culture. They appealed to the audiences who had delighted in rococo painting and the playful novels of Marivaux, while displeasing those who preferred the neoclassicism of David and the stern Roman cadences of Rousseau's *Discourses*. The paradox of Beaumarchais was that he sought to insert himself into the most exclusive circles of French society even as he crafted his public image before a largely middle-class reading public. For a time, the strategy worked surprisingly well. Despite the incessant quarrels and court cases, his writing gave him acceptance and made him rich, allowing him to build a vast mansion in the Faubourg Saint-Antoine.

The strategy couldn't, however, survive the replacement of the culture of publicity by revolutionary politics. Despite late claims to the contrary ("No man on this continent has contributed more than me to making America free"), Beaumarchais actually cared very little for politics. His efforts to funnel money and weapons to the American revolutionaries had almost nothing to do with their cause and everything to do with making himself indispensable to the French Crown. During the

Revolution, he again tried to procure weapons on a large scale, getting once more into a series of convoluted quarrels that, this time, almost cost him his life (although by good luck he survived the Terror and died of a heart attack in 1799). But he showed his true feelings for the Revolution in a letter he wrote to a Russian prince: "You hear 'liberty' shouted where you once heard sighs, 'live free or die" instead of 'I adore you.' These are our games and amusements."

Beaumarchais himself, of course, much preferred the sighs and adoration, especially when directed at himself (and preferably from a member of the royal family). He did not like trading the delicate games and amusements of the Ancien Régime for the new ones, which involved angry calls for social justice, and the guillotine. And the last thing he wanted was the destruction of all social hierarchies. Such a change, after all, would have made his life's work of social ascension—a work he transmuted into art—entirely meaningless.

7

Where Do We Come From? The Enlightenment and the Age of Revolutions

THE FINAL ESSAY IN THIS PART is the broadest, considering the Enlightenment as a whole and its relation to the great political revolutions of the end of the eighteenth century. It does so through a consideration of one of the most ambitious and comprehensive histories of the Enlightenment ever written—but also one of the most problematic.

I

There's something about the Enlightenment. Today, few educated men and women spend much time debating whether Western civilization took a disastrously wrong turn in the High Middle Ages. They do not blame all manner of political ills on Romanticism, or insist that non-Western immigrants adopt Renaissance values. But the Enlightenment is different. It has been held responsible for everything from the American Constitution to the Holocaust. It has been defended as the

---

Book under Review: Jonathan Israel, *Democratic Enlightenment: Philosophy, Revolution and Human Rights* (Oxford University Press, 2011). Essay originally published in *The New Republic*, February 8, 2012.

birthplace of human rights and condemned as intolerant, cold, abstract, imperialist, racist, misogynist, and antireligious. Edmund Burke, in one of the most eloquent early attacks, excoriated "this new conquering empire of light and reason." One hundred fifty years later, Max Horkheimer and Theodor Adorno declared bluntly that "enlightenment is totalitarian." It remains very hard to shake the sense that something fundamental about the modern world owes its form to the intellectual revolutions of eighteenth-century Europe—and that to repair the world, we may need to start by identifying what those revolutions got wrong.

As in all such intellectual controversies, misunderstandings abound, for no one can even agree on what is being argued about. Everything about "the Enlightenment"—its unity, its goals, its methods, its chronological and geographical boundaries—remains in dispute, providing activity, if not always gainful employment, for a sizeable academic industry. While some scholars limit the Enlightenment to a small cadre of eighteenth-century philosophes, others identify it with tendencies in Western thought that may stretch all the way back to classical antiquity. The title phrase of Kant's famous essay "What Is Enlightenment?" is a question that has launched a thousand—ten thousand!—dissertations.

Despite this strife and confusion, over the past century a few scholars have dared not only to define and survey "the Enlightenment" as a whole but also to proclaim its unity and to defend it forcefully against its critics. Interestingly, the most prominent among them have been secular-minded European-born Jews who perhaps feel gratitude to the Enlightenment for their social and intellectual freedom. In 1932, the German-Jewish philosopher Ernst Cassirer, who later fled to America, published *The Philosophy of the Enlightenment*, which traced the development of critical reason through the eighteenth century. Subtle and difficult, the book showed how the same patterns of thought emerged in the realms of epistemology, religious thought, historical thought, and aesthetics. Overall, Cassirer argued that the heart of Enlightenment philosophy lay in a dialectical interaction between the great schools of Descartes and Leibniz, and that it culminated in what he saw as one of the great achievements of the human mind: German idealism. Cassirer took for a motto Spinoza's lovely injunction "Smile not, lament not, nor condemn, but understand." But he concluded, in implicit response to criticisms of the Enlightenment's supposed sterile rationalism, with a measured celebration of its ability "to reconvert criticism to creative activity."

A generation later, Peter Gay, born Peter Fröhlich, a childhood refugee from the Nazis, published his own synthesis, *The Enlightenment: An Interpretation*. Shifting the focus to political and social thought, Gay also cast the Enlightenment as a dialectical process, in his case a Freudian one. (He would later publish an impressive biography of Freud and write an explicitly Freudian history of bourgeois culture.) In Gay's telling, a "little flock" of philosophes, taking inspiration from classical antiquity, engaged in a filial rebellion against their Christian heritage, emerging as "modern pagans" and establishing the "science of freedom." The word "science" mattered as much as "freedom" to Gay, for he highlighted the Enlightenment's dedication to empiricism and experimentation, contrasting it forcefully to religious systems of belief, and to the sort of rationalism that rested on deduction from a priori principles. And his dialectic did not culminate in a philosophical achievement, but in the American Revolution, which Gay (grateful immigrant and friend of Richard Hofstadter) called "the program in practice."

Since the appearance of Gay's work in the late 1960s, his and Cassirer's visions of a unified and largely beneficent Enlightenment have not fared well. Postmodern critics, taking inspiration from Horkheimer and Adorno, among others, have blasted a hyperrationalist "Enlightenment project" that supposedly enabled modern racism and imperialism, among other sins. In the hands of Jean-François Lyotard and Michel Foucault, the Enlightenment's universalism and confidence came off looking distinctly sinister and repressive. Meanwhile, historical scholarship has moved toward expanding and fragmenting the subject. Inspired by the redoubtable historian of political thought J. G. A. Pocock, much of the current generation of historians likes to speak of "multiple Enlightenments," including religious, conservative, and Caribbean Enlightenments, a whole variety of national European Enlightenments, and even, perhaps, an English Enlightenment.

At its best, this new research has moved away from Gay's narrow concentration on a handful of mostly Parisian philosophes. It has cast the Enlightenment as a broad and complex cultural movement that turned cities such as Edinburgh and Naples into exciting intellectual marketplaces, and that involved booksellers, journalists, salon hostesses, Freemasons, liberal theologians, and many other foot soldiers of Burke's "conquering empire." Yet this more diversified scholarship has sometimes seemed to fracture the subject so deeply as to render the term "Enlightenment" almost meaningless.

Over the past decade, flying directly against these two tendencies, there has appeared a third champion of a united and beneficial Enlightenment: Jonathan I. Israel, a distinguished English historian who first made his reputation working on the early modern Netherlands. *Democratic Enlightenment* is the third of three massive volumes, totaling nearly three thousand pages. Whereas Cassirer and Gay and other scholars limited themselves mostly to the eighteenth century, Israel burrows back deep into the seventeenth century. Whereas Cassirer and Gay and other scholars concentrated on France, Germany, and Scotland, Israel's first volume gave pride of place to the Netherlands, and this most recent one soars over a dazzling variety of landscapes. Like Cassirer and Gay, Israel sees a fundamental tension at the heart of the Enlightenment, in his case between the tendencies that he labels "radical" and "moderate." He goes so far as to speak of "two consciously opposed and rival enlightenments." But unlike Cassirer and Gay, he is no dialectician. For him, the only truly significant Enlightenment was the radical one.

In Israel's account, this "Radical Enlightenment" took shape as a coherent "package" of ideas in seventeenth-century Holland, around the titanic figure of Baruch Spinoza. For Israel, it is not enough to say that this brilliant Jewish-born Dutch philosopher challenged European thought with his contention that the entire universe is composed of a single fundamental substance, rather than divided into material and spiritual realms. Israel insists on "an inextricable and universal connection" between Spinoza's "monist" philosophy and "genuinely democratic radical politics." From the very start, he argues, the "Radical Enlightenment" bore the seeds of modern democracy, social equality, religious toleration, freedom of expression, and even sexual equality and toleration of homosexuality. The moderate Enlightenment that rose up to challenge it was a weak imitation, all too willing to trim its sails and compromise with existing beliefs, practices, and institutions.

Most of what today goes by the name "the Enlightenment," without a modifying adjective, properly belongs, in Israel's view, to the latter moderate movement. But he confers his most sustained and sympathetic attention on the radicals, whom he sees as carrying on in the face of heavy persecution, elaborating on but not fundamentally altering the original monist "package," and eventually bringing about the French Revolution in 1789. It is this event, rather than its American counterpart a few years earlier, that Israel takes as the culmination of the Enlightenment—but only the revolution's initial liberal phase.

There is a great deal to criticize in the series as a whole, and in *Democratic Enlightenment* in particular. But there is also a great deal to praise. Israel's work now stands as the most monumentally comprehensive history of the Enlightenment ever written. The scope is absolutely stunning. Sources parade by in English, French, German, Dutch, Spanish, Italian, and Portuguese. Here, a footnote testifies to explorations in the National Archive and Library of Bolivia; there, to material dug out of the Wrocław University Library. Halfway through this newest book, Israel tells us how the Spanish Inquisition put the Peruvian-born writer Pablo de Olavide on trial, confiscated his property, and sentenced him to eight years of reeducation in a monastery. Three chapters later we have moved on to a Cherokee chieftain named Dragging Canoe. And a hundred pages after that, we get an informative disquisition on Rangaku, or the Japanese study of the West, with Israel learnedly telling us that the word was actually an abbreviation of Oranda-gaku, or "Holland-knowledge."

Israel also insists, admirably, on taking ideas seriously as motive forces in history. In the years since Peter Gay's synthesis, historians of the Enlightenment and revolutionary eras largely turned away from the straight history of ideas, embracing various forms of social and cultural analysis in its place. While this shift brought many benefits, it could also have some strange effects. Twenty years ago, for instance, the French historian Roger Chartier produced a book called *The Cultural Origins of the French Revolution*, which included no discussion whatsoever of the ideas of major Enlightenment thinkers. As far as political change was concerned, Chartier maintained that the content of books mattered less than the way they were read, which in turn depended on changing social practices. The thesis was seductive—after all, books do not generally impress their ideas on readers like seals on soft wax.

But generalizing about readers as a whole does not necessarily explain radical historical change. It is the frustrated, hotheaded, eccentric minority of readers who start and lead radical movements. And as Israel's work has made very clear, Enlightenment books did indeed have a life-changing effect on some such readers. In *Democratic Enlightenment*, he argues forcefully that we cannot ignore the striking overlap between the ideas that they absorbed and then passed on, often at great risk, and the ideas that triumphed, if sometimes only briefly, in the democratic revolutions of the late eighteenth century.

The first two volumes of Israel's opus have already provoked enormous debate. Antoine Lilti, perhaps France's most talented younger historian, subjected them to a particularly searching critique in the pages of the venerable journal *Annales*, challenging Israel on nearly every aspect of his thesis. Did Spinoza's work really have all the social and political implications Israel attributes to it? Did a coherent "Radical Enlightenment" really take shape in the way Israel suggests, achieving such strong ideological unity as to constitute a veritable intellectual party? Did its ideas have the reach and the durability Israel claims? Throughout his work, Israel relies heavily on assertions about "Spinozism" made by eighteenth-century polemicists; but as Lilti observed, these writers used "Spinozism" as a scare word, to tar their enemies with the brush of atheism, and many alleged "Spinozists" were nothing of the sort. Critics have also chastised Israel for largely neglecting Enlightenment attempts to develop a "science of society" (led by "moderates" like Montesquieu), and for failing to prove the necessary link between philosophical monism and modern liberal values. It is hardly insignificant, after all, that the most prominent self-proclaimed "materialists" of the twentieth century were communist totalitarians. Israel has responded to the criticisms at length, although he believes so passionately in his thesis that he has often found it difficult to take his critics seriously. The debate shows no sign of slackening.

II

Yet *Democratic Enlightenment* does not merely continue the debate. It takes it to a new level with Israel's claim that the "Radical Enlightenment" brought about the French Revolution. Israel only comes to the Revolution itself in the last two hundred pages of this massive book, but it represents the climax of his entire enterprise. It was the moment at which, in

Israel's view, the promise of the Enlightenment began to be realized, but then, tragically, was "arrested by kings, aristocracy, and Robespierre's Counter-Enlightenment." The interpretation is deeply ambitious, deeply provocative, and deeply problematic.

As Israel himself notes at length, his interpretation is not exactly new. At the end of the eighteenth century, radicals and reactionaries alike attributed the French Revolution to what they called "philosophy." Radicals saw it as liberating the French from the shackles of superstition; reactionaries, as clouding minds with beguiling lies. Both accounts were self-interested enough to be treated with serious suspicion, and for the past two hundred years most historians have done exactly that. Even those who took Enlightenment ideas seriously as a contributing factor came to prefer interpretations that stressed class conflict, or the political dynamics of the Old Regime state, or even pure accident. Israel will have none of it and takes the contemporary perceptions as self-evidently true. "What I am arguing is that the Radical Enlightenment...is the only important direct cause of the French Revolution." Full stop.

Israel insists that although the radicals remained, in his own words, "socially and politically marginal" throughout most of the eighteenth century, they nonetheless managed to diffuse their ideas widely. He calls them "deliberate, conscious revolutionaries...not in the sense of being planners of revolutionary action but rather as ideologues preparing the ground for revolution." And no other factor really mattered, including anything that might involve the experiences of the vast majority of the French population who never came into any but the blurriest contact with Enlightenment ideas. In a particularly provocative passage, Israel declares that "the agenda of 1788–9 obviously had nothing to do with the habits and experiences of the people except insofar as they responded to the summons to rise and establish a new order. Where the agenda sprang from was the thinking of the twenty or thirty philosophes-révolutionnaires leading the Revolution in Paris."

Israel knows quite well that in making these assertions, he is challenging nearly everything written on the subject for the past two centuries. "A correct understanding of the Radical Enlightenment is impossible," he declares, "without overturning almost the whole current historiography of the French Revolution." He is clearly not lacking in intellectual self-confidence. Indeed, throughout his opus he has often found it very difficult to muster patience for those who cannot see what he thinks is so self-evidently true. To take just one example: in a single paragraph dealing with the *Encyclopedia* of Diderot and d'Alembert, Israel characterizes other historians' judgments on the subject as "obviously untrue," "could scarcely be more mistaken," "fundamentally incorrect," "seriously misleading," and "completely untenable." He rejects the philosophy of Michel Foucault as "false" (all of it?) and calls François Furet, the past century's most innovative historian of the French Revolution, "doubly confused."

In writing history this sort of self-confidence is risky, and nowhere more so than in the methodological minefield that is the history of ideas. A generation of intellectual historians, led by Quentin Skinner, have identified the most dangerous of the mines very clearly. It is all too tempting to assume we know what particular statements "must" have meant, rather than placing them firmly within their original intellectual contexts. We can all too easily gloss over the contradictions, incoherences, and evolutions of particular individuals, treating them instead as followers of a single ideological line. We can all too quickly persuade ourselves that an earlier thinker necessarily influenced a later one who expressed a similar idea. And it is all too seductive to attribute a particular event to the conscious activity of those who hoped something like it might come about.

Some historians of ideas have become so wary of these explosive obstacles that their work barely advances at all. Others act more in the spirit of Marshal Zhukov, who once explained to Dwight Eisenhower that he cleared minefields by marching the infantry across them. Jonathan Israel is closer to the latter. It is not always an absurd strategy—Zhukov, after all, reached Berlin; and Israel scores some important points along his own intellectual journey. But finally I do not think the argument of *Democratic Enlightenment* is correct. Showing why requires some digging down into the details of the argument—but the details are, after all, where God resides (perhaps even for a Spinozist).

Consider Israel's claim that the torchbearers of the "Radical Enlightenment" were "conscious revolutionaries." The claim presupposes that these men had a clear vision of what a "revolution" would entail. But did they? It was once assumed that before the French events of 1789, the word "revolution" retained its original etymological meaning of a circular return to a starting point. Israel insists that long before then it had come to mean "fundamental, sweeping change." But the story is much more complicated, and more interesting. As Keith Michael Baker demonstrated many years ago, before 1789 the word "revolution" denoted something essentially unpredictable and uncontrollable. It meant something that happened to people, and rapidly, rather than something that people consciously brought about over a period of years. When Rousseau wrote, in 1762, that "we are approaching the state of crisis and the century of revolutions," he was warning of violent upheavals, not predicting anything that Robespierre or Lenin would have recognized as a true revolution. Baker argued persuasively that the modern concept of revolution as a consciously willed and drawn-out political process only emerged after 1789, in the course of the French Revolution itself.

In *Democratic Enlightenment*, Israel quotes many eighteenth-century writers who denounced injustices, warned of violent upheaval, and demanded that monarchs bring about reforms. But he fails to provide evidence that anyone called for anything like a revolutionary movement to overthrow existing regimes. He does come up with one apparently convincing quote, drawn from Raynal's and Diderot's influential anti-imperialist *History of the Two Indies*. "The tyrants will never freely consent to the extinction of servitude," the text reads, "and to lead them to this order of things, it will be necessary to ruin them or exterminate them." On this basis Israel concludes that the book "clearly summoned the world's oppressed to rise against their rulers in the name of liberty." But the quote comes from a section of the *History* that deals specifically with the institution of Russian serfdom. The French word *servitude* here translates as "serfdom," while the word "tyrants" refers specifically to Russian estate-owners, not tyrants in general. Israel has taken the passage seriously out of context.

Israel's book also runs into difficulty with its sweeping claim that just twenty men, who supposedly belonged heart and soul to the "Radical Enlightenment," provided the entire agenda for the early revolution. Many of the men Israel includes on his list were quite marginal, but he concentrates on four who were undoubtedly revolutionaries of the first order: Mirabeau, the dazzling orator of the early Revolution; Sieyès, the author of its single most influential pamphlet, "What Is the Third Estate?";

Condorcet, greatest of the late philosophes and an important revolutionary politician; and Brissot, a prominent revolutionary journalist and leader of the radical Girondin faction. Israel calls Sieyès a "hardened ideologue" and treats the other three in much the same fashion.

It is a very hard case to make. Most historians would contend that all four of these men were, first and foremost, flexible and self-interested politicians, not early incarnations of Lenin or Trotsky. Mirabeau, for all his supposed devotion to the principles of the "Radical Enlightenment," was quick enough to strike a secret, corrupt bargain with King Louis XVI in 1790, and to work for the monarchy in the revolutionary National Assembly. Brissot struck his own corrupt bargain with the king a year later, so as to drag France into a war against the other European powers. As for Sieyès, he ended his political career by sponsoring Bonaparte's coup d'état against the French Republic, from which he emerged a very rich man.

Nor is it at all obvious that all four belonged, intellectually, to a radical Spinozan Enlightenment. In fact, the greatest single intellectual influence on most of them was a figure Israel mostly banishes to the "moderate" Enlightenment: Jean-Jacques Rousseau. Israel asserts that "Sieyès was always inflexibly anti-Rousseauist as well as anti-absolutist; and Brissot frequently was." Yet Brissot's principal work of philosophy, from 1782, mentioned Spinoza only glancingly, while calling Rousseau the greatest philosopher of all time. Sieyès disagreed vehemently with Rousseau on the issue of representative political systems, but disagreement hardly implies a lack of influence. A large portion of Sieyès's "What Is the Third Estate?" followed Rousseau's *Social Contract* point by point. And if Mirabeau, Sieyès, and Condorcet bore the mark of a common intellectual influence beyond Rousseau, the other most obvious candidate was not Israel's "Radical Enlightenment," but the school of early economic thought called Physiocracy, developed in part by Mirabeau's father, which advocated free trade and the rational management of social resources—and was by no means democratic. The portions of "What Is the Third Estate?" that dealt with economics and social rights stemmed directly from Physiocratic writing. But Israel barely mentions Physiocracy, which does not fit well into his typology of "radicals" versus "moderates."

Israel is in equally dangerous territory when he tries to trace the origins of a key revolutionary concept: the sovereign "general will." This is a classic problem in intellectual history, which most scholars address by starting with Rousseau, the thinker most famous for popularizing the concept. Before Rousseau, the trail is murkier, but the political philosopher Patrick Riley has made a very good case for seeing the origin in Christian debates about the sovereignty and will of God. Israel is sure, however, that the real source must have been Spinoza. Somewhat tortuously, he argues that while Rousseau framed his concept of the general will within a specifically national framework, the French revolutionaries cast their own version as universally applicable—just as Spinoza and the "Radical Enlightenment" had done. And he adds that what the revolutionaries did take from Rousseau, Rousseau himself had copied from Spinoza.

Unfortunately, neither of these arguments holds up. While a few revolutionaries did insist on applying their principles to the entire human race, most of them—including the key figure of Sieyès—agreed with Rousseau that the fundamental framework for politics was the nation. "Everything is in the nation" was the way Sieyès put it, and the thought went straight into the Declaration of the Rights of Man and Citizen, which, despite the universalist aspirations of its title, defined most of the rights it enumerated in relation to national law. Its third article proclaimed, forthrightly enough: "The principle of all sovereignty resides essentially in the nation." As for the idea that Rousseau copied part of his thinking on the subject from Spinoza, the evidence is thin. Israel calls particular attention to Rousseau's argument that if you rebel against a state to which you have given your consent, you are effectively rebeling against yourself, and that if the state then compels you into obedience, it is doing no more than "forcing you to be free." Israel asserts that Rousseau took this idea directly from Spinoza. But the main evidence he cites is an article by a Spanish scholar, Maria José Villaverde, which actually says only that Spinoza's thought on the point "recalls" and "prefigures" Rousseau. While Rousseau's idea certainly had things in common with statements by Spinoza, it had just as much in common with statements by Thomas Hobbes, in the eighteenth chapter of *Leviathan*. And while Rousseau hardly ever mentioned Spinoza, he wrestled long and hard with Hobbes. Once again, there is simply no evidence for a direct, unproblematic tradition leading straight from Spinoza and Israel's "Radical Enlightenment" to 1789.

But Israel stubbornly insists on this connection, and in the concluding chapters of the book he triumphantly holds up a smoking gun of sorts, namely the Declaration of the Rights of Man and Citizen itself. The Declaration's roots, he states firmly, "were in philosophy, and especially in radical thought." And not only that. He insists that a mere handful of ideologues in France's National Assembly managed, by careful maneuvering and sheer force of argument, to win over a much larger number of deputies to their side, and to push through a far more radical document than this majority originally intended. It is certainly a tempting theory. Most historians of the Declaration have emphasized the chaos that presided over its confection, in the astonishing summer of 1789, when the people of Paris rose up in revolt, the French countryside exploded in the greatest violence seen in 150 years, and everyone wondered how much change the royal family would tolerate before trying to claw power back. In the middle of all this the deputies—all twelve hundred of them—hammered out the Declaration, writing and rewriting dozens of drafts, and almost failing at the task entirely.

Was there indeed a secret, powerful force at work behind the scenes, guiding the hand of radical change? Some sort of conspiracy of the righteous? The answer, again, is no. Israel claims that the text of the Declaration was based on a draft written by Mirabeau, one of his alleged ideologues, and pushed through the Assembly by the radical party. But his account is simply mistaken. Strangely, Israel has not consulted the principal source used by nearly all previous scholars of the Declaration, namely the actual records of the Assembly's deliberations (known as the *Archives parlementaires*), which were published in the late nineteenth century. He has relied instead on memoirs and correspondence written by his alleged radicals, who naturally exaggerate their own role. But the Assembly's records show very clearly that the initial attempts to write the document indeed came close to ending in stalemate. Early versions by Sieyès and Mirabeau were rejected. In the end, the exhausted deputies seized on an uncontroversial draft composed by the Assembly's Sixth Bureau, a collection of decidedly nonradical nonentities. To this was added a few articles composed by moderate royalists and Mirabeau's eloquent draft preamble. It was this document, and not Mirabeau's text, that passed the Assembly on August 20, 1789, and became the basis for the final document.

No project conceived on the scale of Israel's is going to be free of errors and misreadings. The history of the development of ideas throughout the Western world—and beyond—over a period of more than a century is an incalculably vast subject. It stretches over far too many political contexts, far too many intellectual idioms, far too many social practices for any one scholar, however brilliant and hardworking, to master completely. Nor should a fear of error deter such a scholar from attempting to generalize about the subject as a whole. Israel's generalizations are particularly appealing, since they seem to uphold an account of liberal modernity that most of his readers will find both familiar and congenial. Particularly at a moment when liberal politics, social democracy, and secularism are under such broad assault across the world, it is deeply tempting to ascribe the creation of the modern political order to heroic revolutionaries who thought much as we do.

But the specific sorts of errors and misreadings that Israel commits in *Democratic Enlightenment* show the real limitations of his project. He has attempted to find order amid chaos: hidden hands, conscious agendas, revolutionary programs. More specifically, he has plucked particular writers and texts out of the vast, sloshing ocean of early modern intellectual production, taken similarities and connections between them as signs of the existence of a conscious and coherent radical party, and attributed to this party responsibility for events that seemed to fulfill its hopes. But history is simply too messy and complicated to allow for such tidy explanations.

Events such as the French Revolution are driven to a frighteningly large extent by accident, improvisation, misunderstanding, and self-interest. The role of ideas should not be minimized, but in practice political figures very rarely follow ideological programs to the letter. They grab ideas helter-skelter from a variety of sources and cobble them together imperfectly in forms they think will work to best advantage. Other people in turn misunderstand, modify, and distort these ideas. To claim otherwise, to insist on the heroic narrative, requires reading texts out of context, ignoring ideas that do not fit, and making assumptions about the course of events that a closer attention to the work of fellow scholars would quickly have corrected.

The result should still not be dismissed. Not only does it make an inspiring story, it also pushes and prods us, with copious new evidence, to reexamine events we thought we knew well from a different perspective. No one who reads Jonathan Israel's pages will ever again doubt the importance of radical materialists in the intellectual changes that shaped the modern political world. But his overall interpretation of the Enlightenment era nonetheless amounts to a projection of his own values and ideas back onto a body of evidence that they fit very imperfectly. His work stands as renewed proof of just how central and controversial the Enlightenment remains in the twenty-first century—but dare it be said that it also suggests that the Enlightenment remains too central, too controversial? We might do a better job of defending our liberal values if we did not see them as having necessarily taken on their full-blown present-day shape in the eighteenth century or before. And we might see those earlier times more clearly if we did not imagine them prefiguring so closely our own dilemmas. "Smile not, lament not, nor condemn, but understand."

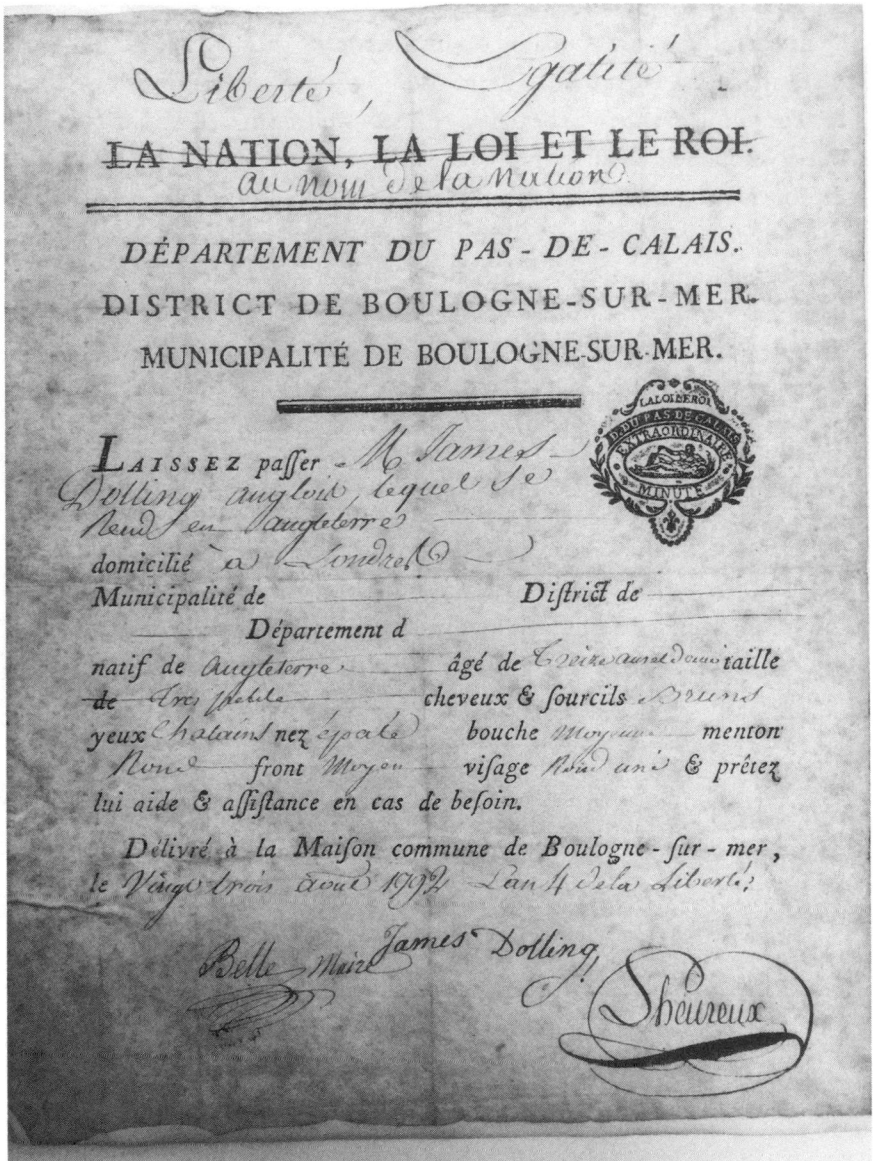

Exit visa, with detailed physical description, issued to the English thirteen-year-old James Dolling, in the Channel port of Boulogne on August 23, 1792. The French monarchy had fallen thirteen days before. The local officials have crossed out the motto "The Nation, the Law, the King," and written in "Liberty – Equality - In the Name of the Nation." Property of the author.

Part III

THE REVOLUTION

─────────◦◦◦◦─────────

I LEARNED EARLY IN MY STUDIES that French historians still feel passionately about the French Revolution, but the point was first driven home to me personally in the spring of 1989, when I was in graduate school. Pierre Chaunu, an eminent pioneer of the "*Annales* school" who had turned deeply conservative in middle age, invited me to speak to his Sorbonne research seminar about my dissertation subject, the politicization of the French legal profession in the eighteenth century. About halfway through the presentation, I quoted a councilor to King Louis XV, who in 1730 demanded that a group of particularly obstreperous lawyers should be divided into three groups, with the first sent to the Bastille, the second exiled, and the third publicly hanged. Chaunu interrupted me, banging on the table. "That's it, that's it!" he exclaimed. "That's what they should have done more of, and then they could have prevented that terrible revolution." Having no idea how to respond, I paused, slightly shell-shocked, and then continued meekly with my paper.

Since then, I have developed more of an appetite for entering into arguments about the Revolution, and some of them have turned very contentious indeed. A good number have concerned my 2007 book *The First Total War*, which several French historians took as an attack on the

Revolution. In the online review *H-France Forum*, Annie Jourdan wrote: "The moral of Bell's story is that the French Revolution was above all bloody." I was not entirely temperate in response. Readers will find here, in the fifth essay in this part, a summary of some of the book's principal ideas. The exchange with Jourdan (and several others) can be found at the website of *H-France Forum*, http://www.h-france.net/forum/h-france forumvol2.html. I have also initiated a few quarrels myself, notably in the essay that concludes this part.

Fortunately, though, French Revolution scholarship is not always a matter of scholarly combat. The first three essays here discuss new approaches to the subject that have generated more light than heat. The fourth essay, meanwhile, reconsiders one of the great English historians of the Revolution and his idiosyncratic approach to it.

I

Un Dret Egal: The Revolution
and Human Rights

ON AUGUST 26, 1789, FRANCE'S REVOLUTIONARY National Assembly issued its Declaration of the Rights of Man and Citizen. Its stirring language and accordance of rights to all "men" everywhere has made it one of the most important political documents in human history. Admirers of the French Revolution continue to cite it, and indeed attribute to the Revolution the "invention" of human rights. But historians, as is their wont, have done their best to make this simple and admirable story complex and contentious. They have pointed out that other declarations of rights preceded the French one, that our own conceptions of "human rights" differ in important ways from those expressed in the Declaration, and that the very text of the document placed some strict limits on the rights it accorded. They have also noted the Declaration's failure to mention women, and the Assembly's supreme hypocrisy in proclaiming rights for all while continuing to tolerate slaveholding in France's colonial empire (which, in 1789, numbered as many slaves as the United States). Nonetheless, they agree that some sort of crucial development in the history of human rights did take place in Enlightenment

---

Book under Review: Lynn Hunt, *Inventing Human Rights: A History* (Norton, 2007).
Essay originally published in *The London Review of Books*, November 16, 2007.

and revolutionary France. Here is a consideration of one of the most inter-esting attempts to interpret this development.

If you want to understand the origins of modern human rights legisla-tion, Lynn Hunt claims, the place to start is not the philosophical back-ground, or the crises that the legislation addressed, but eighteenth-century fiction. The path she follows is not obvious, by any means—particularly as she has not chosen the fiction that most directly confronted issues of injustice (*Candide*, say, or Montesquieu's *Persian Letters*). Instead, Hunt draws attention to epistolary novels of private lives and loves, above all Richardson's *Pamela* and *Clarissa*, and Rousseau's *La nouvelle Héloïse*. These books received frenzied popular and critical acclaim, but not be-cause they said anything about constitutions and rights, even allegori-cally. What they did do, according to Hunt, was to encourage readers to identify with weak female characters who struggled to preserve their autonomy and integrity against various forms of domestic oppression. "How many times," Diderot wrote after reading Richardson, "did I not surprise myself, as it happens to children who have been taken to the theatre for the first time, crying: 'Don't believe it, he is deceiving you . . . If you go there, you will be lost.'" By creating such bonds of iden-tification, Hunt argues, the novels helped eighteenth-century readers understand that all humans resembled them on a fundamental level and that all humans intrinsically possessed natural, equal rights.

Hunt's longtime readers will find this linking of fiction and politics familiar. Some twenty years ago, she popularized the term "the new cul-tural history" to designate scholarship that emphasizes the role of lan-guage and "cultural practices" (e.g. habit, ritual, forms of reading and play, etc.) in driving historical change. Since then, the loose school that embraced the label has made cultural history the most dynamic area within the profession. Hunt herself has done as much as anyone to dem-onstrate its promise in a series of luminous studies on the French Revolution that draw profitably on anthropology, literary theory, and psychoanalysis. For instance, in *The Family Romance of the French Revolution* (1992) she explored how changing visions of family relations in eighteenth-century French society lay behind the radical left's hyster-ical demonization of Marie-Antoinette, and, more broadly, behind the transition from a paternalistic monarchy to a fraternal republic. That book delved into eighteenth-century art and literature, gathering up representations of the family from diverse sources and showing how they fit into coherent patterns.

In *Inventing Human Rights*, Hunt has shifted the focus from revolutionary democracy to human rights but retained something of the earlier book's thesis. Once again, she argues that a key modern political phenomenon sprang out of changes within the supposedly private, intimate sphere in mid-eighteenth-century western Europe. At first glance, the move seems perilous, not because the personal and the political aren't linked (something historians accepted long ago) but because of the chronology. Can we really say that human rights were "invented" in any single time and place? Ludger Kühnhardt, in his 1987 study *The Universality of Human Rights*, began as far back as the Greeks. Such historians generally devote considerable space to Thomas Hobbes, who had much to say about "natural rights," and carefully follow the labyrinthine debates among Grotius, Pufendorf, Locke, and Wolff on the same and related subjects, before even reaching the late eighteenth century. Hunt has little to say on any of this material. And having established the "invention" of human rights in the age of revolutions, she finishes off the rest of their history, to the present day, in a breezy thirty-eight pages, concentrating on the Universal Declaration of Human Rights of 1948. The historian Samuel Moyn has taken her to task for these omissions, and particularly for ignoring the 1960s and the Helsinki process, which arguably brought a new concept of "'human rights" to the center of modern world politics.

Hunt has invited this criticism by giving her book the title *Inventing Human Rights*, but the criticism is partly misplaced. As befits a "new cultural historian," she cares less about providing an intellectual genesis of a concept, or following its particular political uses, than about asking why, at a certain moment, it became widely accepted—indeed, widely recognized as wholly and irrefutably obvious. A better title might have been *How These Truths Became Self-Evident*, because that is the problem that actually concerns her (she starts with Jefferson and the Declaration of Independence). As she notes, between 1689, when the Bill of Rights spoke only of the particular rights of Englishmen, and 1776, when Jefferson claimed that all men "are endowed by their creator with certain unalienable rights," something changed fundamentally. Moyn makes a good case that another large shift occurred in the twentieth century, but Hunt's point still stands.

For her, the eighteenth-century discovery that rights were self-evident depended on two factors. First, people had to learn to see one another as separate, autonomous individuals possessed of free will. And second, they had to be able to empathize with one another, to see themselves in one another's shoes. Only when they came to feel, viscerally, that all others deserved the same rights as they did could the notion of universal, equal, natural rights take hold. Hunt notes further that "autonomy and empathy are cultural practices." They have histories, and both changed remarkably during the eighteenth century. Which is where the novels come in.

Happily, Hunt does not depend solely on novels to make her point and rapidly sketches in a much broader cultural background. She draws on Norbert Elias, and his story of the "ever-rising threshold of shame about bodily functions," to trace the rise of personal autonomy. She follows Charles Taylor, in his great philosophical history *Sources of the Self*, to elucidate the evolving eighteenth-century concept of "sympathy." She also devotes a fascinating chapter to changing attitudes toward torture. Here she notes that "an almost complete turnabout in attitudes took place over a couple of decades." Up to the mid-eighteenth century, most educated Europeans accepted the legitimacy of the most grisly forms of torture: stretching on the rack, pincers, forcing gallons of water down the throat, and a form of execution that involved crushing a person's bones, dislocating his or her limbs, and then leaving the person to die, stretched over a cartwheel. When Voltaire condemned the judicial murder of the Protestant Jean Calas in the 1760s, he did not initially consider the victim's "breaking on the wheel" worthy of comment. But some years later he denounced the punishment as inhuman, and by the 1780s torture in general had come to be almost universally denounced as barbaric and impermissible.

But it is the novels that matter most to Hunt. She wants to understand how people came to think in new ways—indeed, literally how their brain chemistry changed. (She cites recent research in cognitive science in an attempt to prove the point.) For her, the only experience powerful and sustained enough to produce these effects was intense reading. Modern readers of *La nouvelle Héloïse* and *Pamela*, however, may find it surprising that these novels in particular could induce any physical effects besides a narcotic one. Our current sensibilities do not generally take well to their massive helpings of undiluted sentiment. But as literary historians have long pointed out, eighteenth-century readers reacted very differently. *La nouvelle Héloïse*, these readers reported, took hold of them like "devouring fire." The climactic chapters left them, in the words of one, "shrieking, howling like an animal." Readers of *Clarissa* and *Pamela* burst into "passions of crying" and wrote to the author that there was "witchcraft in every page." Indeed, the Scottish philosopher Lord Kames spoke of the "waking dream" induced by novel-reading, while the cultural Cassandras of the day denounced the genre as a threat to public morality (they considered women particularly susceptible to its contagion). This emotional impact, Hunt argues, powerfully reinforced the lesson in empathy that arose from the particular form of the epistolary novel, which allowed readers to peep over the shoulders of supposedly "real" letter-writers and to imagine themselves in their place. The result was deeply felt instruction in "imagined empathy."

In this new cultural context, Hunt suggests, an older language of rights quickly flowed into new and powerful channels. Even before the American and French Revolutions, political writers started to refer not only to "natural" rights—which might not apply outside the state of nature—but to "human" rights that every individual possessed intrinsically by virtue of humanity. They began to speak of "the rights of man." By 1776 the existence of such rights had therefore become "self-evident," at least to Jefferson. Thirteen years later, the authors of the French Declaration of the Rights of Man and Citizen echoed him in their endorsement of man's "natural, inalienable and sacred rights." As Hunt notes, this document in turn "transformed everyone's language virtually overnight," as the phrase "the rights of man" and its many translations proliferated in political debates across the Western world.

But it was not just the language of rights that proliferated. Hunt argues that, in its wake, a "logic of rights" spread as well. It drove the rapid abolition of official torture across the West. It spurred a curtailment of cruel, unusual, and unequal punishments (if not of the death penalty), and a perception of institutionalized social hierarchies as presumptively unjust. In a nice turn of phrase, Hunt speaks of "the difficulty of maintaining social distinctions in an impatiently equalizing world." In France and its empire, the logic led to granting full civil rights to religious minorities (first Protestants, then Jews), and then, if only temporarily, to black slaves. It did not do similar things for women, but Hunt implicitly takes a stand against those authors (especially Carole Pateman and Joan Scott) who see a symbiotic relationship between the rise of equal rights for men and female subjugation, arguing that modern forms of individuation depend on radical sexual differentiation. What matters, Hunt argues, is not that the American revolutionaries did not even consider granting full civil rights for women, or that the French revolutionaries did consider it, only scornfully to deny it. The very idea of equal rights laid the groundwork for later liberation. "The promise of those rights," Hunt pleads, a little whiggishly, "can be denied, suppressed, or just remain unfulfilled, but it does not die." She does concede that the very assertion of equal rights, by undermining traditional assertions of racial and sexual difference on the basis of custom and tradition, helped provoke the "explosion in biological explanations of difference" that occurred in the nineteenth century. But she holds fast to her faith in the "logic," citing the 1948 Universal Declaration as its twentieth-century vindication.

All this makes for a rich, elegant, and persuasive essay. But like all such essays, *Inventing Human Rights* raises more questions than it can answer. To begin with, why does Hunt concentrate so intently on the novel to the exclusion of other cultural phenomena? She points to the fact that epistolary novels in particular appeared to remove the authorial point of view, voyeuristically heightening the sense of their characters' "reality," and hence the ability of a reader to identify with them. Yet remarkably, a similar shift of perspective took hold simultaneously in several different creative arenas. Paul Friedland has shown that striking new practices arose in the theater during precisely the same decades Hunt highlights. Actors stopped interacting explicitly with audiences and started trying to give the impression that they were engaged in "real" action that the spectators just happened to be watching, as if an invisible wall stood at the front of the stage. And, as Michael Fried has argued, painters in the same period began to depict characters deeply absorbed in their own activities, no more conscious of the spectator's gaze than Pamela seemed to the readers of her letters. So here, too, the creators of art strove to efface their presence, to present their work as a piece of reality that the audience could spy on—and therefore to encourage a bond of identification between the audience and the subjects of the works.

It might also be noted that the eighteenth century was a period obsessed with the idea of "emulation"—of putting representations of "great men" before the eyes of the population so vividly that their example would lead to widespread imitation. In France, the century saw the brief transformation of eulogy into an important literary genre. We should not forget that some of the strongest bonds of identification in the period were not with fictional characters but historical ones, created through the reading of classical writers such as Plutarch; they dominated the cult of emulation. Rousseau may have led his readers to identify with the fictional Julie, but as a boy he imagined himself rather as Pericles and Cato: "I thought myself Greek or Roman; I became the person whose life I was reading," he wrote in the *Confessions*. A few decades later, Saint-Just lamented that "the world has been empty since the Romans," who seemed more real to him than his own contemporaries.

There is also the question of the longer-term causes behind the rise of "imagined empathy." What caused readers to react as they did to the novels (and plays and paintings) of the mid-eighteenth century? Hunt hints—but, frustratingly, only hints—at one important factor. "Adherents of the novel," she writes, "understood that writers such as Richardson and Rousseau were effectively drawing their readers into daily life as a kind of substitute religious experience." In talking about the decline of torture, she notes that "pain, punishment, and the public spectacle of suffering all gradually lost their religious moorings." In speaking of older, Christian notions of human dignity, she observes that "the equality of souls in heaven is not the same thing as equal rights here on earth." Indeed. By any measure, changes in religious observance, and the decline of specifically Christian notions of sin, had an enormous amount to do with the developments chronicled in Hunt's book. To most educated western Europeans before the eighteenth century, nothing would have seemed less "self-evident" than the possession of copious natural rights by the wretched creatures of sin who went by the name of humans, who properly could hope for nothing other than God's grace to save their souls. Only once this gloomy shroud of assumptions had seriously frayed could deists such as Jefferson start to see things in a new way. It is no coincidence that the greatest pre-Enlightenment theorist of rights—Thomas

Hobbes—was also the man who did most to unmoor Western under-
standings of politics from Western understandings of God (what Mark
Lilla nicely calls "the Great Separation"). Seen from this perspective,
Hunt's cursory treatment of Hobbes becomes somewhat less defensible.

A final question that she prompts is why and how the idea of human
rights appealed so powerfully and so deeply to people who did not read
novels—or go to plays, view paintings, or read Plutarch. We have plen-
tiful evidence that millions of ordinary American and French people
from well outside the cultural elites eagerly embraced the new creed of
human rights at the end of the eighteenth century. In my own research,
I came across a speech in large part about the rights of man that was
delivered in Toulouse in 1790 to a unit of revolutionary National
Guardsmen who probably did not even speak standard French, as the
speaker used the local dialect. He insisted "that there is no one, absolutely no one... who does not have an equal right to justice and to life's
rewards" (nou ny a pas cap, absouludoment cap... que n'ajo un dret egal
à la justiço & à las recoumpensos). What did these words mean to the
peasants and artisans in his audience? They had not undergone the same
instruction in empathy as their novel-reading contemporaries. But it
was thanks to their actions that the Revolution that proclaimed the
Rights of Man was not stamped out (and stamped out, moreover, by
counterrevolutionaries whose leaders most definitely did read novels,
and probably abhorred torture as well). Historians who want to trace
the intellectual genesis of rights can elide these questions. I wish Hunt,
with her focus on how rights became "self-evident," had done more to
raise them.

Problems of this sort in fact point to some of the limits of the "new
cultural history," enormously fruitful though it has been. Closely linked
to the trend in literary studies known as new historicism, it generally
involves close analyses of texts—and, still more, treating events themselves as "texts" to be read. But in doing so, it tends to flatten the distinction between texts and actions—or, if you will, between actions and the
meanings attributed to actions. At one point, Hunt writes: "Reading
accounts of torture or epistolary novels had physical effects that translated into brain changes and came back out as new concepts about the
organisation of social and political life." It is a striking statement. But
how do the physical effects of reading about torture—powerful as Hunt

shows them to have been—compare to the physical effects on the brain of actually witnessing torture, to say nothing of actually undergoing it? Many different sorts of experience can arguably produce a heightened sense of empathy. In the case of the common people in revolutionary America or France, one might include the experience of witnessing a blatant injustice, of taking part in a crowd action, of receiving a National Guardsman's uniform, even of confronting shared starvation.

Taking on all these different questions would have led Lynn Hunt far afield and stretched her elegant essay into something much more awkward. But the questions, however difficult, need to be posed. As she has shown, in this book and throughout her career, there is much to be learned by drawing connections between the political events that shaped modern politics and the literary developments that shaped modern sensibilities. *Pamela* and the Declaration of the Rights of Man do indeed belong in the same conceptual sphere. But drawing these connections takes us only so far. It leaves a great deal else about the age of revolutions and the politics that it engendered a mystery.

2

Cherchez la Femme: The Revolution and Women

WHAT IS THE SIGNIFICANCE OF THE REVOLUTION'S denial of equal rights to women? As several of the preceding essays have already discussed, historians have divided sharply on this question. Some emphasize the fact that at least the revolutionaries discussed the issue (far more than their American counterparts, incidentally), and that several influential voices did call for extending the vote, and other rights, to female citizens. The Revolution, in this interpretation, therefore opened the door for women's eventual progress toward equality. Others counter that what matters above all is the denial, which was all the more damning and influential for being explicit, and carefully argued. Perhaps modern notions of citizenship were "gendered" from the start. The debate remains one of the most important, and troubling, about the French Revolution's long-term legacy. This essay considers one of the most creative recent attempts to address it from a new angle.

Looming high above the rooftops of the Left Bank sits a lugubrious monument of the French Republic: the Panthéon, final resting place of

Book under Review: Carla Hesse: *The Other Enlightenment: How French Women Became Modern* (Princeton University Press, 2001). Essay originally published in *The New Republic*, April 15, 2002.

the "great men of the *patrie.*" Its oppressively severe classicism, an exaggerated evocation of republican Rome, betrays the anxieties of its eighteenth-century architects, and recalls Heine's line about the impossibility of introducing republican severity into a city of 150,000 stylists, perfumers, and hairdressers. Downstairs, the claustrophobic crypt houses a very peculiar selection of illustrious French corpses. The Panthéon has admitted no kings and few generals, but many *engagé* intellectuals and intellectual politicians, in a very French marriage of politics and higher learning.

For more than two hundred years after the monument's opening in 1791, its roster of national heroes had one further peculiarity: it included not a single woman. Only in 1995 did Marie Curie finally take up belated residence in one of its somber mausoleums. And when she did, it was in the company of her husband, Pierre.

At first glance, this exclusion of women would seem to confirm a story about the French past that feminist historians have been developing for some time now. As they tell it, the eighteenth century's new birth of freedom for men entailed nothing less than a new birth of servitude for women. Before the Revolution of 1789, women had exercised a surprising degree of influence in French public life, as courtiers, aristocratic patrons, or hostesses of intellectual salons. Yet the Revolution brought this influence to an end, and prescribed new and far more rigid gender distinctions.

If, after the Revolution, all men could vote and speak freely and stand for office, women were confined to the household, to serve as helpmeets and mothers, unable even to publish a line without the explicit consent of their husbands. And this "separation of spheres" did not crumble away until the belated extension of the suffrage to women in 1944, and the establishment of legal equality within marriage in 1965. Until then, women unwilling to accept their prescribed fate could do little more than wrestle with the paradoxes of a politics that both offered and denied them the "rights of man," as Joan Scott argued in 1996 in *Only Paradoxes to Offer.*

It is a gloomy story, and one that not all feminists and historians entirely accepted. But it had a great influence, in large part because no scholar stepped forward to offer a persuasive alternate story of French women's journey into modernity. Carla Hesse has now done this, in her short, suggestive, and brilliant book. She offers a story that does not ignore the evidence of the Panthéon, but seeks instead to put it into a different, more complex, and more interesting perspective.

Hesse, who trained as a historian of the book, has a keen sense for how cultural hierarchies work. She has argued in other writings that modern interpretations of the Enlightenment unjustly prefer certain genres over others: Rousseau's formal treatises over his more widely read sentimental novel, for example. In her new book Hesse develops a similar idea with reference to French women.

If we are to find what Hesse calls an "arena for female self-constitution" in modern France, a place where women carved out a space of autonomy, it could not have been within the supposedly "higher" realms of politics and higher learning, in which their subordination was clearly prescribed. The realm in which women achieved autonomy, Hesse contends, was the realm of literature. It was less valued by the male mandarins of the Panthéon (and the nearby École Normale), and consequently more open to women's participation. The central chapters of Hesse's book illustrate how women of the revolutionary era not only found an outlet for their ambitions in the writing of novels but also used their novels to criticize, if sometimes obliquely, the cultural order that the Revolution brought into being. Hesse briefly traces out a female canon of authors who continued this tradition, from Germaine de Staël through George Sand and Colette to Simone de Beauvoir.

This bold and imaginative interpretation unfortunately gets off to a slightly shaky start, in an introductory chapter given to overreaching generalizations. In Old Regime France, Hesse asserts, it was women who defined the extremes of unacceptable forms of speech: on the one hand the vulgar slang of Paris fishwives, on the other hand the pretentious patter of aristocratic *précieuses*. Yet much evidence suggests that the fishwives and the *précieuses* figured among a great many groups who all symbolized uncouth language in their ways, including *patois*-speaking peasants, pedantic bourgeois, pettifogging lawyers, and urban artisans.

"Female eloquence," Hesse also argues, "became a central and dangerous element in revolutionary politics." Yet by any measure the revolutionary authorities paid less attention to women's speech than to the grain supply, diplomacy, educational reform, the counterrevolution, or any of a dozen other pressing issues. Most ambitiously, Hesse claims that the French Revolution saw "a shift from a regime of rhetoric to a regime of philosophy," in which "script eclipsed oral performance as the basis of cultural as well as political legitimacy." It is hard to know how she might prove such a statement, which ignores the centrality of written law to the early modern French monarchy as well as the continuing significance of rhetoric in French political culture during the Revolution and long afterward. Does such a complex thing as a culture really "shift" in such sweeping and simple ways?

Luckily, the rest of Hesse's book resists such claims. One crucial chapter even does something that has become sadly unfashionable in cultural history of late: it quantifies, in the classic manner of the *Annales* school. Hesse here makes the obvious point (obvious once she has stated it, that is) that if a rigid sexual "separation of spheres" had indeed taken place in revolutionary France, one would expect to find the number of female authors declining during the period. Instead, after an exhaustive combing of bibliographies and card catalogues, she produces the following eloquent figures as to the number of French women in print:

1766–1777	55
1777–1778	78
1789–1800	329

That last hard-won number goes a long way toward exploding the story of a new birth of servitude.

True, in the absence of comparable figures for male writers in the 1790s, Hesse cannot say for sure that the *proportion* of women writers increased, although it most likely did. And since this proportion almost certainly remained under 4 percent, many men may still have regarded women writers as little more than unthreatening curiosities. But the basic point is made. Far from driving women out of public life, the Revolution brought them into it.

This entry into print was also, Hesse emphasizes, an entry into a new and anarchic literary marketplace. The Revolution destroyed the cultural order of the Old Regime, in which a leaden system of pre-publication censorship and official permissions stifled literary inventiveness, leaving much of the Enlightenment to be published in the shadows and sold "under the cloak." In its place, initially, came chaos, with copyright law in flux, piracy rampant, and readers abandoning books for the periodical press to keep abreast of the political whirlwind. Old-line publishing houses went under (as Hesse herself showed in an earlier book), and new ones increasingly followed a strategy familiar to modern observers of the industry: diving deep in search of the lowest common denominator.

By the late 1790s, France was awash in sensational gothic novels and romances, often purportedly translated from English: *Miss Belhowe and Lord Clarendon, or the Trials of Love and Virtue; The Enchanted Knots; The Black Castle, or the Sufferings of the Young Ophelle; An Uncovered Pot with Nothing In It, or the Mysteries Underneath the Street of the Moon;* and so forth. These works were not only written in large part for women; they were also increasingly written by women. In France, women's writing marched hand in hand with print capitalism, even if the law still gave virtually complete control over married women's writings to their husbands (an arrangement actively reinforced by the French state as late as 1957).

This commercial success by no means endeared women to an emerging cadre of intellectuals and legislators, who loathed the literary chaos unleashed by the Revolution almost as much as they feared the political chaos. In its place, they longed to implement a new literary order: a rational, sober, enlightened, republican dispensation that would have no place for enchanted knots, black castles, or Miss Belhowe. These men mostly believed in the separation of spheres and frowned on women who "unnaturally" sought to publish romantic fiction instead of staying home as good republican housewives. After the end of the Terror in 1794 they founded new institutions, open only to men, to embody their ideals: a National Institute to serve as a sort of national cultural directorate, and the system of *grandes écoles* to train a new (male) elite. They also sought to develop new philosophical and ethical systems to undergird their creations.

To one sharp-minded observer, all these efforts amounted to nothing but an overwrought exercise in déjà vu. "The philosophical clergy," she wrote scornfully, "is as much a clergy as any other, and it was not worth the trouble to drive the curé from Saint-Sulpice in order to ordain the priests of the Panthéon." Her name was Isabelle de Charrrière, and she was an assiduous reader of philosophy, a novelist, and the lover of Benjamin Constant. On the surface, her novel *Three Women,* written in 1795, fit easily into the fashion for melodramatic romances. Its heroines were a maidservant facing ruin after becoming pregnant, a noble orphan plotting to elope with a dashing aristocrat far above her own social station, and a wealthy widow raising orphaned twins. But Charrrière's treatment of these women, Hesse argues, was anything but conventional. The protagonists, each faced with ethical dilemmas, refused to invoke an absolute, general moral law, for the legal restraints on them as women supposedly denied them the status of autonomous moral actors. Instead they followed what Hesse terms an "outlaw ethics," pragmatic and skeptical, holding their own interests above socially prescribed rules. Not surprisingly, male critics railed against the novel's "immorality."

Hesse explains that Charrrière intended *Three Women* as a critique of Kant's influential ethical treatise *On the Proverb,* which the new cultural establishment had seized on as a philosophical foundation stone for their new order. Her reading explicates the philosophical background with impressive economy, but more important, it casts Charrrière as the exemplar of those women writers who turned from philosophy and politics to fiction in the revolutionary era.

Novels, Hesse argues, are not simply a fallback for women excluded from formal philosophical training and formal involvement in political life. The form itself, with its highlighting of contingency, moral ambiguity, and the constant making and remaking of character and personality, perfectly suited women wrestling with manifold restraints on their own personal autonomy. "This formal indeterminacy of the novel," she observes, "made it possible for women to constitute moral identities that were in some fundamental sense always unfinished and always open to the possibility of radical change." Germaine de Staël, the great novelist and critic (and another lover of Benjamin Constant), recognized this point when she wrote that "literature, properly speaking, becomes women's domain, and men consecrate themselves uniquely to higher philosophy."

The second half of Hesse's book consists of readings in what amounts to an alternate literary canon. Besides Charrière, Hesse considers Louise de Kéralio, who published radical journalism and histories during the Revolution, but later turned to novel writing; the prolific Mme de Genlis; and especially de Staël. And in connection with these last two Hesse develops her most intriguing theme, that of the "doubled self." Modern women writers, she suggests, have faced a danger unknown to their male counterparts: that their public personae will be interpreted as simple reflections of their inner female selves, and therefore dismissed as unworthy of consideration because of women's supposedly inferior moral and intellectual capacities.

In response to this predicament, Hesse argues, writers such as Genlis and de Staël sought in their work to emphasize the gap between inner selves and outer selves, to defend the opacity rather than the transparency of language, and to distinguish women's writing from men's as more naturally restrained, delicate, and veiled. Once again, it was fiction, above all other forms of writing, that gave women a refuge and a medium suited to their message. De Staël warned of the dangers of female self-revelation in her novel *Delphine,* and herself became the thinly disguised protagonist of a novel titled *The Woman Author,* which depicted a woman wooing, under an assumed name, a general modeled on Napoleon.

Hesse limits her sustained analysis to the revolutionary era, but in a last, brief tour de force of a chapter she extends her story an additional century and a half, touching suggestively on the careers of George Sand and Colette and ending with Simone de Beauvoir. In *The Second Sex,* Hesse notes, de Beauvoir constructed her own canon of French female writers—first and foremost de Staël and Colette—whose works she drew on in developing her diagnosis of women's condition. In her central section on the possibility of women's emancipation, nearly every citation came from French women's fiction. De Beauvoir thereby highlighted an alternate, dissident, female Enlightenment, constructed out of very different prose materials from its male counterpart. But by the very act of writing *The Second Sex,* after having herself initially ventured into public life as a novelist, de Beauvoir reversed the journey taken by Louise de Kéralio 150 years before, and reclaimed the domain of philosophy and politics for women's voices. She thereby helped to bring the "other Enlightenment" to a symbolic end and opened the way to contemporary feminism.

All this is a powerfully crafted historical vision, presented by Hesse in lucid and engaging prose. In stressing women's success in the literary marketplace, and the new opportunities that opened up there after 1789, Hesse dispels the idea that the French Revolution was an unmitigated disaster for women. In her emphasis on women writers' subsequent search for moral autonomy, she gives depth and nuance to a history that had previously focused too sharply on the quest for the vote. And by emphasizing the success of writers such as Charrière, Sand, and Beauvoir, she shows that it was possible for women to step outside the deep and gloomy shadows of the Panthéon.

Yet this brief book also leaves important questions hanging. In an appendix Hesse provides a comprehensive bibliography of French women's writing for the years between 1789 and 1800, but she does not subject it to a thorough analysis, or ask whether the period's less well-known women writers engaged in the same sort of criticism that she finds in Charrière, Genlis, and de Staël. Hesse's treatment of the nineteenth and twentieth centuries, meanwhile, is so brief that it unintentionally places George Sand and Colette in a subordinate position to their female predecessors, as if these two much greater novelists were producing only variations (if sublime ones) on established themes.

Most significant, Hesse gives very little sense of how readers other than de Beauvoir actually read, understood, and reacted to this alternate canon of writers. A few scattered quotations, some buried in the footnotes, hint that the books in question stirred controversy and drew predictably misogynistic scorn from male defenders of the literary status quo. So they arguably possessed the power, and posed the sort of threat, that Hesse attributes to them. But how many women readers of the nineteenth and early twentieth centuries saw in these books what de Beauvoir saw and what Hesse sees?

The question is particularly pressing because seven years before *The Other Enlightenment*, one of the most eminent women historians in France published a book quite similar to it, but offering a strikingly different reading of some of the same writers. Mona Ozouf, best known for a landmark study of French revolutionary festivals, is one of the very few living French historians who is also a great prose writer: elegant, witty, even haunting. In *Les mots des femmes* (translated in this country as *Women's Words*), she sketched out richly textured portraits of ten French women writers, including Charrière, de Staël, George Sand, Colette, and de Beauvoir. Unlike Hesse, she had precious little sympathy for the last, titling the essay "Simone, or Greed," and criticizing the writer's "hypocrisy," "bad faith," lack of genius, and servile relationship to Jean-Paul Sartre.

Ozouf also appended to the book an unfortunate, caricature-laden "Essay on French Singularity," which accused "American feminism" of identifying all sex with rape and of trying to erase all sexual differences.

In contrast, Ozouf praised French women for celebrating those differences and for developing a distinctive voice without falling into "extremism." Overall, Ozouf interpreted French women's writing not as a critical response to the Revolution's new cultural order (which she did not find particularly exclusionary or misogynist) but as something complementary to it. So where Hesse sees a sharply critical tradition culminating in de Beauvoir, Ozouf saw a much gentler tradition of female self-expression that largely bypassed de Beauvoir and remains alive in writers such as herself.

Ozouf's evocation of a distinctly French style of women's writing was surprisingly ahistorical, and her downplaying of the revolutionary period's misogyny and exclusionary tendencies failed to convince. I much prefer Hesse's version of the story. But I find it unfortunate that Hesse does not even mention *Les mots des femmes*—not only because she should confront Ozouf directly, but because Ozouf's interpretation has value as historical evidence: it shows how at least one enormously intelligent and eloquent French woman has read the female literary canon.

Perhaps Ozouf's reading is an untypical one, driven less by her reading of the texts themselves than by the political conjuncture of the mid-1990s, in which centrist French intellectuals such as Ozouf were recoiling from the American import that they dubbed *le politically correct*. But if Ozouf's reading is at all typical, then Hesse's women writers start to look either less radically critical or more like figures whose critical intent went largely unremarked and unappreciated by their readers. It is a pity that Hesse does not deal with this issue more directly.

So were French women writers burrowing subversively under the heavy pillars of the Panthéon, or were they helping, perhaps unintendedly, to prop the building up? Without adding an analysis of novel-reading to her discussion of novel-writing, Hesse cannot provide an entirely satisfying answer to this question. Yet she has satisfyingly changed the terms in which the subject will be discussed from now on, and provocatively illuminated the changing contours of female experience in modern France. And in her deft combination of quantitative research and critical readings, Hesse provides a model of how to pursue the social history of ideas.

3

Words and Tumbrels: The Revolution and Language

THIS ESSAY TURNS TO THE OVERALL INTERPRETATION of the Revolution, with particular attention to the question of the Terror. Why was it that a historical process that began drenched in hope and enthusiasm turned so violent so quickly? How are we understand the relationship between the extraordinary effusions of utopianism of 1793–1794, and the equally extraordinary effusions of blood? The essay surveys the cultural and linguistic approaches developed by historians of the Revolution in the last quarter of the twentieth century, returning again to the crucial figure of François Furet. It then goes on to consider a particularly promising new approach.

I

"Words, like things, have been monstrosities," wrote the reactionary critic Jean-François de La Harpe in the wake of the French Revolution, and it is hard to disagree with him. The Terror's leading figures justified the unjustifiable with a creative mendacity that can still evoke shudders. "Terror is nothing but . . . an emanation of virtue" (Robespierre). "Sacrifice

---

Book under Review: Sophia Rosenfeld, *A Revolution in Language: The Problem of Signs in Late Eighteenth-Century France* (Stanford University Press, 2001). Essay originally published in *The New Republic*, November 26, 2001.

two hundred thousand heads, and you will save a million" (Marat). "Every new faction will discover death in the mere thought of crime" (Robespierre). "Following the orders that you gave me I have crushed children under the feet of horses, massacred women who at least...will engender no more brigands. I have no prisoners with which to reproach myself" (General Westermann in the Vendée).

Not surprisingly, historians have been fascinated by French revolutionary language since the events themselves. It makes for a vast field of study, for the revolutionaries obsessively discussed, justified, and commemorated everything that they did or tried to do. "The world thinks," Michelet once remarked. "France speaks." And speaks, and speaks: in the decade following 1789, French politics floated on a great crashing tide of words, written down in newspapers and pamphlets and meticulously preserved by archivists and librarians.

Yet it is only since the 1980s that French revolutionary language itself, as opposed to warfare, or political factions, or social class, has become the central preoccupation of the leading historians of the upheaval. This shift is owed to the broader "linguistic turn" taken by the human sciences over the past generation. Whereas scholars once tended to treat political language as the product or the reflection of "deeper" social and political forces, they now argue that things are never so simple and transparent, and that language helps to structure the very reality it describes. Moreover, since reality can only be perceived through the deceptive veils of linguistic representations, the representations themselves necessarily constitute the historian's first object of study. The French Revolution has served as a sort of laboratory for "post–linguistic turn" history, and in the process our understanding of it has radically changed.

The scholarly trip has been an exciting one, but not without its drawbacks. The fascination with the careful parsing and dissection of speeches and pamphlets, engravings and statues, has tended to obscure the great human drama of the Revolution, so vividly conveyed in the nineteenth century by Michelet and Thomas Carlyle and more recently by R. R. Palmer and Simon Schama. The new work also puts an almost exclusive emphasis on the small percentage of the French—mostly bourgeois or noble, and mostly male—who had the education and the leisure to engage in high-level political debate. François Furet, the pioneering figure in the new revolutionary history, once wrote with unconscious condescension that "the revolutionary lower classes continued to confuse the grain issue with politics," as if feeding a starving population mattered less on some existential level than high-minded debates about the embodiment of the general will. Finally, the new work tends to return discussion of the origins of the Revolution to the even smaller percentage of the French who engaged in high-level political debate before 1789, and especially the philosophes of the Enlightenment. Since the generation of 1789 itself often ascribed the Revolution entirely to the action of the philosophes, we have now come full circle.

It is one thing to state these drawbacks, but it is quite another thing to overcome them: to place the Revolution back into a fuller historical canvas, and to relate its politics to something other than the elite languages of political theory, without throwing out the lessons of the linguistic turn. It is in this context that Sophia Rosenfeld's book is such a welcome development. At first sight it would not seem the most likely work to suggest a path that historians can follow out of their current dilemmas. It is itself an intellectual history, concentrated on the same small number of elites who have already received such intensive examination. Within these limits it ranges marvelously over such different fields as ballet, pantomime, hieroglyphics, telegraphy, and the education of the deaf, but always with a penchant for the theory over the practice. Readers drawn to the Revolution by Simon Schama's palpitating prose will find little drama in Rosenfeld's detailed explications of philosophical debates and her sinuous, complex sentences. And yet her book represents a significant advance.

II

To understand Rosenfeld's contribution, a little more needs to be said about the school of historical writing with which she is engaging, and especially the historiographical legacy of Furet, the twentieth century's greatest historian of the Revolution. Following a brief youthful fling with the French Communist Party in the years after World War II, Furet became a lifelong anti-communist, consumed with the question of how revolutionary regimes turn radically repressive. According to the Marxist orthodoxy in vogue in France at the time, the Revolution had radicalized because of a pitiless class conflict between bourgeois and aristocrats, and because France's enemies threatened to destroy the Revolution, forcing its leaders to adopt exceptionally harsh measures in self-defense. (French Communists made similar arguments on behalf of Stalin.)

In the 1970s, Furet brilliantly exploded these assumptions, showing that they were nothing but a repetition of the excuses that had been offered by the architects of the Terror themselves. Drawing on Anglo-American work mostly ignored by his French colleagues, he pointed out that the competing revolutionary factions did not come from significantly different social backgrounds. As for the "circumstances" of war and civil war, they had certainly placed the radical Jacobin regime in desperate danger in 1793–1794, when France faced an Austro-Prussian assault from the east and several internal revolts. But when the military threats receded, the pace of executions did not slacken in its turn. In fact, it accelerated. The Terror had a momentum independent of "circumstances."

In place of the Marxist orthodoxy, Furet offered his own theory of radicalization in 1978 in a brilliantly difficult essay called "The Revolution Is Over." The crucial factors behind the Terror, he argued, were neither social nor economic nor military, but purely ideological. For the years 1789–1794 were a moment when political language became detached from social interests and took on a life of its own. Centuries of absolute monarchy, combined with the powerful influence of Rousseau's political philosophy, had left French elites in thrall to the idea that sovereignty was utterly indivisible and based on a single, necessarily unitary national will. As a result, any notion of governmental checks and balances, or of a "loyal opposition," was absurd to them. The line between disagreement and treason was vanishingly thin.

In such an atmosphere, competing political factions could establish their legitimacy only by posing as the sole authentic voice of the people, and in this game the most aggressively egalitarian and violent stance always won out. From the beginning, therefore, revolutionary politics amounted to a fatally unstable spiral into Terror, as faction after faction rushed to embrace ever more radical and populist positions: the subjection of the Catholic Church to state management; universal manhood suffrage; the replacement of the monarchy by a republic; the execution of King Louis XVI; price controls; the abolition of Christianity; draconian "revolutionary justice" for dissenters; the utter extermination of the

Revolution's enemies. The repressed and fanatical Robespierre played the game best of all, casting himself as the pure avenging angel of the popular will. But finally, like an infernal machine pushed far beyond its operating parameters, the whole system violently collapsed in the coup d'état of 9 Thermidor, in which Robespierre was arrested and guillotined.

An avowed Tocquevillian liberal, Furet had little in common with such patron saints of French postmodernism as Foucault or Derrida, but his arguments resonated with theirs in surprising ways. His notion that the revolutionaries were fundamentally incapable of thinking in terms of mixed government and genuinely contestatory politics recalled Foucault's vision of the power of hegemonic "discourses" throughout a culture. Furet's description of revolutionary politics as an unstable "semiotic circuit," and his emphasis on language rather than individuals as the driving force behind events, recalled Derrida's remarks on the primacy of texts over authors and on the ways texts constantly subvert their own authority. And so Furet offered a form of history well suited to the linguistic turn that these French philosophers were helping to inspire across the human sciences.

It took an American historian, Lynn Hunt, to make the connection explicit, in her book *Politics, Culture, and Class in the French Revolution*, which appeared in 1984. Unlike Furet's essays, Hunt's work steered clear of the jagged edges of contemporary French politics. Starting with the words of La Harpe quoted earlier, Hunt splendidly highlighted the way language itself served as an instrument of political change in revolutionary France. She argued that revolutionary reforms, such as the new rational calendar, the new forms of political ritual (solemn oathtakings, the burial of political heroes in the Panthéon, grandiose national festivals), and new national symbols (notably a massive Hercules representing the People as an indomitable Colossus) represented considerably more than simply propaganda or an outgrowth of revolutionary utopianism. They amounted, in Hunt's view, to nothing less than "the institution of a dramatically new political culture," centered on democratic republicanism and the "compelling intensity of revolutionary change." Given that the revolutionaries in the end failed to overturn France's social structure or centralized system of government, this new culture constituted their principal accomplishment and legacy. Hunt's book has become a classic of what she herself dubbed "the new cultural history," an American movement conducted very much under the sign of the linguistic turn.

The most rigorous application of linguistic analysis to the Revolution has come from the pen of Keith Michael Baker. His densely written *Inventing the French Revolution*, published in 1990, drew eclectically and eruditely on such diverse sources as German *Begriffsgeschichte* (the "history of concepts"), Foucault's "archaeology of knowledge," and Quentin Skinner's history of political languages. But on the question of the relationship between language and historical reality, Baker's book was absolutely uncompromising. Furet and Hunt had erred, Baker asserted, in assuming that political language had exercised an unusual and extraordinary power during the French Revolution. Politics, he insisted, is always and everywhere a linguistic phenomenon: a contest for linguistic authority. "Social interests" do not exist independently of the language that gave them meaning. "The action of a rioter in picking up a stone can no more be understood apart from the symbolic field that gives it meaning than the action of a priest in picking up a sacramental vessel."

Unlike Hunt, with her sweeping panorama of symbols and rituals, Baker concentrated more dryly on the history of particular words: "public opinion," "constitution," "representation," "revolution." The chapter on the last of these momentous terms offered a particularly clear illustration of Baker's method. Before the late eighteenth century, he showed, the range of meanings we now attribute to the word "revolution" simply did not exist. When the French talked of revolutions, they meant political events that were unpredictable, disorderly, rapid, and largely beyond human control. (The word had already largely lost its original sense of a return to a point of origin.) In no sense were revolutions seen as planned occurrences that could extend into an indefinite future.

People did not yet "make" revolutions, according to Baker. Revolutions happened to them. Therefore, the noun and the adjective "revolutionary" did not exist and would have struck contemporaries as nonsensical. Yet during the second half of the eighteenth century, as French political writers engaged in increasingly acerbic and open public debate, the range of meanings for "revolution" gradually expanded; and by 1789 the word had come to denote more or less what it does today. Only with this "invention" of the concept, Baker audaciously claimed, could the thing itself—the French Revolution—have taken place.

Baker's theory was hugely controversial. Does a thing have to have a name in order to exist? (The classic example is the feeling known as schadenfreude.) But a "revolution," in the modern sense, is not simply a "thing," but an intellectual construct. We can speak, if we wish, of an "Aztec revolution," but could Aztecs have seen themselves as "revolutionaries," engaged in a conscious project of reshaping the human world in accordance with their own wishes, and without any reference to the divine? For that matter, could the French of 1750 have seen themselves as "revolutionaries" in this sense? And if not, could they have carried out anything like the Revolution of 1789 forty years before the fact? Baker compellingly suggested that they could not have done so, and thereby he gave powerful support to Furet's and Hunt's view of the Revolution as first and foremost an upheaval in the realm of culture and ideas.

Baker's work has been widely attacked, but I do not believe that it has been convincingly refuted. In combination with Furet's and Hunt's books, it has fundamentally reoriented the study of the "age of revolution," turning historians back from investigations of personalities and war and class struggle to where the entire subject began: to the Enlightenment, and the great effusion of ideas that preceded the Revolution's great effusion of hope and blood. Baker's description of the political culture of the ancien régime as a virtual terra incognita became the phrase that launched a thousand dissertations.

Yet it is precisely on this terrain that Baker's linguistic analysis has been most unsatisfying. Why *did* French political culture change in the manner he describes? Why *did* the modern concept of "revolution" take shape? Baker, a good student of the linguistic turn, refuses to attribute these linguistic phenomena to "deeper" social causes, rejecting the notion that culture can only be set into shuddering motion by shifts in the tectonic plates of society and the economy. He is equally uncomfortable giving principal credit to a few great minds—making the Revolution *la faute à Rousseau*, as the French phrase has it. He dislikes the very term "Enlightenment," judging it a label retroactively slathered across a somewhat arbitrarily designated set of canonical thinkers. In good Foucauldian fashion, he prefers to trace the flow of impersonal "discourses" through a broad intellectual field, giving equal weight to famous philosophes and to minor figures of interest principally to specialists: Jacob-Nicolas Moreau alongside Voltaire; Chrétien-Guillaume de Malesherbes next to Montesquieu; Guillaume-Joseph Saige in the company of Rousseau.

For Baker, the ultimate motive force is language itself: "At the limit, no one is safe from the potential play of discursivity." Thus he has constructed a model in which French politics "burst out of the absolutist mold" in the 1750s, when the symbolic authority of France's monarch broke apart into separate discourses that considered sovereignty as essentially grounded in justice, reason, or will. In the end, it was the "discourse of will," expressed most forcefully by Rousseau (but not only by him), that prevailed: a way of thinking about politics that ascribed sovereign legitimacy solely to the general and unanimous will of the entire population. With this discourse's success, Montesquieu's idea of dividing and limiting sovereign power came to seem nonsensical to most of the leading figures in political debate, who now concentrated their efforts on finding a way to embody the general will. This shift set in motion the revolutionary dynamic of radicalization described by Baker's close friend and collaborator Furet. The Terror began with an idea of sovereignty.

It is a strikingly abstract and colorless vision of political change, although one supported at every point by meticulous and often brilliant readings of the texts in question. Baker's story seems to have taken place in an altogether different dimension of existence from the country described by earlier generations of historians, with its languorous plumed aristocrats, its burgeoning cities awash in new luxuries, its great armies of the indigent poor desperately scrabbling to fill their stomachs, and its great bloody dramas of the Bastille, the Terror, the Vendée, and Thermidor. But Baker's logic is impeccable, and his arguments are convincing. No serious reader can dismiss him, however much she may prefer the thundering cadences of Carlyle, the lyrical hosannas of Michelet, or the gritty cynicism of Richard Cobb.

So should historians move beyond Baker's vision of the Revolution, and if so, how? Is it possible to interpret the great acts of political imagination that he describes as something other than simply the "play of discursivity"? Must political history consist of nothing more than a meticulous tracing of the sinuous, slippery currents of language? Is any attempt to construct a larger historical narrative linking past and present nothing but a futile exercise in mythmaking, as certain postmodern historians (though not Baker himself) have insisted? It is at this frustrating juncture that Sophia Rosenfeld has appeared, with her apparently odd strategy of considering revolutionary politics from the vantage points of ballet, pantomime, and the education of the deaf.

III

The educated classes of eighteenth-century France, most of them drilled in the rhetorical arts by demanding Jesuit schoolmasters, had a facility for words rarely equaled in the history of the planet. Open almost any book of French revolutionary writings, and you will come across page after page of impeccably eloquent French prose, to all appearances set down as fast as the author could wield a quill. (Had it taken them much longer, figures such as Robespierre would have necessarily spent the entire Revolution behind a writing desk, given how much they wrote.) Yet these same individuals had a deep fascination, indeed often an obsession, with nonverbal forms of communication. They flocked to pantomimes and to the experimental ballets of Jean-Georges Noverre, debated the merits of Chinese characters over their own writing system, eagerly purchased accounts of "wild children" living in the forests without language, and made a cultural hero out of the abbé Charles-Michel de l'Épée, pioneering inventor of one of the first sign languages for the deaf. Is it a coincidence that the decipherer of Egyptian hieroglyphics was a Frenchman?

This apparently paradoxical fascination is not difficult to explain. Their very facility with words made French writers and orators all too aware of language's capacity for deception: of the way crystalline prose too often amounts to a sort of conjuror's trick, distracting and misleading the unwary. Matters were further complicated by the fact that eighteenth-century France was a heavily multilingual country.

The dominant trends in French philosophy in the eighteenth century reinforced this suspicion of language. From Locke's immensely influential *Essay on Human Understanding* to the writings of Condillac, Diderot, and Rousseau, the French were bombarded with impeccably eloquent warnings about the dangers of impeccable eloquence. Words, it was argued, could never completely describe the thing that they signified, and the more abstract the concept, the more imperfect the fit. Thus language inherently gave rise to vain disputes over meanings and to the "abuse of words" by the ill-intentioned. In reaction, French thinkers, notably Diderot and Rousseau, very self-consciously speculated about whether a purely figurative "language of action" might possibly avoid the traps and the treasons of spoken language.

Some of the most fascinating chapters of Rosenfeld's book deal with the search for this "language of action." She highlights Noverre's quest to develop a *ballet d'action* capable of presenting the full range of meanings expressed by tragic drama through choreography and music alone. Noverre and his supporters actually argued for the superiority of ballet and pantomime over spoken drama, claiming for gesture a range and an energy lacking in spoken language, and asserting that gestures were incapable of conveying falsehoods. Noverre's efforts, including an ambitious attempt to stage one of Corneille's tragedies entirely in music and pantomime, were ultimately judged more impressive in theory than in practice. Still, they drew unprecedented numbers of spectators to the ballet in the 1770s.

Rosenfeld also devotes impressive pages to de l'Épée's school for the deaf, in which a new sign language was taught through the use of pantomime, beginning with basic gestures and gradually building to ever more complex and abstract signs. The priest claimed that this method allowed him to derive language from nature itself, and indeed many ecstatic observers believed that Noverre and l'Épée had recreated the actual primeval "language of action" of mankind that had allegedly prevailed in the state of nature before the invention of speech. Rosenfeld carefully demonstrates how these ideas and enthusiasms were widely diffused by academies and other popular educational institutions.

But what did this all have to do with politics? Quite a lot. At the start of her discussion Rosenfeld makes a very simple point. If, following Furet, Hunt, and Baker, historians are to treat language itself as an instrument of political change, then they need to examine the ways different societies understood how language itself operates—something that is by no means constant over time. If the French of the eighteenth century had an obsessive suspicion of language, a heightened sensitivity to "abuses of words," and a desperate desire to devise more perfect forms of communication, then these sentiments would have deeply informed the way they understood language to work in politics. To understand the past languages of politics, then, we need to read them in the light of the epistemological assumptions that underpinned them.

This is the ambitious task Rosenfeld sets herself in the second part of her book, which covers the Revolution and its immediate aftermath. For a start, she demonstrates that the Enlightenment dream of a more perfect language survived intact into the revolutionary upheaval. Even while attempting complete overhauls of French administration, law, and customs, the successive revolutionary assemblies also found copious time to ponder the reform of the French language, to debate how best to end "abuses of words," and even to discuss somehow establishing a gestural "language of action" as the basis of French legislation. The polymathic priest Henri Grégoire blamed peasant resistance to the Revolution on linguistic misunderstandings, and devised a massive project for the "eradication" of local dialects and regional languages in favor of standard French. Faced with economic collapse, impending military disaster, and numerous internal revolts, the delegates to the Revolutionary National Convention turned to the pressing business of grammar and punctuation.

The most utopian of revolutionary projects evaporated after the fall of the Jacobins on 9 Thermidor, but plans for the reform of language survived, and in some ways they intensified. The perpetrators of the coup, far from rejecting the Jacobins' linguistic point of view, adopted it wholeheartedly, denouncing the Terror itself as the ultimate "abuse of words." La Harpe was only one of many figures at the time to denounce the "monstrosities" of revolutionary political language, and their analyses summoned forth more plans for the revision of grammar, the elimination of "aristocratic" tendencies from French, and even the formulation of a hieroglyphic writing system that might represent any spoken language in perfectly rational form.

The story of revolutionary language politics only really came to an end, Rosenfeld shows, when members of the influential group known as the *idéologues* finally broke with linguistic utopianism at the end of the 1790s. In the name of social stability, they argued, legislators needed to concentrate on improving existing systems of French-language education, and on making use of the language already at their disposal—the language of the people—to promote an acceptance of the Revolution on rational and scientific grounds. With the dawn of the nineteenth century, the idea of a perfect language gradually receded from the realm of politics into that of utopian fiction.

It is a fascinating story; but its larger significance, Rosenfeld forcefully argues, was not simply that the dream of a perfect language led legislators to contemplate dialectical differences when they might more profitably have occupied themselves devising new ways of protecting food supplies. It was rather that their linguistic assumptions led politicians of all stripes to consider political difference as the result of faulty or deceptive communication. "Revolutionary political culture," Rosenfeld observes, "with its emphasis on consensus and harmony and its antipathy to factionalism or even contestation . . . should be viewed as a direct result of its framers' historically specific epistemological suppositions and assumptions. The first of these was the idea that the *abus des mots*, rather than legitimate differences of opinion, constituted the root cause of most dissension and strife. The second was that a perfected language, modeled after the " 'methodical' language of signs, could be . . . a vehicle of peace in the social sphere."

This short passage has large implications for any understanding of the French Revolution as a cultural event. It suggests that the revolutionaries' basic mental assumptions about the way the world worked predisposed them to precisely the sort of trust in a unitary sovereign will that was identified by Furet and Baker.

For if political disagreements derived from various forms of miscommunication, then limiting the power of government so as to protect minority opinions, and designing a system of government to accommodate and to balance a range of political positions, was self-evidently absurd. Whatever Montesquieu might have said on the issue, working a system of checks and balances into a constitution made no more sense than working it into an astronomy class. Protecting a person's right to deceive the people through the "abuse of words" was not simply foolish, it was also criminal. For this reason, liberal political ideas, with their emphasis on limiting executive power and guaranteeing individual rights, could start to find purchase in France only after the dream of a more perfect language lost its quasi-occult aura in the years around 1800. And by that point, of course, the political chaos had grown so great that Napoleon had arrived to pick up the battered pieces.

Rosenfeld is proposing a way of understanding political change that goes a significant step beyond tracking the careers of particular words and concepts. "The rhetoric of politics," she writes in her introduction, "always stems from a wider variety of sources and is supported by a wider set of beliefs than simply the political theories or political languages of the past." In other words, if we can identify significant epistemological shifts, such as the rise of new ways of understanding language itself, then we can begin to figure out why particular visions of the political succeeded while others did not. We can gain a sense of why political languages changed and begin reintegrating the sort of analyses Baker has conducted into a wider analysis of past cultures.

IV

But is Rosenfeld correct? Has she really demonstrated the connection between epistemological change and political change? For all its nuance and its intellectual sophistication, the book does have a flaw, namely, a tendency to generalize too easily from the available evidence. In her first chapter, for instance, after having briefly illustrated the interest shown by prominent thinkers in the workings of language, Rosenfeld leaps to the conclusion that the philosophes as a whole had a "desire to explain the workings of the world in linguistic terms." This is true enough in one sense, but the French Enlightenment was famously and voraciously eclectic. Its leading figures could gorge themselves one month on linguistic theory, and the next month turn to law, or commerce, or religion, or even opera as the object of their intellectual passions. They did indeed have a desire to explain the world in linguistic terms—but also in political terms, psychological terms, social terms, material terms, scientific terms. To prove her case beyond a doubt, Rosenfeld would need not simply to track concern about the "abuse of words" through the philosophes' explicit writings on language, but to demonstrate that the concern pervaded the entirety of their works. This would have been an enormous and even quixotic undertaking, and Rosenfeld does not attempt it.

The same problem arises in her treatment of the Revolution. Figures such as Robespierre shared the philosophes' eclecticism. They were great amateurs, and also great joiners, attending meetings of all manner of societies for the improvement of mankind. Henri Grégoire, whom Rosenfeld presents principally as a linguistic reformer, spent the revolutionary years dilating to his colleagues on topics that ranged from the emancipation of the Jews to the abolition of colonial slavery, the reform of the Catholic liturgy, and the origins of the "liberty tree," as well as the eradication of local *patois*. It is certainly significant that Robespierre belonged to a Society of Amateurs of the French Language, but Rosenfeld cannot say whether he devoted more than a fraction of his time to its activities. She is on firmer ground when she shows how, under the Terror, Robespierre grew ever more fearful, even paranoid, about the "abuse" and the "dominion" of words, and ever more strident in his denunciations of eloquence.

If Rosenfeld sometimes assumes rather than demonstrates the political importance of ideas about language, it may be because she has too easily embraced the diagnoses of the Terror that were offered in the immediate aftermath of Thermidor. Figures such as La Harpe and the *idéologue* Destutt de Tracy (who may have invented the word "ideology") have a peculiar appeal today, because their remarks on the importance of language jibe so well with postmodern thinking on the subject. Not surprisingly, it is the period of their own greatest political influence, after 1794, that provides Rosenfeld with her richest and most persuasive evidence. The *idéologues'* conception of precise language as an instrument for reshaping the social order undergirded their plans for a hierarchical national educational system, one whose legacy is still alive in France today.

But language arguably loomed so in post-Thermidorian politics for very specific and limited political reasons. The perpetrators of the coup against the Jacobins faced the almost impossible task of accounting for and denouncing the Terror without calling into question the democratic republican ideals to which both they and the Jacobins appealed. Calling Robespierre an abuser of words gave them a convenient method of surgically separating the "abusive" man from his sound political principles. Rosenfeld tends to read the intensity of post-Thermidorian engagement with the question of language back into the politics of the Terror, the early Revolution, and even the Enlightenment. So while her history of linguistic politics itself is masterful and convincing, her broader conclusions as to the Revolution's underlying epistemological basis remain suggestive rather than definitive.

And yet they are enormously suggestive. Not all of Rosenfeld's claims may survive further research, but her ideas on how to place political languages into a broad historical canvas deserve to have a powerful and lasting influence. Not surprisingly, she is not the only historian presently working along such lines. In the field of French revolutionary history, Paul Friedland has developed a strong and provocative argument about how changes in abstract notions of representation—how one thing stands for another—shaped the emergence of new forms of political thought. He has uncovered remarkable and surprising parallels between changing ideas of representation in politics and in the world of theater, and between the ideas of counterrevolutionary royalists and those of the most radical Jacobins. He uses these parallels to show why liberal ideas of representative democracy had such difficulty gaining acceptance in revolutionary France, in a conclusion fully consonant with Rosenfeld's (and, more generally, with those of Furet and Baker). Lynn Hunt, in her recent work on the origins of human rights, draws striking connections between notions of the individual self first expressed in eighteenth-century novels and the languages of individual rights during the Revolution. In sum, the field is turning toward the elusive territory of epistemological shifts; and Rosenfeld deserves the credit for giving this interest its first sustained and explicit demonstration.

We may hope that such new approaches may lead historians to fit the French Revolution into new large-scale narratives of Western history. Rosenfeld herself does not have such grandiose ambitions, but her work does suggest some possible paths to follow. The idea of a perfect language has obvious religious roots, in the story of the Tower of Babel, and in the case of Christ's apostles being heard in the native tongues of each of their listeners. In the seventeenth century, some French clerical scholars believed that the Celtic languages still retained traces of the original, perfect language of Eden. Arguably the Enlightenment dream of a perfectly expressive primeval language of gesture amounted to a secularization of the scriptural stories, while the projects of Noverre, de l'Épée, and the revolutionaries transposed the longed-for linguistic paradise from the mythic past to the future, and therefore from the realm of history and legend to that of politics. It might be possible, then, to link

Rosenfeld's evidence to the decline of outward forms of religious observance chronicled by a host of historians in recent decades. The theme awaits its historian.

More materially minded historians might explore the connections between concerns over the "abuse of words" and the rise of a commercial economy. In the eighteenth century, the French became more dependent than ever before on instruments of credit, forms of paper money, stock shares, and complex state annuities: on words signifying things of value, but eminently subject to abuse in the form of default, fraud, and counterfeit. At the same time, the burgeoning group of nouveaux riches found it increasingly easy to purchase traditional markers of high status, from elegant mansions to sumptuous clothing to nobility itself, leading critics to lament that these symbols had turned into empty and deceptive words. In an era of mobile wealth, the most sacred of words seemed to bow before the pursuit of lucre. This relationship between eighteenth-century commerce and epistemology is also ripe for exploration.

The difficulty with these hypotheses, of course, is that they rest mostly on inference, as does Rosenfeld's own interpretation of the Revolution. Historians making her sort of argument will never find "smoking gun" pieces of evidence lying forgotten in dusty corners of obscure provincial archives. Rosenfeld cannot hope to stumble across a letter from Robespierre to Saint-Just confessing that he got the idea for the Terror at the ballet. And while Robespierre's executioners may have explicitly blamed the Terror on abuses of the language, they were no more exempt than anyone else from practical and ideological influences on their own choice of words.

Any worthwhile "epistemological history," therefore, cannot content itself simply with quoting sources such as La Harpe, whose remarks about revolutionary language happen to resonate so powerfully with our own postmodern preoccupations. It must patiently sift through as broad and as deep a body of evidence as possible, piling up the citations and considering possible objections, until patterns of resemblance and contrast emerge with unmistakable force and clarity. It is not an easy undertaking, and it should not be confused with the "collage" method all too present in contemporary cultural studies, in which a critic finds a few chance similarities in disparate cultural forms (ideally involving some form of sexual transgression) and announces—*voilà!*—a cultural shift of

"Foucauldian" proportions. A serious "post–linguistic turn" kind of history requires a deep and powerful familiarity with the most important philosophy and literature of the age in question (and an unfashionable readiness to identify certain works and authors as more profound than others). It demands backbreaking work and painstaking explication. There are precious few examples of the method, but Sophia Rosenfeld has given us a fine one.

4

Bastille Days: The Revolution's Great Eccentric Historian

As the previous essay noted, the new cultural and linguistic approaches to the history of the Revolution, for all their intellectual merits, have often failed to convey the enormous human drama of the events and what they meant for ordinary people. Readers frustrated by this shift have other places to turn, however. This essay considers one of them, but warns that the historian in question had important limitations of his own.

Richard Cobb, the legendary historian of the French Revolution who died in 1996, owed his reputation as much to his exuberant eccentricity as to his scholarly achievements. It was not every Oxford don who organized chariot races in the Balliol Senior Common Room or invited a convicted murderer (and school friend) from Dublin to High Table, sitting him next to an emeritus professor of law with the words, "My guest is keenly interested in the Irish penal system."

Yet Cobb's historical writing was memorable as well, not least because he injected so much of his personality into it, and David Gilmour, the author of books on Curzon and Lampedusa, deserves thanks for gathering ten representative pieces, many of them long out of print, in *The French and Their Revolution*. They include a thick, rich slice of Cobb's masterpiece, *The People's Armies*, classic essays on police repression and daily life in the revolutionary era, and more speculative reflections on the "revolutionary mentality" and on writing history through the lens of biography.

The great strengths, but also the great weaknesses, of Cobb's work derived from his lifelong love affair with the urban France of the mid-twentieth century, where he lived for many years (he despised the later technocratic Fifth Republic for its "excessive vulgarity"). Few native French had a better knowledge of the old working-class neighborhoods of Paris and Lyons, of their accents and slang, and of the novels that celebrated them. So strongly did Cobb strive to blend in that he wrote much of his early work in French and spoke of having "a second identity." When a French historian told him that he wrote, spoke, and thought like a Parisian street urchin, Cobb called it the greatest compliment he had ever received.

Drawn to France by such powerful personal ties, Cobb was never content to write its history in terms of colorless abstractions like "the rising bourgeoisie" or "discourses of power." He insisted on seeking out the men and women of the eighteenth century at street level: garrulous and bellicose *aubergistes*, unemployed law clerks who took part in the Terror out of idleness and greed, the luckless servant girl for whom 9 Thermidor marked not the fall of Robespierre but the date of her seduction and abandonment. He had a peerless talent for finding, in the vastness of the French archives, the gritty details that evoked the experience of living through the Revolution and stories demonstrating just how fully the course of events had depended on accident, resentment, boredom, and bullheaded folly.

So intently did Cobb focus on individuals and random factors that some critics asserted he wrote history without organization. Organization was admittedly not Cobb's strong suit (neither was concision), but as in a pointillist painting, the details added up to a coherent whole. *The People's Armies*, for instance, vividly portrays the squadrons of *sans-culottes* who roamed through France during the Terror, repressing "enemies of the interior" and protecting food supplies. It implicitly argues that these were armies neither of efficient revolutionary heroes nor of proto-totalitarian villains. They were fragmented groups of poorly trained men, motivated principally by vanity and avarice, who vented their resentments and fears on unfortunate peasants and were so badly disciplined and commanded that a high-ranking aristocrat could successfully hide in their ranks (a typically marvelous Cobb note). An essay on Lyons and the counterrevolution shows deliciously how Lyons's rugged topography made it a perfect setting for escapes and murder: "Indeed, Lyons was such a good place to murder people in, that people came from a long way off to do it."

Yet Cobb's intense attachments and prejudices also set distinct limits on his achievement. It was not so much that he passed judgment too easily (on an officer in the Revolutionary Armies: "a thoroughly nasty piece of work"; on cavalry officers: "the corps fully deserved its poor reputation"). This habit was part of his style and charm. It was rather that he tended to see revolutionary France through the prism of mid-twentieth-century French popular culture, particularly its fascination with lurid crime and its celebration of a particular type of working-class hero: hard-drinking, quarrelsome, cynical, unambitious, sexually aggressive, and fiercely loyal.

In his essay "The Biographical Approach and the Personal Case History," for example, Cobb compares Nicolas Guenot, a coach driver and crook turned brutal and corrupt policeman, and Cochon de Lapparent, a lawyer turned high administrator. Cobb had an obvious fascination with and even a sneaking admiration for Guenot. He chronicles his career at length and gives an unforgettable picture of what happened after his dismissal on embezzlement charges and his return to his native Burgundy: "Clad in skins and stinking rags, his feet wrapped in sacking," he led "a hermitlike existence in a hide-out made of branches and ferns, suffering agonies in the bitterly cold winters."

Cobb deals with the more successful Cochon far more quickly, disdainfully noting his readiness to obey repellent orders and to direct repression from a comfortable distance. The conclusion: "Guenot was an unusual, even interesting, monster; Cochon is a boring, very ordinary administrator." Along with them, Cobb profiles a rank opportunist and a murderer he calls "a witness for extreme human folly," but does not give much hint that other revolutionary types existed.

In other words, when it came to the political issues for which so many willingly gave up their lives, Cobb reacted with something of the cynicism of a disillusioned 1930s Parisian. He could not take the radical revolutionary leadership seriously, preferring to dismiss its awesome ambitions and excesses with quick, mocking references to "the regimented prissiness of the Republic of Virtues" and "Saint-Just's hideous cardboard Sparta." Nor did he linger over what the language of liberty, equality, and fraternity might have meant to men and women who sincerely thought they were building a better world. Because his sympathetic insight did not extend from the monsters and opportunists to the true believers, he ended up, for all the richness of his work, presenting only one side of the Revolution. He even made it somewhat difficult to understand why a revolution happened in the first place.

5

The Culture of War in Europe, 1750–1815

ANOTHER STRIKING FEATURE OF THE NEW CULTURAL and linguistic works on the Revolution was their neglect of a phenomenon that earlier generations of historians had taken as absolutely central: war. In 1792, revolutionary France declared war on the Austrian Empire and on Prussia. The conflict quickly became the largest and most intense seen in Europe in centuries. It began a series of wars that lasted until 1815 and significantly touched every part of the continent (and, indeed, much of the world). My 2007 book The First Total War *represented, in part, my attempt to apply the new cultural and linguistic methods to this story, but without sacrificing the human drama intrinsic to the history of the subject. As noted earlier, the result was controversial. While many reviewers praised the book, it received sharp criticism not only from French scholars who believed I had condemned the Revolution but also from military historians who preferred to see the revolutionary and Napoleonic wars as fundamentally following from earlier patterns. The debates have continued for years. (See, for instance, Hervé Drévillon's 2013 book* L'individu et la guerre, *and my subsequent exchange*

Originally published in Proceedings of the British Academy 184, *The Crisis of the Absolute Monarchy*, edited by Julian Swann and Joël Félix, © The British Academy 2013. This earlier version of the essay contains full footnotes to all sources cited.

with him in H-France Review, *vol. 14, no. 209.) This essay summarizes some of the main themes of the book and explains why the "continuity" thesis is mistaken.*

———

For an essay on war, this is going to start in a somewhat unusual manner. I am not going to plunge straight into a discussion of battles, or grand strategy. Instead, I am going to examine two classic passages from French literature, which deal not with war, but with the problem of how to seduce a virtuous married woman. The first comes from Choderlos de Laclos's great novel of 1782, *Dangerous Liaisons*. It is an epistolary novel, and the letter in question is one of its climaxes. The Viscount de Valmont is describing to his correspondent, the Marquise de Merteuil, how he has finally accomplished the seduction of the angelic Madame de Tourvel:

> You will find, my friend that I used a pure method that will give you pleasure, and that I remained absolutely true to the principles of this war, which, as we have so often remarked, resembles so much the other sort. Judge me, therefore, as you would judge Marshal Turenne or Frederick the Great. The enemy wanted only to delay, but I forced it to do battle. Thanks to skilled manoeuvering, I was able to choose the terrain and the positions of the opposing forces. I managed to inspire in the enemy feelings of security, so as to be able to close with it more easily as it retreated; I managed to sow terror in its ranks before the battle; I left nothing to chance.... Finally, I only launched my attack after ensuring that I would have a secure line of retreat, so as not to risk everything I had gained up to this point.

The second passage comes from a book published some forty-eight years later: Stendhal's *The Red and the Black*. It describes the first steps by which the young hero, Julien Sorel, seduces the mistress of the house where he works as a tutor, Madame de Rênal, taking her hand in his:

> His expression, when he saw Madame de Rênal... was singular. He looked at her as if she were an enemy he was preparing to fight.... He cut short the children's lessons, and then, when [her] presence... recalled him to the pursuit of his glory, he decided that tonight she absolutely

would have to allow her hand to remain in his. As the sun set, and the decisive moment approached, Julien's heart beat in a singular manner.... The horrible struggle that his duty was waging against his timidity was so painful for him he could not notice anything outside of himself. The clock sounded out nine forty-five and still he had not dared do anything. Outraged at his own cowardice, Julien said to himself: At exactly ten I will do what I have been promising to do all day, or I will go upstairs and blow my brains out.

The first point I want to draw attention to is that in *both* these passages, the act of seducing a virtuous woman is compared to fighting a battle. But there are differences—striking differences. In Laclos, the tone of the seducer is utterly assured and confident. If seduction is like a battle, then it is like a battle in which absolutely nothing is left to chance. Everything is calculated, planned, down to the last detail. The forces are deployed perfectly, and even then, a line of retreat is carefully guarded. The commander never has a moment's doubt. The battle as a whole amounts to a grand and strangely impersonal performance. Of course Laclos is setting up a terrific irony, for nothing would be less assured, or predictable, than the outcome of this particular encounter. But what matters here for the moment is the tone of this particular letter, before Valmont's "victory" turns in strange directions. With Julien Sorel, of course, almost everything has changed. The tone of the seducer could not be less confident, or more anguished. In this battle, nothing is prepared meticulously, and nearly everything is left to chance. The attacker depends on sheer force, and luck. There is no question of any sort of impersonal performance. What is at stake is Julien's very soul.

I would like to suggest that the contrast between these two passages amounts to rather more than just two different literary visions of the same act. It also helps us see a large and interesting shift in European understandings of warfare from the Old Regime to the early nineteenth century. In both cases, warfare is a metaphor used by a novelist, but the kinds of war evoked are very different. One might attribute the differences simply to the vagaries of two different literary imaginations. Both authors, however, reflected at length in other writings on the conduct of war, and themselves had extensive military experience. (Laclos wrote his novel while a serving officer; Stendhal had fought for Napoleon as a dragoon and then accompanied the French army during the 1812 invasion of Russia.) So the contrast might well reflect an evolution of war itself, rather than just the evolution of literary style. To show that it does, though, I need to shift gears, and reflect in more general terms about the period 1750–1815. I will come back, however, to these passages and to their significance.

The period between 1792 and 1815 saw an astonishing change in the physical intensity of European warfare. The figures speak for themselves. More than a fifth of all the major battles fought in Europe between 1490 and 1815 took place just in the twenty-five years after 1790. Before 1790, only a handful of battles had involved more than one hundred thousand combatants. In 1809, the battle of Wagram, the largest yet seen in Europe, involved three hundred thousand. Four years later, the battle of Leipzig drew five hundred thousand, with fully 150,000 of them killed or wounded. During the twenty-three years of war, France alone may have counted close to a million war deaths, including possibly a higher proportion of its young men than died in World War I. The toll across Europe may have reached as high as five million. In a development without precedent, these wars brought about significant alterations in the territory, or the political system, or both, of every single European state. It is not surprising that the great strategist Clausewitz saw in the wars of this period something that approached the ideal that he called "absolute war." As early as 1812, he expressed what he saw as the essential point about how warfare had changed from the prerevolutionary period: "Formerly...war was waged in the way that a pair of duellists carried out their pedantic struggle. One battled with moderation and consideration, according to the conventional proprieties....War was caused by nothing more than a diplomatic caprice, and the spirit of such a thing could hardly prevail over the goal of military honor....There is no more talk of this sort of war, and one would have to be blind, not to be able to perceive the difference with our wars, that is to say the wars that our age and our conditions require."

"One would have to be blind..." Unfortunately, in recent years, historians of this period have in fact suffered, if not from blindness, then at least from extensive cataracts when it comes to perceiving these changes.

They have done so for several reasons. To begin with, there is the influence of the diplomatic historian Paul Schroeder, who has argued in his magisterial work *The Transformation of European Politics, 1763–1848* that the French revolutionary and Napoleonic wars followed naturally from what he characterizes as the fundamental instability and violence of European international relations before 1789. Schroeder emphasizes this continuity because he sees military and diplomatic history as the story of attempts to solve what he calls "the permanent, structural problems of international politics." He takes for granted that most European statesmen have always had peace and stability as their principal goals (that they wanted "a solution to war"). He therefore assumes that because both the periods before and after 1789 were characterized by virtually continuous warfare (in the entire eighteenth century, there were only one or two years in which no major power was at war), they were essentially similar: periods when statesmen "failed" to stabilize the "international system." He does not really consider the possibility that, in an age when most European statesmen belonged to hereditary aristocracies that still defined themselves, ultimately, in terms of military service, these statesmen might have actually seen perpetual peace as undesirable. They might have sought only to limit the destructive effects of war—not end it forever. If we admit this possibility (and, I will argue, we should), then the fact that the major powers fought so frequently both before and during the revolutionary and Napoleon periods matters much less than the *way* they fought. And in this case, the huge differences in the scale, intensity, and political consequences of war after 1792 to which I have just drawn attention recover their full importance.

Incidentally, Schroeder offers as principal evidence for his thesis the fact that "overall, the ratio of battlefield deaths to the total population of Europe was about seven times as great in the eighteenth as in the nineteenth century." The comparison is only superficially impressive. First of all, by his own evidence (which he does *not* cite in his book, but only in an article), the actual *number* of eighteenth-century battlefield deaths amounted to less than twenty-four thousand a year for the entire continent—a level that statesmen might well have considered acceptable, indeed normal. Second, he omits the period 1792–1815 from this comparison (again, without saying so in the book). During this period, the number of battlefield deaths rose to at least one hundred thousand per year: more than four times the pre-1792 figure.

Schroeder's work on diplomacy fits in well with an influential trend among military historians that likewise plays down the rupture of the French Revolution and the Napoleonic Wars, instead emphasizing the broad continuities in military technology and tactics from the eighteenth into the early nineteenth century. These continuities were certainly very real. The period did see technical innovations, but none of them had a decisive effect on the actual battles. Indeed, a soldier from as far back as the War of the Spanish Succession (1702–1714) would have found himself relatively at home on the Napoleonic battlefield, where the principal weapons remained woefully inaccurate and difficult-to-load muskets with ring-lock bayonets, cannon firing either solid balls or grapeshot, and swords wielded by cavalry. Similarly, such basic tactics as the mustering of infantry into square, line, and column remained highly recognizable between the eras of Marlborough and Wellington. For these reasons, a number of military historians have passionately rejected the idea (which I have defended in a book) that the French revolutionary and Napoleonic wars can be considered a "total war."

These military historians of course recognize the massive political changes that accompanied the French Revolution. But they generally go on to argue that these political changes, particularly after the fall of Robespierre, had relatively little effect on the conduct of war. "With Napoleon's seizure of power," writes Ute Planert, "the legitimization of war by revolution came to an end. The *Grand Empire* justified its wars in the interests of the *grande nation*. These interests closely resembled those of the French monarchy in the eighteenth century, be it mercantile and colonial rivalry with England or securing France's supposedly natural frontiers." Planert's analysis (which recalls the classic work of Albert Sorel) leads in the same direction as Schroeder's, namely stressing the continuities between the pre-1789 period and 1789–1815.

The analysis, however, seems misguided to me in several respects. First, it downplays the significance of the intensifying number of battles, and the intensifying death tolls. It also effectively discounts the importance for the conduct of warfare of the political upheavals that continued throughout the period (significant alterations in the territory, or the political system, or both, of every single European state). And in this connection, it entirely disregards a critical political *fact* about the wars, namely that unlike under the Old Regime, neither side ever fully recognized the legitimacy of the other's regime, but instead most often aimed at its overthrow. Yes, Bonaparte on many occasions managed to sign peace alliances and peace treaties with his "brother monarchs." But these agreements nearly all ended in failure, and the allies ended up treating him exactly as the Jacobins and their enemies had treated each other: as a criminal: "In returning to France with plans for upheaval and disruption, he has deprived himself of the protection of the laws, and shown the entire universe that there can be neither peace nor truce with him. The Powers therefore declare that Napoleon Bonaparte has placed himself outside of civil and social relations, and that as an enemy and disturber of the peace of the world, he has subjected himself to public condemnation." Would any European monarch before 1789 have found himself the object of such a statement?

Yet if we accept that warfare did change in extraordinarily important ways during the revolutionary and Napoleonic period, what brought the changes about? As already noted, technological and tactical innovation cannot be held responsible. If we look to older standard histories of the period, which (unlike Schroeder and the new military historians) agree that the French Revolution marked an important rupture, we instead generally find the most attention given to two broad political factors. First: revolutionary ideologies. These were wars between radically incompatible belief systems, one of which was making radically new claims for its universal validity and sought to spread itself by any means possible. Second: nationalism. These were no longer wars between dynastic houses, but between entire nations that were coming to new states of self-consciousness. Both explanations date back to the period itself. For ideology, we could quote Edmund Burke: "It is with an armed doctrine that we are at war... if it can at all exist, it must finally prevail." On the nationalist side, Clausewitz: "The present war is a war of all against all. It is not kings who wage war on kings, not armies which wage war on armies, but whole peoples who wage war on other peoples."

I hardly wish to dismiss the importance of revolutionary ideology during this, of all periods. And having written an entire book on the origins of nationalism in revolutionary France, I don't wish to dismiss that subject either. Still, whenever we find an explanation of revolutionary events that seems to echo the explanations given by the revolutionary actors themselves, it is a good idea to be suspicious.

On the subject of revolutionary ideologies, the most obvious reason for suspicion comes from the chronology. Even during the radical period of the French Revolution, the French leadership disagreed violently on whether France should be fighting a war of liberation. After 1795, reason of state reasserted itself decisively in French foreign policy. And after Bonaparte took power, while the scale of warfare, and the political stakes, continued to intensify, there nonetheless followed a rebirth of naked dynastic politics: he put three brothers and a brother-in-law on various European thrones, and himself married the great-niece of Marie-Antoinette. There have been endless debates about the extent to which Napoleon remained a revolutionary, but no one has yet, as far as I am aware, suggested that he became *more* of one in the course of his imperial rule. But it was precisely during the later years of his Empire that the wars turned most radical, and most intense.

The subject of nationalism is more complicated. There is no doubt that this period saw the rise of distinctly nationalist language, and nationalist political projects, throughout Europe. The concepts of forging nations, and mobilizing them entirely for war, played a role in everything from France's 1793 *levée en masse* to Spain's 1808 rising against Napoleon, to the German war of liberation of 1813. But there are still reasons to doubt nationalism's centrality to the transformation of war. For one thing, as I have argued in *The Cult of the Nation in France*, the concept of national war did not burst forth ex nihilo in the Revolution. It was already present in the middle of the eighteenth century, at least in France and Britain. And after 1804, in France, the regime increasingly downplayed nationalist language, in keeping with its revived dynasticism, and imperial ambitions. "I must make all the peoples of Europe one people," Napoleon told his police minister, Fouché, on one occasion.

Nationalist concepts had a surprisingly restrained effect on the actual conduct of military affairs as well. As revisionist military historians have convincingly argued, the ill-trained and ill-equipped soldiers of the *levée* helped the French war effort much less than is generally thought, while during most of the Napoleonic period, a majority of French soldiers were professionals, not conscripts. In Austria and Prussia, attempts at general levies were even less impressive. The Prussian Landsturm of 1813, whose founding document was described by no less than Carl Schmitt as the Magna Carta of modern partisan warfare, proved ineffective in practice and was drastically curtailed after just three months. As for the Spanish war, which textbooks still generally portray as a spontaneous rising of the entire Spanish people, fighting in the newly named *guerrilla*, it was anything but. As Charles Esdaile has argued, most of the population remained aloof from the war. The guerrillas themselves drew heavily from the ranks of professional soldiers and outlaws, and their activities sometimes resembled organized crime as much as national liberation.

We need, in short, to move away from these explanatory factors. Not only do they echo rather too neatly the explanations of the actors themselves, they also reduce warfare itself to nothing more than an instrument of changing political goals. Of course, the idea of war as continuation of politics by other means (to coin a phrase) was itself very much a product of this period, and of its most famous Prussian staff officer. Rather than accepting Clausewitz's perspective without question, however, we need instead to consider war as a meaningful and dynamic activity in its own right, and to look for changes within what could be called the cultural field of warfare, both before and during the period 1792–1815.

To understand this cultural field of warfare, we need to start with the ancien régime and its armies. This is a world we know a great deal about in some ways, thanks to the work of military historians. And the most important point to underline is that it was fundamentally a world dominated by hereditary aristocracies. In every European state before 1789, the officer corps of the armed forces came overwhelmingly from the nobility, with the highest ranks, so to speak, dominating the highest ranks. In many states, *only* nobles could become officers, and in the rest, commoners had very limited opportunities for promotion. But what consequences did these social practices have? For the most part, military and cultural historians alike have failed to address this question very seriously. They have noted certain salient facts: for instance, in almost all eighteenth-century European military schools, the pupils spent a considerable amount of time in dance classes. High-ranking officers brought sumptuous silverware and china with them on campaign and paid enormous attention to dress and makeup. One French officer killed in battle in 1745 had seven extra pairs of silk stockings in his luggage. These facts are known, but they are mostly presented as amusing details, or worse, as signs of weakness and frivolity, as evidence of the decadence of a declining caste of play actors that was just waiting to be swept aside by the "real soldiers" of the revolutionary era.

There is, however, a certain cultural logic that links these practices to aristocratic culture in general, and to the general nature of old regime war. The work of Norbert Elias reminds us that early modern European court societies cultivated remarkable forms of daily behavior, based on astonishingly difficult standards of self-control. Aristocrats were expected to make their public personas conform to carefully developed models of behavior, and to make use of a rigorously defined and limited repertory of acceptable movements, gestures, language, even facial expressions. Emotional responses had to be channeled into well-defined, acceptable forms. Noble life often deviated from this ideal standard, but the ideal remained powerful. What Elias did not consider, though, is that the same practices deployed in the "theater of the aristocracy" that was the court could also be observed in that other "theater of the aristocracy" that was warfare. Memoirs and letters from the period show that noble officers put an enormous premium on maintaining courtly standards of self-control while on campaign. Their reputation depended on a meticulously splendid appearance, unquestionable courage, perfect equanimity, and absolute devotion to the service of the prince. From this point of view, a training in dance, or the ownership of a few extra pairs of silk stockings, were not in the least decadent or hollowly ostentatious. They were integral to the identity of the aristocratic officer.

I would also like to suggest that these aristocratic practices were intimately related to the limits on war, as they were conceived of before 1789. These limits were quite real, even if we can hardly give full credence to observers like the French officer and moralist Vauvenargues, who wrote scornfully that "war today is fought so humanely, and with so little profit that it can be compared to a serious of tedious civil trials." That was hyperbole. But war was not yet "absolute." Major battles, it is true, saw dreadful carnage, with casualties ranging as high as a third of the combatants (at Poltava, for instance). But major battles were rare: armies had a tendency to avoid them where possible, favoring campaigns of maneuvers. And armies showed historically unusual restraint toward civilian populations. As late as the 1680s and 1690s, French armies invading present-day Belgium left an appalling reputation behind them. But when the French returned in the first decades of the eighteenth century, they largely spared civilian populations (sometimes in return for large, up-front payments). And at the time of the next French invasion, in 1745, Belgian civilians largely went about their business unmolested.

This conduct is usually ascribed solely to such pragmatic factors as balance-of-power politics. But it was also, quite clearly, an expression of the aristocratic values of the court society. The hesitation of commanders to risk battle reflects not only pragmatic calculations but also the need for absolute self-control characteristic of the courtly ideal—think again of the way Valmont describes his "battle" against Mme de Tourvel. The same idea of self-control, linked to a strong aristocratic code of honor, demanded that respect be shown to civilian populations. As Carl Schmitt points out in *Der Nomos der Erde*, noble officers had a tendency to view war as a sort of personal duel on a grand scale, in which the adversaries recognized each other's honor and social standing. Not only did war have its rules; its conduct could be seen, somewhat paradoxically, as a form of aristocratic civility.

The overall point here is that in the Old Regime, war was still considered an essential, and absolutely ordinary, part of the social order. In keeping with this idea, most European states saw war as their principal business and spent well over half their budgets on military affairs—90 percent for Prussia. In the eighteenth century, most European countries spent at least one year out of three actually fighting. And for these very reasons, the destructiveness of war had to be kept within strict limits.

And yet, well before the French Revolution, this vision of war had itself come under concerted attack. Was war in fact an ordinary part of the social order? Or was it an exceptional, and exceptionally horrid, state of affairs? Christian pacifists had made this argument for centuries. But in the decades around 1700, the idea of war as exceptional came to be tied to the idea that human societies, if properly constituted, could achieve a natural harmony, in keeping with scientifically discernable laws, making war unnecessary. As Keith Michael Baker has argued, this idea, and the very concept of "society" as an autonomous field of human existence, came into being precisely in the late seventeenth century. We can see the idea fusing together with more traditional Christian teachings, and inspiring a new sort of pacifism, above all in the work of Fénelon, the Catholic bishop and critic of Louis XIV, whose 1699 novel *Telemachus* condemned military adventurism in scathing terms, and sketched out utopian visions of societies that eschewed war altogether. Significantly, *Telemachus* became the single most popular European book of the early eighteenth century.

Following on this success, the eighteenth century saw a long stream of works that offered plans for perpetual peace. And their critique of war was increasingly integrated into broader works of social thought, especially those that held that all human societies evolved along a linear scale from conditions of savagery toward refinement, civilization, and commerce. In this schema, which counted a large proportion of Enlightenment thinkers among its adherents, the development of commerce and civilization was in fact leading to the imminent extinction of war. In 1813, Benjamin Constant could sum up the now-conventional wisdom: "We have reached the age of commerce, which must necessarily *replace* the age of war." Any modern government that seeks wage wars of conquest was guilty of "a crude and deadly anachronism."

And yet, even as this conventional wisdom was spreading, it was eliciting a critique of its own. As is well known, the genre of universal history could generate not just approval for civilized refinement, but also a longing for the alleged lost vitality of primitive societies—a vitality for which military prowess stood as the most obvious measure. Particularly in Germany, critics came on the scene who rejected linear schemes of evolution altogether, in favor of an emphasis on the unique qualities and destiny of each particular people. Prominent among them was the statesman and philologist Wilhelm von Humboldt, who, rather than condemning war, praised it as the principal means by which societies could make historical progress. In a 1792 tract, he wrote: "War is one of the healthiest phenomena for the cultivation of the human race. It is unwillingly that I see it disappearing more and more from the scene. It is the admittedly fearful extreme, through which courage, labor and fortitude are tested and steeled." Humboldt went on to indulge in a frank military primitivism, which celebrated the hand-to-hand combat of ancient societies, while condemning firearms, and the kind of Prussian drill that turned soldiers into automata. He lamented that only in classical antiquity had the profession of war achieved its "highest beauty," allowing for the full expression of physical and moral strength.

Obviously, this quick overview can hardly do justice to a deep and complex intellectual history. The principal point I want to make, though, is a simple one: while the visions of a Constant and a Humboldt might seem entirely opposed, in one vital sense they shared the same perspective. Both departed entirely from the aristocratic conception of war as an ordinary, unexceptional element of the social order. For both, war was something entirely extraordinary and exceptional—destructively so, for the one; dynamically so, indeed perhaps sublimely so, for the other. Neither saw it as compatible with any sort of social stability.

These new visions of warfare that developed in the eighteenth century were deeply subversive, both of the aristocratic order and of absolute monarchy. Warfare, along with the court, provided both aristocrats and kings with the most important theater for the demonstration of the values that underpinned their social superiority and their right to rule. These men did not merely protect the kingdom and its Catholic faith. They brought it glory and honor. The King of France was a *roi de guerre.* As Thomas Kaiser has argued, under the reign of Louis XV the French monarchy did begin, hesitatingly, to move away from this model of royal legitimization. Its publicists began celebrating the king's virtues as a peacemaker, in accents not too far removed from those of Fénelon and his followers. But France remained far too often at war for such ideas significantly to displace the centuries-old symbolic linkage between the king and his armies. Meanwhile, the idea of warfare's regenerative capacity fed into the increasingly popular proposals at the end of the Old Regime for replacing the professional, noble-led royal army with a new, national one commanded by men of talent, and appropriate for a nation striving to regenerate itself. These were proposals that ultimately threatened the French aristocracy's very raison d'être.

Nonetheless, before 1789, these debates had very little practical effect in France. While the French government took important steps toward professionalizing the armed forces, it did so while reinforcing the hold of the nobility on the officer ranks and the dominance of the high aristocracy at the top of the military pyramid. Hopes for perpetual peace did not stop the French monarchy from using the War of American Independence to take revenge on Britain, even at the cost of national bankruptcy. But then, in just two extraordinary years, everything would change.

———

During the years 1790–1792, which of course saw the formal abolition of the nobility, and then of the monarchy itself, an astonishing ferment of military thinking took place. It began in May 1790, when war seemed to be looming between France and Britain. King Louis XVI asked the new, revolutionary National Assembly for funds to equip warships, but the Assembly balked. In the first instance, its more radical members insisted that the sovereign right to declare war belonged to them, not an unelected monarch. Then, as the debate proceeded, certain figures, starting with Maximilien Robespierre, came to argue that France should renounce "aggressive warfare" altogether. Constantin-François Volney proposed the following measure: "Resolved: that the National Assembly considers the entire human race as forming but a single and same *society*, whose object is the peace and happiness of each and all of its members." A few days later, after a remarkable if confused debate in which the Assembly struggled with the questions of who had the right to declare war, and whether France needed to rethink its foreign policy goals and alliances, the deputies in fact voted to renounce aggressive war for all time.

It was a vote that seems more than a little ironic in hindsight, given that less than two years later, France declared war on Austria and Prussia. But during these two years, the most radical advocates of war, mostly from the so-called Girondin faction, kept insisting that if France did have to fight, it would do so entirely in self-defense, to protect itself against a conspiracy between enemy powers and counterrevolutionary émigrés. They even suggested that war would in fact bring about perpetual peace. The philosophe and Girondin Condorcet published a fantasy, supposedly written in the future, that described the coming war. It recounted that French troops had needed only to step across the frontier for the enslaved peoples of Europe to lay down their arms and embrace the French as liberators. Soon after the war started, General Charles-François Dumouriez told the National Convention: "This war will be the last war."

In this sense, even in its most aggressive moments, revolutionary France was remaining loyal to the new language of peace. Yet in the same debates, we can also see something very different taking shape, something closer to Humboldt's vision of war as a moral test. As early as June 1791, the guiding spirit of the Girondin faction, Madame Roland, was writing to a correspondent: "It is a cruel thing to think, but it is becoming more clear every day: peace is taking us backwards. We will only be regenerated by blood. Our frivolous and corrupt morals can only be reformed by the rasp of adversity." In the following months, the theme sounded out again and again in Girondin writings and speeches, particularly those given by the faction's leader, Jacques-Pierre Brissot. France was "listless" and "dessicated." It was choked by "poison." It needed "strong explosions" to purge itself. Only war would cleanse the country.

In their writings, both before and during the war, the Girondins subscribed to exactly the sort of primitivism Humboldt had expressed. They poured scorn on the "automata" who filled the ranks of the enemy armies, and sneered at the use of firearms. They even went so far as to advocate the return of a weapon not seen on European battlefields for a century: the pike. In mid-1792, the French government ordered smiths in the frontier regions to put aside all other work in favor of pike-making. Admittedly, this order reflected fears of a shortage of muskets, but within months the pike had taken on a life of its own, and no less a figure than Lazare Carnot argued for its distribution to the entire population. In the Legislative Assembly, a deputy criticized Carnot for holding up the pike-bearing ancients as models. France's enemies, he observed sensibly enough, "do not use slings and pikes, the weapons of savages, but firepower directed by scientific calculations." But another deputy immediately shot back, to huge applause: "If we have not been either Spartans, or Athenians, we should become them."

The rise of these twin concepts—that of the "war to end all war," and that of regenerative war—soon had an impact on military affairs. The first led directly to the conclusion that France's enemies could in no sense be considered honorable adversaries. They were, rather, criminals against whom any means were justified. Carl Schmitt has explicated this point very concisely. As he puts it, a war fought to abolish war is "necessarily unusually intense and inhuman because, by transcending the limits of the political framework, it simultaneously degrades the enemy into moral and other categories and is forced to make of him a monster that must not only be defeated but utterly destroyed." Schmitt was thinking of World War I, but the comment applies just as well to the revolutionary period. Consider, for instance, the thinking of Maximilien Robespierre, who had initially opposed the war. By 1793 he had come to a very different conclusion: "Those who wage war against a people to block the progress of liberty...must be attacked by all, not merely as ordinary enemies, but as assassins and as rebel brigands." By 1794, Robespierre's ally Bertrand Barère was forthrightly calling for the "extermination" of the entire British people, and the Jacobin Convention even ordered that no British prisoners would be taken alive. France's officers in the field did not generally enforce this order, and between 1792 and 1815, uniformed armies probably did not carry out more cold-blooded murders against each other than under the ancien régime. But more generally, the apocalyptic notion of the "last war" was one factor lying behind the steady intensification of war during the period.

The concept of regenerative war had a strong effect as well. Consider, above all, the *levée en masse*, the declaration that all able-bodied men must fight for the Republic. Historians have usually interpreted it as a quintessentially modern law, the forerunner of modern conscription, but it was nothing of the sort. It was, at least in its original conception, an expression of the same military primitivism expressed by the Girondins. The men who demanded it did not summon up images of lines of well-drilled musketmen. They spoke of swords and pikes and clubs, of heating sulfur to pour on enemy heads. They spoke of the nation rising up as one great, pike-bearing colossus.

Even after the fall of the Jacobins in 1794, the concepts of war to end war, and regenerative war, did not lose their force. They continued to define the meaning that war held for educated elites, in France and beyond, and to shape the actual conduct of warfare in Europe, down to Waterloo. This continuity is particularly striking, given that with the proclamation of the First Empire in 1804, the Napoleonic regime explicitly sought to reconnect with the language and imagery of dynasticism, and of medieval chivalry. But these innovations were widely ridiculed at the time, and could not disguise the more fundamental similarities between revolutionary and Napoleonic military culture.

Napoleon himself, needless to say, was hardly a serious advocate of perpetual peace. Nonetheless, the point is again worth stressing: despite strenuous efforts, he never managed to reestablish with his principal enemies the relationship of honorable adversaries that had prevailed under the Old Regime. In practice, his treatment of enemy powers swung erratically between the maudlin embrace of "brother sovereigns," as with Tsar Alexander at Tilsit, and angry condemnations of "criminal monsters," as with the British after the breakdown of the Peace of Amiens in 1803. In an 1806 message to his Senate, he candidly acknowledged this breakdown in "civilized" warfare, even while placing the blame squarely on the enemy: "It has cost us dearly to return...to the principles that characterized the barbarism of the early ages of nations, but we have been constrained...to deploy against the common enemy the arms he has used against us." I would not go as far as Paul Schroeder and label Napoleon's policies themselves "criminal." But clearly the language of criminality dominated international relations throughout the Napoleonic Wars and structured Napoleon's own captivity afterward.

The concept of regenerative war underwent several inflections during the Napoleonic period as well. First, while previously regeneration had been seen as something that swept impersonally through all of society, under Napoleon, increasingly, it was tied to the work of specific agents: the armed forces or the commanding general himself. This shift began to take place as early as 1797, when conservatives threatened to take power in France. In response, the remnants of the Jacobin left called for the active intervention of the army. To quote one left-wing newspaper: "The great deluge was necessary to purge the earth. We now need the armies to purify France." The so-called coup d'état of Fructidor duly followed. Over the next two years, the armies routinely portrayed themselves as the last bastion of republican purity, in contrast to the corruption and backsliding of the Directorial regime. Well before taking power in 1799, Napoleon Bonaparte was already portraying himself, in copious written propaganda, as the savior of the Republic. After he took power, he would routinely refer to himself as a "regenerator."

With this shift we see, as well, the arrival of modern militarism on the European scene. As I would define it, militarism is predicated on the understanding of "the military" as a sphere of society that is fully distinct from, and opposed to, the "civilian" one—and morally superior to it. Under the old regime, this distinction simply did not exist. True, common soldiers were often held to be social outsiders. But the aristocratic officer corps was wholly integrated into elite society. Indeed, aristocratic officers rarely spent more than three to four months a year at their posts. During the French Revolution, the Jacobins likewise resisted any separation between the military and society at large, through the cult of the nation in arms. But after 1794, as Rafe Blaufarb has shown, this cult gave way very rapidly to a new sort of military professionalism. Now officers as well as men were expected to spend the bulk of their time in uniform, in physically separate settings from civilian society. Now officers identified themselves principally as officers, rather than as members of a particular social class. Their political loyalties lay mostly with the armed forces itself. Tellingly, it was at precisely this time in history, the 1790s, that the opposition between the words "military" and "civilian" arose in the French and English languages, with the latter meaning a nonmilitary person. Before the Revolution, the noun and adjective "civilian," or *civil* in French, had not existed in this sense.

Second, understandings of regeneration through war came to focus more and more on the individual self. A striking thing about this period, from the point of view of cultural history, is how Europeans were beginning to take an interest in war as an individual, personal experience— indeed, with Clausewitz, as a *psychological* one. Literally thousands went so far as to publish first-person accounts of their adventures. But this was something quite new. There is virtually no equivalent in relation to the Seven Years' War, which occurred just forty years earlier. Obviously, the explosion of memoirs was a complex phenomenon, which depended heavily on increases in literacy and the general expansion of print culture. But it also had a great deal to do with the rise of new understandings of the self, new ways in which the self was coming to be seen as a unique entity possessing a heightened sensitivity to its own inner voice. These new understandings had particularly important echoes in the cultural field of war, for they allowed the rather abstract "courage" and "fortitude" praised by Humboldt to be reimagined as intensely personal qualities. Now, war was not simply the place courage was tested, but the place where the self could express itself most fully. With this shift, I would add, we have moved fully from Valmont to Julien Sorel: from war as a theater of aristocratic self-control to war as a theater of Romantic self-expression.

As the most vivid example of this shift, consider the Saxon writer and soldier Theodor Körner. In 1813, at the age of twenty-one, he gave up a promising career as a playwright to enroll in one of the *Freikorps* of volunteers forming in Prussia to fight Napoleon, and was killed a few months later. Today, he is largely forgotten, but his work was enormously popular in the nineteenth century, and he remained an icon of German nationalism through the Nazi period. The copious poetry he wrote in 1813 was very different from the bombast of older, more established literary patriots like Ernst Mortiz Arndt. It was intensely personal, concerned with his innermost feelings. As one literary critic has put it, Körner seemed to take the war equally as a German crusade and a vehicle for self-realization. Much of his work treats war as a rather boyishly glorious adventure. But it also has a much darker side, which expresses a frankly erotic fascination with death—indeed a sensual longing for it, as in the lines "honor is the wedding guest and the fatherland the bride. He who lustfully embraces it has wedded death itself." In a letter to his father, Körner even spoke of battle as a *Todeshochzeit*—a death wedding. And in one of his most famous poems, he stated frankly that full happiness could only come with the complete immolation of the self in sacrificial death: "Nur in dem Opfertod reift uns das Glück." It is a statement we might place in the mouth of Julien Sorel.

The *most* powerful example of war as self-expression, though, comes in a much more obvious place: in the person of Körner's great enemy, and Julien Sorel's hero: Napoleon Bonaparte. It is, perhaps the greatest of historical clichés to speak of Napoleon as an extraordinary individual, which is one reason why so many historians avoid the subject altogether. But I would like to take another look at it. We have to remember, first, that Napoleon himself worked very hard, throughout his career, to shape this image of himself as extraordinary. Thanks to his early literary ambitions, he was a brilliant melodramatic writer, with a deeply literary sensibility: sometimes novelistic, sometimes more theatrical. Like characters out of the novels of the day, he was deeply conscious of his own originality, prone to constant self-questioning, and constant marveling at the turns of his fortune.

For this reason, Napoleon himself is the single best illustration of the shift in the culture of war that I have been describing here—from war as an ordinary, unexceptional part of the social order, a theater for the performance of aristocratic life, to war as the extraordinary extreme experience that is either to be ended altogether, by whatever means necessary, or celebrated as a means of testing and steeling societies and individuals. In the Old Regime, in the world of Valmont's careful maneuvers, there was simply no place for a self-consciously "extraordinary" military figure like Napoleon. Only with the end of the aristocratic order in France could a figure like him take shape: the extraordinary extreme personified. Not surprisingly, then, under Napoleon, despite all his imperial and dynastic conceits, and despite his strongly stated desire to lead a civilian government, the actual practice of war continued to radicalize, to tend closer and closer to the apocalyptic, absolute ideal.

With Napoleon's fall and exile, the victorious allies tried their best to squeeze "absolute war" back into the Pandora's box from which it had escaped in 1792. But they failed. Their very treatment of Napoleon as a criminal, and their own attempt to impose a permanent peace on the continent in the shape of the Concert of Europe, showed just how much they had internalized the new conceptions of war I have been discussing. By the time Clausewitz came to write *On War*, in the 1820s, it was already almost impossible to see the old aristocratic codes as anything other than archaic and artificial obstacles to the supposedly "natural" course of absolute warfare.

And while I would not want to push the point too far, I would argue that in important ways, the twin concepts of an end to war, and of regenerative war, have continued to structure the way Western elites have understood warfare during the past two centuries. Among intellectuals, the pacifist, liberal critique has remained so strong that, as the sociologist Hans Joas has written, few eminent social theorists have seen war as anything but an aberration, an almost inexplicable anachronism. Throughout the nineteenth and twentieth centuries, a long line of liberal thinkers continued to predict the coming end of war in strikingly similar terms, and often in complete ignorance of their predecessors: from Richard Cobden in 1835 to Norman Angell in 1910 to John Mueller in 1989. The task of theorizing seriously about war has been left largely to the likes of Carl Schmitt, the unapologetic supporter of Hitler whose hatred of liberalism led him to formulate one of the keenest modern critiques of it.

Even in just the years since 1989, in the United States there has been a wild shift from visions of the imminent end of war—the "end of history," "retreat from Doomsday," "democracies don't fight each other," and so forth—to the widespread claim (after 9/11) that the country was engaged in an apocalyptic struggle, testing and steeling the nation. What these perspectives of course have in common is the vision of war as an unmasterable Other, as something that can never really be understood, even by those who have gone through it. And this idea lends war a dangerous mystique, even among its opponents. It gives rise to the sort of judgment expressed by William James in his famous essay on the moral equivalent of war: "The horrors make the fascination. War is the strong life; it is life *in extremis*." But as I have tried to suggest in this essay, such ideas are much less timeless than we might think. They are, to a very large extent, products of the Enlightenment and revolutionary era.

6

The Conductor: Maximilien Robespierre

JULES MICHELET MEMORABLY CALLED THE FRENCH Revolution "a great epoch without great men." Many figures attempted to seize control of events—and of France—between 1789 and 1794. Instead, events seized control of them and in nearly every case ground them into dust. When Emmanuel Sieyès, one of the few leaders of the early Revolution to avoid this fate, was asked what he had done during the Terror, he replied, laconically: "I survived." One figure, however, generally stands out from the others as the man who came closest to truly dominating the radical Revolution of 1792–1794: Maximilien Robespierre. He is an endlessly tempting subject for biographers, but at the same time, as this essay shows, his enigmatic life has proven frustratingly resistant to a definitive portrait.

For a man often vilified as one of the greatest monsters in European history, Maximilien Robespierre lived the first five-sixths of his life in remarkably conventional fashion. As an earnest, prize-winning scholarship boy, and then an ambitious young provincial lawyer in late

Book under Review: Peter McPhee, *Robespierre: A Revolutionary Life* (New Haven: Yale University Press, 2012). Essay originally published in *The New Republic* online, April 5, 2012.

eighteenth-century France, he gave few hints that he would soon become the major figure in a revolutionary Reign of Terror. His early life did have its share of destabilizing tragedies: the death of his mother when he was six, followed by his father's effective abandonment of the family. But whatever demons these events engendered manifested themselves mostly in a ferocious work ethic, personal rigidity, and quite possibly a severe case of sexual repression. By the time he was thirty, in 1788, Robespierre was heading smoothly toward a future as a lonely, irritable pillar of his small town bar association.

A year later, his world changed. The Old Regime collapsed, creating a political vacuum filled in large part by the twelve hundred members of the raucous, newly elected National Assembly, many from backgrounds as obscure as Robespierre's own. (Edmund Burke, not entirely inaccurately, ridiculed them as "fomenters and conductors of the petty war of village vexation.") In this company, men who worked hard and spoke persuasively, along a consistent line of argument, quickly drew attention. Robespierre was one of them, all the more because the line he advocated was daringly radical. Among other things, he argued that France should abolish the death penalty, renounce aggressive warfare, and move toward the elimination of slavery in its colonies. Although ridiculed as verbose, pedantic, and physically unprepossessing (he was short and had an embarrassing facial twitch), Robespierre slowly gained a reputation for rigid, unswerving dedication to the public good. He even acquired a flattering nickname: "the Incorruptible." The British observer William Augustus Miles called him "a character to be contemplated," and predicted he would be "a man of sway in a short time, and govern the million."

He gained his opportunity in 1793–1794, after successive efforts to end the Revolution and establish a stable new constitutional regime had failed. Instead, France's new republican regime seemed to teeter on the edge of catastrophe, threatened by an armed coalition of European powers, and a series of dangerous domestic rebellions. Under these conditions, power passed increasingly into the hands of a dictatorial "Committee of Public Safety," which claimed sweeping emergency power. Tens of thousands of political opponents were executed, and many more perished in the repression of the provincial uprisings. Christian worship was suppressed and utopian projects introduced for making the French, in Robespierre's own words, into "a new people." Robespierre himself virtually invented a new, deist religion for France: the Cult of the Supreme Being.

He never held the dictatorial power his enemies attributed to him, but he did the most of anyone to set the Terror in motion, and after the autumn of 1793 he fell into the grip of something approaching paranoia. As Peter McPhee puts it in this new biography: "Robespierre's mental universe was crowded with unrelenting conspiracies." By midsummer 1794, enough members of the National Convention feared for their lives to stage a coup against him and his allies. From the crest of the revolutionary movement, he was swept under and crushed, dying on the guillotine to which he had sent so many of his enemies.

Robespierre makes an exceptionally difficult figure for biographers. Colorless, intensely private, and doctrinaire, a creature of cold, high abstraction, his political success is mysterious. Not only did little in his previous life foreshadow it, he seemed largely lacking in political ambition of the ordinary sort. He disliked the adulation that increasingly came his way, lived ascetically, and was driven close to physical and mental collapse by the pressures of revolutionary politics. While many fine historians have tried their hands at his life, including Ruth Scurr in a lively volume in 2006, none have been truly successful. The best of them, like Scurr, have echoed his enemy, the philosopher and politician Condorcet, who in 1792 already grasped a key aspect of Robespierre's mindset: "Robespierre preaches, Robespierre censures, he is furious, grave, melancholy, shamming exaltation, logical in his thoughts and conduct; he thunders against the rich and the great; he lives frugally and feels no physical needs; he has but a single mission, which is to speak and he speaks almost all the time.... He has all the characteristics, not of a religious leader, but of the leader of a sect; he has built up for himself a reputation for austerity which borders on sainthood.... Robespierre is a priest and will never be anything else." But as François Furet perceptively observed, the best way of all to understand Robespierre may be simply as a pure, unalloyed conductor of revolutionary ideology. In that case, what matters is not so much to understand the man himself but the Revolution that spoke through him.

Peter McPhee, a distinguished Australian social historian, has chosen very much the opposite path in this new biography, and dwells heavily on the prerevolutionary life and career. Robespierre's upbringing in a broken family led directly, McPhee argues, to a later devotion to the rights of children and education reform, and from there to a broader concern with social improvement. His experience as a scholarship boy in a northern province known for sharp social divisions instilled a radical sense of social justice. McPhee highlights Robespierre's close ties to his sisters and to a select number of friends, and so he rejects the stereotype of "the emotionally stunted, rigidly puritanical and icily cruel monster of history and literature." As for the delirium of Robespierre's final months, McPhee puts more stress than previous biographers on the man's sharply deteriorating physical health. Robespierre routinely worked from dawn to past midnight, complained incessantly of exhaustion and fevers, and spent several crucial weeks in the spring of 1794 confined to his bed. As Colin Jones nicely puts it in the book's cover blurb, "Robespierre emerges less as the man who ruined the Revolution than as a man the Revolution ruined." In short, McPhee tries to sketch a much more human and sympathetic Robespierre than the one who appears in most history books.

It makes for an interesting exercise, and the book has much to be said for it. It is a fine piece of work. McPhee has a sure command of the period, has mastered the voluminous sources on Robespierre, and writes a robust, clean prose. And he practices a virtue that has become all too rare among present-day biographers: concision. (Among current studies of the American founders, a book this length would most likely be "Part One of Six.") McPhee is also quite right to point out that Robespierre was in no sense a pathological freak. He was perfectly capable of ordinary human emotions, relationships, even passions.

And yet, paradoxically, by making Robespierre more human and more frail, McPhee actually makes his revolutionary career even more mysterious. How could a figure so ordinary in some respects, and so weak in others, rise into the leadership of one of the most radically transformative political movements in history? How could he have persuaded so many people to follow him? What made him different from the many others who shared his background? For historical figures of this magnitude, we expect a person with the inhuman stamina of a Churchill or the sinister charisma of a Hitler—not a man who whined, as Robespierre did in June 1793, "exhausted by four years of difficult and fruitless work, I sense that my physical and moral resources are no longer at the level required by a great revolution."

A part of the problem is that McPhee underplays the real hardness and determination of Robespierre's mind, if not his body, throughout most of the Revolution. And perhaps because McPhee sympathizes with Robespierre's ideals, and admires Robespierre's self-denial, he largely misses the colossal sense of self-righteousness that came along with these qualities and were fed by them. Among other things, Robespierre's revolutionary speeches and writings were infused with a ferocious and brutally effective sarcasm deployed against anyone who disagreed with him or fell short of his impossibly high standards. Robespierre also had the true preacher's gift of shifting effortlessly from a savage excoriation of human flaws to a brilliant, hopeful invocation of human spiritual potential: "In our country we wish to substitute morality for egoism, honesty for love of honor, principles for conventions, duties for decorum, the empire of reason for the tyranny of fashion, the fear of vice for the dread of unimportance. We want to substitute pride for insolence, magnanimity for vanity, the love of glory for the love of gold." The passage directly echoes one of the most famous pages in Rousseau's *Social Contract*, and here we come to another remarkable quality: Robespierre's ability to cast his every opinion as faithful to the spirit of the thinker whom so many of the revolutionary generation worshiped as a virtual deity. Robespierre in fact felt a particularly intense bond of identification with Rousseau, and McPhee might have done more to explore this crucial aspect of his personality: the kinship felt by one awkward, intense man, son of a mother who died in his early childhood and a of distant father, for another.

But above all, McPhee does not do enough with Furet's crucial insight into Robespierre as a conductor of revolutionary ideology—and therefore, with the French Revolution itself. It is worth stressing here just how different the French revolutionary leadership was from the leadership of most revolutions. Figures such as Robespierre, Danton, Sieyès, or Saint-Just did not occupy positions of political prominence before the Revolution, as many of the American revolutionaries had done. They had not fought elections or led political parties. They did not spend years in struggle or exile, like Lenin or Mao, dreaming of what they would do once they came to power. In a mere blink of time, they hurtled from banal obscurity to world-historical importance, and so it is perhaps fair to say that the Revolution made them more than that they made the Revolution.

In one sense, the Robespierre of 1793–1794—a man who helped destroy an ancient monarchy and kill its king, who tried to create a new religion, who helped send France's armies into a war of annihilation against the continent's major powers—really did have very little in common with the Robespierre of 1788, a fussy provincial lawyer. He himself famously remarked on the Revolution's transformative power when he said, in 1794, that it had thrust the French two thousand years ahead of other peoples, "so that one is tempted to see them as a different species."

Of course Robespierre was a not a mere empty vessel for revolutionary ideas. And of course the values, the instincts, and the personal qualities instilled into him during his early years mattered. But what mattered above all were the ways these things were transmuted when placed into the hottest, most dynamic political crucible the world had yet seen. What Yeats wrote of John MacBride in 1916 might be said as well of Robespierre in the French Revolution:

> He, too, has resigned his part
> In the casual comedy;
> He, too, has been changed in his turn,
> Transformed utterly:
> A terrible beauty is born.

7

A Very Different French Revolution

THE SHARPEST QUARREL ABOUT THE REVOLUTION that I myself have initiated began with this essay. After writing a long consideration of Jonathan Israel's history of the Enlightenment in 2012 (reprinted as chapter 7 of part II here), I had no intention of engaging again with his ambitious attempt to reinterpret my chosen period of history. But when his massive study of the Revolution appeared just two years later, I felt I could not leave unchallenged his approach, his conclusions, and his blanket criticism of nearly all the works I admired on the subject (indeed, of nearly everything modern historians have written on it). At the same time, I used the opportunity to present a different vision of the Revolution. Israel wrote a sharp response that was longer than my original essay. A shortened version of it appeared, along with my reply, in The New York Review of Books, *October 9, 2014. His longer version can be found on the website of the History News Network (historynewsnetwork.org).*

Did a secret society bring about the French Revolution? In the classic fictional version of this widely believed conspiracy theory, Alexandre

---

Book under Review: Jonathan Israel, *Revolutionary Ideas: An Intellectual History of the French Revolution from the Rights of Man to Robespierre* (Princeton University Press, 2014). From *The New York Review of Books*. Copyright © 2014 by David A. Bell.

Dumas's novel *Joseph Balsamo*, a Masonic society known as the Illuminati gather in a ruined castle in 1770 and plot the overthrow of the French monarchy. Their leader, called the "Great Copt," speaks of the day when "the monarchy is dead...religious domination is despised...social inferiority is extinguished."

Dumas would have found a great deal to appreciate in Jonathan Israel's *Revolutionary Ideas*. Israel does not present the French Revolution of 1789 as the result of a literal conspiracy. But he repeatedly characterizes it as the work of a "small minority" or "unrepresentative fringe" of disaffected Frenchmen who, in his view, consciously and deliberately sought to bring about the greatest political upheaval the Western world had ever seen. Israel does not contend that they belonged to a secret society. But he does argue that they shared a common creed, which they acted deliberately to realize. It is very much the same creed outlined by the Great Copt, although Israel would add sexual and racial inequality to the list of injustices his heroes sought to overthrow.

Israel makes this case in one of the most unusual histories of the French Revolution ever written. He calls it an "intellectual history," but by this he does not mean that he has restricted himself to one part of the subject and left the political, social, economic, and cultural histories of the Revolution to others. He means that only ideas matter for understanding how the Revolution came about and what course it took. A particular set of ideas was its "sole fundamental cause," and conflicts over these ideas drove it forward.

As a result, despite its great length, *Revolutionary Ideas* has surprisingly little to say about the most famous revolutionary events. The fall of the Bastille in July 1789, to which writers like Jules Michelet and Thomas Carlyle devoted many brilliant pages, flies by in two terse paragraphs. The "October Days" of 1789, when angry Parisian crowds, led by market women, marched on the royal palace of Versailles, invaded Queen Marie-Antoinette's bedroom, and forced King Louis XVI and the royal family to return to Paris with them, get the same. The dramatic execution in January 1793 of King Louis, who just four years earlier had claimed a divine right to rule over France as its absolute monarch, is dispatched in two sentences.

Personalities also get short shrift. Previous historians and biographers have speculated endlessly about the psychology of the prim, tightly coiled Maximilien Robespierre, the fanatical Jean-Paul Marat, or the erratic, vainglorious Georges Danton, going back over their childhoods, inquiring into their sex lives, combing their correspondence for intimate revelations. The troubled marriages of Louis XVI and Marie-Antoinette and of Napoleon and Josephine have come in for endless dissection. Even in seven hundred pages of text, Israel has no time for such matters, in general providing no more than an economical line or two of background for each of his dramatis personae (although there is also a helpful "Cast of Main Participants" in an appendix).

The vast majority of the French population fare particularly poorly in *Revolutionary Ideas*. As even readers of the most basic textbook know, the French Revolution began at a moment of economic crisis, in which spiraling prices for the population's staple food—bread—had driven millions to the brink of indigence and starvation. They also know that the Revolution might easily have been strangled in its cradle, had not the common people risen up at a moment of political crisis, stormed the Bastille, and then asserted their power in cities and towns across the country.

Again and again, it was the actions of common people that broke political stalemates and drove the Revolution forward. In scarcely more than three years, from 1789 to 1792, a land of absolute monarchy transformed itself into a democratic republic that gave the right to vote to all adult men. Less than a year later it lurched into civil war and the horrific repression known as the Terror, in which many thousands of innocent people were executed as alleged "enemies of the Revolution," even while France was simultaneously embarking on an extraordinary experiment in utopian social reform. None of this could have happened, for better and worse, without the participation of ordinary French men and women.

Jonathan Israel, in some remarkably cavalier passages, treats these popular actions almost with annoyance. He ignores several generations' worth of historical inquiry into how ordinary French people of the revolutionary era lived and thought. Rising literacy rates, declining patterns of religious observance, and a consumer revolution that put books within the reach of millions do not concern him. He takes no interest in the common people's culture, and never considers the possibility that they might have conceived and articulated revolutionary political ideas on their own. "Bread prices were high and the urban and rural population restless," he writes. "But this was nothing new. Popular disaffection, experience suggested, could mostly be shepherded wherever the elites wished."

On several occasions, he deplores the inability of "the most ignorant part of the population, the illiterate and semi-illiterate," to appreciate what revolutionary ideologues had to offer. "Most ordinary folk did not read their books and would scarcely have understood had they tried." The work of historians such as Robert Darnton, who have shown how the public read and responded to the ideas of thinkers like Rousseau, gets little attention here.

Revolutionary Ideas continues directly from Israel's earlier work on the Enlightenment (see part II, chapter 7), and shows that he has the courage of his convictions. He has accepted very few of the criticisms made of this earlier work and remains entirely committed to his original line of argument. Not only did a "radical Enlightenment" cause the French Revolution, but in 1789 it was still essentially the same radical Enlightenment that originally took shape in seventeenth-century Holland. Its proponents were committed to the creed first elaborated, in his view, by Baruch Spinoza: democracy, religious toleration, human rights, and social, racial, and sexual equality. Faced with an established order that ferociously opposed these ideas, they saw no path forward but radical and, if necessary, violent revolution. And while they did not achieve anything like full success, they still laid "the foundations of democratic modernity." The thesis is shockingly simple.

Of course, Israel recognizes that the actual events were considerably more complicated and that the French Revolution was a bloodily contentious movement, not a unified and coherent one. But he gets around this problem easily—too easily. The 1789 apostles of radical Enlightenment may not have been the whole Revolution, he explains, but they were the "authentic Revolution"—even the "real revolution." He speaks of the Revolution's "essential principles," its "core principles," its "veritable course," its "soul." Everything else was false, inauthentic, unsatisfactory, counterproductive, or worse. Robespierre, whom most historians take as the exemplar of French revolutionary radicalism, was, for Israel, quite the reverse. He had an "approach . . . directly contrary to the Revolution's core values" and was in fact the incarnation of "authoritarian populism prefiguring modern fascism." As this language suggests, Israel is not in the least interested in taking an impartial view of his subject. Rather, he has taken sides, with gusto, and has decided to fight out the original battles once again in the pages of his book.

Who are his heroes, those he calls his "unrepresentative fringe"? For the earliest years of the Revolution, he particularly singles out the flamboyant Comte de Mirabeau and the dour clergyman Emmanuel Sieyès, who together were the most important figures in transforming France's antiquated Estates General, which the king had summoned to deal with a major financial crisis, into the revolutionary National Assembly in 1789. Both men were adept politicians, and both had a strong debt to the intellectual school known as the Physiocrats, which originally supported a strong French monarchy. Israel, however, characterizes them as lifelong dedicated followers of the antimonarchical radical Enlightenment, and, as in his earlier work, describes Sieyès in particular as a "hardened ideologue."

As for the later years of the Revolution, after the Terror, Israel looks especially to the group of intellectuals known as the *idéologues*, who imagined a "science of ideas" that would serve as the basis for a new system of public education (they invented the word "ideology"). A well-educated and rationally organized society, they hoped, could resist the temptations of political turmoil. Most historians believe the *idéologues* owed more to John Locke than to Israel's radical Enlightenment, and do not consider them particularly egalitarian (let alone feminist). But they did have a commitment to the democratic Republic.

The *idéologues* also supported Napoleon's 1798 invasion of Egypt, something that leads Israel, their admirer, into a surprising defense of this early imperialist venture. He acknowledges that Napoleon hoped above all to challenge Britain's hegemony in the East. But he adds, none too convincingly, that "the French sought to emancipate Egypt from her enslavement to tyranny, religion, ignorance, and the Turk, and improve the lives, economy, and society of the Egyptians." Napoleon, he writes, "sincerely nurtured plans for harmonious friendship," but his efforts to bring "revolutionary Enlightenment" to Egyptians "failed entirely with the Muslims."

The most important group for Israel, however, is the one that briefly dominated France at the height of the Revolution. This was the so-called Brissotin or Girondin faction, of whom the most important members were the intellectual and journalist Jacques-Pierre Brissot and the philosopher the Marquis de Condorcet. Although active in revolutionary affairs from the start—and more genuinely radical than either Sieyès or Mirabeau—they only came to real political prominence in the winter of 1791–1792, when they led calls for France to declare war on its neighbors and spread revolutionary ideas beyond its borders. Historians have endlessly debated the extent to which the Brissotins constituted an organized political faction, and whether they held consistent political ideas.

But Brissot and Condorcet themselves had undeniable political importance, and a credible case can be made that they embraced a wider creed of universal rights than almost any previous Western political figures. Both were early supporters of granting full civil rights to French Jews and worked toward the emancipation of black slaves in France's Caribbean colonies. Condorcet in particular was an early and enthusiastic advocate of women's political rights. He also initially drafted the never-implemented French Constitution of 1793, the most expansively democratic such document produced up to that point in history, which Israel examines in the strongest and most original chapter of *Revolutionary Ideas*.

The Brissotins had a vicious rivalry with the political faction called the Montagne (for their habit of taking the highest seats in the National Convention). Led by Robespierre, Saint-Just, and Marat, the Montagne had close ties to the popular activists known as the *sans-culottes*, and supported their agenda of price controls on staple products and harsh repression of suspected counterrevolutionaries. The Brissotins, by contrast, developed sources of support in provincial cities and eschewed Montagnard populism.

By the spring of 1793 the two sides had fallen into a death struggle in which each accused the other of treason and counterrevolution. The Brissotin deputy Maximin Isnard (who, incidentally, first proposed the creation of the Committee of Public Safety, which later helped direct the Terror) declared at one point that if *sans-culotte* insurrections continued, then "Paris will be annihilated, and men will search the banks of the Seine for signs of the city." Finally, in the late spring, heavily armed *sans-culottes* surrounded the National Convention and forced it to expel the Brissotin members. The Montagne, now triumphant, showed their enemies no mercy. Brissot and many of his allies died on the guillotine. Condorcet went into hiding after being pronounced guilty by the Convention of the capital crime of denouncing the constitution that replaced his own. After he was caught, he committed suicide by taking poison.

Jonathan Israel admires the Brissotins enormously and does not have a critical word to say about them. "They were, in fact," he writes, "the founders of the modern human rights tradition, black emancipation, women's rights, and modern representative democracy...the first organized champions of democratic, rights-based, secular modernity." He considers their fall an unmitigated tragedy, which very nearly led to the complete extinction of their cherished causes (the *idéologues'* revival of these causes being partial at best, and crushed in its turn by Napoleon's 1799 coup d'état). Israel quotes copiously and uncritically throughout the book from their newspapers and memoirs and speeches. Indeed, it is not going too far to say that these works constitute his most important source. By contrast, he reviles the "Montagnards," Robespierre especially, and uncritically repeats the Brissotins' invective against them. Robespierre had "debased" and "half-baked" ideas. He lusted for dictatorship, and his personality was characterized by "megalomania, paranoia, and vindictiveness."

Israel is, in fact, quite credulous when it comes to Brissotin accusations against the Montagne. One striking example appears in his treatment of the notorious September Massacres in the late summer of 1792. On the news that the Prussian army had broken through French lines and was marching on Paris, crowds of *sans-culottes* stormed the prisons and killed at least twelve hundred alleged counterrevolutionaries. Afterward, the Brissotins and the Montagne accused each other of instigating the slaughter. Israel admits that "little documentary evidence survives proving the premeditated complicity of leading Montagnard politicians" (for "little," read "none"). But just ten pages later he casually writes of "the Montagne's obvious complicity." Incidentally, while historians have established that nearly all adult male Parisians of the revolutionary era could read and write, Israel here refers blithely to "gangs of illiterate Parisians" who had supposedly fallen under Robespierre's spell.

Overall, too much of Israel's argument depends on this unconvincing use of evidence. Against nearly all other historians of the Revolution, he insists that his heroes Sieyès and Mirabeau "in the main" rejected "the principle of monarchy" from 1789 on, without quoting a single line from them to support his allegations (or fully confronting the fact that Mirabeau became a close, paid confidant of Louis XVI). Israel claims that another of his heroes, the writer Volney, had an "especially prominent" role in prerevolutionary agitation in Brittany while citing nothing other than Volney's own writings. He claims that "many eyewitnesses agreed" with a prominent Brissotin's attack on the Montagne while citing only the attack itself.

Then there is the question of what he calls Robespierre's "dictatorship"—one of the hoariest counterrevolutionary legends about the French Revolution. Robespierre had enormous influence in the Jacobin Society, whose branches extended through the country. He served on the twelve-member Committee of Public Safety, which, along with the Committee of General Security, organized ferocious repression during the Terror. For much of the Terror, Robespierre was the dominant figure on the Committee of Public Safety and used the position to purge many of his enemies and rivals in the larger political universe.

But the Committee was a volatile and contentious body, and Robespierre was often too sick to attend its meetings—his most recent biographer, Peter McPhee, portrays him as a physical and emotional wreck in the spring of 1794, when the Terror was most intense. No serious historian of the French Revolution of the past century has accepted the idea that Robespierre ever exercised a true personal dictatorship, and Israel has no new evidence to present on the subject. Nonetheless, he accepts the Brissotins' accusations that Robespierre did, in fact, become a dictator—a term he never defines, and that therefore inescapably comes freighted with twentieth-century connotations. In keeping with his belief that the Montagne's "authoritarian populism" foreshadowed fascism, he even refers to the purge of the Brissotins in the spring of 1793 as "Robespierre's Putsch." As usual, he gives the *sans-culottes* no credit for independent action and without clear evidence assumes that they acted at Robespierre's instigation.

It is, in the end, impossible to accept an interpretation of the French Revolution that takes sides so completely with one group of its actors, and that is based so heavily on their own highly polemical writings. The sheer volume of Israel's research is impressive, but when it mostly reflects such a narrowly partisan point of view, what does it really amount to? Israel certainly gives us reasons to admire many things about Mirabeau, Sieyès, and the Brissotins, but he is too ready to cast them as principled, idealistic intellectuals. The overwhelming evidence is that most of them were first and foremost politicians. They compromised, made dubious and sometimes corrupt bargains, indulged in hyperbole, and not infrequently lied through their teeth to get what they wanted. Condorcet was largely an exception to this rule—an authentic visionary who came closest of any of the revolutionaries to Israel's ideal. But one man does not make a movement. And it is also a fact that all of the Brissotins, in large part for their own domestic political advantage, advocated a European war that would last, on and off, for twenty-three years and cost millions of lives.

Israel has the confidence to say that nearly all other historians of the subject have been wrong. But that same confidence has kept him from evaluating his evidence with the necessary critical eye. And it has also kept him from giving serious consideration to the thought that anything other than a certain elevated set of ideas might have driven such a vast and complicated upheaval, while leading him to treat most of the men and women who actually fought its battles with unfortunate condescension.

It is still, in one sense, very easy to sympathize with Jonathan Israel. "Democratic, rights-based, secular modernity" looks very frail of late. The "color revolutions" and the Arab Spring, which ignited such strong hopes that revolutionary action might yet have positive effects in the world, have so far mostly trickled out into the sands of cynical disillusion. How inspiring to think that the Enlightenment values we cherish today once had conscious, courageous defenders. How tempting to think of their death struggle against their enemies as a simple duel between good and evil, and to imagine them as martyrs from whose graves "a glorious Phantom may / Burst, to illumine our tempestuous day," as Shelley wrote.

But history does not have the neatness, or the moral clarity, of conspiracy fiction. There was no Great Copt plotting out the events of the French Revolution and driving it forward. And, alas, there was no unified, coherent radical Enlightenment either—at least not as Jonathan Israel has imagined it.

Napoleon Bonaparte, in Antoine-Jean Gros's rendering of his courageous role in the 1796 battle of Arcola. Gianni Dagli Orti / The Art Archive at Art Resource, NY.

Part IV

NAPOLEON BONAPARTE

WHETHER OR NOT THE FRENCH Revolution lacked great men, as Michelet maintained, the period that followed most certainly did not. Germaine de Staël noticed the difference from the moment Napoleon Bonaparte seized power in 1799. As she later wrote: "It was the first time since the Revolution that a proper name was in everyone's mouth ... people talked about nothing but this man who was to put himself in the place of all and to make the human race anonymous by monopolizing fame for himself alone."

In the first essay in this part, originally published in 2003, I remarked that despite Napoleon's stature, serious scholarship had neglected him, especially in comparison with the French Revolution, and its vast buzzing swarm of historians. The statement was true at the time, but the situation has since changed considerably, thanks in large part to a series of high-profile Bonaparte bicentennials, commemorating the events that stretched from the imperial coronation (1804) to the final defeat at Waterloo (1815). Half a dozen new full-scale scholarly biographies have now appeared, along with countless more specialized studies. Conferences have proliferated, and in Paris, a scholarly team has published a magnificent new edition of Napoleon's voluminous correspondence. As a historian specializing in the period, I have been swept along by all this activity, as the essays here testify. I have even written a short biography of my own (*Napoleon: A Concise Biography*, Oxford University Press).

The debates around Napoleon are by no means as contentious as those around the French Revolution, even if books published in France during the bicentennials, including by former Socialist prime minister Lionel Jospin, have tarred him as a criminal who left a disastrous legacy. While he indeed has few unalloyed admirers in modern France, many people there still appreciate the civic institutions he built and the glory he brought the country, if only evanescently. But there are still more than a few serious historical controversies around him, in no small part because he himself offered so many different, conflicting accounts of his actions, and because contemporaries' accounts of him are likewise contradictory. The principal point of agreement seems to be that he remains endlessly fascinating.

I

Just Like Us: Writing Napoleon's Life

OVER THE YEARS, I HAVE WRITTEN about many biographies of Napoleon. In some cases, it has been a depressing experience. Reviewing the first, deeply flawed volume of a planned two-volume set, I gently suggested that the author learn from his subject and stop before he got to Russia (the author, needless to say, failed to comply). I have also been amused at the way authors have claimed originality for their books by highlighting the previously untapped sources they have used. If Napoleon had been like Shakespeare, who left few traces in the historical record beyond his plays, new sources would indeed matter. But given the ocean of material we have about Napoleon's supremely well-documented life, no new material is going to matter much, unless it reveals some truly spectacular new facts. (Did he escape from Saint Helena, leaving a double to take his place? Did he die of poison, as conspiracy theorists have long believed?) Not the least of the merits of Steven Englund's biography, which I discuss in this essay, is that instead of protesting its originality, it simply demonstrates it, through its writing and analysis.

Book under Review: Steven Englund, *Napoleon: A Political Life* (Scribner, 2003). Essay originally published in *The New Republic*, May 17, 2004.

In his *Foundation* trilogy, Isaac Asimov imagined a future civilization in which the social sciences attain such sophistication that it becomes possible accurately to predict the future. A group called the "psycho-historians" apply the techniques to the Galactic Empire in which they live, and find, to their horror, that it will soon collapse. So they create a secret organization to carry out strategic interventions in the course of events—not to halt the collapse (it is too late for that), but to accelerate the rebirth of order and civilization out of a new Dark Ages. For a time, the organization carries out its plan with complete success. But then disaster strikes, in the form of a human mutant called the Mule, who uses sinister telepathic powers to carve out a new empire of his own. The psycho-historians initially react with consternation to this creature, whom they have failed so completely to foresee or to explain. It takes several hundred closely plotted pages for them to regroup and to set the course of history back on its predetermined path.

I often think that modern historians react to Napoleon Bonaparte in much the way that Asimov's psycho-historians do to the Mule: as a freak of nature, endowed with sinister and superhuman powers, who fits into few accepted categories or theories. As a result, amazingly, they often ignore him altogether. To be sure, popular interest in the man remains great—in the past decade, biographies have appeared from major publishers at the rate of more than one per year, from Alan Schom's exhaustive and exhausting narrative to Paul Johnson's caustic and careless pencil sketch. Yet *The American Historical Review*, the flagship journal of the profession, has not devoted a single article to Napoleon in thirty years. Even in France he attracts relatively scant scholarly interest. Perhaps one can expect little else from a discipline that for many years has preferred the *longue durée* to the play of events, and large-scale impersonal forces to exceptional individuals, and history "from the bottom up" to history from the Napoleonic heights, and "microhistory" to epic narrative, and society and culture to diplomacy and war. Nor can Napoleon be said to have benefited from the profession's burgeoning interest in gender, race, class, and sexual orientation. He is the ultimate Dead White Rich Straight Male.

All these preconceptions make it difficult for historians to regard the sixteen years of Napoleon's rule, with their massive, bloody reshaping of the European order, as anything other than a giant historical deviation.

Napoleon is arguably central to many stories of modernity: the advent of what Clausewitz, writing in his shadow, called "absolute war"; the rise of modern dictatorships and cults of personality; the development of militarism and nationalism (two words that first came into common currency in his period). But despite some heroic efforts on both sides of the Atlantic, most scholars have preferred to anchor their accounts of modern history in the democratic revolutions of 1776 and 1789, while leaving Napoleon's triumphs, disasters, and crimes largely in the hands of the popularizers.

Steven Englund is something of a popularizer himself, but in the older and more estimable fashion of the man of letters. In *Napoleon*, he eschews close analysis and makes the sort of minor errors common to writers who have not pickled their brains in historical journals since early adulthood. Still, he has serious and suggestive points to make, and he makes them in a luminous prose that few professional historians can match. His book is by far the best of the recent batch of Napoleoniana and the best biography currently available.

The subtitle, *A Political Life*, is somewhat misleading. Englund presents the book as a study of how Napoleon crafted himself as a figure above petty party politics, strove to incarnate the French nation, and constructed a well-oiled, domineering state that has survived to the present day (which is to say, at least fifty years too long). In one of the brilliant quotations that Englund sprinkles generously throughout, he cites Balzac on this Napoleonic state: "The nosiest, most meticulous, most scribbling, red-tape mongering, list-making, controlling, verifying, cautious, and finally just the most cleaning-lady of administrations—past, present or future." (Its heritage, by the way, lives on not only in France, but everywhere that French models and the Napoleonic Code have penetrated, which is to say much of Europe, Latin America, and Africa.)

Yet this political story is a familiar one, and a book truly centered on it would be of limited interest. Fortunately Englund, who confesses disarmingly that he initially came to Napoleon through a boyhood love of lead soldiers, cannot resist actually focusing on Napoleon's personality, and on war, about which he has more original things to say. Indeed, his signal achievement is to cover these subjects in a way that highlights not only Napoleon's genius—that is, his freakish Mule-like qualities—but also his place in a larger European historical context. Without reducing Napoleon to a mere expression of impersonal historical forces, Englund suggests how a figure such as Bonaparte became possible.

Englund starts with the interesting observation that, among the great figures in history, Napoleon is one of the most accessible to us. This is so, I would suggest, for at least two reasons. For a start, unlike the cases of earlier conquerors such as Alexander, Caesar, or Charlemagne, we know almost everything about Napoleon's life. We know what he read as a child. We know what he dreamed of as an adolescent (he kept notes). We know what he did in bed with Josephine. We know what he ate on Saint Helena (and it does not look likely that arsenic was on the menu, Englund insists, despite the claims of some conspiracy theorists). We know his actions as a general and a ruler in minuscule detail. Indeed, far more is known about Napoleon than is possible for any single biographer to read—and that is without even mentioning the literally tens of thousands of articles and books on the subject.

Of course, we possess similar floods of information about later conquerors as well, Hitler and Stalin in particular. But with those men any sense of sympathy or identification is instantly short-circuited by our knowledge of their pathologies and their atrocities. Not so with Napoleon. No one would ever label him psychologically normal, and a modern tribunal would probably have little trouble convicting him of crimes against humanity—but it is almost impossible not to feel a connection with him. This is the man who, a moment after crowning himself emperor in Notre Dame in 1804, turned to his elder brother and whispered: "If only Daddy could see us now" ("Si Babbù ci vidi"). It is the man whose love for the unfaithful Josephine overwhelmed him even as he was overwhelming northern Italy, spilling into letter after letter of soppy, painfully embarrassing, utterly human passion. It is the man who remained genuinely captivated by great literature all his life, and tried his hand at writing history, philosophy, political treatises, and even a sentimental novel. It is hard to read about Napoleon without wondering, if only for a moment, what it might have been like to lead his life. Small wonder that the surrounding history, when set next to the vibrant colors and sharp details of his portrait, starts to look fuzzy and wan.

The ability of ordinary people to identify with Napoleon was also the key to his success. Napoleon did try hard, on occasion, to craft an aloof

and majestic image in keeping with his imperial title. Ingres's emblematic portrait from 1806 depicts him as a splendid but strangely lifeless
icon: the face peeks out, stiff and pale, from between lace collar and
laurel wreath, while a hand shoots up at an unnatural angle from under
ermine robes to grasp a suggestively elongated scepter. But this sort of
display, and the kitschy imperial court with its Ruritanian titles (Prince
of Benevento, Duke of Ragusa), never had its intended effect. Napoleon
was no Louis XIV, capable of awing subjects into respectful silence by a
show of pure, self-confident, princely grandeur. If the French loved
him—and they did, for a long time—it was because they saw him as one
of their own, even after he became emperor. To them, he was still the
"little corporal" who joked with his troops and shared their dangers; still
the provincial upstart with the uncouth accent who deliciously forced
the flower of the old aristocracy to bow and scrape before him; still the
clever little boy who could never quite believe that he had grown up to
conquer Europe.

For this reason, Napoleon remained, to the end, very much the egalitarian embodiment of the French Revolution. But as Englund grasps
very well, he embodied something else, too. To the Europeans of his age,
he seemed something like a character out of a novel, and indeed he understood himself in precisely this manner. "What a novel my life has
been," he allegedly remarked on Saint Helena in 1816. The various aspects of his story and character—the picaresque twists of fortune, the
lachrymose sentimentality, the constant self-questioning, the intense
awareness of his own originality—might have been the product of some
wild literary collaboration between Richardson, Rousseau, and Goethe.
Small wonder that he so bewitched the greatest novelists of the nineteenth century, from Stendhal through Hugo to Tolstoy.

Napoleon, in sum, embodied a truly modern sensibility, and it was
his genius to be able to translate that sensibility into political terms. As
Englund reminds us, he was himself a powerful writer, a master of self-
presentation. From his early moments campaigning in Italy, he founded
newspapers to report back on his achievements to the French public. He
penned his own military dispatches with such verve and suspense that,
as Englund comments, "contemporaries...enjoyed them for the serial
novel that they were." Even—especially—in exile, he dictated his reminiscences with such force and pathos that the *Memorial of Saint Helena*

became one of the best sellers of the century. He knew, in short, how to address himself to millions of followers in a modern language so as to create a bond that was both strikingly powerful and intimately personal. "What a pity," Valéry, who recognized the emperor's literary abilities, once remarked, "to see a mind as great as Napoleon's devoted to trivial things such as empires, historical events, the thundering of cannons and of men." Englund quotes Valéry, and then, at the end of his book, answers him: "Napoleon chose to 'write' his novel on the world, not on paper."

Napoleon's modern sensibility even had its echoes on the battlefield. Before the French Revolution, aristocratic generals commanding relatively small armies of expensively trained professional soldiers had tended toward cautious campaigning. They fought for limited political aims against adversaries whom they considered honorable equals. The French Revolution swept away this sort of warfare, unleashing huge conscript armies, toppling regimes left and right, and making it incumbent on commanders not merely to outmaneuver but to annihilate their enemies.

Napoleon, despite his training under the Old Regime, grasped the essence of this new sort of war more quickly and more completely than anyone else. As Englund suggests, it resonated on the deepest level with his character and his cultural outlook. Discussing Napoleon's aristocratic opponents, Englund comments that "war was their métier, not their self-expression and their meaning...not their titanic personal struggle, the imposition of their very selves." For Napoleon, possessed of a keen, novelistic sense of the self, war was exactly such an act of expression. He was never so alive as when he was throwing everything into battle with a gambler's verve, praying that large, dispersed bodies of men would come together in just the right place at just the right time. At the battle of Marengo, in 1800, he famously succeeded, but it was, as the Duke of Wellington would later say about Waterloo, "a close run thing." At one point in the fray Napoleon sent the despairing message to General Desaix, "For God's sake, come up if you still can"—and Desaix did, dying heroically in the process. The resulting victory secured northern Italy for France, and Napoleon's place at the head of the French state. At Waterloo, an older Napoleon commanded more falteringly, and the dice rolled out a different number. But the legacy of his wars, and the notion that the modern personality can be fully tested and expressed only on the battlefield, hung heavily over the next century and played its part in bringing about the horrors of the World War I trenches. For Napoleon and his followers, war was a "total" experience in a way that it had not been for his aristocratic predecessors.

It is somewhat surprising that Napoleon's modern sensibility has attracted so little attention from the recent crop of biographers. But then, while modern, it is not quite our own sensibility. Like most French Romantic fiction, it is too mawkish and grandiloquent, too lacking in irony, for contemporary tastes. Little surprise that Napoleon's recent chroniclers have mostly been military buffs such as Robert Asprey, interested in the man of action, or ideologues such as Paul Johnson, who want to see in Napoleon a forerunner of modern totalitarian horrors.

Englund has a romantic streak of his own, which allows him to grasp what the others have missed. To see this streak, one need only read the book's opening scene, a description of Napoleon's tomb at the Invalides:

> Visiting Les Invalides is like visiting the Lincoln Memorial: amid all the funereal marble and the airless geometric space, something is alive.... The imperial sarcophagus is a costly slab of reddish porphyry—a hard and expensive crystalline rock—that is sculpted like a wave, a shape cut from a continuum: dense and heavy, frozen in stone yet eternally cresting. The stone is unexpectedly, almost shockingly, flesh-colored.... It is livid and living, the color of a flayed chest in an autopsy, exposing a raw, still-beating heart.... Most present in this place is the awe-evoking sense of human possibility, which is a different thing from hope. The wave of this tomb becomes a sleigh that will carry us off into an unknown future, even if only a hundred days' worth.

Throughout the book, as he follows the familiar path from Corsican boyhood to Parisian triumph to lachrymose South Atlantic exile, Englund gives us many more such set-pieces (although none quite so brilliant) depicting the various decisive moments of Napoleon's career. Critics may object that these passages come close to reproducing Napoleonic propaganda, but Englund has an answer for them. "Consider

David's portrait of Bonaparte crossing the Alps on a sleek, light gray charger in 1800. 'Wrong,' some say, 'propaganda! He crossed the St. Bernard Pass on a mule, and he was wrapped in furs, without a flowing red cape.' Not all people naïvely believed David depicted literal reality; rather they understood that there are literal and metaphorical truths."

The prose of the introduction, lushly appealing as it is, does stray dangerously close to the cliff's edge of sheer melodrama. An entire book's worth of it would be unreadable. But generally Englund employs a more conversational tone, and he makes good use of a dry wit. On the Austrian reoccupation of northern Italy in the late 1790s: "It was enough to make the Italians miss the French (at least until they returned)." On Napoleon's seizure of absolute power: "At a public reading of the new constitution, a woman was reported asking her neighbor what it all meant. She replied: 'It means Bonaparte.'" Or, quoting Napoleon himself on the same subject: "Moving into the Tuileries [Palace] isn't everything. You have to stay there." Moreover, the tart and sardonic tone does not simply serve to entertain. It also provides a frame against which to highlight the full, sentimental flood of Napoleon's own writings, which Englund quotes at luxuriant length. In one of the best passages of the book, he sets the scene for the coup d'état of 18 Brumaire: "At the end of his life, Bonaparte got off a line—the valediction of his will, hence his last public utterance—which reads thus: 'The love of glory is like the bridge that Satan built across Chaos to pass from Hell to Paradise: glory links the past with the future across a bottomless abyss.' But in autumn 1799, Bonaparte had not yet reached either Paradise or Hell, he was only contemplating the Republic of France from the quarter deck of the frigate *La Muirion*, as it hove into view in the port of Fréjus." Overall, Englund's prose and, yes, his romanticism, allow him to take Napoleon's "metaphorical truths" seriously, and therefore to appreciate a quality that was central to the Napoleonic experience but has virtually disappeared from contemporary political life, namely, grandeur.

But alas, metaphorical truths sometimes conflict with literal ones, and grandeur has a tendency to inspire adulation instead of analysis. When it comes to Napoleon, some admittedly go much more deeply and disastrously in this direction than Englund, notably French interior minister Dominique de Villepin, whose recent study of the Hundred Days whipped past straight hero-worship into the furthest reaches of hagiography. Englund, too, cannot always resist undue admiration, and has a tendency to minimize the uglier side of Napoleon's rule: the internal repression; the criminal sacrifice of hundreds of thousands of soldiers to little purpose; the savage quelling of revolts across Europe.

True, Napoleon locked up relatively few political opponents, and he remained genuinely popular for much of his rule. He was not a totalitarian so much as the last of the great Enlightened despots, with newly efficient systems of censorship and internal espionage. But to say, as Englund does, that Napoleon "only" faced resistance to his rule "under special conditions in Calabria, Spain, and the Tyrol" is rather like saying that Lyndon Johnson "only" faced resistance to his foreign policy in Vietnam. Spain, in particular, as Napoleon himself acknowledged, was his empire's bleeding ulcer. The war there from 1808 to 1814 not only popularized the term "guerrilla," it gave the world the modern phenomenon. Spanish partisans ambushed French soldiers, destroyed French outposts, waylaid French convoys, and then melted back into the general population. The French army tried desperately to contain them, but its expeditions had no more effect than "plowing furrows in water," as one frustrated French officer put it. In desperation, he and his colleagues turned to increasingly cruel means of repression: forcing Spanish peasants into towns, taking and executing hostages, even wiping out whole villages in reprisal for attacks. The war pinned down hundreds of thousands of French soldiers who might have saved Napoleon from disaster elsewhere (say, Russia), confirmed for much of world opinion his reputation as the "Corsican Ogre," and, most important, irreparably punctured his image as unbeatable. The episode deserves more attention than the scant four pages Englund devotes to it.

In general, Englund is weakest on this period, the last years of the Empire, when exhaustion and disease took their toll on Napoleon, and the metaphorical truths of grandeur vanished under the chill waves of a remorseless reality. The epic calamity of the Russian campaign of 1812, which cost nearly a million lives to little purpose, gets no more space than Spain. The awakening of German resistance to Napoleon, and the fateful exposure of Germany to the idea of absolute war, flits by with similar speed. Part of the problem—beyond the understandable exhaustion any biographer incurs in following Napoleon through his labors—is that Englund's own expertise is largely confined to France and Italy.

Once Napoleon's principal theater of operations moves beyond their borders, he becomes notably less sure of himself. As a result, the book rushes from the triumphant harmonies of Austerlitz to the plangent violin solo of Saint Helena, while largely missing the thundering chorus of Russia (the *1812 Overture*, so to speak). The omissions may not bother patriotic French readers, but most others will find themselves wishing for an additional hundred pages of Nemesis.

Still, this is an enthralling work. Not only does it present Napoleon in the vivid detail he deserves, it also begins to suggest how to fit him back into the broad sweep of European history—in other words, how to avoid treating him as a Mulish freak. It helps us to see that Napoleon succeeded because, embodying a modern novelistic sensibility, he managed to create a personal, intimate bond between mass politics and ordinary citizens. He put a human face on mass politics in a way that the French revolutionaries, with their cold and high abstractions, had failed to do. As Germaine de Staël justly remarked, "the only new proper noun to come out of the Revolution is Bonaparte." He did not rise above politics so much as incarnate politics, the state, and the nation in a personality with which ordinary French people could identify. Unfortunately, for all his state-building talent, he built his regime on police repression rather than democratic institutions, and he legitimized it through the promise of conquest rather than free elections and the guarantee of human rights. When his conquests finally faltered, his regime blew away like dust, and his country resumed the wild and violent dance of political instability that had begun in 1789 and would last until well into the late nineteenth century (with echoes in the twentieth). This makes Napoleon's story criminal. But, as Englund shows, the story is also tragic—all the more so because it comes across to modern readers as so intensely human.

2

When the Barracks Were Bursting with Poets:
Napoleon's Life Writing

SINCE NAPOLEON PROVED HIS MILITARY genius at an absurdly early age, it is hard to think of him as anything but a soldier. (He won some of his greatest victories, and arguably established himself as the greatest general in French history, before his twenty-eighth birthday.) But in fact, he did not originally plan to make his name in the field of war. Until the French Revolution made promotion a matter of talent and political connections, rather than of seniority and social rank, this junior officer from the lowest rung of the gentry in France's least regarded province could hope for little in the way of an exciting military career. Instead, as this next essay discusses, he had dreams of becoming a write and showed surprising literary talent. As the essay also notes, this ambition was surprisingly common for eighteenth-century military men. Looking at the "soldier-poets" of the age not only reveals an unexpected side of Napoleon, but shows just how differently his social world was constructed from our own.

Andy Martin is unlikely to convince many readers that Napoleon conquered Europe only as compensation for his inability to write a sentimental

Book under Review: Andy Martin, *Napoleon the Novelist* (Polity, 2001). Essay originally published in *The London Review of Books*, September 6, 2001.

novel. His attention to the emperor's literary ambitions is, however, not unreasonable. Napoleon dreamed of literary as well as military glory, wrote copiously at various moments in his life, and had real talent for it. (Sainte-Beuve called him "a great critic in his spare time," while Thiers elevated him to "greatest writer of the century.") The trouble with Martin's choice of subject is his failure to acknowledge just how ordinary it was, two hundred years ago, for military and literary ambitions to intertwine. It is an intertwining that says a great deal about eighteenth-century culture and its distance from our own.

On receiving his commission as a second lieutenant in the French army in 1785, the young Napoleon Bonaparte embarked not on the conquest of Europe, but on seven years of mostly undemanding peacetime soldiering, interrupted by long and frequent leaves of absence. Friendless and penurious, he did not devote his ample leisure time to the stereotypical debauches of the idle army officer. Instead, as he later recalled, "I lived like a bear, always alone in my little room, with my books, which were my only friends." He devoured Voltaire, Rousseau, Bernardin de Saint-Pierre, and Raynal, and filled volume after heavy volume with reading notes. He sketched out a sentimental novel, *Clisson et Eugénie*, started a history of his native Corsica, and worked feverishly on a *Discourse on Happiness*, which he submitted to an essay competition sponsored by the Academy of Lyon. (Rousseau's career, as he knew, had taken off after victory in a similar contest four decades earlier.) He also found time to get mixed up, disastrously, in Corsican politics, and, while on yet another extended leave, ended up having to flee the island with his family in June 1793.

Following his return to the mainland, Napoleon quickly made a name for himself at the Siege of Toulon, and from there embarked on the unbelievably accelerated career that would make him master of France in six years, and all Europe seven years after that. Yet even in the midst of rebuilding French institutions and society, marching his armies across most of the continent, and earning a widespread reputation as the devil incarnate, he still cultivated his love of letters. When embarking on his Egyptian expedition of 1798, he took along a thousand-book library, as well as a group of 167 scientists, artists, poets, architects, "and one ex-baritone from the Paris Opera" to study Egyptian antiquities and prepare a monumental *Description de l'Egypte*. Their work became the basis of modern Egyptology. Even after crowning himself emperor, Napoleon followed closely the careers of Europe's leading authors (Martin has interesting things to say about his relationships with Goethe and Chateaubriand), and worked hard on his speeches and dispatches, often with memorable results. "Soldiers, from the top of these pyramids, forty centuries look down on you."

And when the Allies had banished him to Saint Helena ("Napoleon's life can be measured in islands," Martin writes), he returned to his literary concerns. He waited with impatience for new shipments of books from Europe—at times he cracked open the crates himself—and staged readings of classic plays for his small entourage. Some followers grew so tired of Voltaire's *Zaïre* that they even considered stealing the emperor's copy to spare themselves further performances. He dictated his reminiscences to Las Cases, who put them together in a book that would sizzle its way into the minds of many aspiring nineteenth-century Romantic heroes, epitomized by Julien Sorel: "He looked sadly into the stream where his book had fallen. It was the one he was most fond of, the *Mémorial de Sainte-Hélène*."

Martin provides an entertaining tour of these Napoleonic obsessions, pausing on the way to take in Boswell's *An Account of Corsica*, Kundera's *Immortality*, Simon Leys's *La Mort de Napoléon*, the invention of the semaphore telegraph, and various other tangential matters. At times, his light touch carries him up into a stratosphere of pure nonsense, as when he writes that since Napoleon did not permanently expand France's frontiers, "his real contribution on the ground was less than nothing. His more durable impact was at the level of imprinting a certain aesthetics of empire on the French mind." Some people might think his effect on the legal code or the state administration would be worth mentioning. And what about the nationalism first kindled in Germany and elsewhere under Napoleonic occupation? Commenting on Napoleon's hasty reading notes, Martin elevates carelessness to the status of existential protest: "Napoleon was in revolt against the very medium he was using. He had to modify everything, irrespective of truth value." Yet Martin does not take himself too seriously, and such excursuses are mercifully brief, as is the book itself. "This may be the first short book on Napoleon," he comments (almost—Felix Markham's classic 1954 *Napoleon and the Awakening of Europe* is even shorter). The problem is not that Martin occasionally loses himself in silliness, but that, like most of the biographers who focus on the battles, he is so dazzled by his subject that he fails to see him in the context of his time. Implicit in the book is the notion that Napoleon's literary ambitions were as extraordinary as his military successes.

Today, they would be: imagine Colin Powell taking time off from his Gulf War command for a brief seminar on the early work of Allen Ginsberg, or officers in NATO's Balkan forces engaging in a philosophical correspondence with Slavoj Žižek. But Napoleon was not the only French officer of his day to devote himself to literature. As the historian Dena Goodman has observed, the barracks were bursting with would-be poets and philosophes. Another famous underemployed artillery officer of the period, Pierre-Ambroise Choderlos de Laclos, for example, started publishing poetry while posted in Grenoble in the early 1770s. A few years later, having helped establish a military school in Valence, he turned Mme Riccoboni's popular novel *Histoire d'Ernestine* into a comic opera and had it accepted by the Comédie Française. Unfortunately, it was booed from the start to the finish of its first and only performance, and the queen's presence in the audience only added to the humiliation. Laclos packed up his resentments and took them off to the Atlantic coast, where he helped construct France's naval defenses, and in his spare time wrote *Les Liaisons dangereuses*.

Jean-François de Saint-Lambert, a longtime military officer, was one of eighteenth-century France's best regarded poets. Known above all for his French version of James Thomson's *The Seasons*, he wrote much else as well: "oriental fables," short stories about American Indians and African slaves, now-unreadable treatises on human nature, articles for Diderot's *Encyclopédie*, and satirical verse on the quarrels of Catholic theologians. He was the lover of Voltaire's friend and collaborator Mme du Châtelet, who died after giving birth to his child. And he expressed, in lines Napoleon would certainly have appreciated, the plight of the sensitive young officer forced to endure the tedium of life in camp:

> I suffered the mortally dull stories
> And the sadly competent songs
> Of our Lieutenant Colonels.
> I suffered the bland puns

> Of a thousand hatefully pleasant men,
> The heavy drunkenness of their banquets
> And their unrefined pleasures.
> Victim of Kings and fools
> I was thoroughly bored for my country.

Not surprisingly, Saint-Lambert did not have a particularly successful military career and left the army altogether after the Seven Years' War. He did, however, win election to the Académie Française.

Then there was Jacques-Antoine-Hippolyte de Guibert, whom historians remember as one of the greatest tacticians of the age, and an important influence on Napoleon's own style of warfare. Born in 1743, he first saw action fighting against Corsican rebels (including members of the Bonaparte family) in 1768–1769, and on his return to mainland France composed an ambitious tragedy about a Renaissance traitor, *The Constable de Bourbon*. Like Saint-Lambert he had a scandalous affair with a much older *salonnière*, after which he was obliged to take an extended leave from the army. He used it to travel through Germany and Austria, observing the military innovations that had served Prussia so well in the Seven Years' War. After a return to active duty, he continued to publish plays, travel literature, political philosophy, and history, and eventually joined Saint-Lambert in the ranks of the Académie. His military masterpiece, the *Essai général de tactique*, also contains encyclopedic discussions of world history and politics, which read more like Montesquieu's *Spirit of the Laws* than an officer's manual.

In Napoleon's personal entourage, too, soldier-poets were anything but unusual. Guillaume-Marie-Anne Brune, born the son of a provincial lawyer in 1763, went to Paris to study law, but found work as a typesetter after his parents cut him off for having married against their will. Full of literary hopes, he published in 1788 a gushing, pre-Romantic account of his travels through western France, full of soppy Rousseauian paeans to the power of nature and sentiment ("my heart overflows, my entire soul has plunged into an inexpressible rapture"). When the Revolution broke out, he dabbled in radical politics and tried his hand at literary journalism, but succeeded only in driving several publications into bankruptcy. In 1791, his fortunes finally took a turn for the better. Along with a large contingent of radical *sans-culottes* he volunteered for the army, and, possibly thanks to his connections with Danton, won election to the leadership of his battalion. He was promoted to briga-dier-general as soon as France went to war against Austria in 1792. Brune's politics might have brought him into difficulty after 9 Thermidor, but he adroitly shifted allegiances from Robespierre to the corrupt Barras, and then proved his political bona fides by taking part in the suppression of his former *sans-culotte* allies. From there success followed success, leading Brune to the exalted rank of marshal of France, until an expression of displeasure with Napoleon's creeping despotism finally led to his summary dismissal. He devoted his retirement to a translation of Xenophon's *Anabasis* and lived to be murdered by a royalist mob after Waterloo.

What accounts for this seemingly unlikely profusion of soldier-poets in Enlightenment France? It wasn't a quirk of the French national char-acter. After all, Frederick the Great of Prussia composed philosophical and literary works, strove to make Berlin a cultural center, and received the sobriquet "philosopher prince" from none other than Voltaire (who soon came to regret his praise). A more likely explanation might start with the tedium of military life evoked by Saint-Lambert. If modern soldiers spend their time preparing to fight the next war, eighteenth-century soldiers often spent their time doing very little of anything. As the *Année littéraire* put it in 1777, "the peace we have enjoyed for several years has allowed our warriors to cultivate other arts than those learned at the school of Mars." But soldiers did not write simply because they had the leisure to do so.

In the eighteenth century the military constituted not a separate pro-fession, but a duty and a calling for the highest elites. In France, not only did the army represent the traditional career for the aristocracy; the law barred them from any profession that bore the taint of trade or manual labor, leaving only the military, the Church, or the law. Things were not that different in England: think of Jane Austen's heroes. On the eve of the battle that cost him his life, General James Wolfe told his of-ficers that he would rather have written Gray's *Elegy* than conquered the city of Quebec.

Nearly every educated person in the eighteenth century seems not only to have read poetry, but to have fancied themselves a poet at one time or another. Look into the private papers and correspondence of members of the nobility or the professions, in Britain or France, and time and again you will come across snatches of satirical verse, love poems, children's verse, and so on. And while few of these authors had any thought of turning a hobby into a full-time calling, the periodical press of the day, particularly local newspapers, offered a means for them to put their best efforts into print. In this way, a New York judge named Henry Livingston published his children's verses beginning "'Twas the Night before Christmas" in a local paper in the 1820s, only to have a more established poet steal the credit after his death and become world famous as a result.

War itself was not in any way considered an unpoetic activity. Voltaire, who in other circumstances lambasted France as a "land of monkeys and tigers," and who lived much of his life in resentful exile across the Swiss border, nonetheless composed a cloyingly sycophantic paean to Louis XV and the glory of French arms after the 1745 Battle of Fontenoy. The verse called the French a "people of Heroes" and carefully singled out each French general for a line or two of praise. Nearly every French poet of the century, established and amateur, had similar verse to his or her credit. After the 1756 seizure of Minorca from the British, one of the rare French triumphs of the otherwise disastrous Seven Years' War, a French publisher brought out a collection of more than 150 poems, songs, and "celebrations" devoted to the victory. The list of authors reads like a cross-section of French society, including courtiers, magistrates, lawyers, doctors, noblewomen, and a heavy sprinkling of military officers. A member of the king's bodyguard contributed a lengthy ode to his master, in alexandrines.

There is no great mystery as to when or why this bond between war and art was broken, or at least twisted into an entirely new form. The mechanized slaughter of the trenches scoured older notions of glory and individual heroism out of the culture. Since 1914, nearly all Western war poetry has been antiwar poetry, and the trend has been true of the arts in general, from Remarque and Owen through Ernst and Grosz and Picasso's *Guernica* to *Catch-22* and *Apocalypse Now*. War and its glorifications have become obscenities.

Meanwhile, the figure of the soldier-poet has fallen victim to hyperspecialization. Soldiers' endless training and retraining, practicing and strategizing, and simply managing their vast organizations demands strenuous, full-time attention. If they are "bored for their countries" it is not thanks to lack of employment. And of course they are segregated from the rest of society, in bases, camps, and barracks, often thousands of miles from their homes. In such settings, gentlemanly figures like Saint-Lambert have no place, and Napoleon would probably have been pushed toward early retirement after a series of unsatisfactory psychological profiles and fitness tests ("easily distracted from the job at hand, little enthusiasm for routine tasks, poor team player").

What made Napoleon unusual was less his dream of literary glory than the single-minded zeal with which he pursued it. Nothing could have been more natural for him, once peacetime ennui had given way to the fury of the Revolutionary Wars, than to transfer this zeal to the profession for which he had been trained since childhood. Napoleon did not embrace war because he had failed at literature. War embraced him and gave him a new opportunity to succeed. There is an irony to the story, however. For by the time his ambitions had collapsed at Waterloo, Napoleon had made war a more "professional," strenuous occupation than it had been before. Napoleon the emperor, in other words, made it likely that there would never again be another Napoleon the novelist.

3

Brushes with Power: Napoleon and Art

Napoleon not only had genuine literary talent, but a keen sense for brilliant visual images, especially of himself. From his earliest military successes in Italy in 1796–1797 he used this sense to present himself to the French people as the incarnation of youth and glory, and as a political savior figure. He knew the importance of newspapers, of engravings, of architecture, and of painting. It is small wonder that some of the greatest visual artists of the age did some of their greatest works in his service, including images of Napoleon that even today remain hugely familiar, and not just in France. This essay considers his relationship with the painter Jacques-Louis David, as revealed by an important 2005 museum exhibition.

In a brilliant scene in Andrzej Wajda's film *Danton*, Robespierre, the guiding spirit of the Reign of Terror, pays a visit to the studio of the painter Jacques-Louis David. On a wall, he sees David's unfinished tableau of *The Tennis Court Oath*, depicting a central event of the early

Book under Review: Philippe Bordes, *Jacques-Louis David: Empire to Exile* (Yale University Press, 2005) (and exhibit at the Clark Institute, Williamstown, Massachusetts). Essay originally published in *The New Republic*, August 22, 2005.

French Revolution. Robespierre points to one of the men whom David has sketched in and says coldly, "He was not there." "Yes, he was," David protests. "He was not," Robespierre repeats, "and besides, he's a traitor. Take him out." And he marches off, leaving the painter mutely to comply with his dictates.

The scene never actually took place. It is the Polish director's allegory of Stalinist airbrushing, produced in the dark time of General Wojciech Jaruzelski. But its plausibility reveals something of the uneasiness that David's career, with its tight braiding of art and politics, can still generate, more than two hundred years after the French Revolution. No great figure in Western art had a more intense involvement with radical politics than this presiding genius of neoclassicism, and none was more compromised by it. From 1792 to 1794, David sat as a member of the French National Convention. He belonged to the Committee of General Security, a key body in the implementation of the Terror. He voted to condemn King Louis XVI to death and narrowly escaped going to the guillotine himself in 1794. (He did spend time in prison.) And in his monumental work *The Death of Marat*, he produced a painting that transforms one of the most repellent and murderous demagogues of all time into a martyr of Christ-like dimensions. The fact that the painting is also one of the greatest pieces of political art of all time, the *Pietà* of the revolutionary age, makes it even more disquieting.

Predictably enough, it is not the political art of the Terror that has prompted the most consistent reproofs of David. Radicalism, however sanguinary, will often be excused on the grounds of its sincerity. David has attracted the most scorn for the work that he produced in the last quarter century of his life, particularly in the service of Napoleon. Consider *Napoleon Crossing the Saint-Bernard*, the painting that first greets visitors to "Jacques-Louis David: Empire to Exile," an exhibition at the Sterling and Francine Clark Institute in Williamstown. It is still the most familiar image of Napoleon—think brandy advertisements—and its astonishing evocation of the whipping wind and the rearing horse, its dramatic rendition of an individual set alone against the elements, represents the closest that David, a cool admirer of Poussin, ever came to Romanticism.

Originally commissioned for the king of Spain, the painting also served an important propaganda purpose, implicitly attributing the successes of the Second Italian Campaign of 1800 to Napoleon's genius alone (rather than, say, to the revolutionary fervor of his armies). It therefore helped pave the way for the replacement of the first French Republic by a hereditary Napoleonic Empire. And it was only the first of many works of fawning adoration that David would produce of the man who would soon appoint him his First Painter, commanding vast fees. The artist's radicalism had apparently decomposed into nothing but simple, selfish opportunism. The speed of the transition disgusts David's critics and leaves even his admirers uneasy.

This unease is one of two reasons why David's work in this period has never before been the subject of a major exhibition. (I will come to the second reason in a moment.) And it is a bad reason. David was never anything remotely like a hack, and his work for Napoleon was often powerful and brilliant. Moreover, it grew out of far more than just opportunism. If some of the paintings done between 1799 and 1815 lack the inspiration of David's prerevolutionary and revolutionary periods, others vividly convey the thrill that so many of the French felt at living in what seemed like a new age of Alexander. The dazzling victories that came between 1800 and 1809—Marengo, Ulm, Austerlitz, Jena, Friedland, Wagram—together with Napoleon's ability to restore order and prosperity to a country wracked by revolutionary chaos and civil war, generated very real support and excitement, and made the emperor a mythical figure. Even Chateaubriand, who despised Napoleon's tyranny, called him a "poet of action."

Today we find Napoleon's militaristic cult of personality sinister and kitschy, rendering David's support for it only somewhat less disturbing than his earlier allegiance to Robespierre. Still, there is every reason to assume that the Napoleonic enthusiasm of the painter, whose twin daughters both married Napoleonic generals, was genuine, and inspirational. Back home in 1807, after a long stay in Italy, he wrote that France seemed to have become a literally brighter, more sharply defined place since the coming of the Empire: "It seemed to me on my return that I had just had a cataract operation."

The works chosen for the Clark exhibition give an excellent sense of what he meant. The Napoleonic grandees who commissioned portraits from David, resplendent in their gaudy uniforms, are the very incarnation of imperially conspicuous wealth and power. Antoine Français de

Nantes, who collected taxes from an empire that stretched from Hamburg to Barcelona and Dubrovnik, seems practically to disappear under his almost comically splendid blue costume. David's son-in-law Claude-Marie Meunier, painted with broad, rapid, very un-Davidian brushstrokes, has an expression of amused boldness, while the red ribbon of the Legion of Honor gleams brightly against his intricate gold-embroidered black uniform.

And then there is Napoleon himself, in the *Saint-Bernard*, and in David's other great portrait of him, from 1811, *Napoleon in His Study*. This work, a civilian pendant to its predecessor, shows the emperor rising from his desk at 4:12 a.m., candles guttering in the lamp, having just put in a full night working on his new Civil Code. Here there are no Alps to conquer, only the mountains of frustrating legal paperwork that had bedeviled the French for centuries, and that the Code indeed reduced to manageable proportions. But David conveys the same sense of Herculean dedication and superhuman ability as before. The *Saint-Bernard* may have been pure mythmaking, but *Napoleon in His Study* gives a perfectly accurate picture of the emperor's eighteen-hour-a-day work habits. As Talleyrand famously quipped, "What a pity the man wasn't lazy."

Art historians have often speculated about a continuing sentimental loyalty to the Revolution on David's part, but there is little trace of it in these works. Perhaps it shows through, faintly, in his sympathetic portrait of the daughter of the Jacobin martyr Le Peletier de Saint-Fargeau, from 1804. Perhaps it comes out in the thicket of bayonets that rise up in the very lower right of *Napoleon Crossing the Saint-Bernard*, recalling revolutionary engravings of the people in arms—but this is a tiny detail. Philippe Bordes, in his engrossing book that is the catalogue to the show, quotes David's supposed words on hearing of Napoleon's coup d'état: "Well, I had always thought for sure that we were not virtuous enough to be republicans." The note of resignation, as well as the false and boastful claim to prescience, rings true.

The best sense of the older David's changing political attitudes comes less in his depiction of his contemporaries than in his paintings of classical subjects. David made his reputation, before the Revolution, with utterly stern, uncompromising visions of classical republican virtue: particularly *The Oath of the Horatii* in 1784 and *Victors Bringing Brutus the Bodies of His Sons* in 1789. In the latter, a hero of the early Roman republic, having ordered the execution of his own sons for treason, sits somberly, in shadow, as their bodies are brought to him: an Abraham who went through with the deed. To highlight Brutus's total dedication and self-command, the painter sets the dark figure off against his brightly lit wife and daughters, who watch the scene in a state of wild, despairing grief. No work of art better captured the mentality that allowed the Jacobins to feel virtuous in sending tens of thousands of their fellow citizens to the guillotine. No work of art helped more to inspire them to do so.

In his later work, by contrast, David preferred Greece to Rome, mythology to history. These paintings (on the whole rather inferior) mostly lack the earlier contrast of light and darkness, preferring cheerful, almost pastel colors. The sharp gender distinctions (which foreshadowed literal attempts to expel women from the public sphere) are missing as well. A painting from 1819 titled *The Anger of Achilles* again returns to the subject of a parent's slaughter of a child—in this case, Agamemnon's sacrifice of Iphigenia to gain a favorable wind from the gods on the eve of the Trojan War. But here David has twisted the story to make Achilles into Iphigenia's betrothed and highlights the great warrior's rage at the manifestly unjust deed. Other works, such as *The Departure of Hector*, a crayon drawing from 1812, infuse the male figures with a tenderness that the earlier David might have frowned on.

Bordes's marvelously produced catalogue, while meticulous and informative, does not really do enough to convey such points. Divided into separate essays on different aspects of David's late career, it assumes a great deal of prior knowledge and never provides a full introduction to the painter's life or to the period in which he lived. Yet if the book will occasionally overwhelm or frustrate the casual reader, cognoscenti will delight in the wonderfully complete detail on each picture, not to mention the oblique, caustic little jabs at colleagues that Bordes occasionally delivers. The world of David scholarship, as befits its subject, is not a gentle place. Bordes also does an excellent job of relating David's art to his more material preoccupations—especially his anxious desire to bestow huge dowries, worthy of an Old Regime nobleman, on his twin daughters. As the catalogue reminds us, David was one of the first Western artists to demand that the public buy tickets to see his work— he needed the money, he explained, to provide himself with "the noble independence proper to genius."

As this quotation suggests, Bordes's readers will also get a very good sense of another crucial factor in David's work: his sense of self-importance. Hailed while still in his thirties as the greatest painter of modern times, David rarely hesitated to describe himself as a "genius," or to boast that he had put the French School "at par with the great period of the Italian School." In the unsatisfying and long-unfinished painting *Alexander, Apelles, and Campaspe*, he clearly meant to compare himself to the most renowned of Greek artists, while casting Napoleon in the familiar role of Alexander, who supposedly gave Apelles his favorite mistress. David's difficulties with the work may well reflect his frustrations with his imperial patron, who in later years disparaged the huge, ambitious tableau *Leonidas at Thermopylae* because he did not like the subject of military defeat, and did not hesitate to play his favorite artists off against each other. On first seeing the sublime *Napoleon on the Battlefield of Eylau*, painted in 1808 by David's former student Antoine-Jean Gros, the emperor said nothing, but removed the ribbon of the Legion of Honor from his own chest and pinned it on the artist. One can only imagine the reaction of the "First Painter" on hearing the story.

David's self-importance may also help explain why he changed his Neoclassical style so little after making his reputation in the 1780s. Viewers of his paintings from the early 1820s may notice some changes in tone and color from the days of *Brutus*, due perhaps to the influence of the Flemish School (he was living in Brussels). It remains hard to believe that in the very same years Delacroix, Géricault, Turner, and Friedrich were producing some of the most powerful works of the Romantic movement in painting.

Mercifully for the casual reader, Bordes avoids the feminist and psychoanalytical approach that has characterized much recent David scholarship, particularly Ewa Lajer-Burcharth's influential book *Necklines: The Art of Jacques-Louis David after the Terror*. Her dense Lacanian study has much to offer, particularly in regard to David's explorations of gender roles, and the changing relation in his work between the body and the sense of individual character—of the self. But like too many art historians today, Lajer-Burcharth has a tendency to zoom beyond such close analyses into the cloudy realm of high-theoretical speculation, as in this riff on David's famous prison self-portrait of 1794 (on display at the Clark), in which the painter put his left cheek in shadow to hide a disfiguring tumor: "David's cheek thus announces itself as the site of that fraught symbolic transaction with language for which one always has to pay with a 'pound of flesh'—a sign, that is, of *symbolic* castration that accompanies all subjects' entry into language." For Bordes, thankfully, an ugly tumor is sometimes just an ugly tumor.

The exhibition at the Clark, laid out with admirable clarity and restraint, generally avoids any risky galloping along the art-historical frontier. Where historians have energetically discussed David's debts to Lavater and the emerging science of "physiognomy," the exhibition satisfies itself with helpfully putting a contemporary book of physiognomic "types" on display; where feminist scholars have debated the meanings of changing female costume after the Terror, the show simply provides a contemporary book of engravings of fashion and lets the visitors draw their own conclusions.

And the exhibition reveals, quite unexpectedly, a pawky, even playful streak in a painter usually regarded as a master of high historical tragedy. After finishing his portrait of the sensually plump Comtesse Daru in 1810, we learn, David could not help confessing to "indiscreet thoughts" about her. In one of two splendid portraits of the Comte Turenne from 1816, he placed the young nobleman's coat of arms inside his hat, where one would expect the manufacturer's label.

Yet there is a problem with this sumptuous and original revival of David's art. It is the other reason why David's late career has never before been the subject of a major exhibition: three of the painter's most important later works—*The Coronation, The Distribution of the Eagles*, and *Leonidas at Thermopylae*—are so mammoth, collectively measuring more than fifteen hundred square feet, as to make their transportation an expensive improbability. They are all in Paris or Versailles, and they have not, to my knowledge, been brought together even there, to say nothing of in California or Massachusetts. Any exhibition of David's last quarter century therefore runs the risk of having a *Hamlet*-without-the-prince quality, and of losing sight of the monumentally ambitious scale on which David worked throughout much of the First Empire.

In an effort to make up for the absence of the three giants, the curators have substituted a series of studies that David carried out while working on them: the head of one of Josephine's ladies-in-waiting for *The Coronation*, a sketch of one of the emperor's guardsmen for the *Eagles*, compositional studies for *Leonidas*, and so forth. Among other things, these studies display David's superlative skill with a black crayon. But set alongside the many other small drawings on display and the impressive series of life-size portraits, they give the misleading impression of a painter most comfortable working on a small scale. It requires careful reading of the exhibition materials, and a certain imaginative effort, to keep in mind that during much of the period David was not, for the most part, working in solitude on portraits and drawings, but directing the efforts of a large atelier to produce paintings of huge size, complexity, and ambition.

For the same reason, the exhibition fails fully to convey the disjuncture between David's career under Napoleon and what followed in the last decade of his life. After the fall of the Empire in 1815, not only did the painter lose his best and wealthiest client, but the restored Bourbon monarchy banished him from France, on account of his vote to decapitate the new king's elder brother in 1793. Nearly seventy years old, David moved to Belgium, where he remained active, painting portraits and private commissions, but on a terribly reduced scale. The artist who had spent much of his career providing the definitive vision of climactic moments in world history was now reduced to sympathetic little portraits of fellow exiles. At the Clark, the striking oil of General Maurice-Étienne Gérard jostles with several far less inspired portraits and some versions of Greek myths that stray toward the insipid.

And so, despite the fact that David preserved a remarkable technical skill until the end of his life, the story ends on a plangent note. Political disillusionment, professional disaster, and old age combine to produce their inevitable result. Yet one has only to remember how close David came to execution in 1794 to realize that for all the trauma of his exile and decline, he was still a very lucky man. One has only to reflect on how many other people he helped send to the guillotine to wonder whether he deserved his luck. And one has only to gaze on the seductively glorious portrait of Napoleon crossing the Saint-Bernard—"the world-spirit... on horseback, stretching out to dominate the world," as Hegel famously remarked after glimpsing the emperor from his window in 1806—to recall that great political art and great political virtue finally have very little to do with each other.

4

One Does It Like This: Napoleon's "Shit in a Silk Stocking"

ONE OF NAPOLEON'S GENUINELY IMPRESSIVE personal qualities was his ability to recognize talent in others and his readiness to surround himself with brilliant men. (Brilliant women were a different matter, as shown by his notoriously difficult relations with Germaine de Staël.) He so valued the companionship of the great mathematician Gaspard Monge that he personally went to plead with Monge's wife to let her husband depart on the Egyptian expedition of 1798. He made the jurist Jean-Jacques Régis Cambacérès the principal author of his law code, and then arch-chancellor of the Empire, despite Cambacérès's homosexuality. And he formed a long and unlikely partnership with the enormously talented—if also enormously corrupt—statesman Talleyrand, the subject of the biography reviewed here. Indeed, even when Talleyrand engaged in high treason, Napoleon did no more than send him into internal exile. He would later pay a heavy price for this act of mercy.

Napoleon and his chief diplomat, Charles-Maurice de Talleyrand, are usually seen as the oddest of history's odd couples. One personified

---

Book under Review: David Lawday, *Napoleon's Master: A Life of Prince Talleyrand* (Cape, 2006). Essay originally published in *The London Review of Books*, November 16, 2006.

boldness, ambition, and overblown operatic passion; the other, subtlety, irony, and world-weary cynicism. One displayed such restless physical energy that contemporaries repeatedly reached for that newly hatched adjective "electric" to describe him; the other was sickly and pallid and had a club foot. Politically, one wanted to conquer the world, while the other thought France would do very well within its "natural boundaries," and even conspired with the country's enemies to put it back there. The two most familiar images of the men express the contrast eloquently. First, there is David's brilliant portrait of Napoleon on his rearing charger in the Alps, seemingly master of the wind, rocks, and sky; second, Chateaubriand's acid description of Talleyrand hobbling into the presence of Louis XVIII with the help of Napoleon's sinister police chief: "A door suddenly opened. Silently, there entered vice, leaning on the arm of crime, M. de Talleyrand walking with the support of M. Fouché."

In fact, the two men had far more in common than is usually recognized. Both had an astonishing intelligence and capacity for work. Both were extraordinarily ambitious, the aristocratic former priest no less than the former junior artillery officer. The story of how Napoleon's ingenuity drove the British out of Toulon and won him promotion to general at the age of twenty-four is well known. But Talleyrand, in his late twenties, managed the equally impressive feat of becoming the "agent-general" of the entire French clergy and defending its interests so well that his colleagues voted him the enormous gift of 100,000 French pounds. Both had oversize cravings, although Napoleon sought power and Talleyrand lusted especially after money (both also had a considerable appetite for women). Despite their political differences, both instinctively resisted fanaticism, and throughout most of their careers worked to heal the scars of the French Revolution—with equal lack of success.

Both were also extraordinary performers, each carefully crafting the persona he showed to the world (this is probably what made them both so exceptionally quotable). From the days of his first Italian campaign in 1796–1797, Napoleon consciously promoted himself as the great Romantic hero, influencing his portrayal in newspapers, engravings, paintings, and the theater. But Talleyrand's world-weary aristocrat, so carefully groomed and powdered, with languorous speech and exquisite manners, was no less of a pose. David Lawday, in his new biography, tells one of the great stories about Talleyrand, which, although perhaps apocryphal, expresses precisely the effect the man intended to have. A Jacobin radical bursts into his study during the Terror, and Talleyrand gives him a glass of cognac, which he immediately starts to guzzle. Talleyrand stops him:

> "No, no, no, that is not the way to drink cognac. One does it like this. One takes the glass in the hollow of the hand, one warms it, one shakes it with a circular motion to liberate the scent, then one raises it to one's nostrils, one breathes it in."
> "And then?" sighs his panicked visitor.
> "And then, Sir, one puts one's glass down and one discusses it!"

While Talleyrand cannot compete with Napoleon in terms of sheer volume of biographical material, his life has nonetheless attracted more than its share of talented chroniclers, including Crane Brinton, André Castelot, Jean Orieux, and the French politician Michel Poniatowski (not to mention the prolific historian Louis Madelin, to whose 1944 effort an American publisher appended the subtitle "A Vivid Biography of the Amoral, Unscrupulous and Fascinating French Statesman"). For authority and learning, it will be a long time before Emmanuel de Waresquiel's recent eight-hundred-page volume is improved on. And as far as sheer literary art goes, the British diplomat Duff Cooper's 1932 study remains unsurpassed. True, the debates about Talleyrand are usually fairly superficial. Until Waresquiel, most French scholars had an understandably difficult time getting beyond Talleyrand's plotting with Metternich and Alexander I against France during wartime, and his engineering of the hapless Bourbons' return to the throne in 1814. The twentieth-century Sorbonne potentate Georges Lefebvre called Talleyrand one of the "most despicable characters in the history of France." British and American writers have been more understanding, perhaps because they find Talleyrand so perfectly expressive of all their most beloved clichés of Frenchness. As Lawday puts it: "To grasp Talleyrand is better to grasp that elusive race, the French."

In scholarly terms, Lawday's work does little to deepen our understanding of Talleyrand. For research, he has relied principally on Waresquiel and earlier biographers, and on printed correspondence. In terms of argument, he mostly takes up the familiar Anglophone pro-Talleyrand position, pushing particularly the idea of Talleyrand as peacemaker and oracle of European unity. It is not an unreasonable idea, but others have formulated it before him, and it requires an uncomfortable reliance on Talleyrand's letters and self-serving memoirs. Lawday also has a shaky grasp of non-Talleyrandian French history. Louis XV did not "rule the country according to the unbudging feudal concepts of his Bourbon forefathers." Louis XVI was his predecessor's grandson, not his son, was not stopped by the "police" at Varennes, and was not executed on January 23. Napoleon was not promoted to "major" after Toulon. The early nineteenth-century Duc de Richelieu was not (rather obviously) a "direct descendant" of Cardinal Richelieu. Minor errors, for the most part, but they do undermine one's confidence.

More significant, Lawday falls into the familiar biographer's trap of consistently exaggerating his subject's importance. From reading this book, one would think that Talleyrand had a major role in bringing about the Revolution of 1789 (he didn't), and almost single-handedly devised the subsequent, disastrous reform of the French Church (he belonged to a large herd of politicians all stumbling in the same direction). Talleyrand had innovative ideas on primary education, but that hardly makes him the father of the modern French education system. He took part in plotting the events of 18 Brumaire and welcomed Napoleon's rise to power, but was not the instigator of the coup (that dubious honor belongs to Emmanuel Sieyès). Was he "the most renowned world statesman of the age"? What about Metternich? And then there is the unfortunate title of Lawday's book. Talleyrand was successively Napoleon's patron, ally, counsellor, betrayer, and enemy, but never his "master." Lawday quotes an exchange between Talleyrand and the restored Louis XVIII in 1814, in which the king asks: "How did you bring down the Directory, and now the colossal power of Bonaparte?" "My God, Sire, I really did nothing like that!" Talleyrand replies. For once, he was telling nothing but the truth, and Lawday should have listened. (Talleyrand added, with characteristic wit: "There is just something inexplicable about me that brings misfortune on governments that neglect me.")

Still, this is a brisk, enjoyable book, which, if it lacks Duff Cooper's flair, also avoids his occasional ponderousness. Starting in medias res with Napoleon's decisive break with Talleyrand in 1809, during which he threatened Talleyrand with execution and called him "a shit in a silk stocking," Lawday then moves in a straightforward manner through Talleyrand's eighty-four-year life. Over three-quarters of the book deals with the period of the French Revolution and Napoleon, but this is entirely appropriate.

Talleyrand himself famously remarked that only those who had lived during the Old Regime truly knew the "sweetness of life" (*douceur de vivre*, which Lawday oddly renders as "joy of life"). Yet this was itself, in part, a postrevolutionary pose, for Talleyrand's own early years under the ancien régime had more than their share of bitterness. He was the oldest son of an ancient noble family, but his club foot kept him from the military vocation of his class, and led his parents to treat him with even more indifference than French aristocrats ordinarily showed their children. In his memoirs, he recounted that an uncle was shocked to find him, alone and in rags, chasing sparrows, and took him to an elegant house where they saw a man and a woman receiving guests. "'Go on, my lord and nephew," the uncle told him. "Kiss this lady, she is your mother."

With the army ruled out, Talleyrand instead headed into the Church. At the seminary of Saint-Sulpice he paid little attention to his studies, preferring to major in seditious literature and minor in actresses, but these choices proved little impediment to a clerical career. (He showed excellent taste in women in establishing a short liaison and long friendship with Germaine Necker, the future Madame de Staël.) After finishing his training, he moved rapidly through the Church hierarchy, doing particularly well as agent-general. At just thirty-four he was consecrated bishop of Autun. Had the French Revolution not occurred, he would most likely have ended up a cardinal.

Instead, he was swept up in a tornado of possibilities. When the Revolution began in 1789, he quickly emerged as a prominent liberal reformer. On July 14, 1790, in his episcopal robes, he celebrated Mass at the triumphant Festival of the Federation in Paris. Not long afterward, his support for the nationalization of the Church led to his excommunication. But he could not keep up with the Revolution's rush to the left, and when the monarchy fell in August 1792, he fled the country, ending up in Philadelphia. There, desperate to revive his finances, he became deeply involved in land speculation and even took a long trip on horseback to inspect some possible purchases in upstate New York. Lawday has a wonderful vignette of the fastidious Talleyrand and his servant spending the night in a trapper's cabin. But unlike his fellow exile Chateaubriand, Talleyrand had no real attraction to the wilderness, and once the Terror ended, he soon returned to France.

Getting back, he found that his disenchanted and cynical mood had become a perfect match for his country's. Mme de Staël introduced him to Paul Barras, strongman of the new Directorial regime, and within a year he had become foreign minister. According to Benjamin Constant, who went with him to thank Barras, he kept repeating "we shall make an immense fortune...an immense fortune...an immense fortune." Indeed, he soon started collecting bribes on a large scale, and his attempt to squeeze £50,000 out of three American diplomats (the "XYZ Affair") helped bring France to the brink of war with the United States. With Talleyrand, self-interest often trumped the demands of diplomacy.

To be sure, as Lawday points out, Talleyrand developed very early on a cautious and consistent vision of international relations. It was grounded in the Enlightenment conviction that the age of war had given way to the age of commerce, making military conquest fundamentally counterproductive, even when waged for a just cause. In 1799, Talleyrand would tell the French parliament that "any system intended to bring liberty by open force to neighboring nations can only make liberty hated and prevent its triumph." Yet these convictions did not stop him from supporting the Directory's relentless expansionism or spouting bile against the British when the political mood demanded it. Nor did they keep him from striking up an alliance with the most successfully aggressive French general of the day, Napoleon, whom he praised most unconvincingly as a reborn Cincinnatus ("far from fearing his ambition, I believe that one day we shall perhaps beg him to return from the comforts of a studious retirement"—oops). Talleyrand even helped devise Napoleon's disastrous Egyptian expedition of 1798–1799. In short, he was already playing a double game, preaching restraint while abetting expansion, and lining his pockets in the process.

This game continued when Napoleon seized power late in 1799 and reappointed Talleyrand as foreign minister. Perhaps sensing the traits they had in common despite their clashing public personae, the two men established a remarkably close rapport that lasted for a decade.

("He has got inside me," Napoleon allegedly confided to his secretary; "what he advises is just what I want to do.") Talleyrand served Napoleon as France launched a second invasion of Italy in 1800 and then as it negotiated a general European peace in 1802. He remained in office as this peace quickly broke down (in large part thanks to French aggression), and then as Napoleon launched his armies eastward in 1805, eventually crushing Austria and Prussia and establishing French control over central Europe. He literally stood by, a wry smile on his face (at least in David's painting of the event), as Napoleon crowned himself emperor in Notre-Dame. And although resigning as foreign minister in 1807, he remained outwardly loyal as Napoleon turned his gaze south, and invaded Portugal and Spain. In return for his support he collected grandiose titles—grand chamberlain of the Empire, Prince of Benevento—and grew very, very rich.

Talleyrand did, admittedly, attempt to restrain Napoleon's ambitions. He tried hard to keep the peace of 1802–1803 from breaking down and after Austria's 1805 defeat negotiated a peace settlement more generous than Napoleon wished. By 1808, when Napoleon sent him to Erfurt to negotiate with the tsar, Talleyrand was actively plotting *against* Napoleon. "It is up to you to save Europe," he allegedly told Alexander, "and you will only succeed by standing up to Napoleon. The French people are civilised, their sovereign is not. The sovereign of Russia is civilised, his people are not. The sovereign of Russia must therefore be the ally of the French people." Talleyrand started sending advice and information to Metternich, and even conspired with Fouché, the priest turned radical revolutionary turned Napoleonic spymaster, to ease Napoleon off the throne in favor of his brother-in-law Joachim Murat. As Duff Cooper inimitably put it: "This was treachery, but it was treachery upon a magnificent scale."

In 1809, Napoleon learned of Talleyrand's plotting, confronted him with it in the melodramatic interview Lawday describes, and then fired him. He could not, however, bring himself to have Talleyrand shot (despite his reputation as a tyrant, he executed very few of his political opponents). By 1812, on the verge of his Russian catastrophe, he even begged Talleyrand to resume the foreign ministry. Talleyrand declined, however, and when the Empire, its strength drained away in Russia and Spain, finally collapsed, Talleyrand was there to welcome the allies into

Paris, arrange the return of the Bourbons to the throne, and help devise a new constitution. The following autumn he represented France at the Congress of Vienna, obtaining unexpectedly favorable terms for his new Bourbon masters. He even managed to draw Austria and Britain into a secret, defensive alliance against Russia and Prussia. Napoleon's improbable return to power in the Hundred Days wrecked these arrangements, but after Waterloo, Talleyrand floated to the surface yet again, becoming prime minister to the rerestored Louis XVIII (*Louis deux fois neuf*, as the Paris wits had it).

In truth, though, the days of Talleyrand's importance had nearly come to an end. While he advocated reconciliation with the revolutionary and Napoleonic past, the Restoration's reactionary parliament did not, and this led to a stalemate. Talleyrand was hardly the man to rally public opinion. He never had Napoleon's rapport with ordinary people, and his physical presence, unimpressive to start with, had only become more so as he passed his sixtieth birthday. Like most people his age in the early nineteenth century, he suffered from a host of chronic physical complaints, in his case above all from debilitating respiratory infections. Charles de Rémusat memorably described his elaborately offensive ablutions, in a passage Lawday quotes at length:

> He first appeared as an enormous bundle of flannel, muslin, twill and cottons, a whitish mass that arrived in laborious hops with scarcely a greeting for the company, then sat before the fireplace where three valets awaited him.... They at once began removing woollen stockings and flannels from his legs, plunging the limbs into a bowl of sulphur water...his head covered by a sort of cotton tiara kept in place by a pastel ribbon over a tight bonnet that came down to the eyebrows to show a pale, inanimate face.... [He consumed] via the nose a large beaker or so of warm water which he then snorted forth like an elephant from its trunk.

Not exactly Napoleon crossing the Alps. And not surprisingly, Talleyrand lasted barely two months before snuffling out of office. For the last twenty-five years of his life he remained largely a spectator, although he did come out of retirement to serve Louis-Philippe as ambassador to Great Britain. He died in 1838, negotiating his final surrender to God (would the former priest take the sacraments?) with something of his old flair and skill.

It's an extraordinary story. But it's also a story that Lawday, like most of his predecessors, has a hard time facing straight on, because it is really a story of massive failure. In the early 1790s, Talleyrand supported a moderate, liberal version of the French Revolution, and it failed. He sought to restrain Napoleon, and to end the bloody sequence of revolutionary and Napoleonic wars, and he failed, time after time. He plotted to ease Napoleon out of power and failed. He struggled to negotiate a "soft landing" for France after the terrible defeat of 1814 and failed, thanks to the Hundred Days. He tried as prime minister to set France on a middle course, and failed yet again. In the end, he succeeded principally in surviving—not such a small achievement in those dangerous days, but not a great claim on posterity's favor either.

Lawday, even more than most earlier biographers, wants to make Talleyrand a success, even something of a hero. Writing of the Treaty of Paris, which ended hostilities in 1814, he quotes two typically self-aggrandizing notes of Talleyrand: "I have finished my peace with the four great powers." "I await the judgment of posterity with confidence." Lawday comments: "Posterity did not disappoint him . . . Europe was spared a general war for all of a hundred years." In his conclusion he adds that Talleyrand had a "paternity claim" on European union. Did he really? The peace that followed 1815 came above all in response to the immense horrors of the wars that had ripped jaggedly through Europe in the previous quarter century, taking the lives of millions, touching every single state on the continent, and devastating most of them. Talleyrand had been in a better position than almost anyone to prevent those horrors. To his credit, he tried to, although not always very hard. But he failed. Ultimately, his life is testimony to the inability of individuals—even, in the end, Napoleon himself—to control the awesome currents of democracy, terror, and total war that surged through Europe in the wake of the French Revolution.

5

Was Tolstoy Right? Napoleon in Russia

IN MOST WAYS, NAPOLEON STANDS comparison with any of history's other great military commanders. As Andrew Roberts has recently stressed (in yet another biography), he won fully fifty-three of the sixty major battles he fought—an astonishing record. But military success rarely depends on battles alone, as the epic disaster of Napoleon's 1812 invasion of Russia demonstrates all too clearly. In Russia, Napoleon actually won, if not by much, the single most important battle of the campaign: Borodino. Immediately afterward, he marched triumphantly into Moscow. But if he outfought the Russians, he did not outthink them. Their strategy of a "scorched earth" retreat, which turned all too literal when they burned Moscow to the ground after it fell, left him no choice but to turn his already-depleted forces around. And then, in the howling cold of the Russian winter, his army dissolved amid scenes of phantasmagorical horror. "They were no longer living hearts, men of war," Victor Hugo would later write. "They were a dream wandering in the gloom, a mystery, a parade of shadows under a black sky." This essay discusses one of

Book under Review: Dominic Lieven, *Russia against Napoleon: The True Story of the Campaigns of War and Peace* (Viking, 2010). Essay originally published in *The New Republic* online, May 12, 2010.

the most persuasive accounts of the campaign and the reasons for the Russian victory.

———

Writing about Napoleon's invasion of Russia in *War and Peace*, Tolstoy remarked: "The historians provided cunningly devised evidence of the foresight and genius of the generals, who of all the blind instruments of history were the most enslaved and involuntary." It is not a comment that Dominic Lieven would endorse. His new book is all about the fore-sight and genius of generals—and politicians as well. More specifically, it is about the foresight and genius of Russian generals and politicians. If Napoleon failed in his bid for European domination, Lieven argues, the credit goes first and foremost to Tsar Alexander I, and to the generals and administrators who served him.

In making this argument, Lieven must take on a host of opponents. First, there are the Western historians of the Napoleonic wars, who have often presented these conflicts as the tragic epic of a single individual's hubris, with the Russians reduced to supporting parts. Then there are the Russian historians and politicians who long downplayed the tsar and his generals, while highlighting the heroism of the Russian people as a whole. And there is the looming figure of Tolstoy himself, with his dis-dain for historians, and his own mystical exaltation of the Russian people and of historical destiny. In *War and Peace*, the great Russian military characters are the common soldier Platon Karataev—"the very personification of all that was Russian"—and General Kutuzov, whose genius and skill "sprang from the purity and fervor of his identification with the people."

Lieven, by contrast, not only downplays the role of the common people, but spends little time with them. In contrast to Adam Zamoyski in *Moscow 1812: Napoleon's Fatal March*, a vivid recent account of the invasion of Russia that highlights the experiences of ordinary soldiers on the French side, Lieven remains for the most part in the palaces of the monarchs and the tents of the generals. This is partly owing to a lack of source material: only two memoirs from ordinary Russian soldiers have survived. But it is mostly because Lieven believes in a very traditional sort of military and diplomatic history. It will also not escape the reader's notice that the book's dramatis personae include an attractive young

Russian major-general—"calm, tactful, self-effacing and hard-working"—named Christoph von Lieven, a direct ancestor of the author.

For the general reader, this method has its costs. While Zamoyski quotes liberally from personal correspondence and memoirs, Lieven cites very little, and then, in the manner of Leopold von Ranke, mostly from dry official correspondence and memoranda. When it comes to the burning of Moscow in 1812, Zamoyski draws on Napoleon himself: "mountains of red rolling flames, like immense waves of the sea, alternately bursting forth and lifting themselves to skies of fire, and then sinking into the ocean of flame below." But Lieven is content to state flatly that "Moscow burned for six days," and then to enumerate the damages.

Still, Lieven has a serious argument to make, and he makes it persuasively. "One key reason why Russia defeated Napoleon," he writes, "was that her top leaders out-thought him." As early as 1810, it became clear to the tsar and his men that the fragile French-Russian alliance would soon collapse and that Napoleon would invade. They understood that the French emperor would attempt to destroy the Russian army in a series of quick major battles, so as to force the country into political subordination. In response, they planned for "a war exactly contrary to what the enemy wants," to quote a key memorandum from 1812: namely a strategy of "deep retreat" to exhaust and deplete the French, followed by a full counterattack that would bring Russia's massive armies back into the heart of Europe, and ultimately (along with its allies) to the gates of Paris.

In 1812–1814, Lieven argues, the Russians followed this strategy, and with brilliant success. In doing so, they could count on several key resources, including superior cavalry (in some ways, Lieven nicely quips, the greatest Russian hero of the war was the horse), and the masses of serfs who were ruthlessly conscripted with little hope of seeing their homes again. In 1812–1814 alone, the Russian army conscripted some 650,000 men. Thanks to their status as semislaves, they were cheap, receiving pay equal to only one-eleventh of what British soldiers received.

Finally, and in sharp distinction to Tolstoy and the Russian nationalist historians of the conflict, Lieven believes that the "aristocratic, dynastic and multiethnic" qualities of the Russian empire constituted a real strength as well. In particular, he highlights the effective cooperation of the nobility and the tsar, and the key role played by military officers of foreign descent, especially Germans from the Baltic states such as his ancestor. (They made up 7 percent of all Russian generals.) While he gives due credit to Tolstoy's idol Kutuzov, he reserves his greatest praise for the war minister and then supreme commander Mikhail Barclay de Tolly, the descendant of Baltic Germans and Scots.

At times Lieven pushes his argument very hard. Were the tsar's fits of hysterical anger a sign of the mental instability for which his family was famous? Lieven prefers to call one of them "the performance of a brilliant actor letting off steam." Maybe. Was the Russian army's escape after the key battle of Borodino a matter of luck and Napoleon's blunders? Lieven thinks the Russians planned well enough that they would have escaped even if, at a key moment, Napoleon had thrown his reserve into the fray. On most of these specific points, though, Lieven deserves the benefit of the doubt, thanks to the heroic job of research that he has brought off. He has explored a wealth of new archival material (some of it only available since the fall of the Soviet Union), and his book will stand as the definitive account of the Russian war effort unless and until other historians go through the same material and reach different conclusions.

When it comes to the war as a whole, however, Lieven's account suffers from being nearly as one-sided as the Western ones he criticizes. He rarely cites the abundant French source material and French works of history even less. He gives scant attention to the strengths and the weaknesses of the French imperial regime that the Russians helped to defeat, and surprisingly little to Napoleon—including such pertinent factors as the painful physical ailments that distracted the emperor during the invasion, and quite possibly made a crucial difference at Borodino. Enormously useful as it is for understanding the Russian side of the equation, Lieven's work cannot fully explain the overall course of events.

Similarly, Lieven's focus on military decision-making limits the extent to which his book can contribute to a broader political and cultural understanding of the period. There is no trace here of the Romantic and occasionally messianic Napoleon who saw himself as the new Alexander the Great and proposed to the tsar a joint conquest of India. Lieven even characterizes Napoleon's invasion of Russia as a "cabinet war fought for strictly limited political purposes," similar to the limited wars undertaken by European monarchs before the French Revolution. One would hardly guess from such a description that it was also the largest military operation in European history up to that point, a colossal gamble by a man who had altered European borders and politics more violently than anyone since the Caesars, and a conflict widely seen across the continent as an apocalyptic battle between good and evil. By 1815, as the historian Paul Schroeder has put it, Tsar Alexander himself dreamed of making the Gospels the basis for European politics, and "banishing war and conflict from the earth," but Lieven's book dwells little on this dimension of the war, even on the Russian side. To grasp it, readers will still need to turn elsewhere—perhaps even to Tolstoy.

6

Violets in Their Lapels: Napoleon's Legend

IT WAS LEO TOLSTOY, in War and Peace, *who wrote perhaps the greatest (not to mention the funniest) literary portrayal of Napoleon. Consider this passage: "The Emperor Napoleon had not yet left his bedroom and was finishing his toilet. Uttering little snorts and grunts, he presented now his stout back, now his plump hairy chest to the flesh-brush with which a valet was rubbing him down. Another valet, with his finger over the mouth of a bottle, was sprinkling eau-de-Cologne on the Emperor's pampered person." Needless to say, Tolstoy's success has not stopped many later novelists from trying their hands at fictionalizing Napoleon—with distinctly mixed results, as this essay shows. But besides towering over nearly all the later efforts, Tolstoy's portrait reveals a great deal about how Napoleon's posthumous reputation has evolved. There are some historical figures whom it is exceedingly difficult to imagine "en toilette." "Did anybody ever see Washington naked?" asked Nathaniel Hawthorne. "I imagine he was born with his clothes on and his*

Books under Review: Sudhir Hazareesingh, *The Legend of Napoleon* (Granta, 2004); Patrick Rambaud, *The Retreat* (Picador, 2005); Max Gallo, *Napoleon: The Eternal Man of St. Helena*, translated by William Hobson (Macmillan, 2005); Sudhir Hazareesingh, *The Saint-Napoleon: Celebrations of Sovereignty in Nineteenth-Century France* (Harvard University Press, 2004); Stuart Semmel, *Napoleon and the British* (Yale University Press, 2004). Essay originally published in *The London Review of Books*, June 23, 2005.

hair powdered." Not Napoleon. He remains, despite his attempts at imperial splendor, a man of the people whom it is very easy indeed to imagine in intimate circumstances. This essay examines the ways Napoleon has been imagined and represented over the two centuries since his defeat and exile.

France, it has often been said, is a democracy with the manners of an absolute monarchy. Think of the ceremonial splendor with which French presidents surround themselves, the haughty, distant style they tend to adopt, or the way relationships within their entourages tend to mimic, with delicious self-consciousness, patterns of favoritism and intrigue developed long ago at the court of Versailles. No Western head of state in recent memory (British monarchs included) has had a more regal touch than François Mitterrand, alleged socialist. Nothing is more alien to mainstream French democracy than American-style "populism." The word *populiste* is a deadly insult.

This aspect of French culture helps explain why France remains so conflicted by the memory of Napoleon Bonaparte, for he was an absolute monarch with the manners of a democrat. Of course, he tried to deny it. He founded an empire, and an imperial court, buried himself under yards of ermine, and hired poets and painters by the cartload to hail him as the new Charlemagne. He turned former drummer boys and schoolteachers into dukes, made a king of Naples out of a onetime grocer's assistant, and married the niece of Marie-Antoinette. But all this pomp entirely failed to produce the desired effect. If Napoleon inspired loyalty and affection, even in defeat, it was not because of the would-be imperial splendor, but because the French people continued to see him as they had done from the start: as the "little corporal" who shared his soldiers' risks and discomforts; as the upstart provincial with the uncouth accent who outsmarted the crowned heads of Europe; as the lover of Josephine. He remained a man of the people despite himself.

If Sudhir Hazareesingh hits a wrong note anywhere in his splendid survey of Napoleon's "legend" in nineteenth-century France, it is when he compares Napoleon to de Gaulle. There are of course numerous parallels between these two generals turned "saviors of the nation," who each sought to rise above the compromises and corruptions of ordinary politics. But they differ not only in their relationship to the French Republic, which de Gaulle saved and Napoleon destroyed, but also in their places in the memory of the French people. De Gaulle, founder of the regal presidency of the Fifth Republic, continues to inspire respect, and a certain affection, but nothing like the powerful emotions felt even today about Napoleon.

Clearly, Napoleon satisfies deep longings in French popular culture, not simply for a lost era of French power and grandeur, but also for a leader with whom they feel an intimate, personal bond. It is the sort of connection that is hard to imagine having with the aloof and imperious de Gaulle. In another age, a figure like de Gaulle might have inspired epic poetry, but Napoleon demands the psychological intimacy of the novel, and indeed has probably featured in more of them than any other figure in Western history, as well as in hundreds of films. "What a novel my life has been," he remarked on Saint Helena, and few of his remarks were more acute or revealing. How many novels have been written about de Gaulle? How often, for that matter, are his name and image used to sell things? (Napoleon's image has appeared on products from brandy to chocolate to condoms, and then there is the ad for Diovol antacid showing him with his hand in its familiar place inside his vest: "Some say it was merely a pose. We think it was heartburn.") Search for "Napoleon" on eBay, and you find thousands of objects for sale: books, films, games, dolls, plates, glasses, ceramic tiles, cat cartoons, sherry decanters, brandy bottles, coffee pots, chess sets, even vintage dog food ads (many of these, admittedly, don't come from France). Type in "de Gaulle" and you find around a few hundred items, mainly stamps.

This difference, as much as anything to do with the two men's records as rulers, explains why the French elite reveres de Gaulle, but looks on Napoleon with something like embarrassed disdain. Napoleon has no grand Parisian squares named after him, only the relatively minor rue Bonaparte. In the great monument to French memory edited by Pierre Nora, *Les Lieux de mémoire*, the only essay on him concerns the pathos-laden return of his body to France in 1840. Which is to say that he receives roughly the same space as the abbey of Port-Royal, the *Larousse* dictionary, or the theme of "visits to great writers." Nonetheless, in the culture at large, he remains the object of enormous, even obsessive—if somewhat guilty—curiosity, and a fair share of devotion.

Two recent series of French novels illustrate these points. Patrick Rambaud's polished trilogy (*The Battle, The Retreat, Napoleon's Exile*) treats the emperor with fascinated scorn. The three parts move from the horrific 1809 battle of Aspern-Essling, in which forty thousand men died in thirty hours, to the disastrous retreat from Moscow in the autumn of 1812, to Paris in the final days of the empire in 1814. Napoleon himself appears only occasionally, through the cynical eyes of others. "What danger can we be in, so close to His Majesty?" one character asks another. "Catching a good bout of diarrhea, for a start," comes the reply. This Napoleon is a coarse, tired, flabby, flatulent monster, almost wholly indifferent to the massive suffering he causes.

Rambaud conveys the horrors and madness of each of his three set-pieces, picking details out of a mass of historical research. In *The Retreat*, for instance, men cut slices out of a living horse (to eat), without the horse noticing, because of the unbelievable cold. The French title of this second volume, *Il neigeait*, is taken from Victor Hugo's great poem about Napoleon, "L'Expiation." But Rambaud, unlike Hugo, sketches a war—and a Napoleon—scoured of glory or grandeur. He gives us, in other words, a powerful version of conventional establishment wisdom, pithily expressed by de Gaulle himself: "Napoleon exhausted the goodwill of the French, abused their sacrifices, and covered Europe with graves, ashes and tears." Appropriately, *The Battle* won the Prix Goncourt.

Max Gallo's million-selling quartet of novels, by contrast, gleefully embraces the myth of the "grand homme" in its most lurid, overblown form. If Rambaud displaces the focus from Napoleon to the ordinary men and women drowning in his wake, Gallo places the man front and center. Much of the novels takes the form of an endless interior monologue: the emperor recounting his own life story to himself, as it takes place. Gallo has an addiction to Napoleon's bombast, without much sense of how to convey the power of the personality that lay behind it. One portentously delivered maxim follows another, on and on. The style even extends, hilariously, to the bedroom scenes:

I am the first male.
He enters her room.
She is mine, as I wish her to be.
He lets her sleep as dawn approaches.

In the annals of bad Napoleonic fiction, Gallo's quartet ranks above even such classics as the 1931 Italian stage drama about the Hundred Days, *Campo di Maggio*, coauthored by Benito Mussolini.

Not surprisingly, serious historians today lean much more heavily toward Rambaud's view of Napoleon than Gallo's. But the repulsion they tend to feel has had the unfortunate effect of leading them to underestimate Napoleon's importance to French political life after 1815. In most accounts, Bonaparte and Bonapartism largely vanish with Waterloo, returning only to fill the vacuum left by the implosion of the Revolution of 1848—and then, in Marx's damning words from *The Eighteenth Brumaire*, as farce rather than tragedy. Both the First and Second empires still tend to be dismissed as simple dictatorships, with popular support for Napoleon and his nephew explained away with reference to longings for postrevolutionary stability or jingoistic pride in military conquest. For fifty years, the most popular interpretation of the Restoration has been that of Guillaume Bertier de Sauvigny, a descendant of a leading 1814 royalist, who portrayed a France exhausted and disgusted by Napoleon, and ready to reembrace the exiled Bourbon dynasty. And it has seemed a reasonable theory, given that Napoleon threw away millions of French lives, wrecked the country economically, and left it smaller than he found it. (When he took power in 1799, France's borders enclosed modern Belgium, Luxembourg and the Rhineland.) Surely his political popularity did not survive his defeat any more than Hitler's did.

Thanks to Hazareesingh, however, this theory is no longer tenable. In *The Legend of Napoleon*, the more ambitious of his two new books, he demonstrates convincingly, and with panache, the continuing power of popular Bonapartism long after Waterloo. Drawing on an impressive range of original sources, especially police archives from across France, he shows that Napoleon remained a popular political idol for much of the nineteenth century. After the restoration of the Bourbons,

Bonapartism was outlawed as a political movement, and open signs of loyalty to the emperor were punishable with imprisonment. Yet his image remained ubiquitous. Hazareesingh has uncovered a healthy trade in Napoleonic objects of all sorts: coins, drawings, cartoons, playing cards, tobacco boxes, tiny statuettes. On one occasion, an attempt to conceal a statuette in a wineglass led to its accidental ingestion: after nearly choking on the miniature emperor, the unlucky Bonapartist ended up in jail. Hazareesingh also reveals that a peasant claimed to see Napoleon's face in the moon, while several compatriots in the Aude insisted that his effigy was visible on the surface of a flattened egg.

Rumors of his second return to France circulated incessantly, reinforced by the regular appearance of impostors claiming the imperial purple—in the 1840s more French madmen took themselves for Napoleon than for any other figure except Jesus Christ. Others expressed hope for his return by wearing violets in their lapels—the flower comes out, as Napoleon came back, in March. His name and image remained important to underground movements, and in the immediate aftermath of the Hundred Days, attempts by the new Bourbon government to punish Bonapartist officials led to serious unrest and even violence. Napoleon's birthday, August 15, which had been France's national holiday under the Empire, remained celebrated as what Hazareesingh nicely calls an "anti-fête": a day of raucous popular exuberance and defiance of the gouty, hugely uncharismatic Bourbon placed back on the French throne by the victorious allies.

Besides Bertier de Sauvigny, Hazareesingh has a more eminent target in mind: the late François Furet, founding father of French neoconservatism. In his historical works, Furet largely ignored the survival of Bonapartism, while positing the survival of an untamed revolutionary tradition that flowed, like a powerful underground river, beneath empire and restored monarchy alike, to burst out into the open again in 1848 (and again in 1871, after the fall of the Second Empire). Hazareesingh sternly but persuasively argues that it is absurd for Furet, whose major work centered on the years 1789–1794, to assume that revolutionary politics took on its definitive form at this time and remained largely unchanged throughout the next two decades. Rather, he insists, it was largely subsumed into Bonapartism; after 1815 the two blended inextricably into each other. Napoleon might have brought the Republic to an end, but he nonetheless protected the revolutionary legacy of civil equality, popular sovereignty, religious toleration, confiscation of church lands, and the tricolor flag. When Napoleon declared, "I *am* the French Revolution," he was not entirely wrong.

Admittedly, by the time of his first surrender and abdication in 1814, Napoleon's revolutionary credentials had faded to near illegibility, thanks to his ever more grandiose imperial pretensions, his creation of a new nobility, and his reestablishment of slavery in France's Caribbean colonies after its revolutionary abolition, all crowned by his marriage to a Habsburg. Had he remained in exile on Elba, he would probably never have served as such a powerful symbol of revolutionary possibility. Indeed, had that pathetic exile continued (British journalists mocked him for needing more "Elba room"), he might never have reemerged as any sort of idol at all in France.

But as Hazareesingh notes perceptively, the Hundred Days changed everything. During this famous episode in which Napoleon returned from Elba, rallied France behind him once again, lost to Wellington at Waterloo, and sailed off to final exile on the British warship *Bellerophon*, he adopted a new, liberal constitution and openly abjured his old projects of conquest. He seduced Benjamin Constant, his keenest and sharpest liberal critic, into becoming a collaborator. And on Saint Helena, enduring the petty humiliations inflicted by his British jailer, Sir Hudson Lowe, the vaguely comic turned intensely tragic; a man mocked as pathetic emerged as a figure of vast and genuine pathos. The record of his reminiscences compiled by Emmanuel de Las Cases under the title *Mémorial de Sainte-Hélène*, and published in 1822 to enormous popular acclaim, sealed this transformation and gave Napoleon a posthumous triumph more durable than any of his military victories. In truth, the liberal turn of the Hundred Days was little more than a desperate political ploy. But for the French public, it served to associate the name of Bonaparte firmly with the Revolution—at least until Louis-Napoleon's coup, which again associated it, for good this time, with tyranny.

Not the least of the accomplishments of *The Legend of Napoleon* is to make the rise of Louis-Napoleon more comprehensible. How could this unimpressive echo of his domineering uncle, the author of two ludicrously bungled coups, rise to power and found a Second Empire more durable than the First? If Bonapartism mattered as little after 1815 as

Bertier de Sauvigny or Furet believed, then the rise of Louis-Napoleon can only be read as a sign of popular desperation, gullibility, or weakness. Hazareesingh shows instead that Louis-Napoleon built on a strong existing base of support, exploiting the association of the name Bonaparte with liberal principles. Indeed, his canny exploitation of the Bonapartist heritage not only brought him to power but kept him there until the catastrophe of the Franco-Prussian War, despite the widely detested coup of 1851 and a series of foreign adventures that ranged from dubious (the Crimea) to disastrous (an absurd attempt to turn Mexico into a client state).

Hazareesingh pursues these themes further in his second, more narrowly focused, but equally instructive new book, *The Saint-Napoléon*. Readers may initially wonder if they have missed a Napoleon among the pantheon of Catholic saints, but no one had heard of him until 1805, when Napoleon asked the pope to canonize a new saint for his birthday. With Rome under the control of the French army, the pope conveniently "discovered" a Roman martyr named Neopolis who had allegedly refused to pledge allegiance to Emperor Maximilian (he almost certainly never existed). Named the patron saint of warriors, Neopolis-Napoleon became the pretext for the most shameless propaganda ever produced by a regime that was anything but reticent in this department (think of the Vendôme column), in the form of icons of a haloed "Saint Napoleon" who bore a suspiciously exact resemblance to his modern homonym. From 1806 to 1813, the emperor's birthday and saint's day replaced July 14 as the French national holiday, and did so again after the foundation of the Second Empire in 1852, accompanied by festivals, parades, and fireworks.

In studying this holiday, Hazareesingh takes on an even more eminent target than Furet: Alexis de Tocqueville, who excoriated the Second Empire as a crass despotism, deprived of any trace of true civic spirit. While historians have long acknowledged that the Second Empire took a liberal turn in its final years, they have nonetheless largely accepted Tocqueville's view of the regime, along with Victor Hugo's scathing assessment of the emperor he dubbed "Napoléon le Petit." Only the Third Republic, it is generally argued, really managed to establish a viable civic culture in France, and to forge its diverse provinces and populations into a nation. In the famous phrase of Eugen Weber, only after 1871 did the Third Republic, and economic modernization, turn "peasants into Frenchmen."

From this point of view, one would expect the Second Empire's celebrations of the Saint-Napoléon holiday to have been sad affairs: dreary propaganda pageants performed by flunkies before a passive and resentful population. Hazareesingh, again drawing on a mass of little-known archival material from the French provinces, shows that nothing could be further from the case. For the most part, the French celebrated August 15 with genuine enthusiasm, and in large numbers. Individuals and local governments frequently took the initiative, and appropriated the holiday to their own purposes, devising all manner of illuminations, fireworks, parades, and even, in one town, "nautical jousts." The Saint-Napoléon became the principal occasion for demonstrations of French patriotism and gave the French state a way of asserting its spiritual authority over the Roman Catholic Church. Napoleon's birthday was also the Feast of the Assumption, and the coincidence allowed imperial officials to fold the religious celebrations into the national holiday, or, when the Church resisted, aggressively to enforce the primacy of the secular observances.

If Hazareesingh's pathbreaking books have a fault, it is their sometimes uncritical reliance on state records. Restoration police officials, all too aware of the regime's dubious legitimacy, were hypersensitive to any hint of resurgent Bonapartism, especially after the Hundred Days. Their meticulous records of minor and even absurd examples of support for Napoleon may testify more to this sensitivity than to anything else. In the absence of reliable statistics as to the overall state of French public opinion, it remains difficult to say for sure how typical Hazareesingh's Bonapartists really were. Similarly, in his account of the Saint-Napoléon holiday, he tends to underestimate the extent to which local officials, journalists, and the police might have found it in their interest to put on a good show each August 15, and to inflate the extent of public participation and enthusiasm in their reports.

More broadly, it is not always clear how well his evidence of popular interest and enthusiasm for the two Napoleons necessarily correlated with political sympathy for them, or, in the case of enthusiasm, with the health of the regime. A great deal of the market for Napoleonic collectibles and artifacts in the 1820s was surely driven by the same simple curiosity and fascination that now drive sales of Napoleoniana on eBay. As for the Second Empire, apolitical concern for French forces abroad may have driven liberals to take part in patriotic celebrations in much the way that some Bush-hating Americans nonetheless plastered "Support Our Troops" stickers onto their cars during the Iraq War. And what does the existence of popular enthusiasm really say about the nature of a regime? Many recent examples (the Nazis, the Chinese Cultural Revolution) suggest caution here.

While Hazareesingh finds unexpected evidence of admiration for Napoleon in nineteenth-century France, Stuart Semmel finds the same, more surprisingly, in nineteenth-century Britain. He demonstrates that even at the height of the Napoleonic Wars, when most Britons were reviling the emperor as the "Corsican Ogre," a significant minority remained admirers. This is not the only way Semmel's and Hazareesingh's work overlap, even though Semmel concentrates on Napoleon's lifetime, rather than his posthumous image. Semmel, too, singles out the Hundred Days as the crucial moment in determining Napoleon's reputation: in Britain almost as much as France, the episode turned him into a figure of genuine pathos and a liberal icon. The British authorities were so concerned about this shift that they ordered the *Bellerophon*, en route to Saint Helena in 1815, to leave British territorial waters, probably out of concern that a sympathetic magistrate might issue a writ of habeas corpus to keep Napoleon in Britain. After his safe arrival on Saint Helena, radicals lambasted the British government for its petty treatment of him there. In the words of the weekly periodical *The Black Dwarf*, Britain spent vast sums "to torture one man abroad, while tens of thousands are starving at home to furnish the expense."

At first glance, the strain of British admiration for Napoleon seems the principal novelty of Semmel's book. His broader contention that representations of the man served mainly as mirrors in which the British saw themselves is not particularly surprising. Nor is his tracing of a broad shift from early enthusiasm, through a period of intense vilification in 1808–1185 (when British soldiers were fighting the French in Iberia), and to the final phase of widely shared sympathy. Semmel makes a good case for the fractured and anxious nature of early nineteenth-century British political society, but historians of the period have been traveling in this direction for some time: it is a predictable corrective to

Linda Colley's argument for Georgian Britain's cohesion and dynamism. What sets Semmel's book apart, however, is the extraordinary richness of his analysis and the wealth of material he has uncovered.

Take the "emperor of Garrat." In the eighteenth century, the community of Garrat, south of London, regularly "elected" a laborer or artisan to the position of mayor or MP. The ritual was what Hazareesingh would call an anti-fête: a raucous, symbolic challenge to constituted authority. As far as anyone knew, it died out in the 1790s. But Semmel has discovered that the electors convened again in 1804, this time to name a muffin-seller called Harry Dimsdale as emperor, with a punchbowl as his crown. The ceremony still carried a whiff of challenge to authority in general, but its principal target was Napoleon, who in December 1804 would take part in a rather more splendid version of it in Notre-Dame.

Semmel has also uncovered the banquet held in Yarmouth to celebrate Napoleon's defeat, which featured a table three-quarters of a mile long groaning under the iconic English dishes of roast beef and plum pudding, accompanied by strong beer. While the townspeople gobbled and guzzled, an effigy of the Corsican Ogre blazed away on top of a pyramid of tar barrels. There was also the loony millenarian who tried desperately to expose Napoleon as the Beast of the Book of Revelation by writing down the Latin abbreviations for the Napoleonic titles of general, consul, and emperor—DVX, CL, I—and triumphantly explained that the numerals added up to 666. Semmel tells, too, the story of the journalist Lewis Goldsmith, who worked for Napoleon in Paris and published an English-language propaganda journal as a sort of Lord Haw Haw *avant la lettre*. Once back in Britain, Goldsmith published a sensational exposé of Napoleon and became the emperor's fiercest vilifier. Somewhere in the course of this ideological journey, incidentally, he passed William Cobbett traveling in the opposite direction, from his original Napoleon-hating conservatism to an endpoint of Napoleon-loving radicalism. By September 1815, Cobbett was publishing odes in the exiled emperor's honor: "Yet how resplendent is thy setting sun; / Transported to a living tomb.... Thy fame still lives in every Freeman's heart."

Cultural historians today often fall into the trap of treating the texts they study as elaborate and spirited word games, neglecting the emotions these texts expressed and inspired. Semmel occasionally slips in this direction, but mostly does an excellent job of recapturing the fears and hopes of this period of perilous, total war. Admittedly, it is now hard to take seriously some of the anxieties he documents as to how Britain would fare under French occupation—English porter and cheese banned in favor of *soupe-maigre* and "sour rat-gut Liquor"; London renamed "Bonapartopolis." Compared with what Hitler might have done, this seems pretty mild. But Semmel insists, rightly, that having witnessed Napoleon extend his empire across all of Europe, threatening British trade and possibly the islands themselves, many Britons thought their way of life was under threat. And during the long years in which they seemed incapable of stopping him, they genuinely doubted if they would ever be up to the task.

Given the intensity of these anxieties and doubts, the survival of a strain of Napoleonophilia throughout the wars seems all the more astonishing. Semmel sticks so closely to the texts that he does not really pay enough attention to this point, or do enough to investigate the threats and harassment that writers like Cobbett and Leigh Hunt must have incurred for supporting the leader of an enemy power in wartime. But the evidence he presents serves as a vivid and depressing reminder that, in some ways, Britain in the era of Napoleon was more open to genuine, vigorous political debate than it, or any other Western nation, is today. When did any writer in the United States openly sympathetic to the nation's enemies last have anything like the influence that Cobbett or Hunt had during the Napoleonic Wars?

Taken together, the works of Semmel and Hazareesingh raise another troubling point. Although the British people obviously were far more hostile to Napoleon than the French, the range of opinions in the two countries was remarkably similar, especially after the Hundred Days. Nearly every British writer had a close French equivalent, and this testifies eloquently to the cosmopolitanism of European elites in the immediate aftermath of the Enlightenment.

In this period, the best-educated classes of Britain and France (and Germany and Italy and America) had a better knowledge of each other's cultures than their successors do today, in the supposed age of globalization. They read more of the same books, developed parallel literary and artistic movements, and participated in more of the same debates. Even war—and even Napoleon's internment of thousands of Britons caught on French soil after the Peace of Amiens broke down in 1803—did not break off these contacts or destroy this sympathy. Napoleon might be emperor of the French, but he was the cultural property of the entire Western world.

Construction of the Eiffel Tower, in preparation for the 1889 Universal Exposition marking the centennial of the French Revolution. De Agostini Picture Library, Getty Images.

Part V

THE NINETEENTH CENTURY

NOT SURPRISINGLY, GIVEN MY TWIN INTERESTS in the revolutionary period and Vichy, my review essays on nineteenth-century France have tended to look both backward and forward. The essay here that deals with Victor Hugo, for instance, pays particular attention to his obsession with Napoleon. The later essays in this part are concerned mostly with the reactionary, anti-Semitic right that would come to power in 1940.

But this Janus-like approach does not simply reflect my own intellectual profile, or even what historians of the nineteenth century have preferred to study. In France, the nineteenth century was the great century both of history-writing and of imaginative visions of the future—of Jules Michelet and Jules Verne, of the faux Roman-Byzantine Sacré-Coeur towering over the Right Bank of Paris, and of that preeminent symbol of industrial modernity, the Eiffel Tower, across the Seine. It was the century in which historical study became professionalized in France, and in which many of the greatest historical works in the French language appeared (the name Michelet figures heavily under both these headings). Four of the century's most important French political leaders—François Guizot, Adolphe Thiers, Alphonse de Lamartine, and Jean Jaurès—wrote notable works of history. Louis-Napoleon Bonaparte, the man who ruled France for longer than anyone else in the century, came to power largely on account of his name's historical resonance. But it was also a century of utopian hopes for the future, even if those on the royalist, reactionary French right imagined the future as a return to an imagined past.

The nineteenth century was also a period in which many of the most ambitious and brilliant French minds found a more satisfying outlet in literature and the arts than in politics, with very happy results. Yet the lure of politics never entirely receded, and so literary and political passions became braided tightly together—more tightly, perhaps, than at any other time in the country's history. Many of the essays here deal with French literature, particularly in its more politicized incarnations. One of them, meanwhile, examines a novel *about* nineteenth-century France that was deliberately written in a pastiche of period style.

I

Becoming France: A Country between Traumas

THE APPEARANCE OF ROBERT GILDEA's excellent Children of the Revolution gave me the chance to offer some generalizations about nineteenth-century France as a whole. It also provided an opportunity to reflect on how historians have gone about trying to survey an entire century of a country's history. It is not an easy task, and in retrospect, the criticisms offered below might have been somewhat more tempered.

The history of France in the "long nineteenth century" is bookended by slaughter. At one end stand the revolutionary and Napoleonic wars, and at the other, World War I, both of which left the country traumatized, exhausted, and grieving for a lost generation. Remarkably, though, these two exercises in exsanguination have failed to overshadow the years in between as heavily as one might expect. France between 1815 and 1914 seems almost to belong to a different, and considerably happier, dimension of history.

Book under Review: Robert Gildea, *Children of the Revolution: The French, 1799–1914* (Harvard University Press, 2008). Essay originally published in *The New Republic*, April 1, 2009.

Seen from the outside, the reason lies mainly in literature and the arts. The names suffice to tell the story: Stendhal, Balzac, Hugo, Flaubert, Baudelaire, Rimbaud, Zola, Proust, Ingres, Delacroix, Renoir, Manet, Degas, Monet, Rodin, Berlioz, to cite only the most obvious. Rarely, if ever, has a century in the life of a nation seen such a dazzlingly intense series of artistic achievements. The French are all too painfully aware that in the ninety years since World War I they have achieved nothing entirely comparable.

In other respects as well, nineteenth-century France can be seen as something of a success story. In politics, it is certainly true that the years from 1800 to 1871 saw the country lurch back and forth between empire, monarchy, and republic, the transitions punctuated by vicious civil unrest—but the unrest was mostly short-lived (even the bloody Paris Commune of 1871 lasted only a few months), and had correspondingly small death tolls, at least in comparison with the earlier bloodletting of the French Revolution. And after 1870, France managed to transform itself into a relatively stable republic that arguably did a better job than any other nineteenth-century democracy in securing the rights and the liberties of its citizens (certainly better than the segregated, post-Reconstruction United States, or a Great Britain dominated by wealthy landed and industrial interests).

Economically, the country remained relatively undeveloped. At the end of the nineteenth century, 41 percent of the French labor force still worked on the land, compared with just 9 percent of the British, and a large majority of the population lived in villages or small towns. The lives of French peasants were hard, sometimes brutally hard, but probably less so than those of industrial workers in a Manchester factory or a Pennsylvania coal mine. Moreover, most French peasants owned their own farms, and their children had increasingly good chances of social mobility, regularly moving from the land into teaching and the civil service. All in all, France probably weathered the century's industrial revolutions as well as any major Western nation.

In foreign affairs, the French avoided repeating the epochal disasters of Napoleon's First Empire for an entire century. True, Napoleon's nephew Louis-Napoleon, who ruled from 1848 to 1870 (first as president, then as emperor), had a weakness for ill-advised military adventures in such far-flung places as the Crimea, Mexico, China, and Italy.

His brainless decision to go to war with Prussia in 1870 cost him his throne, led to a German occupation of northern France, and deprived the country of Alsace-Lorraine. Still, by the bloody standards of modernity, the mercifully short Franco-Prussian War remains a relatively minor conflict.

The country's most dubious collective enterprise during this period was the one the French themselves took the greatest pride in: the acquisition of a vast colonial empire. By 1914, the tricolor flag flew across most of western and northwestern Africa, Indochina, and a score of islands and enclaves across the world. In the twentieth century, France would pay for the conquests, the expropriation of resources, and the violent disruption of indigenous societies with its agonizing defeats in Vietnam and Algeria, and the dangerous social tensions connected with immigration from former colonies. But in 1914, few people could yet glimpse this imperial tragedy in the making.

The art of reducing a long and varied history of this sort to a book-length narrative is not an easy one. All too often, historians boil away the complexity and the flavor, leaving nothing but an insipid textbook broth of familiar facts. Yet occasionally a talented and seasoned historian can undertake the exercise in such a way as to shape understandings of a subject well beyond the academy. Nineteenth-century France has attracted more than its share of such historians. In *France in Modern Times*, which covered the Revolution and the twentieth century as well, the liberal American Gordon Wright called attention above all to ideological conflict, and lucidly showed how ideology shaped the memory and interpretation of events, as well as the events themselves. The brilliantly eccentric Briton Theodore Zeldin, who wrote many volumes on the period 1848–1945, developed what he called a "pointilliste" method, which rejected traditional chronologies and built a larger picture out of thousands of tiny snapshots of lives and events, grouped under such idiosyncratic headings as "happiness and humor," or "logic and verbalism." Francois Furet kept the focus relentlessly on politics and political philosophy, casting the period 1770–1880 as one in which France first succumbed to, and then slowly freed itself from, the great pathologies of modern politics, as expressed especially in the revolutionary Reign of Terror.

Robert Gildea has aimed to produce another work of this caliber, as part of a high-level new series. He does not match these illustrious predecessors, but he has produced a stimulating and highly readable, if somewhat uneven, volume. Despite its title, its story really begins in 1815, with only cursory treatment given to Napoleon I and his Empire. (The catastrophic Russian campaign of 1812, for instance, gets one-quarter of the space devoted to a trip to the Middle East by the poet Gerard de Nerval.)

With Zeldin as a large exception, nearly all previous students of the subject have seen their job as a kind of historical seismology, tracing out the profound and complex effects that the earthquake of the French Revolution wrought on France's political and social terrain. This is understandable enough. The French themselves remained obsessed with the Revolution and defined their politics in relation to it until well after 1914. Furet went so far as to call his volume *La Révolution: 1770–1880*. Yet this choice of frame is also a pity, for it risks reducing some of the most interesting and original aspects of the story to little more than echoes of, and reactions to, the primal event. Most obviously, it is utterly inadequate as explanatory background for the stunning literary and artistic achievements. Yes, Stendhal and Victor Hugo were obsessed by Napoleon, and yes, the arts attracted brilliant and ambitious young men who might earlier have ventured into politics, but these facts tell us nothing about the character or quality of what was created. And while a longing for lost Napoleonic grandeur surely lay behind France's launching itself into the race for empire, this point explains little about the nature of the empire, or its future trajectory. Even in politics, historians run the risk of reducing a complex and continually evolving series of conflicts to an endless replaying of the same original revolutionary scenario.

Gildea's title would suggest that he has fallen into the same familiar pattern, and in fact the book begins with a rousing salvo of clichés on the subject: "On every generation to which it gave birth the French Revolution left its mark.... The Revolution divided the French into two irreconcilable camps." The introduction then continues with a reductionist survey of the nineteenth century as the story of five generations, each of which supposedly struggled with the revolutionary legacy in its own lockstep way. The "generation of 1800" was "intensely self-aware." The "generation of 1830" was "a generation of builders rather than dreamers." The generation of 1890 tended toward ideological extremes and had a "taste for action." Like clichés about "the greatest generation" and the "baby boomers" (perhaps not coincidentally, Gildea, born in

1952, belongs to the most talked-about generation in history), such generalizations are far too broad and shallow to tell us anything serious about the periods in question.

Fortunately Gildea is too good a historian to rest his work on such a flimsy scaffolding, and after the introduction the five generations vanish from the book almost entirely. More conventionally, but also more sensibly, *Children of the Revolution* actually divides the century into two broad parts, with the dividing line at 1870–1871, when a stable republic came into being following the disaster of the Franco-Prussian War. Moreover, despite occasional references to the marks, scars, wounds, traumas, and so on of 1789, the Revolution looms over the book much less than the title would suggest. Somewhat like Zeldin, Gildea has chosen to move away from any overarching narrative at all, by dividing each of his two parts into seven chapters that look, in turn, at politics, the provinces, class structure, religion, women, the arts, and the relation between France and the wider world. (An additional chapter at the start of part 2 tells the story of the Franco-Prussian War and the Paris Commune.) At its best, this strategy works like a narrative son et lumière to illuminate different facets of the subject.

Like many British historians of France today, Gildea writes under the shadow not only of Zeldin, but of another great Oxford predecessor, Richard Cobb. Cobb devoted his career to the French Revolution, and told the story at street level, through the experiences of ordinary, often eccentric men and women struggling to survive in the political maelstrom, whom he adamantly refused to collapse into anonymous "masses" acting at the behest of abstract historical "forces." Writing from the perspective of the cynical, hard-bitten working-class Parisians among whom he lived for many years, Cobb had particular scorn for ideology and high-flown rhetoric. Gildea leaned particularly toward Cobb in his recent book *Marianne in Chains*, which examined the experience of ordinary French people under Vichy. Controversially, he reached the conclusion that collaboration with the Germans was not only more common but also more defensible than earlier historians had maintained.

Children of the Revolution is a more conventional book than Cobb or Zeldin would have written, but it bears their influence. Except for the two political survey chapters, which cram a century's worth of events into clear but rushed narratives, the book makes its points mostly through snapshots of individual lives. To illustrate the religious revival of the early nineteenth century, Gildea uses the tireless peasant-born priest Jean-Marie-Baptiste Vianney, curé of Ars (later canonized), whose confessional had an eight-day waiting list by 1845, even though he sometimes spent fifteen hours a day hearing confessions. Female work in the 1870s is personified by Jeanne Bouvier, who started in a silk mill at age eleven, went on to a dizzying series of positions in domestic service, and then successively made her living as a hat-, corset-, and dressmaker, earning anywhere from 10 to 45 francs a week, at the mercy of the economy and the season. As for literary figures, Gildea fails to resist the irresistible Germaine de Staël, daughter of the last chief minister of the Old Regime, lover of Benjamin Constant, eloquent novelist, and penetrating liberal thinker. He also makes excellent use of the aristocratic salon hostess and feminist Marie d'Agoult, the lover of Liszt and romantic rival of George Sand.

In keeping with his delight in quirkily human exceptions to grand narratives, Gildea artfully deploys the sort of ironic quotations that quietly disrupt the expected story line. In retrospect, Emperor Louis-Napoleon may well appear reckless, erratic, and not overly bright, but just four months before he fell, Leon Gambetta, the future founder of the Third Republic, could declare that "the Empire is stronger than ever." Stendhal's *Le Rouge et le noir* may now stand as one of the greatest triumphs of French fiction, but at the time of its publication the public and the critics alike considered it a disaster, and in its first year it sold barely fifteen hundred copies. On learning in 1831 that Simon Bolivar had died, Stendhal wrote to a friend: "Do you know from what? From envy at the success of the *Rouge*." The playwright Sylvain Maréchal has a reputation as one of the most radical defenders of revolutionary republicanism, but in 1801 he could still publish a pamphlet entitled *Bill to Prohibit Teaching Women to Read*. And who was it who attacked Russian Jewish immigrants in 1890 as "these despicable people [coming] into a country that is not theirs"? None other than the wealthy, assimilated Sephardic Jewish literary critic Bernard Lazare.

Gildea's methods work well for the themes that he has identified as central. The chapters on the provinces show brilliantly how a generation of Romantic writers began to identify particular personalities for the different regions of France, rooted in a combination of geography, language, folklore, and custom. Gildea traces the growing tension between this vision and the demands of the rigidly centralized state apparatus inherited from Napoleon. "Everything moves towards Paris," he quotes the Second Empire's great urban planner Baron Haussmann, in 1859: "main roads, railways, telegraphs. Everything moves out from it: laws, decrees, decisions, orders, officials." Gildea particularly shows how state officials started to see the profusion of dialects and local languages as a threat to national unity, and made instruction in standard French a priority for the school system. Yet the state did not attempt to eradicate these languages and provincial identities altogether, recognizing the need for provincials to identify with a folkloric "petite patrie" as well as the big national one.

Gildea's chapters on religion likewise manage the difficult feat of treating French Catholicism and anticlericalism alike with sensitivity and understanding, while explicating the long, bitter quarrels between the two and also giving a full picture of French Jewry and French anti-Semitism. Gildea does not neglect the ferocity with which the French right attacked Jews in the last two decades of the century (culminating in the Dreyfus Affair), but he also shows the remarkable success achieved by French-born Jews at a time when most other Western countries still threw up far higher barriers to their social advancement.

The discussion of literature and the arts is less successful. Gildea does his best to fit them into a broad social and cultural context, but the pressure of covering so much greatness—not to mention such broad topics as "mass culture"—in fifty-odd pages leaves little room. He provides telling statistics, for instance, on increases in the reading public and book publishing (the first more than doubled between 1801 and 1871, while the second increased more than fivefold just between 1814 and 1866); but he fails to provide a key part of the explanation, which is that the replacement of expensive rag paper by cheap wood pulp allowed publishers to slash their production costs. In general, the treatment of modernism suffers from being kept separate from discussions of technological change and the industrialized "modern life" that it struggled to represent. Here the dividing line of 1870 also becomes overly rigid, because it separates Baudelaire (pre-1870) from the symbolist poets he did so much to influence. And then there are odd omissions: Renoir, Rodin, and the entire subject of photography, which the nineteenth-century French largely created and then turned into an art form.

Most egregious is the way Gildea neglects the many things that do not fit into his chosen themes. He has no chapters on science or social science, so that major figures such as Comte and Pasteur go unmentioned. Marie Curie wins a brief mention only because of her gender, and Durkheim an even briefer one only because of his Judaism (something that would have distressed to no end this proud republican Frenchman). Material on technological change and the rise of industrial capitalism gets into Gildea's book only when relevant to class conflict, so that such large topics as the rise of the factory system pass essentially undiscussed. In his brief, rather scattershot treatment of international relations, Gildea neglects to mention most of Louis-Napoleon's adventures, including the interventions in China and Mexico, and the Crimean War.

Strangest of all, Gildea has little to say on the French colonial empire, particularly before 1870. In one of the two lengthy and informative chapters on women, he quotes the feminist Flora Tristan, in 1843, calling women "the last slaves who still remain in French society." Left painfully unmentioned is the fact that in 1843 French plantation owners in Guadeloupe and Martinique still kept enslaved hundreds of thousands of blacks, who had been freed during the Revolution, only to be reenslaved by Napoleon. (The Second Republic, as readers will not learn from this book, finally abolished slavery for good in 1848.) Nor does Gildea give more than passing mention to the fact that by 1914 Algiers and other areas of North Africa had become in large part French, with considerable European settler populations, impressive French architecture, and the legal status of French departments. By 1914, few people in France actually thought of Algeria as a "colony" at all, preferring to see it the way Americans today see Hawaii. In practice, the French denied citizenship to those living under "Koranic law," and equally managed to keep the indigenous populations of West Africa in a subservient position, even while touting France's "mission to civilize" these supposedly benighted areas of the globe. Yet the rhetoric of "civilization" cut both ways, leading the French to invest considerable amounts in schooling, language instruction, and physical infrastructure in the overseas empire, and providing paths to full citizenship for a "meritorious" minority of the conquered (notably North African Jews). These policies would all have huge consequences for the history of France and its empire after 1914.

Until relatively recently, historians tended to play down this imperial history. Following the decolonization of the 1950s and 1960s, French commentators and historians tended, defensively, to redefine France's imperial ventures as a temporary phase in the country's history, whose natural arc led to the independence of the now "mature" colonies. But these ideas obscure the very different, and very central, place that the colonies held in French visions of their country in the previous century, and the very real interpenetration of colonial and metropolitan life, in economics, politics, and culture. It is too bad that Gildea reinforces the prevailing postcolonization views rather than challenging them, as so many historians have recently done. (Today roughly half of all dissertations on French history in North American universities focus on the overseas empire.)

Still, no general survey can hope to treat all subjects equally. Furet, for instance, neglected far broader areas of the French experience in the nineteenth century (including imperialism), so as to focus intently on the alleged pathologies of French democracy. Robert Gildea has drawn very effectively on recent research in the areas he chooses to explore, and he presents his material in admirably lucid and entertaining prose. And, above all, he succeeds in one central task: showing just how surprisingly livable and creative France was during this golden century-long interval between two moments of horror. No wonder that so many remain nostalgic for it, and not just within the country's borders.

2

La Même Chose: Americans Abroad

WHILE THE END OF THE NAPOLEONIC WARS left France politically and economically exhausted, it also allowed the country to reclaim its status as the Western world's most desirable travel destination. The artistic and literary efflorescence described in the previous essay only added to the attraction, as did France's preeminence in many of the sciences, especially medicine (this was, among other things, the century of Louis Pasteur). This essay is concerned with the Americans who flocked to France in the period. Writing it made me feel a certain kinship with these predecessors of mine—especially those who crossed the Atlantic to study. And it left me intensely grateful not to have repeated some of their experiences—notably that of the American trapped in Paris during the Commune who wrote of discovering the difference in taste between brewery rats and sewer rats.

Ever since the eighteenth century, the French have held a contradictory place in the American imagination. When we need a frivolous, effeminate, weaselly antagonist to highlight our supposed simple and manly

Book under Review: David McCullough, *The Greater Journey: Americans in Paris* (Simon and Schuster, 2011). Essay originally published in *The New Republic* online, July 3, 2011.

virtues, we call on them. Yet when we search for an ideal of refined, worldly sophistication to place above our own more rough-hewn tastes, they also fit the bill. How many jingoistic senators have gone hoarse denouncing "cheese-eating surrender monkeys," only to soothe their tired throats at the very next congressional recess with a silky Gevrey Chambertin, accompanying a delicately herbed *gigot d'agneau*, followed by, yes, a delectable slice of *Brie au lait cru*, at a sumptuously decorated gastronomic temple of the *rive droite*?

In the history of America's obsession with France, two periods generally stand out. There is the age of Jefferson and Franklin, two men who played the contrast between aristocratic Old World decadence and democratic New World simplicity for all it was worth. And then there is the interwar era of Hemingway, Fitzgerald, and Gertrude Stein, most recently fetishized in Woody Allen's *Midnight in Paris*. But the intervening period has received far less attention, despite such literary highlights as Mark Twain's *Innocents Abroad* and Henry James's *The Ambassadors*. Yet thousands of Americans crossed the Atlantic every year in the nineteenth century, heading to Paris for business, pleasure, education, and artistic inspiration, and left behind voluminous accounts of their experiences.

These are the experiences David McCullough sets out to describe in *The Greater Journey*. He certainly has wonderful material to draw on. Among the Americans who lived in Paris for extended periods was the painter Samuel Morse, who came to the city as a disconsolate widower (leaving his children behind in the care of relatives) and spent long months there preparing his masterpiece, *The Gallery of the Louvre*. It was in France that Morse took notice of the "telegraph" network of semaphore towers that relayed messages across the country and became obsessed with the idea of building a more efficient electronic equivalent. He also spent time in Paris with his friend James Fenimore Cooper, whose novels of the frontier delighted French as much as American audiences. (Balzac wrote of Cooper that "in his hands the art of the pen has never come closer to the art of the brush.")

McCullough gives particular attention to the Illinois politician Elihu Washburne, who kept a vivid journal of events while serving as American ambassador during the Prussian siege and Paris Commune of 1870–1871. And he makes a hero of the sculptor Augustus Saint-Gaudens, the son of a French shoemaker in New York, who prepared his great sculpture of

Admiral Farragut while living in Paris. Many other famous Americans make appearances here (rather like in Woody Allen's movie): Hawthorne, Emerson, Thoreau, Harriet Beecher Stowe, and Mary Cassatt, among others. McCullough has nice details on the way that regularly scheduled luxury steamship travel replaced the long, dangerous sailing voyages of the early nineteenth century. By the 1850s, "floating palaces" such as the *Arctic* and the *Pacific* included grand dining saloons, gentleman's smoking rooms, wine cellars with thousands of bottles, and tons of ice for refrigeration.

McCullough's best chapter tells the little-known story of the hundreds of American medical students who came to study in Paris at a time when the French led the world in medical science. In 1833, McCullough notes, Paris's twelve hospitals treated more than sixty-five thousand patients, while Boston's two saw barely eight hundred. In America, aspiring doctors had trouble gaining access to cadavers for dissection, but in France they could purchase a dead adult body for $2.50, and a child's corpse came even cheaper. In the main anatomical amphitheater of the Paris Medical School, six hundred students could dissect at the same time, with discarded tissue fed to dogs kept in cages outside. The school suspended the exercise in summer, when the stench of decomposing bodies grew too foul even by the malodorous standards of central Paris. (It was in this period, McCullough might have noted, that the city finally emptied out its mephitic communal cemeteries, transferring the bones of millions to the underground catacombs.)

McCullough, well known as the biographer of Theodore Roosevelt, Harry Truman, and John Adams, has a smooth, practiced style and a well-honed eye for the colorful anecdote. To describe the imperious manner of the French surgeon Guillaume Dupuytren, he turns to an account by the medical student Jonathan Warren: "If his orders are not immediately obeyed, he thinks nothing of striking his patient or abusing him most harshly. A very favorite practice of his during his consultation is to make a handle of the noses of his patients. Whenever a man enters with any disease of the head, he is immediately seized by the nose and pulled down onto his knees where he remains half in sorrow and half in anger at the treatment until he is allowed to rise and describe his disease." To illustrate the conditions of a starving, besieged Paris in the

winter of 1870–1871, McCullough cites the Chicago academic and journalist Nathan Sheppard, who noted that cats were selling for four times
the price of dogs, and that "the flavor of a brewery rat surpassed that of
the sewer rat, due to its diet." Rat meat, Sheppard recorded, tasted surprisingly like bird.

Most American observations about Paris were admittedly less piquant
or surprising, and McCullough includes a few too many of the banal variety. We hear an American medical student praising the "peculiarly exquisite" aroma of French coffee, and Harriet Beecher Stowe gushing over
Parisian women's instinct for stylish dress, and Saint-Gaudens noting, yes,
that "Paris in the spring is wonderful." There are the expected letters about
the temptations of Parisian gambling, nightlife, and women, leading to
the entirely predictable lament of an art student: "I am entirely out of
money." And lest McCullough's readers think that all Americans rushed
headlong into Parisian fleshpots, he also gives us the educator and wom-
en's rights advocate Emma Willard's shocked reaction to the naked statues
in the Jardin des Tuileries. In "our America," she wrote home prudishly,
"the eye of modesty is not publicly affronted, and virgin delicacy can walk
abroad without a blush." Even when reinforcing clichés about Franco-
American interactions, *The Greater Journey* is perfectly enjoyable.

Unfortunately, the book is also often disappointingly superficial.
Particularly in its latter half, Paris becomes little more than a colorful
backdrop for a series of amusing but disconnected American stories.
The major events in the city's history—the 1848 revolution, Haussmann's
boulevards, the Franco-Prussian War, the construction of the Eiffel
Tower—pass by in familiar textbook fashion. Where an American visitor took particular interest in events, McCullough provides further
detail—for instance, in the case of the Commune, witnessed with horror
by Ambassador Washburne. But other significant elements of the city's
history go unmentioned, notably the corrosive religious politics of the
late nineteenth century and their culmination in the Dreyfus Affair. (It
is an interesting question, left unasked here, why visiting Americans apparently turned a blind eye to this subject.) At one point, McCullough
casually mentions that in the late 1870s an English-language newspaper for the American community in Paris began publication, but says
nothing at all about who published it, or what impact it had.

Few French people receive sustained attention in McCullough's book, and even then we only see them through the eyes of the Americans. In fact, McCullough has done little serious research on the French setting. His bibliography includes few of the standard scholarly studies of nineteenth-century Paris and no works at all in the French language. A particular shame is that he appears not to have visited the major research library for the history of Paris, the Bibliothèque Historique de la Ville de Paris, which contains, among its many treasures, a massive catalogue that cross-indexes descriptions and travelers' accounts of the city—the proper first stop for anyone working on a book such as this one.

Yes, the subject of the book is the Americans, but thanks to McCullough's concentration on their personalities to the neglect of the historical context, there are things about their history that he simply misses. When discussing medical education, for instance, *The Greater Journey* underscores how the great early nineteenth-century doctor Pierre-Charles-Alexandre Louis inspired American students: "Louis did nothing for show. He was neither spellbinding nor flamboyant.... Yet he had a power. What set him off from the others was his clear-headed approach to the treatment of disease, his insistence on the need for analysis based on evidence, on 'facts.'" But McCullough neglects to mention the principal reason for Louis's fame, namely his leadership in introducing then-novel epidemiological approaches to medicine, which for the first time drew on aggregate observations of thousands of patients to determine the most effective treatments. Among other things, Louis used these approaches to discredit the age-old practice of therapeutic bleeding. It was his role in this intellectual revolution, not just his personal magnetism or his hardheaded empiricism, that drew aspiring American doctors across the Atlantic to study with him.

The Greater Journey will undoubtedly sell for summer reading, especially for the masses lamenting the demise of the luxury steamships of 160 years ago as they endure the horrors of contemporary transatlantic travel, en route to the endless admissions queues at the Musée d'Orsay and the T-shirt vendors of the Champs Élysées. The book will entertain them greatly and do little to disturb their enjoyable preconceptions about the City of Light. American fantasies about France will remain, as ever, highly resistant to empirical evidence. But for a more textured and instructive view of the same subject, today's traveler might also pick up the Library of America's lovely volume *Americans in Paris: A Literary Anthology*, edited by Adam Gopnik, in which Cooper and Stowe and Washburne—and Mark Twain, Henry James, Edith Wharton, and Ernest Hemingway, among others—speak for themselves.

3

Big: The Napoleon of Literature

EARLY IN MY ACADEMIC CAREER I had an hour-long commute to work and became addicted to audiobooks to ease the frustrations of the Washington Beltway. One day, at the local public library, I found an audio copy of Victor Hugo's Les Misérables, *unabridged, on several dozen CDs. On a lark I borrowed it, and quickly became hooked by the stories of Jean Valjean, Javert, Cosette, the Thénardiers, and several hundred other characters. It took many months of heavy traffic on the Beltway and I-95, but I eventually listened to the entire novel. On more than one occasion, my wife came out to the driveway at the end of the day to find me still sitting in the car, determined to learn how a particular chapter ended. Ever since I have had a very soft spot indeed for Hugo's work, both the novels and the exquisite poetry. This essay, a consideration of Graham Robb's fine biography of Hugo, gave me the chance to consider his position both in the context of nineteenth-century French history and in French literature more generally.*

Every few generations, a writer comes along whom the French decide to anoint as their Literary Genius and National Conscience. There are a

---

Book under Review: Graham Robb, *Victor Hugo* (Norton, 1998). Essay originally published in *The New Republic*, April 6, 1998.

number of recognizable requirements for the position. The Genius must be enormously prolific, ready to whip off a poem, a newspaper article, or at the very least an aphorism, at a moment's notice. He (no women need apply) must have strong, though not necessarily consistent, political opinions. He must have a busy and irregular sex life, the better to give pleasurable outrage to the *grandes dames* of the Faubourg Saint-Germain. He must have aristocratic pretensions (or the twentieth-century equivalent, an education at one of France's ultra-elite *grandes écoles*). He must have a towering ego. Oh yes, he must also be a great writer, though no one expects perfect consistency on this score either.

In the eighteenth century, the demiurge in question was, of course, Voltaire. In the sadly diminished twentieth century, the closest the French came to casting the role successfully was Sartre. It was the nineteenth century that fixed on the most perfect example of all, when it culturally beatified Victor Hugo.

Of Hugo's lack of a writer's block, there can be no doubt. *Les Misérables*, for example, is thirty-five-hundred-odd pages long. Graham Robb nicely observes that the book changes your life in part because you spend so much of your life reading it. As for the other requirements, Hugo began his career as a fiery defender of the divine-right monarchy, and finished it as a thundering prophet of socialism and the secular republic. His sex life makes ordinary libertinism look monastic. He belonged to both the Bonapartist and Orleanist nobilities. He wished to found a new religion and compared himself to Jesus. Most amazingly of all, he was indeed a great writer.

These various attributes make Hugo an irresistible subject for biographers, but also an unusually challenging one. In the first place, he demands stamina. Merely reading through his collected works took Robb four years. Reading everything contemporaries wrote about him, to say nothing of subsequent literary criticism, would be wholly impossible. More important, a biographer cannot write about Hugo the man and Hugo the writer without confronting something utterly inseparable from them: Hugo the public phenomenon. From the early admirer who wanted his tombstone to read "Here Lies One Who Believed in Victor Hugo" to the later one who wanted Paris renamed Hugopolis, and to the Vietnamese Buddhists who made him literally a saint, Victor Hugo was the center of a cult.

More to the point, he reveled in it. His apartment on Henri IV's Place des Vosges in the 1840s, bedecked with pieces of armor and medieval tapestries, was less a private dwelling than a bizarre public showcase for an endless stream of visitors. (Dickens keenly described it as "a most extraordinary place, looking like an old curiosity shop, or the Property room of some gloomy, vast old Theatre.") His diaries can read like dispatches from the farthest reaches of clinical narcissism: "4 October: The popular photograph of myself is being sold in the streets. I bought one"; "20 October: The papers report that the Victor Hugo balloon has landed in Belgium"; "1 December: "On the Boulevard Victor-Hugo a Victor Hugo orphanage is being founded" ...

In 1878, Hugo wrote the following words about Voltaire, fully intending them to apply to himself as well: "He was more than a man, he was a century. He had exercised a function and fulfilled a mission." The first sentence is an exaggeration, but the second is not; and for this reason a biography of Hugo must also be, at least in part, a history of the culture that defined that function and mission. It is not an easy task, and Robb has not wholly succeeded at it.

Robb has certainly brought the requisite stamina to the job. He has read through the Hugo oeuvre from the sublimities of "Tristesse d'Olympio" and *Les Misérables* to the awfulness of the early gothic novel *Hans of Iceland*, which featured a demon dwarf, bodies torn to shreds by the dozen, and a hero named Thorvick—Victor backward. (A British reviewer called it "the most extraordinary and ultra horrible production of a disordered imagination that has ever frozen the blood and blanched the cheeks of romance readers.") More important, Robb has read Hugo's writings with the sort of care that allows him constantly to draw previously unseen connections. When he turns to the way Hugo described his daughter and son-in-law's tragic drowning, for instance, Robb immediately recalls "the consummation-in-death at the end of Notre-Dame de Paris, thirteen years before: 'Two skeletons were found, locked in a curious embrace. One of the two skeletons—the skeleton of a woman— still wore a few scraps of dress of a material which had once been white.'"

Robb also manages to tell Hugo's life story with the sort of wit and lightness of touch his subject singularly lacked: "Hugo could talk for hours about concision"; "The young Duchess ... knew his poems by heart, which was more than could be said for Hugo, who once complimented his daughter on a poem he had written himself"; "A statistical analysis shows that from 1847 to 1851, he had sex with more women than he wrote poems." To late twentieth-century sensibilities, Hugo's Olympic-scale pomposity presents an almost irresistible target, and it is to Robb's credit that he indulges us with these pleasurable pinpricks while still taking Hugo and his work seriously. Only occasionally do the worst aspects of Hugo's own prose appear to have infected his biographer's, as in this truly dreadful analysis of some late verse: "Its main verb straddles the caesura like a soul yearning to cross the great divide."

Thanks to his hard work and wit, Robb manages to make the well-known story of Hugo's life fresh and entertaining. First, there was the unusual childhood as the son of one of Napoleon's generals. Born in eastern France in 1802, Hugo lived for a time in Spain, where, if the First Empire had survived, he would have grown up to become Count of Siguenza at the Bonapartist court of Madrid. ("My works would have been written in a language which is not widely spoken and would thus have had little effect.") Instead the First Empire crumbled, and the adolescent Hugo found himself living in genteel poverty in Paris. But obscurity did not last long, thanks to a facility for verse so remarkable that poems formed themselves in his mind at all hours, even during sleep. "Hugo actually complained about this involuntary activity as a nuisance," Robb writes, "as if it had been a speech impediment or a tic." By age twenty Hugo had already won important literary prizes, gained powerful patrons, and become a leading figure in the nascent French Romantic movement.

From then on, his life was a constant performance, acted out before an ever-swelling audience. At twenty-two, he served as official poet at the coronation of the reactionary Charles X. Soon afterward, he published his *Préface de Cromwell*, designed to serve as the official manifesto of French Romanticism. There followed the famous "battle" of *Hernani*, Hugo's play that, from its very first line (with its famous enjambment) deliberately violated the rigid rules of classical French versification. The work became a rallying cry for a literary generation, provoking street battles and even duels. Robb shows just how carefully Hugo and his literary allies orchestrated the public confrontation and crafted his public legend.

But the legend grew very nicely on its own. In following years, rumors circulated that Hugo could eat half an ox at a single sitting, go without food for three days, see and hear more keenly than mere mortals. "According to the authoritative testimony of Hugo's barber, his bristles blunted the razor three times as quickly as a normal beard." Embarrassingly adoring letters arrived by every post. Fed by this sort of adulation, the poet's ambition quickly vaulted beyond mere literary revolutions. In his poetry he conflated his own life story with that of the human race. As Robb rightly remarks, he had "begun to think of himself as a Messiah."

While not attempting a sustained psychoanalysis, Robb does suggest plausibly that this egomania verged on serious mental illness. Insanity ultimately claimed both Hugo's brother Eugène and his daughter Adèle (she was the subject of François Truffaut's film *The Story of Adèle H*). But in Hugo's case, his admirers accepted any eccentricity as a manifestation of Genius, while the manner in which some expressed their Hugo-worship ensured that none of his desires went frustrated. In the 1820s, he put his young family on display as an example of domestic bliss. Ten years later, he acquired an "official" mistress and embarked on a dizzying odyssey of sexual conquest, the details of which he meticulously recorded in secret, but none-too-subtle code in his notebooks. ("The word 'spontinian' has been interpreted, inexplicably, as an allusion to the composer, Spontini," Robb writes drily; "Hugo's later notes show it was his code word for ejaculation.")

The remarkable thing is that Hugo's talent was not crushed under the weight of his swollen ego, or swamped by the adulation, or left to wither as he indulged himself with mistresses and "live pornography." Quite the contrary. It flowered. In the 1830s he produced his greatest Romantic poetry and his novel *Notre Dame de Paris*, which provided a brilliant vision of a gothic and grotesque fifteenth-century Paris and bequeathed to literature the world's most famous hunchback, Quasimodo. In the 1840s came more great poetry and the beginnings of *Les Misérables*. Unsurprisingly, these achievements inflated the Hugo legend to new dimensions. By 1848, after King Louis-Philippe, he was the most famous Frenchman alive, a figure whose recommendation could transform obscure villages into major attractions for the nascent tourist industry and whose utterances carried political as well as literary weight.

Politics, in fact, increasingly dominated Hugo's life, and Robb quite properly makes the Revolution of 1848 the dramatic center of his story. By that date, Hugo had long abandoned his early Catholic legitimism in

favor of the solid bourgeois moderation of the July Monarchy. A friendship with that most bourgeois of kings, Louis-Philippe, earned him
both a peerage and high-placed protection when an affair with an artist's
wife threatened to land him in prison. (The king bought the cuckold's
silence with a commission, and, "a few months later," Robb quips, "the
Château de Versailles acquired some unusually mediocre frescoes.")
When the Revolution broke out, however, Hugo hastily rallied to the
new Second Republic and won election to parliament.

The decisive moment came in late June 1848, when the people of Paris
rose in revolt against a newly elected Assembly that was more responsive
to conservative peasants than to poor workers. Hugo found himself
face-to-face with the Parisian barricades, and Robb evokes the encounter
by quoting Hugo's own unforgettable description of a barricade in *Les
Misérables*: "It was a collaboration of the paving-stone, the rubble-stone,
the beam, the iron bar, the rag, the shattered window, the broken chair,
the cabbage-stalk. . . . It was enormous and living, spitting thunder and
lightning as if from the back of an electric beast. The spirit of revolution
covered that peak with its cloud in which the voice of the People rum-
bled like the voice of God. . . . It was a pile of rubbish and it was Mount
Sinai." Still, as Robb strikingly points out, the Hugo of 1848 actually saw
the barricades from the side of the forces that suppressed the revolt.
Indeed, he personally led a detachment of Republican Guards against
the rebels.

It was a turning point. The bloody, ruthless suppression of the workers left Hugo at an uncharacteristic loss for words, one that speaks of a
deep personal crisis, perhaps even of deep guilt. Whatever the case, in
the next years he finally stopped trimming his politics to fit the regime
and abandoned the pose of a great lord for that of a radical prophet.
When Louis-Napoleon Bonaparte assumed the presidency of a France
exhausted by Revolution, Hugo initially flirted with him, as he had
done with Louis-Philippe. As Bonaparte steadily suppressed freedoms
in the name of order, however, Hugo slid into opposition; and the president's coup d'état against his own parliament in 1851 led the poet to flee,
first to Belgium, then the Channel Islands. The Genius was now the
Exile, flinging anathemas against "Napoleon the Little" (his book of the
title did much to discredit and ridicule the regime), holding court for
the usual procession of adoring visitors, and finishing *Les Misérables*,

which finally appeared in 1862. The book garnered one of the most rapturous popular receptions ever granted a novel. As Robb notes, it was one of the last great masterpieces of Western literature wholly accessible to a popular readership.

In his exile of nearly two decades, Hugo only grew more eccentric. He communed with spirits and gradually acquired an impressive collection of otherworldly interlocutors. The list, Robb notes, included Cain, Jacob, Moses, Isaiah, Sappho, Socrates, Jesus, Judas, Mohammed, Joan of Arc, Luther, Galileo, Molière, the Marquis de Sade, Mozart, Walter Scott, Androcles's Lion, Balaam's Ass, a comet, and an inhabitant of Jupiter called Tyatafia. Shakespeare, in conversation with Hugo, admitted that English was an inferior language to French.

And yet Hugo's stature continued to grow. Worshipful letters arrived in Guernsey for him by the boatful, some addressed only to "Victor Hugo, The Ocean." The last years of his life represented an apotheosis that eclipsed even that accorded to Voltaire a century before. As the farcical reign of Napoleon the Little came to a tragic end in the Franco-Prussian war and the Paris Commune, Hugo staged a triumphant return to French soil, and became a sort of unofficial royalty for the new Third Republic. Twentieth-century fiction writers should not even dream of the sort of celebrity he enjoyed, lest they curl up in despair. The memorization of his poems became mandatory in the schools. The state renamed his street Avenue Victor-Hugo. His every utterance received prominent coverage in the newspapers. He was, Robb says, "the most famous man on earth." His funeral in 1885 was one of the great civic festivals of the Third Republic, with up to two million mourners flooding into Paris as the pallbearers laid him to rest in the Panthéon, near the tombs of Voltaire and Rousseau.

Robb tells this amazing story with great verve, some fascinating new information (particularly on Hugo's role in 1848), and many acerbic swipes at previous biographers, one of whom he does not even deign to name, merely referring to "the last life of Victor Hugo in English." He wisely avoids providing plot summaries of the novels, and indeed spends remarkably little time on the works at all. The occasional quotations from letters and novels give a good sense of Hugo's prose style, but Robb does not even try to evoke the poetry, frankly admitting the impossibility of doing so in an English-language book. It is a pity, though, for unsuspecting readers will imagine a Hugo who spoke mostly in basso profundo, in majestic declamations that verged on bombast. They will not easily guess the lyrical delicacies of which the poet was capable.

While this particular unevenness is probably unavoidable, Robb's more formal excurses into literary analysis go wrong in a different way and reflect a more serious problem with his book. Consider these judgments. Hugo's early travel book about the Rhine is nothing less than an early "roman-fleuve." A passage describing a railroad makes one think "a theory of relativity was just around the corner." Hugo's letters "are filled with what looks like surrealist imagery." The last novels, and particularly the bizarre *L'Homme Qui Rit*, "stand like weird towers on the frontier of Romanticism and Modernism."

Each of these judgments is certainly defensible, but collectively, they produce the wrong impression. Victor Hugo's anticipations of modernism are the least interesting thing about him. He was emphatically not an avant-garde artist. Indeed, he did not *want* to get too far ahead of his day. Even his early literary rebelliousness was carefully calculated, and involved the embrace of a movement that had swept England and Germany many years before and in France faced little serious competition from a moribund neoclassicism. When Hugo remarked that "the poet exists for the people," he meant it. He mostly gave his public what they wanted, not what he thought they should have. The "magnificent delusions" of the strange late novels were what prompted Robb to write his biography in the first place, and clearly he prefers them to most of the better-known, less proto-modernist work; but they represent the relatively rare moments when Hugo's manias started to bubble out of control and his relationship with his public grew frayed.

Yet this relationship was everything to Hugo, and it largely determined the direction of his work. For what is a messiah without followers? Robb, unfortunately, while citing many examples of the public's adulation of Hugo, rarely gives the public itself serious attention. Above all, he generally fails to reflect on the ways France's military humiliation in 1815, and the ideological exhaustion produced by an unending merry-go-round of regimes (fifteen or so of them between 1789 and 1870), might well have led the French public to seek in literature something it could not find in politics. The nineteenth century, of course, was the great era of the writer-politician in France: Hugo shared the stage with Chateaubriand, Lamartine, Tocqueville, and many others. Robb might profitably have compared Hugo's career to theirs.

Most strikingly, the cult of Victor Hugo eerily recalls the earlier cult of Napoleon, a fact that Robb notes in passing and then seems to forget. It is likely that Hugo's intense, visceral loathing of Napoleon III, "Napoleon the Little," stemmed not just from an admirable hatred of tyranny (compounded, perhaps, by guilt over the events of 1848), but also from a sense of jealousy and competition. Certainly, his readers appreciated the comparison between Hugo's lonely vigils on Jersey and Guernsey and Napoleon I's exiles on the even lonelier islands of Elba and Saint Helena. "L'Expiation," Hugo's single best-known poem, which Robb barely mentions, is about Napoleon. In that corner of the national psyche where Americans keep "The Midnight Ride of Paul Revere," and the British "The Charge of the Light Brigade," the French still repeat its lines "*Waterloo! Waterloo! Waterloo! morne plaine...*"

It may be that Hugo owed his station as France's Genius to this well-gratified Napoleon complex. His great works derive not just from enormous talent, but from the fact that he, more than any of his contemporaries, had the manic drive and the titanic arrogance to pose convincingly as a savior in a country that desperately needed one. The greater the need, the stronger was his response; and it is no coincidence that in a career that spanned nearly seventy years, so much of his most enduring work stems from the two different decades that followed the crashing political disillusionments of 1832 (a year of unsuccessful insurrections against the July Monarchy) and 1851. The resounding moral truths of *Les Misérables* have a power independent of the circumstances of their composition. Nonetheless, they clearly spoke most powerfully and directly to the France in which a great outburst of revolutionary fervor had just fizzled into the crass and tyrannical regime of Napoleon the Little.

Victor Hugo was undoubtedly a little mad, as Robb suggests more than once, chronicling the family history, the sexual obsessions, the spiritualism, the prodigious versifying, the preternatural self-centeredness. But to see the madness as the key to Hugo's literary genius, as Robb does, with his modernist preference for Hugo's maddest, strangest literary productions, is somewhat to miss the point. Victor Hugo was Victor Hugo not because he was mad, but because the public thought he was sane. Or rather, because the public happily joined him in his madness, finding in his art exactly what he found in it: a world preferable to the complex, frustrated, and disillusioned one in front of his eyes.

4

Who Mended Pierre's Leg? Lourdes and the Catholic Right

MANY OF THE ESSAYS IN THIS PART deal with nineteenth-century French best sellers. Victor Hugo's Les Misérables *was one, of course. Another was the* Mémorial de Sainte-Hélène, *which recounted Napoleon's exile on Saint-Helena, in large part in Napoleon's own words. A third, discussed here (as well as in chapter 1 of part II) was Édouard Drumont's mephitic classic of anti-Semitism,* La France juive. *But all of these books were outsold by Henri Lasserre's* Lourdes, *a melodramatic account of the apparitions at what would become one of the world's most popular Catholic shrines. The book's success testified to the strength of religious belief in France a century after the "Age of Reason" and the French Revolution—and to the political implications of that strength. This essay, prompted by Ruth Harris's excellent book on the subject, discusses the overall phenomenon of Lourdes and the importance of Lasserre's book within it.*

On the surface, no two people in nineteenth-century France had less in common than Louis Pasteur and Bernadette Soubirous. Pasteur, the great

---

Book under Review: Ruth Harris, *Lourdes: Body and Spirit in the Secular Age* (Allen Lane, 1999). Essay originally published in *The London Review of Books*, November 11, 1999.

icon of modern biological science, was a French national hero, a pillar of the academic establishment: the very embodiment of modern, rational, liberal civilization. Soubirous was a miserably poor, tubercular peasant girl, illiterate, unable to speak anything other than Pyrenean *patois*, who claimed, in February 1858, to have seen a miraculous apparition in a grotto near the village of Lourdes. "Que soy era Immaculada Councepciou," the apparition said to her: "I am the Immaculate Conception."

Yet both Pasteur and Soubirous came to stand as symbols of healing. Within a decade of the apparition, Lourdes had become one of the great pilgrimage sites of the world, and people flocked there by the thousands to bathe in water from a spring Soubirous had found, in order to gain relief from one debilitating illness or another. Sufferers have been flocking there ever since, usually after Pasteur's successors in the medical profession have failed to heal them, and every year brings its host of supposedly miraculous cures.

Pasteur and Soubirous have more recently been brought together to symbolize the remarkable shift in perceptions of science and religion over the past two generations. It was once the case that few secular writers would have dared mention the biologist and the peasant girl in the same sentence, except to dismiss the latter as a benighted, superstitious, embarrassing relic of the past, the sort of person who would vanish altogether from the bright scientific future pointed to by Pasteur and his like. But that was before the Frankfurt School, Michel Foucault, the environmental and antinuclear movements, the "linguistic turn," and the new academic field of "science studies" (carried out largely by sociologists, anthropologists, historians, and literary critics). Thanks to them it is much harder to see the history of science as a triumphal pageant, steadily advancing toward that bright future. Pasteur in particular has variously been denounced as a coldhearted exploiter of his patients, a falsifier of data, the ruthless servant of an oppressive patriarchal order, while figures such as Soubirous are more likely to be respected even by nonbelievers. Their faith is honored, their visions are described in a determinedly neutral manner, and the supposed miracle cures are examined with the eye of a sympathetic anthropologist, rather than a skeptical doctor. At its reductionist and polemical worst, this new approach treats science with the sort of scorn and vitriol that French freethinkers once directed at the Roman Catholic Church.

Ruth Harris's book exemplifies the promise of this approach rather than its excesses. Pasteur appears only incidentally in its pages, yet he lurks behind them, for the book's great theme is precisely the confrontation between modern, scientific, secular society and religious passion. *Lourdes* is a general history of the shrine from its origins to World War I, but the last section, which examines the power of faith in a secular world, the rituals of modern pilgrimage, the cures themselves, and the influence Lourdes eventually exerted even on its secular critics, is the richest. It is here that Harris combines analysis with sympathy for her subjects and vivid, evocative prose, as in this passage:

> During the 1897 Jubilee pilgrimage to Lourdes, after a long day full of exertions, Père Picard asked for a drink. Rather than drawing some water afresh, he asked a stretcher-bearer to fill his glass from an infected pool, filled with the pus, blood and scabs of the sick pilgrims. When the father had received the water, he made the sign of the cross and drank slowly, right to the end. Then, he gave back the glass and concluded with a smile: "The water of the good Mother of Heaven is always delicious."... Picard both enacted a nineteenth-century vision of medieval fervor and underlined his belief in the power of faith over science at the height of the Pasteurian "revolution."

This is the first substantial history of Lourdes not written from a Catholic perspective, and it would be quite wrong to suggest that Harris's earlier chapters are lacking in interest. She begins by providing a sort of microhistory of Soubirous and her apparitions, which movingly recounts how the fourteen-year-old girl, accompanying her sister and a friend in a hunt for firewood, sat down to rest in front of the grotto and first saw the childlike figure she called simply "aquéro"—"that." Over the next month, it appeared again and again, as crowds eventually numbering seven thousand (three thousand more than the population of Lourdes) came to the wooded area to watch the girl kneeling ecstatically in the mud, drinking the dirty water and recounting what she had heard. Aquéro asked for prayer, penitence, bathing and drinking in the fountain, a religious procession, and a chapel. The local authorities disapproved and tried to keep Soubirous from the grotto, but without success.

Harris sketches out a number of contexts in which to make sense of what happened. Lourdes suffered a major economic decline in the 1850s—the Soubirous family, for example, was reduced to living in a former prison. Bernadette was ill-treated at the hands of the woman for whom she was a maid-of-all-work and shepherdess. "Far from being a rural idyll," Harris writes, "it seems her life was toilsome and grim, even by the standards of the region." She also underlines the importance of the woodland, as a site of conflict between the peasantry and the state and as a place where earlier miraculous apparitions had occurred. Aquéro fitted in with Pyrenean traditions about the Virgin Mary, but also with local lore about sprites and fairies. Finally, Soubirous's words about the Immaculate Conception came at a particularly convenient time for the Church, as the Vatican had recently translated this belief into doctrine.

In short, many different observers had good reason to believe Soubirous, and to consider the apparitions miraculous. Her story gained the support not only of the local peasantry, but of a Pyrenean bishop determined to bring his diocese onto the national scene, of a Catholic press eager for continuing evidence of divine intervention in human affairs, and even of figures close to the imperial court of Louis Napoleon. It was a powerful combination, and it soon overcame the initial resistance of the local authorities: within a few years the phenomenon of Lourdes had grown to astonishing proportions. From being simply one miraculous apparition among many (other women claimed visions not only in Lourdes but in the same grotto), the story came to animate a cult that would, by the turn of the century, bring hundreds of thousands of visitors every year. By the mid-1860s an enormous basilica had been built, and word of Lourdes's miraculous cures was starting to attract sufferers from across Europe. The town would be changed forever, becoming, among other things, one of the world's capitals of religious kitsch. "At Lourdes there is such a plethora of vulgarity," an otherwise sympathetic Huysmans wrote, "such a hemorrhage of bad taste, that the notion of some intervention by the Prince of Depravity inevitably springs to mind." Meanwhile Soubirous, her visions accomplished, was packed off to a convent in distant Nevers, where she died of tuberculosis in 1879, and there she remains, waxed and preserved as a relic. The business of saying what the visions meant was left to others to argue about.

The key figure here is the Catholic journalist Henri Lasserre, who attributed his own recovery from blindness to treatment with Lourdes water. His *Notre-Dame de Lourdes* sold more than a million copies: more than the works of Victor Hugo, Jules Verne, or Alexandre Dumas; more probably than any other book published in France in the nineteenth century. It ran to 142 editions in just seven years, was translated into eighty languages, and remained in print until the 1960s. It did so well because it was highly melodramatic, was simplistic to the point of gross inaccuracy, and turned both the obstructionist local authorities and the religious order that first oversaw the shrine into cartoon villains. The meticulous Jesuit Léonard Cros attempted a more accurate account of the apparitions but went too far in a different direction, laying out absolutely all the evidence, even where it contradicted itself. Catholic critics warned that he would destroy the credibility of the apparitions altogether. A combination of these criticisms and the pains he took in his researches meant that his book was not published until the 1920s and did not appear in full until 1957.

However expertly done, these sections pale beside the last one, which so brilliantly illuminates the bizarre world of nineteenth-century French Catholicism, still suffering from the trauma of the Revolution, and yearning to return to an imaginary medieval past of deep faith and organic social cohesion. For Catholics who saw themselves, despite their social position and often considerable wealth, as an oppressed island of faith in a hostile secular sea, the miraculous apparitions and cures gave reassurance of divine support as well as offering hope for the conversion of the faithless, and thanks to the pilgrimage that developed, providing an annual opportunity for mobilization in defense of the Church and true believers.

Catholic anxieties became more acute after the Commune, when anticlerical workers seized control of Paris, persecuted priests, and shot the archbishop. Among Catholic responses to this event was the construction of the Sacré-Coeur, built expressly to expiate the sins of the city and to stand guard over it, permanently, inescapably. These anxieties might have been allayed had France reembraced the Bourbon dynasty after the Commune's failure, but instead it opted for the Third Republic, elected anticlerical leaders like Jules Ferry, and drove Catholics once again to despair. In these circumstances every miracle cure reported at Lourdes and every new account of Soubirous's apparitions was seized on as further proof of the Catholic verities, to be flung in the face of the Republic and its secular supporters. The priests of the Assumptionist order, who organized the pilgrimages to Lourdes, led by such charismatic figures as François Picard, saw themselves as crusaders battling for their country's salvation. Against Marianne, symbol of the Republic, they held up the Virgin Mary. Against the will of the people, they held up the will of God.

Unlike earlier historians, Harris not only discusses the priests but gives equal time to their female sponsors and supporters, who contributed just as much to the way Lourdes developed. They ranged from the Duchesse d'Estissac, who had a replica of the grotto built in the grounds of her château, to the humblest nuns, clerical assistants, and lay disciples, whose relationships with the priests often had a sexual tinge. "Our Lord wants you more for himself every day," the head of the Assumptionists wrote to one of his female charges. "There are delicate things in your soul that he wishes to penetrate completely. You have to open up wide to him, and, when you are open, open yourself to him still further, because the divine Master has an insatiable need for your love and intimate sacrifices." She warns, however, against reading such relationships as nothing more than expressions of repressed sexual desire. "To reduce the feelings between priests and women to some kind of sexual perversion is to misunderstand the benefits women gained from such encounters.... In a pre-Freudian world, these encounters enabled them unselfconsciously to act out and play with many imaginary roles." Of one priest and nun she writes that "their spiritual 'love affair' was possibly the greatest human relationship of their lives." At the same time she suggests that the relative weakness of French feminism owes a great deal to this sort of Catholic activism, which gave women alternative outlets for their energies and ambitions.

The annual pilgrimage to Lourdes, organized by the priests and their followers, saw thousands of people trekking to the far south of France in the hope of a cure. Members of some of the country's wealthiest aristocratic and bourgeois families assisted them, acting as stretcher-bearers and nurses in what Harris calls "a temporary inversion that paradoxically reinforced social hierarchies at the journey's end." For the sick, the journey involved agonizingly long hours on the train and then four or more hours getting from the station to the shrine. The last rites often had to be administered en route. But suffering was so much the point of the exercise that priests might call out "no remedies" to the doctors who sometimes accompanied their patients. "Bodily sacrifice was admired above all else," Harris writes, "with the sick on stretchers using their last bit of strength to imitate the Passion by putting themselves in the position of Christ on the cross." After the Calvary of the journey would come, it was hoped, the resurrection of the cure. As for the nobs, by participating in the rituals, helping the afflicted, and exposing themselves to the "harrowing atmosphere" of the trains, hospitals, and pools, they were acting out an ideal of Christian solidarity that they dreamt of extending to French society as a whole.

The cures themselves caused the greatest controversy. At the very moment when the triumph of science seemed assured, when Pasteur and his germ theory seemed to be stripping away mystery and fear, the pilgrims of Lourdes were asserting the claims of the supernatural. The paralyzed stood up and walked, the blind saw, the deaf heard. Secular critics mocked it all as an anachronistic farce in which unscrupulous priests and charlatans preyed on the gullible and the hysterical. In *Lourdes*, his most popular novel, Zola scandalized Catholics by fictionalizing the case of a tuberculosis sufferer cured at the shrine and falsely claiming that she had relapsed afterward.

Anticlerical doctors descended on the town, eager to expose the cures as a fraud, or to find proper scientific explanations for them. Sometimes their task was relatively easy: one deaf woman regained her hearing after repeatedly syringing her ears with Lourdes water, washing away wax that had hardened there over several decades. At other times they resorted to the notion of "suggestion," or invoked that quintessential nineteenth-century malady, hysteria. On a few occasions they were simply stumped. Pierre de Rudder, a Flemish laborer, broke his leg so badly he spent a year in bed in terrible pain. His doctors found a three-centimeter gap separating the two parts of the unset bone and counseled amputation. Instead de Rudder went to Lourdes and was cured. Today, the leg bone resides in a glass case in the Lourdes museum, with only a fracture line visible.

In large part to avoid giving ammunition to the secular enemy, a medical bureau, staffed by Catholic doctors, was set up to separate true cures from false ones. It had strict standards, and in its first year of operation, the numbers of the cured fell by nearly half. As Harris points out, adopting the methods of modern science to verify the miraculous was more than a little paradoxical, and like Cros's researches, the medical bureau risked writing the miraculous out of Lourdes altogether.

Ironically, Harris, though not a Catholic, sometimes seems to take a less critical approach to the miracles. She doesn't endorse the thesis of divine intervention, but she considers it possible that the cures demonstrate something more interesting than temporary "suggestion," pointing to powerful, as yet poorly understood, ways the mind can act on the body. She even calls these mental capacities "miraculous"—though she puts the word in inverted commas. Harris is hardly the first to have concluded that something was at work that we still don't understand. Her last chapter shows that many of the secular intellectuals and physicians who observed the phenomenon were forced by what they saw— not just the "cures" but the degree of religious feeling, particularly on the part of women—to question their own assumptions about the workings of the mind, and the relationship of mind and body, notably in regard to the developing notion of the unconscious. Among them were a number of pioneers of the new science of psychology, including Charcot. "Psychoanalysis," Harris writes, "is built on religious foundations, on the 19th-century attempt to reinterpret the physical and psychological dimensions of the religious imagination." In this sense, it represents a retreat from nineteenth-century positivism and foreshadows the change in attitudes to science that is now taking place.

It is a pity that Harris decided not to take the story up to the present, leaving us to wonder about Soubirous's canonization, Franz Werfel's tremendously popular *Song of Bernadette*, the transformation of pilgrimage in the age of the global tourist industry, and the twentieth-century's own spectacular wave of Marian apparitions, from Fatima to Medjugorje. Between 1980 and 2000 alone there were more than two dozen widely reported apparitions in the United States alone, leading in some cases to lawsuits by neighbors incensed by the resulting parking problems.

Harris's failure to take on the twentieth century is a minor problem. A somewhat more serious one concerns her treatment of the links between Lourdes, extreme right-wing politics, and anti-Semitism. As the book makes clear, the architects of the Lourdes pilgrimage had a visceral hatred not only of republicans but of Protestants, Freemasons, and Jews.

Le Pèlerin, edited by the Assumptionist priest Vincent de Paul Bailly, regularly printed caricatures of Jews and accounts of Jewish ritual murder of Christians. The Assumptionists helped lead the campaign against Dreyfus, strongly supported the anti-Semitic monarchist Action Française, and in 1898 even toyed with the idea of a coup. As a result, in 1900 the republican government expelled them from France. Harris says that for these men and women "anti-Semitism was an integral part of their piety, the dark side of their veneration for the Virgin and the Eucharist."

"Integral" is a strong word. Yet in the following sentence, she tries to separate Lourdes and the pilgrimages from this political pollution: "In the enclosed world of pilgrimage, devoid of republicans, Freemasons and other 'enemies,' the venom and rancor of life under a distasteful regime faded, and the positive aspects of the Catholic program came once again to the fore." In this way she justifies restricting her own discussion of anti-Semitism to a couple of pages, although she devotes more to the overall political context.

The problem with this argument is, first, that it goes against what Harris herself has previously said: namely, that many of those who took part in the pilgrimage saw it in large part as a way to rebuild their strength against their enemies—republicans, Protestants, Freemasons, and Jews. Second, it avoids the question of the overall impact of Lourdes on French politics. To the extent that Lourdes was an effective means of mobilization for the extreme Catholic Right—and Harris leaves very little doubt that it was extremely effective—it directly strengthened the forces of reactionary monarchism and anti-Semitism. In most cases, a secular observer "converted" by the experience was another voice against Dreyfus, another vote for the Far right. Finally, both the stories of the cures and the anti-Semitic propaganda juxtaposed images of twisted, unhealthy, corrupt bodies with healthy, normal ones. How often were the Jews themselves referred to as a "sickness" or a "plague," calling, perhaps, for a drastic "cure"? Representations of suffering, diseased bodies can't be seen as altogether innocent when they feed directly into representations of a suffering, diseased body politic. It is not that easy to separate the "positive aspects" of Lourdes from its "dark side."

5

Conspiracy Porn: Fictional Anti-Semitism

During the French Revolution, an obsession with conspiracies became a characteristic trait of the radical left, which detected behind each of its setbacks the malign, hidden hand of counterrevolutionary plotters. In nineteenth-century France, however, it was the radical right that particularly excelled at spinning out tortuous, elaborate conspiracy theories. As the previous essay pointed out, the pious pilgrims who descended on the shrine at Lourdes everywhere saw evidence that dastardly plots were in motion to persecute and enslave Catholics of ancient French stock like themselves— plots by anarchists, revolutionaries, Protestants, Freemasons, Illuminati, and, above all, by Jews. This essay examines a novel by a famous present-day author, Umberto Eco, that takes these conspiracy theories for its subject. In the process the book proves remarkably illuminating about nineteenth-century France (if less successful, alas, as a piece of story-telling).

Barack Obama is a Kenyan-born communist jihadist. The Mossad staged the attacks of September 11. Vince Foster was murdered on the

Book under Review: Umberto Eco, *The Prague Cemetery* (Houghton Mifflin Harcourt, 2011). Essay originally published in *The New Republic*, November 9, 2011.

306

orders of his lover, the notorious lesbian Hillary Clinton. The U.S. government is concealing the wreckage of an alien spacecraft that crashed in New Mexico in 1947. A secret society named the Priory of Sion protects the living descendants of Jesus Christ and Mary Magdalene.

It is tempting to think that we are living in a golden age of conspiracy theories. The Internet has certainly made it easier than ever before to disseminate sensational revelations about mysterious, tentacular organizations and their nefarious plots. Other digital technologies, such as Photoshop, have made it possible for ordinary computer users to take on a role once reserved for master forgers, and fabricate sophisticated "evidence" to support these conspiracy theories, thereby giving them even greater credence and circulation. And yet conspiracy theories have always been with us—they are, alas, an integral part of our culture.

They took on their modern form at the same moment that so many other elements of European civilization did, with the invention of the printing press. The first great explosion of popular print in the early sixteenth century consisted in large part of shocking revelations about conspiracies: that Martin Luther had entered into a secret pact with the devil, or that the Catholic Church was itself a giant conspiracy to enslave Christendom. Fears of a malign British conspiracy against the thirteen colonies had a crucial role in bringing about the American Revolution. Robespierre justified the Reign of Terror as a response to counterrevolutionary intrigue. With the Nazis and the communists, the obsessive pursuit of conspirators led to the greatest mass murders in history.

Contrary to what one might assume, the advent of stable democratic politics does nothing to reduce the popularity of conspiracy theories. Democracy, after all, rests on the belief that governments are better directed by the common sense of ordinary people than by the esoteric wisdom of exclusive elites. (The historian Sophia Rosenfeld has fascinating things to say on this subject in her book *Common Sense*.) By its very nature, democracy tends to nourish a populist suspicion of elites, and from there it is just a short step to the conviction that these elites are involved in active conspiracies. The most influential populists in America today—right-wing talk show hosts—see politics largely in conspiratorial terms. Rush Limbaugh has repeatedly accused liberal Democrats of deliberately plotting to bring about the 2008 economic collapse, so as to advance their agenda of turning the United States into the USSR. Glenn

Beck has notoriously embraced a host of conspiracy theories, inspired in some cases by the work of crackpot anti-Semites, and often centering on the Jewish financier George Soros. But conspiracy theories are not exactly lacking on the left, either.

Conspiracies are the sinister doppelgängers of our attempts to understand the world around us in rational terms. And, of course, we love them. With its promise of initiation into occult mysteries, and its revelation of order where others only see chaos, the conspiratorial frame of mind brings distinct psychological pleasures. Hence the enduring popularity of fiction that might be characterized as conspiracy porn, exemplified in recent times by Dan Brown and Stieg Larsson. It is hard to say which of these two writers has more turgid prose, more impoverished capacity for description, or thinner, more stereotyped characters. But both of them are remarkably adept at slowly, teasingly pulling away one layer after another of a hidden plot, each time giving tantalizing new glimpses of the secret truth, but always holding back the full story until the final climax. Brown, in particular, has perfected the "Key to All Mythologies" as striptease.

Neither Brown nor Larsson, however, can hold a candle to some earlier practitioners of what has been a long and proud tradition. In particular, they pale before the great nineteenth-century master of conspiracy fiction, Alexandre Dumas. *The Man in the Iron Mask*, with its story of terrible intrigues against the brother of Louis XIV, and *The Three Musketeers*, featuring the dastardly plots of Cardinal Richelieu and Milady, are perhaps the best remembered of Dumas's novels; but in most of them the plot centers on, well, plots. Perhaps the single most lurid, sensational, spine-tingling fictional evocation of a secret conspiracy ever written comes in the first chapter of Dumas's now largely forgotten novel *Joseph Balsamo*, which appeared in 1846. Here he brought together all the iconic elements of the phenomenon. On the grounds of a ruined castle, on a remote mountain in Germany, in the year 1770, a series of cloaked figures emerge from the gloom. They verify their identities by exchanging passwords. They subject new members to frightening initiation rites. And then they finalize a sinister plan to change the course of history, in this case by destroying the monarchy of France. Unfortunately, nothing in the rest of the novel lives up to its opening, as the book laboriously follows the career of its title character, a real figure better known as Cagliostro, who badly damaged the reputation of the French royal family in the Diamond Necklace Affair of the 1780s.

It is precisely this opening scene from Dumas that provides one of the starting points for *The Prague Cemetery*. Umberto Eco is probably the world's best-selling postmodernist novelist, who famously declared, in the postscript to *The Name of the Rose*, that "books always speak of other books, and every story tells a story that has already been told." *The Name of the Rose* is itself an explicitly postmodern tissue of allusions to other texts, from Aristotle to Sherlock Holmes, larded with philosophical meditations on the construction of truth, but enlivened by a sensational murder mystery, vivid descriptions of the medieval setting, and a healthy dollop of transgressive romance (a cruel French critic once called Eco "Dan Brown for Ph.D.s"). Now, in this most recent novel, Eco has put aside most of the sex and much of the mystery, and abandoned himself almost entirely to intertextuality, borrowing copiously and overtly from Dumas and a host of other nineteenth-century novelists. (He even illustrates the story with nineteenth-century engravings.) This is a book about the making of books, which tells the story of a conspiracy to manufacture conspiracy theories.

Conspiracy theories, and their fabrication, are of course well-worn themes for Eco. In *The Name of the Rose*, his protagonists uncover a plot by figures in the Catholic Church to suppress a dangerous text: Aristotle's treatise on comedy. Eco's second novel, *Foucault's Pendulum*, centers on a group of Italians who concoct a giant conspiracy theory as a game, only for it to turn—or so it seems—frighteningly real. Illuminati, Rosicrucians, Knights Templar, Jesuits, the Priory of Sion, and the Elders of Zion are all familiar sights along Eco's curriculum vitae. With an insistent postmodern playfulness that can become repetitive, he uses novels to comment on the genre of the novel, on verisimilitude, and on the boundaries between fact and fiction. Deliberately concocted conspiracy theories— that is to say, fictions masquerading as fact, and bringing the orderliness of an imaginary world to the messiness and complexity of the real one— are perfect grist for his fictional mill.

The Prague Cemetery, which extends Eco's meditations on the subject, tells the life story of one of the most extraordinarily repulsive individuals in recent fiction. Raised in Turin in the 1840s by a bitter, twisted, reactionary grandfather who blames all the ills of the world on the French

Revolution and on the Jews, Simone Simonini grows up cruel, repressed, and numb to ordinary human emotion. Dismissing women as "a repulsive sex," he feels desire for nothing but food, and the novel at times seems to read like a series of recipes and restaurant menus: *agnolotti alla piemontese, tartare all'albese, écrivisses bordelaises, mousses de volaille, mauviettes en cerises, petites timbales à la Pompadour, cimier de chevreuil,* and so on. Reduced to poverty by an unscrupulous lawyer, Simonini discovers a talent for forgery, and thereby comes to the attention of the Piedmontese secret service at the very moment that the Kingdom of Piedmont is spearheading the unification of Italy. It employs him in various intrigues involving the revolutionary nationalist Garibaldi, at one point sending him to war-torn Sicily in the company of none other than Alexandre Dumas (who did in fact travel there on his yacht in 1860). But having carried out his assignments with somewhat too much zeal, Simonini is handed off by the Piedmontese to the French secret service. He spends the rest of the century in Paris, taking part in intrigues involving everything from the Paris Commune of 1871 to the Dreyfus Affair, and working for everyone from Napoleon III to the Prussian secret services to the tsarist Okhrana, while also consorting with a host of notorious fraudsters and forgers.

As Eco explains in a final section titled "Useless Learned Explanations," he has taken all these characters, except Simonini himself, from actual history. Simonini, in fact, comes across as a nineteenth-century Zelig, although far more active and malign. Among other things, we discover that it was actually Simonini who framed Captain Dreyfus for supposedly selling French military secrets to Germany, thereby precipitating the greatest crisis of the French fin de siècle. The great crisis of Simonini's own career, meanwhile, arises from his connection with the notorious French journalist known as Léo Taxil, who spent twelve years industriously publishing sensational revelations about lurid anti-Catholic conspiracies, only to cause an enormous scandal by announcing, in 1897, that he had made it all up to embarrass the Church.

In the course of these adventures, Simonini slowly puts together his greatest work of all—and this is where *Joseph Balsamo* comes in. A number of his employers ask Simonini to forge eyewitness accounts of the secret meeting of a great conspiratorial organization. He obliges, and explicitly takes Dumas's scene as the template: "Let us imagine conspirators who come from every part of the world and represent the tentacles of their sect spread throughout every country. Let us assemble them in a forest clearing, a cave, a castle, a cemetery or a crypt, provided it is reasonably dark. Let us get one of them to pronounce a discourse that clearly sets out the plan, and the intention to conquer the world." The actual identity of the conspirators does not entirely matter: depending on the needs of the particular employers, it can be the Illuminati or the Jesuits, the Freemasons or the Jews. "Here's a form to be filled out at will, by each person with his own conspiracy." The location shifts back and forth as well, as Simonini and a host of collaborators and competitors continuously revise the account, adding in allusion after allusion, borrowing from one printed account after another, in an orgy of intertextuality.

Most often the meeting takes place in the old Jewish cemetery in Prague, whence Eco's title. Only at the end of the novel does Simonini finish the manuscript, giving it to the Russians, and it is hardly a spoiler to reveal the title under which it becomes known, for Eco has hinted at this denouement for hundreds of pages: it is *The Protocols of the Elders of Zion*. This is of course the notorious forgery, in reality concocted by the Russian secret services, and purporting to reveal plans for Jewish world domination, which twentieth-century anti-Semites put to frighteningly effective use, and which continues to be regularly reissued throughout the Arab world. In the final pages of *The Prague Cemetery*, Simonini confesses that "the whole purpose of my life has been to bring down that accursed race," and delights in the fact that "thanks to my work, all the Mordechais in this world are on their way to a tremendous raging pyre." (Mordechai was the name of a Jew who supposedly confessed plans for world domination to Simonini's grandfather.)

Of course, since the author of this horrific story is Umberto Eco, none of it comes across straightforwardly. The novel opens with Simonini as an old man, in 1897, apparently trying to recover from some sort of trauma, and writing a journal at the suggestion of a brilliant young doctor he has encountered, a "whingeing little Jew" named, rather too obviously, "Froïde." Simonini discovers mysterious traces of a stranger, a cleric, in his apartment, and soon the cleric begins leaving him notes that betray a surprising knowledge of his life. Who is this man? An enemy? A ghost? A fantasy? Or perhaps an alter ego, the other side of a split personality? The narrative voice shifts back and forth between Simonini and the cleric, with occasional interventions by an omniscient narrator, as Simonini struggles to recapture a suppressed memory and to deal with the traumatic event behind it. Only at the end of the novel, even as Simonini frames Dreyfus and gives the *Protocols* to the Okhrana, does Eco reveal the nature of this trauma, in a macabre scene that reads like X-rated Dumas. Alas, readers originally drawn to Eco by the young monk's sexual escapade in *The Name of the Rose* will have given up long before they reach this point.

From a historical and philosophical point of view, *The Prague Cemetery* is a smart and intricate success: a fiction, hammered together out of spare boards of fact, about the concoction of a real historical document that itself tells a deeply and malevolently false story. All of this comes into focus only slowly, as the reader pieces together clues from the fragmentary writings of a deeply unreliable narrator who fears he is himself delusional, unable to tell fact from fiction, and uncertain as to whether the trauma that induced the delusion in the first place ever actually happened. Negotiating Eco's circles within circles within circles quickly induces a degree of vertigo—exactly as the author intended, no doubt. In the end, however, the playfulness is ingenious, but it is not particularly profound.

In Europe, one particular element of Eco's concoction provoked criticism: its depiction of Jews. Simonini describes the stereotypical Jew as having "the profile of a vulture, with fleshy lips, the lower lip heavily protruding like a Negro's, deep-set watery eyes, eyelids less open than those of other races." At one point he encounters a renegade Jew named Brafmann, who tells him the story of the secret Jewish organization known as the Kahal, which acts as a "secret government" behind the scenes, manipulating Christian governments and working for Jewish world domination. The Kahal was in fact central to nineteenth-century accounts of Jewish conspiracies, including the wildly popular ones of the French anti-Semite Édouard Drumont (who, needless to say, also appears in *The Prague Cemetery*) as well as the *Protocols of the Elders of Zion*. Still, Brafmann himself was an all too real historical figure—a Russian Jewish convert to Christianity who had taught Hebrew at the Orthodox seminary in Minsk and published copious anti-Semitic propaganda—and a writer can hardly hope to portray an anti-Semite with any verisimilitude if he does not put anti-Semitic stereotypes into the man's mouth.

This is not an anti-Semitic book. In fact, it is precisely the figure of the Jew that, from a historical and philosophical perspective, provides its most fascinating and subtle elements. As the historian David Nirenberg has argued, Jews have played a surprisingly important role in the genealogy of the philosophical and linguistic issues with which Eco is wrestling. In Christian thought, the Jew has often served as a sign of carnality and corruption. If the Christian believer strives for a higher and transcendent truth of the spirit, the Jew represents the low, limited, sordid reality of matter. In the world of the flesh—that is, the world of the Jew—all exchange, and therefore language itself, is corrupt, imperfect, and false: "for now we see through a glass, darkly, but then face to face." The Jew himself can therefore become the sign of forgery and fiction. Except that in *The Prague Cemetery*, it is the Jews who instead become the subject of one of the most evil and effective forgeries and fictions ever devised, a book concocted (in Eco's telling) by a forger disgusted with his own flesh but unable to overcome it, whose exterminationist anti-Semitism is clearly a manifestation of his own infinite self-loathing.

In Eco's novel, the figure of the Jew knits together forgery and fiction, conspiracy and carnality. In the climactic, trauma-inducing scene of the novel—a Black Mass, no less—a renegade priest denounces the "false god Jesus Christ" and then declares, in mockery of the Gospels: "In the beginning was the flesh, and the flesh was with Lucifer, and the flesh was Lucifer." Is it a coincidence that Eco has named his protagonist Simon, recalling both the given Jewish name of the apostle Peter and the name of the sorcerer Simon Magus, who tried corruptly to sell the blessings of the Holy Spirit (and who thereby gave his name to simony)?

It would have been wonderful if Eco's talent as a storyteller had, in this novel, fully lived up to his philosophical and critical ambitions. Unfortunately, it does not. (The same was true of *Foucault's Pendulum*.) For all the fascination of the questions Eco poses, and the intellectual pleasure involved in teasing out the successive puzzles, the book's exposition is often labored and confusing. "The Narrator is aware," Eco writes in his afterword, "that, in the fairly chaotic plot sequence of the diaries reproduced here . . . the reader might have difficulty in following the linear progression of events." Well, yes. Doubtless, Eco means this statement as yet another whirling, playful gesture, but it raised too loud a laugh from this reader. And the chronological table of events provided by Eco proved all too necessary to make sense out of the preceding 439 pages. Names and dates flew past so quickly that I sometimes found it almost impossible to keep track—and I teach modern European history for a living. I do not see how anyone could easily appreciate, or even follow, the pages on the Dreyfus Affair without a detailed knowledge of its events and its protagonists. Between virtuosity and pretension, erudition and obscurity, the lines are thin.

Then there are the masses of detail Eco throws in. He may have included them so as to play even further with the conventions of novelistic verisimilitude, but they have a crushing effect. "Today," one character remarks all too casually, apropos of bomb-making, "there's more interest in nitrobenzene and nitroaphthalene. Or if you treat paper and cardboard with nitric acid, you obtain nitramine, which is similar to xyloidin." Glad to have that explained. Forty pages later Eco tells about the animal corpses that piled up in the Paris sewers in a single six-month period: four thousand dogs, five calves, twenty sheep, seven goats, eighty hens, sixty-nine cats, nine hundred fifty rabbits, a monkey, and a boa constrictor. At least the list has a certain morbid entertainment value. But then there are the recipes and the menus.

Worst of all, Eco does not give the reader enough reason to follow the long, tortuous story of the misanthropic Simonini, who not only lacks all redeeming features but finally, and more fundamentally, lacks interest. Eco does better with many of the minor characters taken from history, including Dumas, Garibaldi, various other motley and bumbling Italian revolutionaries, and a cunning Russian spy. But nearly all of them flit by in a few pages and then disappear. The romance and the mystery that enlivened *The Name of the Rose*, and saved it from drowning in a froth of philosophical speculation, are mostly absent from *The Prague Cemetery*. In the end, Umberto Eco has forgotten the single most important ingredient for successful conspiracy theories and novels alike. They can be outlandish, outrageous, and even frankly unbelievable; but, as even the crudest generator of Internet rumors remembers as he spins out the latest tale about how the KGB secretly altered President Obama's birth certificate, they should never, ever be boring.

6

Pogroms of Words: The France of the Dreyfus Affair

In POLITICAL LIFE, NOTHING HAS GREATER explosive potential than a spectacular revelation that apparently demonstrates the truth of some long-suspected malfeasance. In 1791, King Louis XVI's botched attempt to flee France proved what his radical opponents had long charged: that he was in league with the counterrevolution. The incident shocked the entire country and did more than any other factor to bring about the king's fall and execution. A century later, in 1894, it was the turn of the French right to declare its conspiracy theories vindicated, when a Jewish army officer, Alfred Dreyfus, was arrested as a spy and a traitor. Unlike the king, Dreyfus was innocent, but so perfectly did the idea of his guilt fit the right-wing mindset that "anti-Dreyfusards" could never acknowledge this fact. Indeed, the more the evidence of his innocence accumulated, the greater their fury. As a result, the Dreyfus Affair became the great conflagration in which all the smoking political passions of nineteenth-century France ignited—the culmination of what the book under consideration in this essay termed the period's "culture wars."

Book under Review: Frederick Brown, *For the Soul of France: Culture Wars in the Age of Dreyfus* (Knopf, 2010). Essay originally published in *The New Republic*, August 27, 2010.

The phrase "culture wars" has a peculiarly contemporary and American sound. Its very hyperbole captures something about our over-excited political culture. It summons up images of Sarah Palin denouncing liberal elites to a Tea Party convention, or of hippies facing off against riot police. It triggers associations with a series of "hot button" American issues: gay marriage, abortion, gun control, prayer in schools.

Yet "culture wars" are in fact endemic to Western modernity. They may be defined as conflicts that divide a country less along regional, confessional, racial, economic, or even ideological lines than according to more inchoate but easily grasped disagreements over basic values, assumptions, and beliefs. The long-standing Russian disputes between westernizers and Slavophiles qualify as a culture war. Germany came close to inventing the phrase with its Kulturkampf ("culture struggle") of the late nineteenth century, although that particular battle had a distinctly confessional and anti-Catholic accent. And it certainly fits modern France. It was in 1820 that the historian Augustin Thierry observed that "we believe we are one nation, but we are actually two nations on the same soil, two nations at war in their memories and irreconcilable in their hopes for the future."

Of course, those who bemoan culture wars are usually waging them at the same time, and Thierry himself offers a good illustration. He may have been commenting on the harsh divisions that persisted even after the revolutionary and Napoleonic traumas, but he was also helping to deepen them, through a particularly corrosive variety of historical mythmaking. A secular liberal, he meant "two nations" in the most literal possible sense, for he cast his conservative aristocratic enemies as literal aliens—invading "Franks" who had remained racially distinct from and socially opposed to the country's native Gauls since late antiquity. His solution to the problem of France's culture wars was simple: victory over the intruders.

By the late nineteenth century, few French people still believed that they could trace their problems directly back to the fifth century. But the country's culture wars were still very much in progress, and Frederick Brown is quite right to use the phrase in the subtitle of his wonderful book. In fact, France's great modern culture wars arguably stretched over an even longer period, taking shape before the French Revolution and lasting into the mid-twentieth century.

Of course, the genealogy of the contending parties is anything but clear. Resisters and Vichyites were not the same thing as Dreyfusards and anti-Dreyfusards, who in turn differed from mid-nineteenth-century republicans and legitimists, Restoration-era liberals and "ultras," revolutionary Jacobins and counterrevolutionaries, and the philosophes and antiphilosophes of the Enlightenment. Yet there were still strong continuities, which the participants themselves recognized. At any moment, France had millions of inhabitants who saw their country as the natural home of reason, of Enlightenment, of science, and of cosmopolitan openness to the world. And it had millions of others who insisted it was properly a land of Catholic faith and mission, monarchical tradition, and a closed, organic social structure. Between the two sides, there was rarely much common ground.

As Brown shows, the late nineteenth century saw two major—and related—shifts in the country's long cultural quarrel. The first was the consolidation of the secular republic. Between 1789 and 1871, France had lurched erratically back and forth between monarchy, republic, and Bonapartist empire, experiencing three revolutions, five coups d'état, and two regime-changing military debacles in the process, as well as countless smaller insurrections. Then in 1870–1871, Napoleon III's Second Empire collapsed after its humiliating defeat in the Franco-Prussian War, and even as the victors proclaimed the new German Empire in the Hall of Mirrors at Versailles, politicians in Paris founded the Third Republic. It got off to an extremely rocky start: in the spring of 1871, Parisian radicals rebelled against it and created the alternative government of the Commune, which the Republic bloodily suppressed. For several years thereafter, a conservative legislature seemed on the verge of restoring the monarchy yet again, only to have the project founder on the intransigence of the pretender to the throne, the feeblest of the Bourbons, who refused to reign under the Revolution's tricolor flag. Republicans also averted the threat of yet another coup, by the charismatic general Georges Boulanger, and by the 1890s the regime finally seemed to rest on solid ground. Its supporters meanwhile proceeded with an ambitious program to remove the Catholic Church from public life, establishing a system of free, state-run primary education and then, in 1905, formally separating church and state.

The opponents of the Republic never accepted its legitimacy, but increasingly—and this is the second shift that Brown recounts—they found another target for their outrage. In 1886, a third-rate journalist named Édouard Drumont published *La France juive*, or *Jewish France*, which became one of the greatest best sellers in French history. France had of course known anti-Semitism before, but in the 1880s it began to take on an astonishing new virulence and became ever more central to French life.

Drumont and his followers spun out bizarre and tortuous conspiracy theories, eventually involving a secret Jewish syndicate they dubbed the Sanhedrin and a secret rabbinic association called the Kahal, supposedly bent on world domination. When a prominent bank, closely linked to conservatives and the Church, went bankrupt in 1882, the anti-Semites blamed Jewish financiers. When an early French-financed attempt to dig a canal in Panama collapsed amid scandal a few years later, with some Jewish figures playing a role, it was a "Jewish disaster." Drumont founded a newspaper, *La libre parole*, to advance his views, and everywhere it found evidence of further Jewish plots.

His message spread throughout the country, relayed in large part by Catholic clergy. "We are being pillaged, dishonored, exploited, and emptied by the Jew," Brown quotes, almost at random, from a diocesan newsletter. "Servile, slithering, artful, filthy, and vile when he is the weaker one, he becomes arrogant when he has the upper hand, as he does now. The Jew is our master.... When one of these vultures swoops down on the finances of a people, he pilfers, ransoms, tears, flays, strangles." In this mephitic climate, it is hardly surprising that when the French intelligence services came across evidence of a high-placed German mole in the French army in 1894, suspicion immediately fell on a Jewish officer.

Army officials quickly conducted a kangaroo court-martial of Alfred Dreyfus, failing to disclose exculpatory evidence. Dreyfus received a life sentence, to be served on Devil's Island, where such sentences were usually short. And then, what had started as a simple, albeit egregious miscarriage of justice turned into the Affair. As the extent of official misconduct became clear, in large part thanks to the heroic efforts of Dreyfus's family, desperate officers brazenly forged further evidence against him. They even went so far as to protect the real mole, Ferdinand Esterhazy, when his guilt became apparent, to preserve the honor of the army. The question of Alfred Dreyfus dominated headlines and public discussion, divided families, and seemed once again to threaten the Republic's survival. It took many years, a tortuous series of trials, and an unprecedented campaign for public opinion—exemplified by the Dreyfusard Émile Zola's *J'accuse*, his famous open letter to the president of the Republic—before Dreyfus finally won exoneration in 1906.

But the real significance of the Dreyfus Affair derives from the torrent of sheer smoking venom that flowed from the mouths and the pens of the anti-Dreyfusards. A few years ago the French sociologist and historian Pierre Birnbaum skillfully demonstrated its full, horrifying extent in a book called *The Anti-Semitic Moment*. In virtually every corner of the country, Jews were vilified and threatened, and mobs paraded in the street calling for their deaths. An Anti-Semitic League founded by Drumont flourished, with hundreds of branches throughout France. Outside observers reacted with horror, including the Austrian Jewish journalist Theodor Herzl, who drew the lesson that Jews could live normal lives only in a homeland of their own and went on to found the Zionist movement.

For French Jews themselves, the Dreyfus Affair had a more ambiguous conclusion. After all, Dreyfus was finally vindicated. Justice, and the Republic, prevailed in the end. And despite the outpouring of anti-Semitism, the Affair led to surprisingly little bloodshed. In metropolitan France, not a single Jew lost his or her life, although two were killed in French Algeria. Fittingly enough for this most verbal of countries, the Dreyfus Affair was a pogrom of words. Still, the place of the Jews in France hardly seemed secure. As historians have often remarked, at the turn of the twentieth century, the European country that seemed most likely to perpetrate a holocaust was not Germany or Austria, but France.

Frederick Brown devotes the longest chapter of his learned book to the Dreyfus Affair, and rightly so, for it was by far the greatest battle in these culture wars. Brown does not enter into debate with other historians, or offer opinions on the largest historical issues posed by the affair—for instance, whether this new anti-Semitic moment differed in fundamental ways from earlier waves of European Jew-hatred. He is content to tell the story, cogently and clearly. His narrative, though, certainly suggests a connection between anti-Semitism and the consolidation of the Republic. It notes that contemporaries themselves saw Jews as symbols of the Republican order and anti-Semitism as a stalking horse for its opponents (in the words of the anarchist Louise Michel, as "a pretext by means of which monarchist Catholics might put the Republic in mortal danger"). But he lets readers draw their own conclusions.

He follows much the same strategy in the rest of the book. He does not try to give an exhaustive history of French cultural conflict in the late nineteenth century. Instead, he offers readers a somewhat meandering but consistently instructive series of episodes and sketches, starting with the controversies around Ernest Renan's attempt to write a "historical" life of Jesus, in the 1860s, which scandalized observant Catholics. He gives short, vivid chapters on the financial scandals, some fine sketches of individual personalities, and a remarkable chapter on the way a tragic fire in a pavilion built for charitable fund-raising temporarily brought a truce in the culture wars, only for animosities to burst out again quickly among the mourners. He concludes with the stark contrast between a gala "banquet of science" held in 1895 and another banquet five years later in honor of the conservative writer Maurice Barrès. The latter included a speech by a conservative journalist who praised "virtuous violence," and insisted that "beating a sick man bloody is better than leaving him to rot." France was still very much two nations in one, and the risk of the culture wars turning real seemed as high as ever.

There are a few strange omissions. Brown might have devoted some space to the outlandish shrine of Lourdes, with its massive pilgrimages and alleged miracle cures, which took on huge significance for Catholics under the Third Republic. Brown also pays surprisingly little attention to France's acquisition of a vast overseas empire during this period. Conflicts between Catholic missionaries abroad and the Republic's famous "civilizing mission" ensured that the French culture wars spilled over to large areas of Africa and other parts of the world as well (although at times there was also surprising cooperation). Brown does observe, though, that the Paris World Fair of 1878 grotesquely included "several hundred 'indigenous people'" who "spent six months in a human zoo called the Negro Village."

As befits the author of celebrated lives of Flaubert and Zola, Brown is at his best in biographical mode. He does particularly well with the industrious, methodical engineer Gustave Eiffel, creator of the eponymous tower. As the book reminds us, initially the Eiffel Tower received as much criticism as applause, and not only from the surprisingly numerous artists who denounced it as "an odious column of bolted metal." The project originally came about as part of an exhibition marking the centenary of the French Revolution and celebrating the triumph of reason and science. And as its frame rose high above the city, it all too obviously challenged the other great Parisian construction project of the period: the lugubrious Basilica of the Sacred Heart, or Sacré-Coeur, which was beginning to loom over the city from the heights of Montmartre. (It was not finished until 1914.) The Catholic Church originally conceived of Sacré-Coeur as a reminder of and "expiation" for the city's sins during the Commune, when the city's archbishop was taken hostage and then shot.

Brown has a particularly brilliant sketch of Georges Boulanger, the charismatic and vainglorious general who came close to seizing power at the end of the 1880s. Boulanger initially posed not as a combatant in France's culture wars but as an "apolitical" solution to them, and in this regard he resembled a succession of generals who tried to play similar roles throughout modern French history, Bonaparte and De Gaulle most successfully. French republicans and monarchists alike have historically distrusted populist appeals to the crowds, preferring to put their faith in impersonal institutions. But Boulanger, like Bonaparte, defied these conventions, highlighting his own heroic life story (including feats of derring-do in Algeria and Indochina, and a serious wound incurred during the Italian War of Independence), and making carefully planned appearances astride a splendid black charger. As Brown nicely remarks, he knew how to create "the illusion of depth."

The figure of the charismatic general in politics actually came closer to the nineteenth-century American political model than to the French— and not coincidentally, as Brown notes, Boulanger formed many of his political ideas during a visit to the United States in 1881. "When left alone," Brown writes, "he concluded that Jacksonian democracy worked better than French republicanism." By the end of the decade, however, Boulanger had lost faith in democracy of any sort and slipped closer to the far right. His story ended farcically, as his opponents charged him with attempting to subvert the Republic and embezzling money from the War Ministry, and his political movement quickly collapsed. In 1891, stricken by grief at the death of his mistress, he traveled to her graveside in Brussels, leaned back against her tombstone, and blew his brains out.

Boulanger could not bring the culture wars to an end. Neither could Dreyfus's vindication in 1906. And despite a so-called holy union in 1914–1918, neither could World War I, which Brown briefly discusses at the very end of his book. In fact, in the 1920s and 1930s the conflicts turned viciously and destructively ideological, with the rise of the French Communist Party, the formation of various fascist and reactionary groups, and a right-wing attempt to overthrow the Republic in 1934. The culture wars ended only when the Catholic monarchist right made its pact with the devil under Vichy, not only accepting Nazi rule but also taking advantage of it to make a final reckoning with its enemies, notably the Jews. The Liberation in 1944 left these culture warriors largely discredited, and despite occasional stirrings since then, the battles of the age of Dreyfus are well and truly over.

Since 1944, in fact, France has known a remarkable degree of cultural consensus. This does not always appear obvious from the American media's coverage of the country, which mostly seems to feature riots, protests, and strikes. But vocal opposition to government reforms, such as attempts to shake up higher education, or to loosen labor laws, amounts in large part to a traditional form of French political theater, and does not point to any fundamental division over values, assumptions, or beliefs. Catholicism, a principal player in the older culture wars, has a shockingly small place in French public life today. In one recent poll, only slightly more than half the population described themselves as even nominally Catholic. Abortion evokes very little passion, as compared with the United States. Neither does the large role taken by government throughout society, including in areas such as health care. To be sure, the problems related to immigrant populations, and particularly the challenge posed by radical Islam, have generated tremendous anxieties. But with the exception of a relatively small minority, most French people agree in general terms about the need to "integrate" these populations. If the Muslim population continues its present rate of expansion (a doubtful proposition), and if radical Islam flourishes within it, then a new and virulent set of culture wars could well break out in the future. But for the moment, this possibility is by no means assured.

So France is no longer the "two nations on the same soil" that Augustin Thierry described almost two centuries ago. Thierry's essay itself now appears somewhat ironic, for it was mostly not about France at all but about the United States. Thanks to the American Revolution, Thierry argued, "America has expelled from its shores the nation that claimed to rule over it," and therefore achieved the sort of ethnic unity and freedom that the divided French could only dream of. But the two countries' more recent history has demonstrated all too clearly that culture wars are not merely the remnants of ancient ethnic animosity. They can bubble up from within a seemingly homogeneous, consensual body politic and split it dangerously apart. It is happening all too obviously in the United States today, and as a result Thierry's lament about "two nations on the same soil" is now our own. We must hope that the divisions begin to heal before our culture wars turn as vicious and ugly as the ones Frederick Brown has described. Or has that already happened?

Anti-Semitic exhibition, entitled "The Jew and France," at the Palais Berlitz in Paris, 1941. It was sponsored by the Vichy government and connected to the introduction of official discrimination against the French Jewish population. Germany, Federal Archives, Bild 146-1975-041-07, 0.Ang.

Part VI

VICHY

───────◦◦◦◦───────

SOON AFTER FRANCE SURRENDERED TO GERMANY in 1940, the great French Jewish historian Marc Bloch wrote a short book entitled *Strange Defeat*. It blamed the country's military debacle not only on the conservatism and rigidity of French military planners, but more generally on the degeneration of French society, which had allegedly fallen prey to pervasive selfishness and greed. For many years, versions of this thesis remained conventional wisdom for historians, who characterized prewar France as a decadent "stalemate society" incapable of modernization, or of resisting extreme ideological passions. In this view, the triumph of the French ultra-right during the Vichy regime represented a natural culmination, the moment when out-of-control putrescence ate away the last beams holding French society together and caused a disgraceful collapse.

More recently, some scholars have persuasively contested this thesis (notably my Princeton colleague Philip Nord, in *France 1940: Defending the Republic*). In their view, the defeat of 1940 was by no means inevitable, and the Third Republic by no means as frail as Bloch, in his despair, had believed. Vichy was not the foreordained conclusion to the Third Republic's culture wars.

This new perspective does not, however, diminish the moral drama of Vichy that originally attracted me to the subject—quite the opposite. If the defeat of 1940 was caused by a particular conjunction of events, rather than by the Republic's general debility, why did it then produce such a crisis of faith in the Republic? Why did so many of the French rally so quickly to a regime pledged to an ultra-right ideology that had never prevailed at the polls? Why did so many of them collaborate with Hitler?

The essays here do not pretend to answer these questions, but they look at numerous individual cases, principally from literature and the arts. Among them is one genuine hero, Jean Guéhenno, and one genuine moral monster, Louis Darquier. And there are many others, of course, who fall in between.

I

When French Irrationality Was Deadly: Vichy's Literary Progenitors

THIS ESSAY DEALS WITH VICHY only in part. In the book it appraises, Frederick Brown continued the project begun in For the Soul of France *(which I discuss in chapter 6 of part V). In particular he looked at the writers, mostly but not exclusively on the right, who were most entranced by the ideological extremes in the last decades of the Third Republic. But the single most interesting writer he examined, Pierre Drieu La Rochelle, became a self-proclaimed poet of fascism and a mainstay of Vichy's cultural establishment. His example helps to illuminate why so many French writers became willing supporters of Vichy—and, therefore, of the Third Reich.*

Dancing with the devil is an old pursuit among French writers. Even such a stalwart of the Enlightenment as Diderot created a fictional character (the seductive Nephew of Rameau) who could remark, "If there is any genre in which it matters to be sublime, it is evil, above all." From Diderot through de Sade and de Maistre, Baudelaire and Huysmans, down to Michel Houellebecq and Jonathan Littell, a powerful tradition

---

Book under Review: Frederick Brown, *The Embrace of Unreason: France, 1914–1940* (Knopf, 1940). Essay originally published in *The New Republic*, May 31, 2014.

in French writing has challenged the bounds of conventional morality, loudly defied the dictates of Enlightenment reason, and expressed an abiding fascination with blood. It is as if the culture that, perhaps more strongly than any other, celebrated reason and geometrical order also provoked within itself a deep, wild, and willfully primitive reaction, a return of the repressed par excellence.

Never in French history did this cultural impulse prove more pernicious than during the troubled decades of the Third Republic (1870–1940). In this period, some of France's most talented writers gazed longingly into the abyss and then turned the full power of their eloquence against the institutions of parliamentary democracy. Even as the Republic lurched from scandal to scandal and crisis to crisis, writers on both the left and the right subjected it to endless, pitiless mockery and abuse. Robert Brasillach, one of the most brilliant writers and critics of his generation, likened it to "a syphilitic old whore, stinking of patchouli and yeast infection." Charles Maurras, an enormously skilled polemicist, endlessly denounced it as "the Jew State, the Masonic State, the immigrant State." Such attacks did much to drain French democracy of legitimacy precisely at its moment of greatest peril. They made it all too easy for a portion of France's elites to treat the crushing defeat of 1940 as history's judgment on a corrupt and senile society, and therefore to embrace Hitler's grotesque New Order rather than to struggle against it.

Frederick Brown has now taken the story he first pursued in *For the Soul of France*, which dealt principally with the late nineteenth century, through the interwar period. This time no single "affair" dominates the landscape, as the Dreyfus Affair did in the earlier book, but the specter of Vichy looms on the horizon, as the final destination at which so many of those who "embraced unreason" eventually arrived.

Although Brown deals with a great many such figures, he reserves his most sustained attention for a handful of writers of real talent. Maurice Barrès, who died in 1923, was a wildly popular novelist and anti-Dreyfusard best known for his work *The Uprooted*, published in 1897. A story of a group of young men from his native province of Lorraine, it excoriated the Republic's secular educational system for supposedly destroying the connection between French students and their native soil and "race." Maurras, a hugely prolific poet, critic, and journalist, became the guiding spirit of the reactionary movement known as the Action Française, and lived long enough to spend his last years in prison for "complicity with the enemy" during the Occupation. On his conviction in 1945, he exclaimed: "It's Dreyfus's revenge!" Pierre Drieu La Rochelle, younger than the others, was a novelist and critic who openly embraced fascism in the 1930s. Rather than face trial as Maurras had done, he committed suicide soon after the Liberation.

As in *For the Soul of France*, Brown tells his story in an episodic, sometimes impressionistic manner. He mixes chapters about Barrès, Maurras, and Drieu together with vignettes about a variety of scandals and causes over which the apostles of "unreason" obsessed. One chapter follows the long campaign to canonize Joan of Arc, which finally came to fruition in 1920. The Action Française celebrated Joan as a symbol of the true Catholic France, and held her up against the godless Revolution of 1789, regularly staging massive processions that ended at Joan's golden statue in the Place des Pyramides in Paris. (In recent years, the National Front of Jean-Marie Le Pen and his daughter, Marine, have continued the tradition.) Barrès, Maurras, and Drieu all had a near-fatal weakness for neo-Romantic medieval kitsch. Another chapter delves into the Stavisky Affair of 1934, which centered on the collapse of a massive Ponzi scheme perpetrated by a Russian-born Jew named Alexandre Stavisky. Thanks to his close connection with government ministers, the affair led to the collapse of the ruling center-left coalition and prompted right-wing rioting that briefly threatened the Republic. Yet another vignette traces the hilarious far right obsession with Maggi, a staid Swiss dehydrated-food manufacturer (still in business and now part of Nestlé), which the Action Française accused of cloaking a vast "Jewish-German" espionage network.

Occasionally Brown's method becomes needlessly distracting. He repeats information, jumps back and forth in time, and returns to themes and characters already discussed in his earlier book—indeed, despite the dates in the subtitle, much of this book's first hundred pages returns to the fin de siècle. Brown never provides an overview of the period's history, and uninitiated readers will find themselves having to flick back continually to a timeline that he provides at the end. Despite some fine pages on surrealism, he does disappointingly little with the visual arts, and largely neglects some writers who would have fit naturally into his story, such as Robert Brasillach and perhaps Céline. Still, the book as a whole is more than engaging enough to assuage these irritations.

Although Brown's principal fascination lies with the far right, he does not ignore the other side of the political spectrum, which offered its own brand of unreason during these years. The Communist poet Louis Aragon weaves in and out of the narrative, and so, more substantially, does the surrealist poet and artist André Breton, who joined the Party in 1927 but could never match Aragon's orthodoxy (leading to his expulsion in 1933). In an atmosphere where the political extremes often touched, both men were for years close friends with Drieu La Rochelle. Brown also has a memorable description of the Paris Exposition of 1937, in which the twin ideological threats to the Republic took an alarmingly physical form. On one side of the Eiffel Tower the Soviets constructed a stone monolith topped by twin heroic figures, each seventy-five feet tall, "thrusting the hammer and sickle skyward like conquistadors setting foot on a new continent." On the other side, Hitler's architect, Albert Speer, answered with an even taller monument, topped by a twenty-foot-tall Germanic eagle, "its wings spread like Dracula's mantle."

Brown also has space for at least a couple of heroes, familiar enough to adepts of French history, but presented here with verve. Even as the French were preparing, in 1914, to march off to a war that Maurice Barrès would celebrate as "a resurrection," at least one French politician had the courage to dissent. "Today you are told: act, always act!" the Socialist Jean Jaurès declared in January 1914. "But what is action without thought? It is the barbarism born of inertia.... To stand for peace today is to wage the most heroic of battles." Six months later, just three days before France declared war on Germany, Jaurès was shot and killed by a nationalist hooligan, who was later acquitted by a prowar jury.

Brown also introduces one of Jaurès's disciples, Léon Blum, a talented writer and politician whose early admiration for Maurice Barrès did not survive the Dreyfus Affair. In 1936 Blum, now leader of the French Socialists, barely escaped Jaurès's fate when a gang of Action Française thugs dragged him out of his car on the Boulevard Saint-Germain and beat him savagely. He survived, led the Popular Front to victory in that year's parliamentary elections, and became France's first Jewish prime minister, whereupon the deputy Xavier Vallat greeted him with a notorious speech in the National Assembly: "Your assumption of power, Mr. Prime Minister, is unquestionably an historic event. For the first time, this old Gallo-Roman land will be governed by a Jew.... I say what I think—and bear the disagreeable burden of saying aloud what others only think—which is that this peasant nation would be better served by someone whose origins, however modest, reach into the entrails of our soil than by a subtle Talmudist." Vallat, a close friend of Charles Maurras, would go on to head Vichy's General Commission for Jewish Affairs.

The really remarkable sections of Brown's book, however, are the ones that deal not with politicians or scandals but with the three writers Barrès, Maurras, and Drieu. And even here, one subject in particular stands out. The portraits of Barrès and Maurras are nuanced and sensitive, but both men, despite their talent, moved too easily and quickly from serious spiritual struggle to glib, simple partisanship to be truly interesting. Indeed, both often put their talent aside entirely in the service of partisan hackery. Maurras, who went almost entirely deaf at age fourteen, certainly had pathos in his life. But his massive output all too often consisted of nothing more than wittily vulgar abuse, littered with all manner of racial and anti-Semitic slurs.

Drieu La Rochelle, although he, too, ultimately failed to become a truly great writer, was different. At age fifteen, in 1908, the mischievous, antic adolescent had a fateful encounter with Nietzsche. *Thus Spake Zarathustra* enthralled him, and he went on, in his penultimate year of school, to tear through Descartes, Schopenhauer, Hegel, Schelling, Fichte, Bergson, Hartmann, William James, Darwin, and Spencer. In 1914, he went off to fight in World War I with a copy of *Thus Spake Zarathustra* in his knapsack. The war only confirmed the lessons he found in Nietzsche about vital energy and the dangers of degeneration. "The trumpet of war sounded in my blood," he wrote later. "At that moment, I belonged body and soul to my race charging through the centuries... toward the eternal idol of Power, of Grandeur."

After the war Drieu joined an eclectic and politically ecumenical literary circle that included the three great Andrés of interwar literary France: Breton, Malraux, and Gide. To Breton, in 1927, he dedicated a memoir called *The Young European*, arguing that parliamentary democracy had driven France to decadence. As Brown points out, Breton's surrealism, with its longing for some new creation, born out of the unconscious and capable of recovering a forgotten human unity, was all too compatible with the post-Romantic sensibility that had also nourished Barrès and Maurras. "With its penchant for the bizarre and the surprising, its contempt for bourgeois morality, its black humor, its glorification of evil genius, its language of rebirth, its messianism, its explorations of the erotic at the margin of death, the postwar literary generation envisaged a new human condition and succumbed to the ravages of a twentieth-century *mal de siècle*."

Drieu himself wrote some works of considerable power. His short novel *Le feu follet* (The Manic Fire), of 1931, although tinged with hackneyed criticisms of European degeneration, gave a darkly disturbing picture of a heroin addict's descent into despair and his ultimate suicide. Drieu's criticism could be acute, and he deserves much of the credit for bringing Jorge Luis Borges to European attention after a trip he made to Argentina in 1933. "My poet walked and walked, striding like one possessed," Drieu recalled of the time he spent with Borges. "He walked me through his despair and his love, for he loved this desolation."

But in the end Drieu's politics overwhelmed and crushed his literary inclinations. In January 1934, he spent a week in Nazi Berlin and was enraptured. A month later, he witnessed the right-wing riots in Paris and cheered on the forces trying to overthrow the Republic. In 1936, he attended the inaugural meeting of the Parti Populaire Français, a fascist party led by a thug-like former Communist named Jacques Doriot. Drieu fantasized that Doriot was the messianic leader who could break through the pettiness, the banality, and the ordinary corruptions of life and recreate "great communions." Drieu thenceforth styled himself the poet of fascism, defending it as "the political movement that charts its course most straightforwardly, most radically toward a great revolution of mores, toward the restoration of the body—health, dignity, plenitude, heroism." His writing turned steadily more crude, and he gave vent to gutter anti-Semitism. "In whatever language decadence slavers," he wrote in an inferior novel called *Gilles*, "whether it be Marxism or Freudianism, the words of Jews inform the drool." The novel portrayed a France undermined by the assimilation of all manner of "alien" elements, including Jews, feminists, homosexuals, and surrealists (a movement with which he had by this time definitively broken).

Drieu was now prepared for his role as a leading impresario of cultural collaboration. During the Occupation, he feverishly supported Marshal Pétain's "National Revolution," and took over the most important French literary periodical, the *Nouvelle revue française*. The fact that he used his influence to save some friends from the Nazis (including a former wife who had been born Jewish) cannot mitigate this record, and to the end Drieu remained loyal to a horrific ideal. "I hope for the triumph of totalitarian man over the world," he confided to his journal in June 1944. "Enough of this dust of individuals in the crowd."

Drieu La Rochelle's darkly fascinating career inspires Frederick Brown to some remarkably fine writing. "Despair was Drieu's homeland," Brown writes of the young author. "The character Drieu could flesh out most convincingly was his shadow." By the time Drieu gave himself over fully to fascism, Brown comments, he "felt alive only within the radiant circle of a hero." Brown brilliantly calls *Gilles* "a picaresque novel with the bones of a thesis regularly poking through the flesh of its characters." All in all, these pages of Brown's book provide one of the most acute portraits I have read of how a writer succumbs to the lure of political fanaticism. They stand with Carmen Callil's brilliant biography of the anti-Semite Louis Darquier as among the most lucid examinations of this chapter in the history of European darkness.

Although Brown finishes the book with a nine-page epilogue on Drieu's role in the Occupation, *The Embrace of Unreason*, properly speaking, comes to an end in 1940. Will Brown now continue his multivolume investigation of French unreason with a third book, on Vichy? If so, he will enter into some heavily trodden scholarly territory, and the sheer weight of events may prove hard to convey in his loose, impressionistic style. Still, it would be wonderful to see him try. There are few writers better positioned to explore this drama, and the way so many of the brightest minds in France failed the test—not only gazing into the abyss but plunging willingly over the edge.

2

The Collaborator: Vichy's Moral Drama

FEW BOOKS ON FRENCH HISTORY have affected me as deeply as Carmen Callil's Bad Faith, *one of the two books discussed in this essay. It is an astonishingly acute and vivid portrayal of a profoundly evil man. When, even today, writers in France like Éric Zemmour try to defend Vichy, parroting Marshal Pétain's line that it saved France from worse evils, I think of this book. What can possibly exculpate a regime that put a man like Louis Darquier in a position of power? Darquier bears direct responsibility for the murder of the French Jews deported to the Nazi death camps, and it is agonizing to think that he avoided punishment and died peacefully in Spain at the age of eighty-two, many years after the end of the war. It was this book, more than any other, that prompted my thinking on Vichy as a moral drama.*

What is it about Vichy France that still exerts such a strong hold on the Western imagination? Publishers bring out large, well-reviewed histories of Vichy at regular intervals. It remains an irresistible setting for historical

Books under Review: Richard Vinen, *The Unfree French: Life under the Occupation* (Yale, 2006); Carmen Callil, *Bad Faith: A Forgotten History of Family, Fatherland, and Vichy France* (Knopf, 2006). "The Collaborator" by David A. Bell from the December 5, 2005, issue of *The Nation.* Copyright 2005–2006, *The Nation.*

fiction, as shown by the success of Alan Furst's novels, which return again and again to wartime France. Films about Vichy, from *Casablanca* and *The Sorrow and the Pity* to *The Last Metro* and *Au revoir les enfants*, attract large and enthusiastic audiences. In 2006 the gorgeous, heart-breakingly incomplete novel *Suite Française*, by Irène Némirovsky (a Jew whom Vichy deported to the death camps), finally published after lying for decades in a suitcase her daughters found it too painful to open, appeared in English translation to rapturous critical acclaim.

In some respects, the attention seems disproportionate. Vichy was a dreadful regime, but just one among many during a dreadful period of human history, and surely one that occupies a lesser realm of horror than Hitler's Germany or Stalin's Soviet Union. Its worst crime, the deportation of some seventy-six thousand Jews to the death camps, involved only a little more than 1 percent of the Jews murdered in the Holocaust—nor did the French operate death camps themselves. Why, then, does Vichy remain such an unusually compelling subject, especially in the United States and Britain? Is it simply that more Americans and Britons speak French than German? Or perhaps there is a double standard at work: The French, unlike the Germans, are "civilized" and so should have "known better."

I think there is a different, more fundamental reason, which has to do precisely with the lesser horror and greater moral ambiguity of Vichy. French singer Jean-Jacques Goldman once wrote a song that begins. "If I had been born in '17 in Leidenstadt / On the ruins of a battlefield / Would I have been better or worse than those people / Had I been German?" The question is simply too painful for most people to confront, because the answer seems all too obvious, and too damning. If they had been born German in 1917, they would likely have become Nazis, or cowards complicit in Hitler's crimes. When faced with this probability, the process of sympathetic identification that draws us into the past is simply blocked.

But what if they—what if you—had been born in 1917 in France, and then experienced the catastrophic defeat of 1940, when the Wehrmacht simply steered around the famed Maginot line and conquered France in a matter of weeks? Would you have fled to fight with de Gaulle? Joined the Resistance? Supported the puppet regime of Marshal Philippe Pétain? Not only were such choices all the more dramatic for being suddenly thrust on the French; they seem more psychologically plausible as well. It is much easier to imagine oneself failing a moral test and turning "collabo" in 1940 than slowly, steadily participating in the Nazi evil from the start. This may be one reason the "collabos" are often the most vividly sketched characters in Vichy fiction and film (think of Captain Renault in *Casablanca*, or Lucien in Louis Malle's *Lacombe Lucien*), and why figures like Pétain, his foreign minister, Pierre Laval, and now Louis Darquier, the regime's notoriously anti-Semitic second commissioner for Jewish affairs and the subject of Carmen Callil's extraordinary book *Bad Faith*, have received such intense biographical scrutiny. It is surely one reason images of female collaborators having their heads shaved at the Liberation, as in Robert Capa's famous photograph of 1944, remain some of the most searing and psychologically resonant ones of the entire war. It is all too easy to see ourselves in their place.

In the introduction to *The Unfree French*, a general history of Vichy France from the perspective of ordinary people, Richard Vinen protests the very idea of putting himself in his subjects' shoes. "When I was working on the French social elite during the Second World War," he writes, "survivors of that period (usually Pétainists), would sometimes ask me what I would have done if I had found myself in their position. This is an understandable but futile question. If I had been alive in France in 1940 I would have been a different person, and how I would have reacted would have depended on the social and political circumstances of my upbringing." Vinen is right, of course, but he is too sanguine about his ability—or anyone's—to avoid the question. Identifying with individuals in the past is central to the writing of good history, and to the experience of reading it.

Practicing what he preaches, Vinen not only guards against identifying with his subjects; he avoids judging them almost entirely. Indeed, in the classic British empiricist tradition, he is leery of generalization of any sort, implying at one point that a great deal of Vichy's history still defies understanding: "Much of what people said and did under Vichy...remains inscrutable." He likes nothing better than to take a particular topic—the flight of refugees from Paris and other cities in 1940, forced labor in Germany, collaboration, resistance, the Liberation— and explain sternly that its complexity and variety make general conclusions almost impossible. Vinen declares at the outset that "I am interested in the French rather than in France...how the French lived rather than abstract ideals," and he concentrates as much as possible on people's ordinary experience. His approach is deliberately episodic.

In some respects, this approach works well, for Vichy's history is indeed far more complex than its popular image suggests. After the sudden and catastrophic defeat of May-June 1940, France did not simply fall under German occupation. Different areas, including Paris, came under various German and Italian administrations, while Germany forcibly annexed the region of Alsace-Lorraine (130,000 of its men went on to serve in the German armed forces, mostly on the Eastern front). Meanwhile, a large area in the south remained autonomous and theoretically neutral until November 1942, governed from the old spa town of Vichy under the leadership of the aged World War I hero Pétain. This "Vichy regime" had a role in running the occupied zones as well, but under conditions of continuous bureaucratic chaos, disarray, and infighting. The histories of these different zones involve at least as much murkiness and confusion as they do stark moral choices.

Vinen has a keen eye for incidents whose sheer absurdity shows just how chaotic and unpredictable things were. For instance, a Canadian insurance company, taking Vichy's theoretical neutrality at face value, continued to pay Pétain a pension throughout the war. Meanwhile, the French children's magazine *Le Journal de Mickey*, with support from Walt Disney, not only went on publishing but solemnly instructed French children in their duty to "the Marshal." So complex were Vichy's criteria for Jewishness, and so rigid the racial bureaucracy, that one woman was deported from France and sent all the way to Auschwitz, only to persuade officials there of her "Aryan" status, on which they returned her safely home. Meanwhile, on the grounds of the Auschwitz-Birkenau complex, an idealistic young French scoutmaster set up a model camp for "volunteer" French workers, leading them in songs, games, and exercises that were occasionally disturbed by the smell of burning flesh. The scoutmaster later turned out to be a Gaullist spy.

Beyond the confusion and unpredictability, Vinen is particularly good at evoking the privations and hardships that served as the backdrop to nearly all French lives between 1940 and 1944. He waxes eloquent on subjects like ration cards, waiting in line (you could pay a mother 7 francs an hour to wait for you; her children would deliver the provisions), and the black market. He explains persuasively that farmers endured their own share of hardships and did not enjoy a plenty denied to city dwellers. He recounts the plot of a novel whose intellectual hero, having gone hungry for too long, declares with bathos: "My son will run a dairy." He also reveals that Parisians kept four hundred thousand rabbits on their balconies as a source of food.

When Vinen takes the time to sketch out individual characters and incidents, his book is especially instructive and revealing. He gives a lively account of collaborationist crime and figures like the gangster Henri Lafont (who counted a black singer and a German Jew among his mistresses, and eventually volunteered to fight in the SS). Vinen also makes a fascinating comparison between three young French Jews who survived the war, showing the determining effect that their prewar social status had on their experiences. Unfortunately, however, much of the book moves too quickly for its own good. To take just one example, in his section on the "exodus" of June 1940, when as many as eight million people fled their homes (including more than two-thirds of the population of Paris), Vinen seldom devotes more than a sentence to any single person or story. It is an admittedly unfair comparison, but Némirovsky's *Suite Française* gives a far more vivid sense of the chaos, confusion, and anguish of this moment, and of the variety of individual experiences.

More serious, Vinen's allergy to generalization often leaves him with little to say that does not sound simply obvious: "German troops in France were not all the same"; "French people often discussed how they should deal with the Germans"; "Prison camps changed over time." At the end of the book, he writes: "The first and simplest conclusion of this book is that life for most French people between 1940 and 1944 was miserable." Did we doubt it? True, some historians of late have put relatively little emphasis on the hardships, but the basic facts have not been in question.

Most surprising, while Vinen details the many different ways the French dealt with the German occupiers, including political collaboration, sexual contacts, forced labor in Germany, and bureaucratic connections, he almost entirely avoids the subject of resistance. He has an entire chapter on French laborers in Germany, but nothing at all on the "Free French" forces in England. And he provides only five pages on the organized Resistance itself—half the amount given over to the headshavings of 1944–1945, and scarcely more than on the black market, or standing in line. True, the book explicitly concerns "the bulk of the population" who did not actively resist, and is partly set against the old myth, long discredited by historians but still tenaciously upheld in some fiction, that France was a "nation of resisters." But in downplaying the Resistance so thoroughly, Vinen ends up diminishing the importance of the choices the French did indeed face during the war, however much their sheer exhaustion and despair, and the ambient chaos, may have led them to pretend that these choices did not exist.

That these choices did exist, despite all the limiting factors that Vinen explores, is brought home with astonishing force and passion by Carmen Callil in her biography of Louis Darquier, who headed Vichy's General Commission for Jewish Affairs between 1942 and 1944, the period that saw the most Jews deported to the death camps. Her book is a brilliant and frightening tour de force, a triumph of research and one of the finest portraits of human evil I have ever read. It is not a story of ordinary people by any means. Darquier stood out even from the leaders of Vichy in his rabid anti-Semitism and ideological hatreds. But it shows all too clearly the sort of monsters, French and German, who had so many of France's ordinary people at their mercy during these terrible years.

Darquier's prewar story was mostly one of pathetic failure. He was born in 1897 into comfortable circumstances in the southern French town of Cahors, the son of a prominent doctor and politician. In the army during World War I, he performed well in action but turned disorderly and disobedient (and usually drunk) away from the front. After the war he tried selling advertising, followed by a stint in the wheat business, but proved incapable of holding down a steady job. He was lazy, sloppy, arrogant, pompous, mendacious, and frequently intoxicated. He also had a penchant for embezzlement, and only his family's political connections kept him out of jail. Between 1927 and 1934 he lived in a series of cheap hotels (constantly dodging bill collectors), spinning ever more fantastic stories about himself. Appropriating the identity of a more distinguished family, he called himself Darquier de Pellepoix and sometimes passed himself off as a baron. Tall, broad-shouldered, and never without a monocle, he at least looked the part.

In the late 1920s he met a mate perfectly suited to him: an Australian chorus girl named Myrtle Jones, who matched him in scrounging ability, outdid him in alcohol consumption, and liked to pass herself off as Sandra Lindsay or Lady Sandra Workman-Macnaghten. In 1927 they married—probably bigamously, because there is no record of a divorce from her first husband—and moved to London as Baron and Baroness Darquier de Pellepoix. There, they lived hand-to-mouth in Darquier's familiar style, and in April 1930 he made it into the pages of the *Evening Standard* under the headline "Monocled Baron Charged" (with being a penniless illegal alien). Later that year they had their first and only child, a girl named Anne, and promptly abandoned her into the care of an English nanny paid (irregularly) by their families, scarcely ever to see her again. The couple had frequent drunken rows, during which he beat her ferociously. Yet even though they were sometimes separated, they could not cut their bonds. Soon after Anne's birth, her parents returned to France.

In the early 1930s, as the ideological climate turned extreme, Darquier followed his older and more successful brother into right-wing politics, and in February 1934 had a life-changing stroke of good luck: he got shot. The occasion was the riots of February 6, in which crowds from a variety of far right organizations attacked the National Assembly and tried to overthrow the weak government of the Third Republic, which much of the population considered unrepresentative of the "real country" and therefore illegitimate. Painfully wounded in the thigh, Darquier immediately became a political celebrity. "It's like having a winning ticket in the lottery," he wrote during his recovery, with characteristic cynicism. "I think I'm going to find influential friends now, as I'm a unique example (the others who were severely wounded are cooks, drivers and shop employees). I believe that I'm going to profit from the accident—I've decided to play this card for all it's worth!" True to his word, he started to cultivate leaders of the extreme right, including Pierre-Charles Taittinger, the champagne magnate (think of him next time you have something to celebrate), and to lead an association of February 6 veterans. In 1935 he won election to the Paris City Council and used it as a platform to spout a message of hatred toward democracy, modernity, Freemasons, and Jews.

There is little sign that Darquier gave particular attention to the Jews before the mid-1930s. He was anti-Semitic, of course, but in the reflexive, unthinking way that characterized nearly all right-wing French people of the day (and a good many on the other side of the political aisle as well). He had cordial relations with individual Jews. But after 1934 a number of hard-line anti-Semites decided he could be a useful spokesman and prompted him to make the Jews his principal political issue. Darquier eagerly complied. He started to put references to Jewish finance, blood purity, and *The Protocols of the Elders of Zion* into his speeches. He demanded anti-Jewish legislation and founded anti-Semitic publications. He acquired a dog named Porthos and taught it to attack at the command "Aux Juifs!" All this time, he and Myrtle were continuing to live their drunken, helter-skelter existence. In 1935 his bar tab alone came to some 50,000 francs (roughly $40,000 today). Several times debt almost derailed him.

In the late 1930s, though, Darquier found a new and sinister source of funding: the Nazi government. With its support, he expanded his loose network of clubs and associations, and turned ever more strident and passionate in his denunciations, calling for the expulsion of all Jews who had entered France since 1918. Repeatedly hauled into court on charges of libel, of defamation, of disseminating enemy propaganda, and of being an enemy agent (the Nazi subsidies were an open secret), he used each controversy to raise his stature on the extreme right. The day after Hitler invaded Poland, he got into a fistfight in the Brasserie Lipp after loudly denouncing the "Jewish War." Soon afterward, Darquier went back into the French army and was captured, along with millions of others, by the Germans. But the Nazis quietly arranged his release, and by the summer of 1941 the Vichy regime had cleared him of all outstanding legal issues. His moment had arrived.

At first, it was not clear that the new regime created under Pétain's aegis would follow Hitler's line on the Jews. Pétain stood for order, for dignity in defeat, for a "national revolution" that would cleanse the country of the corruption and weakness of the Third Republic, but not necessarily for official anti-Semitism. As Vinen points out, several Jewish deputies to the National Assembly joined that body's infamous vote to award Pétain full powers (which gave Vichy the status of the Republic's legitimate successor). Among Vichy's most enthusiastic initial supporters, there were far more Catholic conservatives than fascists, who remained a tiny minority of the population.

Yet as the regime began to consolidate, extremists like Darquier wriggled out into the open, and both they and the Germans began to push for French counterparts to the Nazis' Nuremberg Laws. The regime willingly obliged. Starting in October 1940, it issued two "Statutes on the Jews," which went further than even the Nazis requested, banning Jews from teaching, journalism, film, theater, the officer corps and civil service, most professions, and finance. Foreign Jews were interned, and in the summer of 1941, 250,000 Parisians visited an anti-Semitic exhibition titled "The Jew and France." Vichy set up its General Commission for Jewish Affairs.

Into this madhouse, in March 1942, came Louis Darquier, to replace the conservative Catholic Xavier Vallat, whom the Nazis and their French soulmates considered too soft. Darquier immediately began to abuse the office, siphoning off funds, sexually exploiting secretaries, and trying to use the commission's investigative unit as his own private police force. But he was right at home. Typical of the commission's personnel were Jean Bouvyer, a thug from the prewar right-wing terrorist group the Cagoule, who tracked down Jews in hiding, and Georges Montandon, a reputable anthropologist who inspected men and women for physical signs of Jewishness and took large bribes to issue "Certificates of Non-Belonging to the Jewish Race." Darquier himself developed a profitable sideline issuing the same certificates, and amassed a small fortune from this and other corrupt practices. His laziness was legendary; the only significant policy he actually formulated and implemented himself was to oblige all Jews in the occupied zone to wear the yellow Star of David.

But by the time Darquier took office, the Final Solution had begun in earnest, and the Germans had serious plans for his commission. Adolf Eichmann demanded that Vichy deport one hundred thousand Jews to the death camps and, through his French subordinates, put pressure on Vichy to make the arrangements. Darquier found himself in the unfamiliar and unwelcome position of having to take responsibility, along with the police official René Bousquet, who actually organized the deportations. The Germans, believing exaggerated propaganda, thought that the Jewish population in France numbered 865,000. In reality there were only 330,000, and fewer than 100,000 of the non-French refugees whom Vichy hoped to expel first were Jews, so the French found it hard to comply with Eichmann's directives.

There followed the sort of bureaucratic chaos and confusion described by Vinen, as the French and the Germans bickered and bargained over numbers, but it had gruesome results. In July 1942, the French police—acting on the authority of the French state, not the Germans—arrested nearly thirteen thousand Jews in Paris, including more than four thousand children, and shut them up for days in stifling heat in an indoor bicycle racetrack (the Vélodrome d'Hiver, or Vel' d'Hiv') without water or proper sanitation. The final destination was Auschwitz. Thousands were gassed on arrival, and hardly any survived. Many more arrests and deportations followed. As a result of macabre bureaucratic logic, young children initially exempted were sent to their deaths later on, when the rules changed. Children born in France, and therefore possessing French citizenship, were separated from their parents. Darquier's chief of staff, Pierre Galien (a Nazi agent), asked to intervene on behalf of a ten-month-old child left parentless by the deportations, replied: "It's a Jew child, let it die." Vinen tells the moving story of a brother and sister, fourteen and ten years old, left to fend for themselves after their parents' disappearance (their landlord coldly insisted that they continue to pay the full rent on their apartment).

Nonetheless, by March 1943 the French had met less than half of Eichmann's target; the Germans were furious with them, and with Darquier in particular. "The result of Darquier de Pellepoix's activity over his past year in office," a German memo concluded, "is nil in all areas." Darquier was continuing to make speeches, to preside over his various clubs and associations, and to embezzle money meant for anti-Semitic propaganda efforts, all the while complaining about his work-load. He and Myrtle (who remained in Paris with him throughout the war, although technically an enemy alien) remained as disorderly as ever in their private lives, although now in the more luxurious confines of the Hôtel Bristol. (As Callil acidly remarks, Darquier was one of very few Frenchmen to gain weight during the war.) The Germans tried to dismiss him, but he saved himself for a time by helping to broker the theft and sale of a large private Jewish art collection. (In the northern zone alone, Vichy stole more than a billion francs in Jewish property, along with one hundred thousand artworks, forty thousand of which were never recovered).

Darquier finally lost his job in early 1944, but he remained in France until after D-Day. And then, as the Allied armies approached Paris, he and a French mistress escaped south, walking across the Pyrenees into Spain. The Franco regime welcomed him (along with many other French exiles), gave him an apartment, found him jobs teaching French and trans-lating, and protected him even as a postwar French court condemned him to death in absentia. Later French governments made no serious efforts to uncover his whereabouts, let alone extradite him, and so, like many other prominent French (and German) officials, he paid no price for his wartime activities. He had another daughter by his mistress, but was eventually reunited with Myrtle. In 1978 a journalist from *L'Express* tracked him down and surreptitiously recorded an interview in which Darquier angrily defended his wartime record, spouted familiar anti-Semitic diatribes, and declared that the only thing gassed in Auschwitz was lice. The interview caused a scandal in France and eventually led to the indictment of Bousquet, who had gone on to a brilliant career in business (thanks partly to the protection of François Mitterrand, himself a former extremist and supporter of Pétain who switched sides at a convenient moment). Darquier finally died in August 1980, near Málaga.

While Darquier was hardly an unknown figure, Callil has done a Herculean job of research to give a far closer, richer portrait of his life than we have for almost any figure of his era. Her bibliography lists nearly one hundred separate archives in seven countries, more than one hundred interviews, and countless letters given to her by individuals, including members of the Darquier family in France. *Bad Faith* is long and detailed, but in this case the details reveal the devil.

Callil is not a professional historian (she is the founder of Britain's Virago Press), and her motivation for pursuing Darquier's story was anything but academic. In the first pages, she explains that soon after she came from Australia to Britain in the early 1960s, she attempted to commit suicide. When she recovered, her doctor prescribed therapy, and for seven years Callil went three times a week to see a half-Australian psychiatrist. She was Anne Darquier, the abandoned daughter of Louis and Myrtle who had been raised in Oxfordshire by her redoubtable nanny, Elsie Lightfoot. Anne died in 1970 at the age of forty, poisoned by alcohol and pills. ("It was not suicide," Callil writes, "though there are slow ways of trying to kill yourself not given that label.") Callil, who was deeply affected by Anne's death, learned of the elder Darquier's identity only later, when she spotted him in Marcel Ophüls's documentary *The Sorrow and the Pity*.

Callil's book, then, is the result of what can only be called an obsessive quest to understand: to understand the unhappy Anne Darquier by understanding the bizarre and terrible legacy that she had the impossible task of living with. While principally a biography of Darquier himself, it is also the story of the entire family, with long, fascinating pages on Myrtle and her Australian family, and on the story of how a hard-edged ambition took Anne Darquier from genteel poverty with Lightfoot to university at Oxford, and then into medicine. Anne, who during the war had idealized the father she had never met (and whom she had very little idea of), finally met him after he arrived in Spain, and the experience left her utterly appalled and distraught. Just before her death she remarked to Callil that "there are some things and some people you can never forgive." Incidentally, Darquier inherited £16,552 from his daughter and used it to purchase his apartment in Madrid from the Spanish government. As one of Myrtle's pallbearers remarked (she had died soon before Anne): "No one, it seems, survives Darquier."

Callil writes with passion (how could she not, under these circumstances?), and it gives her book a force and drive that keeps the reader going through its four-hundred-some pages of narrative. Occasionally she overwrites: "The threnody of [Myrtle's] Tasmanian family and the money she would one day inherit trills through all her letters like the sound of a piccolo." More often, however, she holds back, giving her prose touches of dry, penetrating wit. For instance: the existence of the unoccupied zone gave France "a sedative pretence of sovereignty." Or, on Darquier's appointment to head the commission: "An even worse punishment for the Germans responsible for his appointment was their discovery that Darquier was a pestiferous bore." Or, on Louis and Myrtle: "Their mutual inventions were one of the strongest cords that held them together." Callil also has an unfortunate line, in her postscript, about what "the Jews of Israel [are] passing on to the Palestinian people." It has caused a predictable controversy and is wrongheaded. Since when does a great crime confer any special moral burden on the *victims*?

But what of the question of Louis Darquier's own moral responsibility? Here, Callil poses more genuinely troubling and difficult questions, and the problem of identification rears its head. On the one hand, by telling the story in the way she has, Callil inevitably relates Darquier's monstrosity in his private life to the monstrosity of his public actions. Callil knows, of course, that most monsters injure no one other than their nearest and dearest, while many great criminals lead impeccable private lives. But she draws a connection nonetheless by characterizing Darquier, in the end, as a sort of wanton incompetent whom chance and tragedy swept up into a position where he could do harm on a bizarrely vast scale:

> Yoked in mutual self-deception with Myrtle, the Baron and Baroness, twin children—wicked children—played games, murderous games, pulling wings off butterflies, dispensing cruelty like liquorice water. Left to himself, Louis Darquier would have destroyed only his own children and any adult...foolish enough to dabble in his fantasy world....Above and around Darquier were the real criminals, the Pétains and Weygands, the Bousquets and Vallats, the cardinals and clergy, the judges and lawyers, the industrialists and businessmen... who put his babbling mouth to work for their own ends....Looking at him, hearing him speak...they stared their own inhumanity in the face....He was ridiculous, he was their fall guy, but he was also the dark essence of *l'Etat français*.

There is something about this judgment that is just a little too easy, and this may perhaps have to do with the many years Callil spent inside Louis Darquier's head. It is not that she sympathizes with him in any way. Darquier was a man almost impossible not to loathe, and Callil loathes him fiercely. But she may have gotten to know him too well to take him as seriously as he deserves. Darquier was indeed a wicked child of sorts—indeed, a certifiable maniac. But World War II was a time when the maniacs emerged from the asylum and nearly destroyed civilization. What was Hitler, after all, if not a more efficient, a more energetic, a more ambitious Darquier? The more sober men of Vichy—the Pétains and Lavals and Bousquets—were indeed criminals. They exploited their country's defeat for their own ideological and personal ends. But left to themselves they would never have devised the idea of sending tens of thousands of innocent men, women, and children to their death for the sin of being born Jewish. That insanity came from the Darquiers. It is relatively easy to imagine being a classic collabo like Bousquet, who doubtless defended his actions to himself better than Darquier could ever be bothered to. Putting oneself in Darquier's shoes is much harder, precisely because of the extent of his mania. Even Callil, understandably, flinches from the task in revulsion. Nonetheless, thanks to her, we now have a portrait of his evil that remains scorched in the brain long after the book has been closed.

3

Everyday Choices: Dealing with the Occupation

*THE GERMAN OCCUPATION AUTHORITIES and their French collaborators did
everything they could to heighten the moral quandaries that the French population faced, and to make resistance a morally indefensible choice. Could
killing a German officer be justified, if, in retaliation, the Germans shot fifty
French hostages? What actions justified putting one's compatriots in danger?
Some historians have flinched from these questions, but Robert Gildea, in a
well-crafted local study of the Loire region under German occupation, addressed them directly. While appreciating much about his book, I disagreed
with Gildea's conclusions, and in this essay, explain why.*

Vichy, a name once associated with strong-tasting mineral water, has
come, over the past sixty years, to signify a strong-tasting morality tale.
Choose your side: the heroic Resistance, or the shameful collaborators?
Humphrey Bogart posed the choice to Claude Rains in *Casablanca* (in
response, Rains threw a bottle of Vichy water in the trash). Charles de

---

Book under Review: Robert Gildea, *Marianne in Chains: Everyday Life in the French
Heartland under the German Occupation* (Metropolitan Books, 2002). This essay was
commissioned by *The New York Times Book Review* but never published.

Gaulle's Free French posed it in their large-scale trials and purges of collaborators in 1944–1945. Writers, artists, and historians have posed it ever since.

As the war has receded, the shape of the story has changed, but its morality tale quality has remained largely unchanged. At the Liberation, de Gaulle and his followers propounded the myth that a "nation of resistants" had overwhelmingly opposed the puppet regime of Marshal Philippe Pétain. But in the 1970s, historians (notably Columbia University's Robert Paxton) placed the French in the dock by insisting on the unpleasant fact that at least through 1942, most of the population had massively supported Pétain. Since the 1980s, attention has come to focus on Vichy's greatest crime: the deportation—carried out without direct German pressure—of seventy-six thousand Jews from France to their deaths in the Holocaust. In 1995, after a series of new revelations, and trials, President Jacques Chirac formally offered atonement for France's wartime treatment of the Jews.

Yet history does not always make for a good morality tale, argues Robert Gildea in this new, fascinating, but problematic, case study of the German occupation in the Loire region of western France. Gildea has modeled his richly detailed work after that of his late Oxford colleague Richard Cobb, the famously eccentric historian of the French Revolution who had a passion for the French local archives, and what they revealed about ordinary men and women awash in the floods of great events. Cobb also had a loathing for cant, hypocrisy, and ideological zeal of all varieties, and it is this perspective that gives *Marianne in Chains* its originality. Provocatively, Gildea disparages the extremists of the Resistance almost as much as he does the ultra-right ideologues of Vichy. His sympathies lie both with the victims—above all, the Jews— and with those men and women who strove to keep local society together, even if the Liberation subsequently labeled them traitors.

Gildea has very little patience indeed for the Resistance. Take his account of Aristide Royer, one of the region's most prominent Resistance leaders. In 1943, the Gestapo captured him and forty-two comrades, most of whom died in concentration camps. Gildea reveals, disturbingly, that Royer had been warned about the Gestapo action, thanks to Hubert Sommer, a German police translator whom a Resistance member had known before the war. But Royer refused to act on the information, and even allegedly denounced Sommer, who was arrested as well, and died fighting in a German penal battalion. Gildea raises the question of whether Royer was a German agent, and deplores the reluctance of the town of Saumur to include Sommer, a former scholar of French literature, on its Resistance monument. In a similar vein, Gildea has kinder things to say about Lieutenant-Colonel Karl Hotz, the cultured, moderate German commander in the city of Nantes, than about Gilbert Brustlein, the French Resistance member who assassinated him on October 20, 1941, leading the Nazis to shoot nearly fifty French hostages in retaliation (including a university student whose only crime had been to raise a French flag above the city's cathedral). Gildea's heroes, in this story, are the community leaders who frantically lobbied the Germans to stop the executions and whose efforts probably saved another fifty hostages from death.

Gildea is properly unsparing on the subject of the Loire region's treatment of its Jews, who suffered humiliation, expropriation, and, in thousands of cases, deportation to the death camps. Whatever justifications the local police and administration offered for their complicity with the Nazis, Gildea concludes tersely that, in the end, they "simply did the dirty work of the SS." But he also notes that the Liberation authorities did little to help returning Jewish survivors recover their property or rebuild their lives, and long refused to acknowledge a distinct Jewish dimension to France's wartime suffering (instead lumping Jewish victims into the total number of French victims). "The Resistance Gospel," he remarks caustically, "always privileged the hero over the victim."

The book's subtitle—*Everyday Life in the French Heartland under the German Occupation*—is somewhat misleading. Gildea's short chapters on food, recreation, and family life add relatively little to existing scholarship on the subject, although he has an eye for arresting details, such as the number of French children fathered by German soldiers during the war years (as many as seventy thousand). He is also illuminating on the barter trade that grew up between hungry city-dwellers and their farmer cousins, and on attempts to circumvent a ban on public dancing that lasted until well after the Liberation. But the bulk of the book deals with the local administrators and community leaders (in French, "notables") who tried to keep French society functioning during this catastrophic period. The long accounts of administrative battles sometimes make for heavy going, especially since Gildea does not share his mentor Cobb's penchant for leavening his text with sketches of colorful misfits, outcasts, and villains.

Overall, Gildea argues that until 1943, local leaders in the Loire region largely managed to protect their communities without making undue moral compromises. He presents an image of moderate French and Germans cooperating with each other, even as the zealots on both sides worked to increase conflict and polarization. As the Allied victory drew near, however, the zealots won out, and the local leaders were forced either to choose sides or play a dangerous double game.

This interpretation is challenging and serious, but ultimately unpersuasive. Robert Gildea has not done away with the story of Vichy France as morality tale (can anyone, yet?), but rather has transferred the moral judgments from large, faceless groups—"the French," "the Germans," "Vichy"—to individuals. The shift is illuminating, but it comes at the expense of the larger picture—namely, the war. Yes, many local leaders acted moderately, and saved many lives and livelihoods. But their collaboration not only served the cause of their localities; it also served the Nazi war machine. The region's farmers fed German troops. The region's factories outfitted them. The port city of Saint-Nazaire became a major U-boat base. The local leaders understandably refused to weigh the lives of their neighbors against the uncertain and intangible prospect of hindering Hitler's war effort. But the historian, perhaps, should not be so eager to endorse their point of view, or to disparage the Resistance figures who insisted on making cruel and dangerous trade-offs for an overridingly important cause.

4

The Humanist as Hero: The Literary Sources of Moral Resistance

MORAL VIRTUE IS GENERALLY MUCH LESS INTERESTING than evil. "Imagine the universe wise and philosophical," quips the character "Him" in Diderot's Rameau's Nephew. *"Admit that it would be frightfully dull." Jean Guéhenno, a writer who steadfastly refused any form of collaboration during the Occupation, was a far less colorful personage than the horrific Louis Darquier. If the wartime diary he kept consisted of nothing but a record of his gloomy daily existence in occupied Paris, and his imprecations against writers who collaborated, it would be a worthy document, but hardly a classic. What makes it a classic, I argue in this essay, is not what Guéhenno says about himself, but what he says about his books. It was through his love for the classics of French literature that this working-class boy from Brittany had raised himself up to become a notable Parisian intellectual. And it was through his intensive reading of particular writers that he not only justified his resistance to Vichy and the Occupation, but found the strength to continue it through four bleak and dangerous years.*

Book under Review: Jean Guéhenno, *Diary of the Dark Years, 1940–1944*, translated and edited by David Ball (Oxford University Press, 2014). Essay originally published in *The New Republic*, September 26, 2014.

The twentieth century dealt a very harsh blow to the idea that moral clarity and courage can be learned from books. Never in history did more nations worship great books more fervently than in 1914. But over the following decades, this love for the humanities did little to prevent crimes against humanity. In fact, a shocking quantity of evil was done by cultivated men who sighed with pleasure at great novels, poetry, and music, adored the old masters, and boasted of their philosophical sophistication. Far too often they defended indefensible actions as necessary to preserve "civilization." A taste for Kant and Goethe was no prophylactic against mass murder.

Given this dismal record, is there any point in searching for the intellectual roots of moral heroism? Surely, to explain the actions of those who have dared to take a stand against the slaughter and the tyrannies, we need to look to the mysteries of individual psychology, rather than to the content of reading lists. After all, the perpetrators had the same educations, committed the same passages to memory.

Every once in a while, however, an extraordinary document comes along to remind us that the books matter. In such a document, we can see how an individual's preference for particular writers, and for particular themes in their works, did indeed shape an outlook conducive to moral clarity and courage. Yes, it may have been a quirk of psychology that led the individual in this intellectual direction in the first place, but what he or she found there nonetheless had a decisive effect. And while the perpetrators may have read the same books, the document also reminds us that there are better and worse ways of reading.

The diary kept by the French writer and critic Jean Guéhenno during the German occupation of France from 1940 to 1944 is one such document. Unlike most French intellectuals, Guéhenno steadfastly refused to publish openly a single word as long as France remained under the control of Germany, and of the collaborationist Vichy government of Marshal Philippe Pétain. Instead he wrote in his diary as an act of private resistance and as a chronicle of his country's "servitude." For four years, with perfect clarity and often astonishing eloquence, he recorded his disgust with collaborators, his anguish at the horrors overwhelming the continent, and his belief in "my real country ... that country which is only an idea, [which] has not been invaded and never will be." Already fifty years old in 1940, Guéhenno did not take up arms for the Resistance.

He did hold clandestine meetings with other writers, and contributed to and distributed underground magazines. And the diary itself, if discovered by the Germans, could have earned him a death sentence.

Published in full in France soon after the war, *Diary of the Dark Years* has long been familiar to the French public and to scholars of French history. It is not a record of Guéhenno's daily activities, and it has little to say about the texture of life during the Occupation, or about its author's intimate relationships. Occasionally he does use startlingly vivid physical imagery, as when he describes a tree where the Germans had tied the victims of their firing squads: "It is really there. The tree has been sawed off, ripped apart by bullets at the level of a man's heart. It was used all last winter, four or five times every week. The earth is all trampled down at the foot of the tree. It has lost its bark. It is black from the blood that has drenched it." Mostly, though, the diary reads like a combination of a philosophical meditation and a political manifesto directed to an audience of one. Like most diaries, it can be frustratingly repetitive.

But this is a genuinely important and enthralling book, and its publication in English in an excellent, fluid, and expertly annotated translation by David Ball is a welcome and long overdue event. Its most famous passages have been endlessly quoted. Guéhenno was wittily critical of his fellow authors. "The man-of-letters species is not one of the greatest species in the human race," he noted bitingly in November 1940. "[He] is unable to live out of public view for any length of time.... 'French literature must go on,' he says. He thinks he is French literature and French thought, and they would die without him." When describing his own situation, Guéhenno could turn deeply lyrical: "Here we are, reduced to silence, to solitude, but perhaps to seriousness as well. And after all, whether our cell is full of light or not depends on us alone." Guéhenno deplored Vichy's participation in the persecution of the Jews, applauded Charles de Gaulle's defiance of Pétain, and repeatedly condemned the "shame" of collaboration.

But what made Guéhenno take this path? French intellectuals mostly had a less-than-pristine war record. Jean-Paul Sartre, although a *résistant*, submitted his plays to the German propaganda office, which barred Jews from all productions. André Gide published in collaborationist journals. Sacha Guitry and Jean Cocteau openly supported, and socialized with, the occupying authorities. Writers from the far right, such as Robert Brasillach and Pierre Drieu la Rochelle, wrote Vichy propaganda and called for the victory of fascism. (Brasillach's writings earned him a death sentence in 1945.) The question of just what explains Guéhenno's choices has received surprisingly little attention.

In his useful and concise introduction, Ball looks mostly to Guéhenno's background and politics for an explanation. He notes that Guéhenno, unlike most Parisian literati, came from a provincial working-class family; his father worked in a shoe factory. At the age of fourteen, Guéhenno himself left school to help support his family in Brittany and never attended *lycée*. But moved by a passion for books, he studied at night, passed the Baccalaureate exam, and then made it into the elite École Normale Supérieure. He also embraced socialism. As a result, Ball writes, "he saw Pétain as the embodiment of the triumph of the reactionary bourgeoisie." During the interwar years, bourgeois intellectuals and politicians, especially on the reactionary right, could display very high degrees of condescension and scorn to men like Guéhenno. It would be easy to interpret his wartime stance as a product, in considerable part, of social resentment. As he wrote in the diary in 1940, "I am...a scholarship student with no respect for the heirs of the earth, a free man with no reasons for being free since he is not rich."

Yet emphasizing the resentment would mean not taking Guéhenno seriously enough as an intellectual. What breathes through the pages of the diary, far more than the occasional traces of class hostility, is Guéhenno's absolute fervor for books and ideas. It was literature to which he devoted himself as an adolescent, literature that helped him escape the world of the shoe factory, literature that he adored teaching to high school and college-age pupils in the day job that he held throughout the Occupation. All through the dark years he took refuge in books: his reading included Tolstoy, a biography of Mallarmé, Montesquieu, Valéry, and Michelet. He subjected the speeches he heard on the radio— Pétain's, Churchill's, even Hitler's—to short, pungent *analyses de texte*. He clearly saw his diary itself as a work of literature, even if he could not count on it ever seeing the light of day. And it is, in fact, in literature that we can find some of the most important sources of Guéhenno's moral heroism.

Guéhenno certainly had catholic and cosmopolitan tastes in literature. He adored Whitman and Goethe (whom he quoted in the diary in German), and took great pleasure in *A Farewell to Arms*. He invokes Chateaubriand and Benjamin Constant, Lamartine and Stendhal. But above all, it was the French classics of the sixteenth, seventeenth, and eighteenth centuries that enthralled him, and three writers in particular. The first was Pascal, and it is easy to see why the seventeenth-century thinker would matter so deeply to Guéhenno at this of all moments. Pascal's wit, as sharp as any other in history, cut through pretense and hypocrisy with unmatched flair. Pascal could satirize his enemies (especially the Jesuits) with terrifying ferocity. But he also adored solitude and willingly retreated from the world to contemplate eternal things in fear and trembling. Guéhenno admired, but also criticized, the mathematical rigidity of Pascal's thought. "What eloquence! But what geometry!"

In the diary Guéhenno even more frequently invoked Montaigne. Like Pascal, the sixteenth-century essayist willingly cut himself off from the world. He retreated to his study to commune with great writers, to wander the corridors of his own mind, and to deplore the barbarities of his age. Guéhenno's frequent use of the antiquated word "servitude" to describe Vichy France harkens back to Montaigne's great friend Étienne de La Boétie, who wrote a *Discourse on Voluntary Servitude* exploring why people surrender their liberty to tyrants. Montaigne invoked La Boétie many times. "Now there's a clean mind," Guéhenno wrote in the diary of Montaigne. "He was horrified by all pretense, the 'ceremony' which...even prevents us from knowing what we are by filling us with reverence for false ideas about ourselves." Seeing a world consumed by violence left Guéhenno musing about the horrific sixteenth-century civil wars between French Catholics and Protestants that Montaigne famously compared unfavorably to cannibal rituals. "I think of what a Montaigne would be like today, caught between the various 'leagues' that are drenching the world in blood."

But above all, there was a third writer and thinker, with whom Guéhenno felt a personal bond, and whom he spent most of the war years systematically studying, in order to write a biography. This figure was Rousseau. Guéhenno himself made the connection between

Rousseau and the Occupation in the preface to the biography, which appeared in three volumes between 1948 and 1952, and stood for years as the standard French critical study. (An English translation was published in the 1960s.) "In 1941," Guéhenno wrote, "in the somber and illusory leisure which servitude imposed upon writers, I looked round for some noble companion, of the kind who never gives in. Around us, all was falsehood. My thoughts turned once more to Rousseau; I opened his correspondence again and began to live in his company."

The reasons for the personal identification could not be more clear. Like Guéhenno, Rousseau came from a lower-class provincial background. (His father was a Geneva watchmaker.) Like Guéhenno, Rousseau was largely self-educated and lived largely on his own from an early age. Like Guéhenno, he had ambivalent relations with the Parisian literary establishment—hugely ambivalent, in Rousseau's case. "There is surely no other writer in our literature into whose life I can enter so easily," Guéhenno noted in the diary in 1942. "From fourteen to twenty, I had the same experiences, the same adventures, the same temptations, and the same humiliations." Like Montaigne and Pascal before him, Rousseau detested artifice and hypocrisy, prized sincerity, and treasured solitude. He, too, made a deliberate choice to isolate himself, to commune with nature and contemplate his own character rather than to live amid the glitter of Parisian literary society.

Guéhenno's Rousseauism was evident long before the war. As early as 1928, he published a lyrical essay called "Caliban Speaks," in response to a play by the philosopher Ernest Renan that had cast Shakespeare's monster as a symbol of democracy in all its imperfections. Caliban, as channeled by Guéhenno, spoke in unmistakably Rousseauian accents. Like Rousseau, he insisted that his homely exterior concealed an "overly honest" spirit that admittedly made him "an impossible man." And "Caliban" argued that what he had objected to, in his famous tirade against Prospero—"the red plague rid you for learning me your language!"—was not learning itself, but sophistry. "We must not confuse culture with knowledge," he wrote in words that directly echoed Rousseau's *First Discourse*. "If the more knowledgeable person were also the more cultivated, then a student in our primary schools would be more cultivated than Plato."

In fact, the diary shows that Guéhenno did not wait until 1941, but committed himself to the biography from the very first moments of the

Occupation. "I will definitely write a Rousseau," he declared to himself in July 1940, praising "the exemplary life of a man who does not surrender." He would sometimes take a day of his own to work through a day of Rousseau's, reliving the adventures of the philosophe at a two-hundred-year remove. "Experiencing as I do the life of my hero day after day, I am sometimes as curious about the next day as he might have been himself." Guéhenno fantasized about traveling back in time to meet Rousseau, "to go back along all the paths of his thought with him and find the living intuition that guided him." This was an intense identification indeed.

For a man deliberately setting himself against the world, in times of turmoil and persecution, it would be hard to find a better inspiration than Rousseau. Arguably, the great themes of his work were independence and self-sufficiency. How can men (women, alas, were a very different case for him) free themselves from subjection to others? Rousseau's *Discourse on Inequality* speculated as to the origins of subjection—political, economic, and psychological. His *Emile* imagined a program for raising a child to become a fully self-sufficient adult. His *Social Contract* is often read, incorrectly, as a manual of collectivism, when it is in fact a profound meditation on the dilemma of how to live as a free and independent person, and still join with others in a political society. The leitmotif of Rousseau's great autobiographical work, *The Confessions*, is his own inability to live with others, his anger at the corruptions and betrayals of society, and the solace that he finds in solitude and isolation. The late, lyrical *Reveries of a Solitary Walker* beautifully celebrates this solitude. In his final years, Rousseau succumbed to what often reads like clinical paranoia, but this tone strangely suited Vichy France, where the line between madness and sanity had become difficult to trace. As Guéhenno wrote in his diary in September 1940: "My thoughts seem to me those of a madman. It is the world which is mad around me. But the effect is the same. The connection between it and me has been destroyed."

Just as Rousseau's work could teach the courage to live independently, so it also provided a witheringly strong diagnosis of the corruptions of social life in general, and literary life in particular. As Rousseau recognized, even egotism is a form of subjection, since it enslaves us to the opinions of others. He mercilessly dissected the vanity of his fellow authors, and deplored their readiness to accept support from the autocratic government of France's Old Regime, fearing that it would ever so subtly bind their thought. Guéhenno's own comments on "men of letters" (the phrase itself is redolent of the eighteenth century) might almost have been taken straight from *The Confessions*: "The piercing eyes of a man of letters preoccupied by his reputation: whether he's leafing through a book or a newspaper, eager to find his way instantly in the confusion of the page, he can always see and recognize his name like a sun."

Among the writers of the Enlightenment, none has received harsher criticism in modern times than Rousseau. He has been blamed for everything from the French revolutionary Terror to modern child-rearing fads. The Israeli historian Jacob Talmon called him the father of totalitarianism. These theories sometimes have a surface plausibility. Before Guéhenno, another French scholarship boy, cut off from his parents early on, who developed a similarly fierce bond of identification with Rousseau was Maximilien Robespierre. But Rousseau—like Nietzsche, like Jesus—cannot be held responsible for the way he has been misread.

Jean Guéhenno was a superior reader. He knew, instinctively, that in the case of great writers it is not the explicit prescriptions that matter. Even the greatest writers can make for woefully inaccurate historians, shockingly bad commentators on current events, and terrible planners in almost every respect. The history in Rousseau's *Discourse on Inequality* is invented, the ideal republic of his *Social Contract* is a fantasy, the child-rearing program of his *Emile* is absurdly unworkable. These books are speculations, and what matters is not the literal programs they lay out but what they tell us about the human condition. In Guéhenno's case, what he found in Rousseau and the other writers he adored not only helped him to justify the courageous choices he made under Vichy, but quite clearly guided him to these choices. In the case of this heroic man, books helped to engender exceptional moral clarity and courage. "Anyone with the determination to live continuously and conscientiously according to the truth is assured of tremendous power," Guéhenno wrote in his biography of Rousseau. He might have been describing himself and his extraordinary book.

5

Poison Pen: A Literary Collaborator on Trial

THE STORIES OF THE DARQUIERS and the Guéhennos, though fascinating and instructive, are also, in an important sense, distracting. Most of the French under Vichy had far less clear-cut experiences, involving far more murky compromise and calculation, as the books by Richard Vinen and Robert Gildea discussed earlier (chapters 2 and 3 of this part) clearly emphasize. After the war, quite naturally, the French found it far easier to celebrate the heroes and condemn the villains than to confront this other, far more complex legacy of the "dark years." In this essay, I turn to the issue of how the French avoided fully coming to terms with Vichy by considering the trial and execution of the collaborationist writer Robert Brasillach—the subject of a brilliant book by Alice Kaplan. I argue that while Brasillach was indeed a literary Darquier of sorts—and very much a traitor—his punishment served to distract attention from many others who collaborated less flamboyantly than he did.

———

On February 6, 1945, a thirty-five-year-old Nazi collaborator named Robert Brasillach went before a firing squad in the fort of Montrouge, south of Paris. A brilliant writer with a particular talent for embedding venomous stings in elegant prose, he had put himself at the service of the extreme right ever since his days at the elite École Normale Supérieure, when he made his name with a mock obituary of André Gide. During the Occupation, Brasillach breathlessly cheered on the Nazis, and used the newspaper he edited, *Je Suis Partout*, to denounce members of the Resistance and applaud the deportation of French Jews to extermination camps. After the Liberation, he was the best-known collaborationist intellectual to stand trial.

As the readers of Alice Kaplan's enchanting memoir *French Lessons* will remember, Brasillach's ghost has haunted her for a long time. In the course of doing research on French fascist writers for her doctorate at Yale twenty years ago, this daughter of a Nuremberg prosecutor not only read through the man's voluminous works (including novels and a much-read history of the cinema), but immersed herself in the repellent milieu of his surviving friends and apologists, carrying out long interviews with his brother-in-law, the fascist literary critic and Holocaust denier Maurice Bardèche. "I ate lunch each day with the extended family," she wrote in *French Lessons*, and told how one day she brought a plum tart as a gift. "Bardèche's wife Suzanne said, 'Robert loved these plums.'...I understood that she lived with her dead brother every day, he was there at the table."

In *The Collaborator* Brasillach sits not at the lunch table but in the dock, as Kaplan tells the story of his trial and execution. The subject is a somber one, but she brings to it the same fluidity and grace and even something of the same light, seductive touch with which she earlier described her lifelong love affair with the French and their language. Kaplan often pauses to give her own personal reactions to the story, deftly explores the many ironies in Brasillach's case (like the fact that his defense attorney was his prosecutor's landlord and lived in a neighboring apartment), and has a genius for concision. Brasillach, for instance, was "a writer who believed that Nazism was poetry." *The Collaborator* is one of the best-written, most absorbing pieces of literary history in years.

But what are the most important questions to ask about the trial of Robert Brasillach? Kaplan, a literary critic, clearly thinks they are the questions posed by the prosecution itself during the trial. What responsibility do writers bear for their work? When do words become crimes? Kaplan struggles with these questions and ultimately comes to the same conclusion the jury did.

Yet there are problems with this approach. First of all, in Brasillach's case, the question of when words become crimes is a relatively easy one. The Brasillach of the Occupation was not merely a writer who lent his talent to a repulsive cause. His words gave aid and comfort to the enemy, and his public denunciations probably led directly to the deaths of members of the Resistance. Whether or not he deserved a death sentence, he was undoubtedly a traitor.

Second, and notwithstanding Brasillach's guilt, there is a different question to ask, concerning not the responsibility of writers but their vulnerability, particularly when the responsibility of others remains hidden from sight. Oddly for a critic, trained in probing beneath the surface of texts (by Paul de Man, no less!), Kaplan takes the trial itself very much at face value. She implies that Brasillach had a real chance to be acquitted, and faults his lawyer, the flamboyant Jacques Isorni, for offering too literary a defense and for failing to connect with the largely working-class jury.

But Isorni, who went on to defend Marshal Pétain, knew exactly what he was doing. Brasillach stood no chance at all with the jury, carefully chosen from members of the Resistance, and certainly not in a six-hour trial held when the Germans seemed at the point of turning back the Allied offensive in the Battle of the Bulge (the jurors took all of twenty minutes to reach their decision). Isorni's only hope, in a proceeding covered intensely by the press, lay in an appeal to a different court: the tribunal of public opinion. Only a wave of public sympathy for a defendant still ranked among the great writers of this most literary of nations might have persuaded General de Gaulle to commute the death sentence. The strategy failed, but it was the only one available.

All the participants in the trial took the issue of the writer's responsibility seriously. But the trial's "lofty tone," as Kaplan puts it, does not change the fact that it amounted to an elaborate theatrical spectacle, and one that served an ugly purpose, even as it administered a just punishment.

As Kaplan notes, the court's authority was undercut from the start by the collaborationist records not only of the defendant but of the judges and prosecutors as well. True, they had had a very different war from Brasillach. Men like the chief prosecutor, Marcel Reboul (Isorni's tenant), were not fascists and had sometimes done what they could to help the Resistance. But they kept the judicial system functioning even when the Nazis insisted on a fundamental perversion of justice, using new laws to impose death sentences retroactively on French hostages. And behind the judiciary stood a French administration, and social elite, much of which had smoothly shifted its allegiance to Vichy in the terrible summer of 1940, and only slipped back when the tide of the war changed. The long-hidden early right-wing career of François Mitterrand is only the most prominent illustration of this history. The accusations against Brasillach risked rebounding on the accusers, along with an extra charge of hypocrisy.

The judges and prosecutors of course went to great length to draw distinctions between their own quiet, prudent collaboration (ostensibly justified by the need to preserve the French from the greater horrors of direct Nazi rule) and Brasillach's noisy, flagrantly treasonous conduct. Kaplan largely accepts the argument, and in one respect she is right to do so. Brasillach's guilt far overshadowed that of his executioners. But as she only notes in passing, putting Brasillach on trial also distracted attention from those within the administration and elite whose guilt, particularly in regard to the seventy-six thousand murdered French Jews, far overshadowed Brasillach's. (Kaplan asserts, far too easily, that the horror of the deportations "was only understood" much later. Did the French in 1945 really want to understand it?) While Brasillach went to his death, men like René Bousquet and Maurice Papon, who coolly dispatched Jews to Auschwitz, glided seamlessly back into the corridors of power, each to serve in a long series of high financial and government positions. In this respect, Brasillach was a scapegoat—a peculiarly repulsive scapegoat, perhaps, but a scapegoat nonetheless.

There were several things that suited Brasillach for this role. There was his indeterminate sexuality—it is uncertain if he ever had homosexual relations, but his writing certainly had homoerotic strains, and he was widely believed homosexual by his peers. There was his flamboyant lack of manners, his absolute inability to restrain his sublimely nasty pen (as in his denunciation of the Third Republic as "an old syphilitic whore"). And there was, above all, his status as a writer: visible and vulnerable. His writing made him an obvious target, and his death removed some of the pressure on the French state to dig beneath the surface of the Occupation into the foul-smelling layers inhabited by powerful men like Papon, who finally came to trial only in 1998.

There is an obvious reason to resist this conclusion. This was Brasillach's own defense and that of his supporters to this day. But we do not have to conclude, as they do, that the greater guilt of the Papons somehow erases Brasillach's own considerable responsibility. Rather, we should keep in mind a fundamental historical point. Words can be crimes, and writers do bear responsibility for them. But no matter how terrible the words, their criminality cannot match that of the hand that softly writes a line on a page, sending thousands to their deaths. "Great is the hand that holds dominion over / Man by a scribbled name," as Dylan Thomas wrote. "Hands have no tears to flow."

6

The President as Narcissist: From Vichy to the Élysée

THIS ESSAY MOSTLY DEALS WITH POSTWAR France, but it follows directly from the previous one. François Mitterrand, Socialist president of France from 1981 to 1995, was one of the many ambitious French civil servants who followed the dictates of calculation more than conscience under Vichy. He flirted with the Resistance while also maintaining ties to Marshal Pétain's regime, and developed close personal ties to high-level Vichy officials such as René Bousquet. At the Liberation, he paid no price for his compromises, but immediately embarked on a long and successful political career in which calculation would trump conscience many more times, even if he never again confronted moral stakes as high as during the war. The appearance of Philip Short's excellent biography gave me the chance to reflect on a man whose career—including, very much, its Vichy chapter—had long fascinated me.

Of all modern European leaders, François Mitterrand was the one most clearly born into the wrong century. He would have made a superb Renaissance cardinal, presiding over Mass with great pomp before

---

Book under Review: Philip Short, *Mitterrand: A Study in Ambiguity* (The Bodley Head, 2013). Essay first published in *The Guardian* on November 28, 2013.

retreating to a sumptuous apartment to engage in a little discreet selling of holy offices, before dinner with his mistress. He would have been a brilliant patron of the arts, a peerless schemer in the Curia, a deadly enemy even for a Borgia. A modern democracy was the wrong place for his talents. He succeeded in his greatest ambition, to rule France, but in the end he accomplished relatively little in the role.

He remains an endlessly fascinating figure, and Philip Short tells the story expertly in this deeply researched and marvelously readable biography. Born into a conservative, bourgeois family in southwestern France in 1916, Mitterrand initially gravitated, like so many others in the feverish final days of the Third Republic, to the political extremes. He even moved in circles close to the right-wing terrorist group known as the Cagoule, without ever joining it himself. He also demonstrated a capacity for flamboyant passion by composing more than two thousand love letters to the first great object of his affections, a young woman named Marie-Louise Terrasse. The war interrupted both his political and romantic plans, landing him in a German prisoner-of-war camp. But he soon escaped back to France, driven in large part by concerns about Marie-Louise's fidelity. And he then began a dangerous political dance, working overtly for the Vichy regime in prisoners' organizations while also flirting with the Resistance. Only in the summer of 1943 did he cast his lot with the latter, and he demonstrated reckless bravery in the cause.

After the Liberation, his work on behalf of prisoners won him quick election to parliament and a cabinet post when still just thirty years old. For nearly half a century thereafter he rarely disappeared from the public eye. He was anything but a populist, or a riveting orator. But he had astonishing personal magnetism. The journalist Françoise Giroud left a memorable description of Mitterrand's effect on women: "When he unwound, he was irresistible.... If he had wanted to, he could have seduced a stone—economical in his gestures, his eyes shining with mischief, his voice velvety, his words enveloping you like a shawl." The same qualities helped him to forge powerful friendships with men as well and to attract a large cadre of political supporters. It also helped that, like many other great politicians, he was a wholly convincing and absolutely shameless liar. As Georges Pompidou once remarked: "Never let Mitterrand impress you. No matter what he tells you, never believe a word he says."

His political odyssey was as vivid as his personality. During the decades after the war, most western European politicians moved steadily away from doctrinaire Marxian socialism; Mitterrand moved toward it. Already in 1940, his experience as a prisoner had shaken his confidence in traditional conservative politics. He was especially impressed by the way, in prisoner-of-war camps, an initial attitude of every man for himself gave way to cooperation. As he wrote, quite movingly, many years later: "One has to have seen the new representatives—nobody knew exactly how they had been appointed—dividing up the black bread into six slices, equal to the nearest millimetre, under the wide-eyed supervision of universal suffrage. It was a rare and instructive sight. I was watching the birth of the social contract." When he entered politics, it was as a member of the broad center left, and he remained there throughout the twelve years of the Fourth Republic (1946–1958), during which he held ministerial posts on eleven separate occasions, and played an important role in the breakup of the French colonial empire.

When the Fourth Republic collapsed amid the debris of the Algerian war, and Charles de Gaulle took power, Mitterrand emerged as the most prominent leader of the opposition. He denounced de Gaulle for having staged a "permanent coup d'état" (even writing a book with this title), and ran unsuccessfully for president against him in 1965. He studied Marx and Lenin, and his rhetoric took on stronger Marxist accents. When a new Parti Socialiste emerged under his leadership in 1971, it had very different ideological goals from Britain's Labour and from West Germany's Social Democrats. The next year, Mitterrand led it into an alliance with the Communist Party, with their so-called Common Programme calling for large-scale nationalizations of industry.

During these years, Mitterrand's personal passions remained as strong as ever. After Marie-Louise jilted him, he fell into what can only be called a rebound marriage with Danielle Gouze, eight years his junior. She would bear him three children, but it was not exactly a marriage of minds. Soon after marrying, she innocently asked him how his day had gone. He snapped back: "I did not marry you under the regime of the Inquisition." He cheated on her incessantly, and with no apparent compunction. Then, in his late forties, he met the twenty-year-old Anne Pingeot, and fell for her as completely as he had for Marie-Louise, although without entirely abandoning his other extracurricular activities.

She became to all intents and purposes his second wife, bearing him a daughter, Mazarine, in 1974. Short's account, however, suggests that Danielle Mitterrand does not deserve too much of posterity's pity. In 1958 she acquired a long-term lover of her own, a gym teacher who sometimes fetched the morning croissants for the Mitterrand ménage, and then sat down to a friendly breakfast with François.

In many other countries, these escapades would have brought Mitterrand's career to a quick, scandalous conclusion. His relationship with Pingeot was widely known in Parisian society. But a compliant and complacent French press not only hid this secret until the end of Mitterrand's presidency in 1995, but two others as well. One, relatively inconsequential, was the youthful flirtation with the Cagoule. The other, much more serious, was that soon after taking office in 1981 Mitterrand was diagnosed with prostate cancer that had already metastasized to the bone. Remarkably, the secret did not leak out, and doctors kept him alive another fourteen years.

The presidency itself saw Mitterrand's political journey to the left reach a sudden stop and then reverse. His platform of large-scale nationalization was not only anachronistic, but unworkable under conditions of global recession. Capital flight and social unrest ensued, and to stave off an economic meltdown, Mitterrand called for "opening a parenthesis in the history of socialism." It is a parenthesis that has never closed. He implemented austerity policies, sought a modus vivendi with French business, and abandoned the full-bore Marxist rhetoric of the 1970s.

Mitterrand's fourteen years in office (among post-Revolution French leaders, only Louis-Philippe and Napoleon III lasted longer) proved a moderate success in some respects. An ambitious decentralization program reduced the power of imperious Napoleonic prefects, and transferred considerable authority to newly created "regions" such as Rhône-Alpes and Aquitaine. Mitterrand barely bothered to disguise his strategy of "embracing" the Communist Party in order to "smother" it, through an alliance that gave it little but four insignificant ministries. The arrangement hastened the Communists' decline, although their fall, in retrospect, looks entirely inevitable. In 1986, when Mitterrand lost control of the National Assembly to Jacques Chirac's neo-Gaullists, the resulting episode of "cohabitation" secured the Fifth Republic's stability, although the two men worked viciously to undermine each other.

Mitterrand strengthened France's place in the Western alliance, and worked effectively with Ronald Reagan, Margaret Thatcher, and Helmut Kohl during the collapse of the Soviet bloc.

Short argues that Mitterrand "changed the ground rules of French social and political debate in ways more far-reaching and fundamental than any other modern leader before him". This is an exaggeration, for to a large extent, Mitterrand did little more than acquiesce in and preside over changes already under way. In fact, he arguably squandered the opportunity to move France toward a more open, flexible form of social democracy, loosening the dirigiste rigidity that still dominates so much of French economic planning and labor relations. He might, for instance, have done more to weaken the influence of the *grandes écoles*: the small, privileged institutions whose like-thinking graduates have a stranglehold on the highest circles of French government, business, and academia. His weak gestures in this direction were summarily reversed by Chirac in 1986 and never reintroduced.

Mitterrand's failures came for two basic reasons. First, he had little understanding of, and less sympathy for, the way France had changed in the "thirty glorious years" of postwar economic expansion. He had a sentimental fondness, born of his wartime experience, for industrial workers and peasants, but looked with distaste on the large new suburban middle class. A man of deep literary culture and respect for tradition, he could not come to grips with men and women who preferred television to Stendhal, and fast food to *cuisine bourgeoise*. Short largely misses this side of Mitterrand. A skilled and fluid biographer, whose previous subjects include Mao and Pol Pot (Mitterrand must have come as something of a relief), he focuses on his subject's activities, often day by day, to the neglect of the larger historical context.

He does, however, capture well the other reason for Mitterrand's failures—a narcissism that was monstrous even by the standards of highly successful politicians. One of his anecdotes reveals it: at a crucial moment in the Algerian war, Mitterrand, then the minister responsible for French North Africa, kept a leading moderate Muslim politician waiting in his anteroom for an hour and a half because he insisted on catching up with the comic strips in the *France Soir* newspaper.

As president, once socialism's "parenthesis" had begun, Mitterrand lost interest in social transformation, and concentrated on manipulating those around him, in a manner that commentators compared, with reason, to the court of Louis XIV. Mitterrand himself was not entirely oblivious to this side of his personality. An earlier biographer, Catherine Nay, quoted his astonishing remark, made with tongue supremely in cheek, in reference to Stendhal's archetypical young man in a hurry: "Look at the poverty of Julien Sorel's ambition."

And, of course, Mitterrand also invested huge energies in the architectural *grands projets* that are one of his principal legacies: I. M. Pei's striking additions to the Louvre; the Grande Arche de la Défense; the Bastille Opera; the finance ministry at Bercy; the hideous National Library at Tolbiac that now bears Mitterrand's name. No other western leader of the last half century did anything remotely comparable. It is a record a Renaissance potentate would have taken pride in.

Top image: ©iStock.com/FrancescoRizzato. Bottom image: The Taking of the Bastille, 14 July 1789 (oil on canvas), French School, (18th century) / Chateau de Versailles, France / Bridgeman Images.

Part VII

PARALLELS: PAST AND PRESENT

———◦◦◦———

ONE OF MY GREATEST AMBITIONS as a historian has been to point, however distantly, to the enduring effects in our own world of patterns of thought and action set long ago. I hoped that my work on revolutionary French nationalism might help readers think about the ties that bind modern nations together (France itself, of course, first and foremost). I hoped my book on "the first total war" might help illuminate the way modern nations deal with questions of war and peace, very much including the United States since 9/11.

On occasion, I have tried to bring out such connections between past and present more explicitly, in short form, for a general audience. The essays here were written in response to events ranging from the introduction of perestroika in the Soviet Union to the turmoil that followed the Arab Spring. In each case, I tried to show the continuing importance of political patterns first established during the age of revolutions, when so much of modern political life came into being—especially in that great political laboratory that was revolutionary France.

Of course, I am painfully aware of the pitfalls involved in any such enterprise, which is why I kept these essays mostly short and speculative. It is all too tempting to impose our own concerns on the past, and to take for real connections that exist mainly in our own retinas. As one of the characters in Montesquieu's *Persian Letters* remarks: "We never judge things without secretly turning back upon ourselves. I am not surprised that Africans depict the devil shining white, and their gods black as coal . . . it has been very well said that if triangles could invent a god, they would give it three sides." But this "secret turning back" is a danger that affects all historical work, not just short speculative essays. In seeking to avoid it, in the end all that historians can do is remember the warning, and make their cases as well as possible.

I

Paristroika: From the Bastille to the Lubyanka

THIS ESSAY, MY FIRST VENTURE into historically grounded prognostication, produced a certain amount of scoffing when it first appeared in mid-1988. At the time, most American commentary on perestroika was still limited to the question of whether Mikhail Gorbachev was a genuine reformer, or a secret hardliner trying to lure the West into lowering its defenses. Few observers yet imagined that the reform process in the USSR might run out of control, regardless of Gorbachev's real motivations—the possibility that the comparison with prerevolutionary France suggested to me. One eminent Sovietologist wrote a letter to The New Republic *in which he condescendingly chided me for imagining that the Soviet leadership would ever let things get to the point where Ukraine might break away. In this case, at least, French history provided a better guide to the future than Soviet precedent.*

For the second most powerful nation in the world, '87 and '88 were extraordinary years. A series of reforms ended some of the autocratic government's worst abuses. A reform-minded leadership experimented with

Essay originally published in *The New Republic*, July 11, 1988.

plans for the liberalization of a calcified and corrupt state. The press flourished, and with each day the limits on what could be published were pushed outward. A young and attractive ruler seemed to articulate popular hopes. Yet the population's material situation remained poor, and notoriously stubborn entrenched elites held on to their privileges with increasing desperation. Attention focused on the convocation of a representative body that had not met for a very long time…

This may sound like a description of the year 1987–1988 and Gorbachev's USSR, but for a historian, what comes to mind is 1787–1788 and the France of Louis XVI. It is often forgotten today, but in the period that preceded the French Revolution, the royal government carried out reforms as shocking and exhilarating as those now taking place in the Soviet Union. These reforms, however, failed to prevent the impending upheaval, and may even have hastened it. As Tocqueville observed, the drama of 1789 began not when things were at their worst but when things were finally starting to improve—as things may now start to improve under Gorbachev.

King Louis XVI was not a particularly charismatic or competent leader. Nonetheless, under his rule France experimented with a series of provincial assemblies, the greatest concession to democracy ever made by the absolute monarchy. In 1787–1788 it abolished the venerable institution of judicial torture and granted defendants in criminal trials the right to attorneys. It also gave official toleration to Protestants, who had within living memory been the target of massacre and deportation. In those years the young and popular king seemed to side with the people against an intransigent nobility. And by the summer of 1788 official censorship had collapsed, and effective freedom of the press came into being, complete with raucous criticism of the existing order.

This was the bright side of Louis's reign. Yet his government made frustratingly little progress against France's mammoth social and economic problems. The most immediate of these was the state's massive debt, incurred in large part through military spending. The country's financial apparatus functioned less as a collector than as a sieve for money and needed radical reform. The nobility obstinately refused to abandon their own considerable financial privileges. And, ominously, a catastrophic harvest in 1788 sent the price of bread skyrocketing and unleashed the familiar specter of famine. In retrospect it hardly seems surprising that revolution soon broke out.

Of course, Louis XVI and his ministers thought they could control the reform process. They did not see a contradiction between rapid political liberalization and slow structural change. Seeing the nobility as the main obstacle to such change, they believed that the pressure of newly liberated public opinion would help overcome noble resistance. For this reasons, the Crown subsidized pamphleteers who peddled its line, and Marie Antoinette, in other contexts the epitome of aristocratic haughtiness, declared herself "the queen of the Third Estate." However, the strategy soon backfired. Independent public opinion, initially supportive of Louis XVI, soon forced the king and the nobility back into each other's embrace, and eventually destroyed both.

Now consider the situation in the Soviet Union. One week a new political party forms in Moscow. The next, Lenin himself comes in for criticism, despite Gorbachev's protestations of following Lenin's true line. Bukharin, Kamenev, and Zinoviev are rehabilitated, and since textbooks have failed to keep up with glasnost, the state cancels high school history exams. The Tatars, brutally exiled from their Crimean home under Stalin, are allowed to start returning. The Orthodox Church is given unprecedented freedom and publicity. Eduard Shevardnadze meets in New York with the prime minister of Israel. Andrei Sakharov gives a quasi-official news conference. A protest march for more glasnost proceeds in Moscow under the gaze of Western reporters without police interference. In short, taboos are collapsing like dominoes. Yet at the same time the new regime has brought about little improvement in the population's material conditions or in the efficiency of the unwieldy economic system.

Needless to say, Gorbachev too hopes to control the reform process. He seems to believe that public opinion, given a voice for the first time in Soviet history, will help him prod a recalcitrant party and bureaucracy into motion. Indeed, he and his supporters seem almost cocky about this strategy. As one Soviet official said recently about the relaxation of religious controls: "Since the power belongs completely to us, I think we are capable of pointing this track in whatever direction is to our interest." To be sure, the Soviet state exercises a sort of social control that

Louis XVI could not have begun to imagine. And Gorbachev is far more able and shrewd than the hapless French king. But he has already underestimated the power and unpredictability of his newly articulated public opinion. Take Armenia and Azerbaijan. If Gorbachev had simply crushed nationalist rumblings there, he would have alienated public opinion and lost crucial support for other aspects of his program. Louis XVI faced similar dilemmas.

So what is in store for the USSR? Obviously any historical comparison with revolutionary France has severe limits. Even in 1917, when the Russian revolutionaries consciously compared themselves to the great figures of 1789–1799, history failed to follow a proven script. It would be absurd to cast the upcoming Communist Party conference as a Soviet Estates General. But the parallels do suggest three general points.

First, Gorbachev's motivations for glasnost and perestroika—the question of whether he is a "true Leninist," for instance—may ultimately prove of little importance. Historians have argued about Louis XVI's sincerity in 1787–1788, yet agree that it mattered far less than the events Louis helped bring on. Even if Gorbachev were a Machiavellian master of disinformation, plotting every *Pravda* letter to the editor in order to lull Western suspicions, glasnost would still have the same consequences.

Second, the greatest opposition to Gorbachev may ultimately come not from the "conservative" Party hierarchy but from those now calling for further and faster reform. In France an entrenched and ambitious aristocracy long posed the greatest apparent threat to Louis XVI. Yet it was very little time before a new force, calling itself "the nation," emerged and took control of the state, even though in 1788 it possessed no political structure and no military strength. The Crown possessed an enormous police apparatus, but the collapse of royal authority made the police a useless weapon.

Finally, by opening the existing order to criticism and by giving legitimacy to public opinion, Gorbachev may well have destroyed the Soviet state's own last vestiges of legitimacy. Tocqueville noted that when Louis XVI called on his subjects to air their grievances, the individual complaints collectively formed nothing less than a call for the abolition of the entire regime. By the time the Estates General convened in 1789 many French people saw little logic or reason in their national institutions and were eager to wipe the slate clean. Today a whiff of that revolutionary spirit is present in the recent call by Moscow political clubs for a new constitution.

So though we are not likely to see Muscovites storming the Lubyanka anytime soon, we may well see considerable turmoil in the Soviet Union. The French monarchy had survived civil war, invasion, famine, and plague. In the end, what it could not survive was glasnost.

2

The Shorn Identity: The End of French Republican Assimilation

THIS ESSAY DID NOT TRY to set up a parallel but to place the condition of France's banlieues, *populated largely by poor, disproportionately Muslim immigrant communities, in historical context. It was prompted by the large-scale rioting that struck the* banlieues *in 2005, and it recapitulated many of the arguments I first made in my 2001 book* The Cult of the Nation in France. *The basic point was that older "republican" methods of assimilating new populations into France had effectively collapsed in the 1960s, without anything new taking their place. Unless the French state made a real effort to devise new methods, I argued, the problems of the* banlieues *would simply get worse. The last lines of the essay, written ten years before the* Charlie Hebdo *and Hyper Cacher massacres of 2015, make for painful reading after those events.*

To the smoke rising from the Paris suburbs, the American press has been adding a generous portion of fog. Typical was a front-page story in the *New York Times.* A "significant proportion of the population," Craig S. Smith wrote, "has yet to accept the increasingly multiethnic makeup of

Essay originally published in *The New Republic*, November 28, 2005.

the nation. Put simply, being French, for many people, remains a ba-
guette-and-beret affair." Put simply, this is distressingly close to nonsense, and not just because berets have been far more scarce on French
streets than baseball caps for many years. What Smith and the many
American journalists who have repeated such ideas for the last few weeks
have not reported is that France has been a multiethnic country for a
very long time, and, for decades, it did as well as any other Western
country—including the United States—at integrating large numbers of
immigrants into its society. The problem that has literally burst into flames
this year is not that France has an innate inability to integrate ethnic
groups, but rather that its method for integrating them no longer works.

To see the multiethnic history of modern France, one need look no
further than the phone book of any major French city. In addition to
the Duponts and the Lebruns, and names of Arab and African origin,
there are long columns of Cohens and Kowalskis, of Chungs and
Nguyens, of Martinis and Gonzalezes and Oliveiras. In the years between World War I and 1965, during which the United States radically
curtailed immigration, France took in a considerably higher proportion
of immigrants than we did.

Nor did most of these immigrant groups experience more prejudice
than their American equivalents. (The Jewish community, mostly descended from nineteenth- and twentieth-century immigrants, constituted
the glaring exception.) Today, throughout the highest ranks of French
society, men and women of immigrant descent are anything but un-
common. Nicolas Sarkozy, the tough-talking interior minister, is the
son of a Hungarian immigrant on one side and the grandson of a Greek
Jewish one on the other. Pierre Bérégovoy, a Socialist prime minister in
the 1990s, was of recent Ukrainian descent. That great icon of French
cinema, Yves Montand, was born in Italy as Ivo Livi. Jacques Derrida,
France's most famous philosopher of the late twentieth century, was an
Algerian Jew.

Furthermore, France's ability to accept and integrate new ethnic
groups has not entirely ceased to function in recent decades. Just minutes from central Paris, areas like Belleville and Porte d'Ivry are home to
hundreds of thousands of French citizens of southeast Asian descent,
who have remained almost entirely removed from the recent distur-
bances. In part thanks to these immigrants, tiny Asian carryouts have

become as common as bakeries in many parts of the city in recent years, suggesting that, if "baguettes" remain central to French identity, it may only be because the word also means "chopsticks." In recent years, Asian surnames appear to have become increasingly common among the students admitted to France's elite institutions of higher education, the *grandes écoles*. For that matter, a steady stream of ethnic North Africans has also been rising into the French middle class, their successes overshadowed by the larger problems of the suburbs.

Admittedly, until recently, this history of immigration had been relatively invisible. Unlike in the United States, immigrant heritage has never functioned as a source of French national pride. There is no French equivalent to the Ellis Island museum, no French holiday like Saint Patrick's Day. Artists and writers from the older immigrant groups have not, for the most part, injected an ostentatiously ethnic flavor into their works. There is no French-Jewish Philip Roth or Woody Allen. And, for this reason, the French themselves long remained largely ignorant of their own history, to the point that, as late as 1986, one of the country's best and most prominent historians, Pierre Nora (himself, ironically, of Jewish descent) could speak of large-scale immigration as "a novelty of the country's present-day situation." The leading French authority on immigration, Gérard Noiriel, had to struggle long and hard just to have his subject recognized as a legitimate one in French academia. But, since the publication of his pathbreaking book *Le creuset français* (*The French Melting Pot*) in 1988, there has been an explosion of studies, hobbled only by the stubborn refusal of the French state to compile statistics on the country's racial and ethnic composition.

This refusal—the official denial that ethnicity can have any legitimate place in public life—reflects the republican ideology that lies behind France's model of immigration. Republicanism resolutely opposes any show of loyalty to an entity other than the nation itself, whether an ethnic group, a geographical area (such as a French province), or a religion. As long ago as 1789, a legislator memorably articulated the key idea in regard to the group that, until very recently, was seen as most different from the French norm, and around which discussions of ethnic difference tended to crystallize: "Everything must be refused to the Jews as a Nation...and everything granted to the Jews as individuals." In recent years, the most ferocious debates over French identity have not concerned immigrant groups, per se, but Islam, and particularly the wearing of headscarves by Muslim girls in the public schools, which the French state has banned. To dedicated republicans, the headscarf is precisely the sort of badge of identity that threatens to trump one's identity as a citizen and endanger civic unity.

To understand why the republican model of integration has begun to fail over the past forty years or so, a bit of older history is necessary. The model dates all the way back to the French Revolution. Large-scale immigration had not yet begun in the late eighteenth century, but, even so, France was perceived as dangerously divided among its own constituent populations. The diversity of language was most striking. By some estimates, less than one-fifth of the population spoke standard French with any degree of fluency (although many more understood it). It was hardly surprising that the great revolutionary orator Mirabeau referred to France as an "unconstituted aggregate of disunited peoples."

To create a cohesive political community, the most radical revolutionaries believed that they had to erase these regional differences, and, in the words of Henri Grégoire, take people and "melt them into the national mass." The revolutionary government embraced ambitious projects of integration, focused above all on the educational system. It envisaged sending thousands of instructors into the countryside, much as the Roman Catholic Church had earlier sent thousands of missionaries. But where the missionaries had worked to forge a united faith, the secular instructors would forge a united nation.

The revolutionaries did not have the means to put their projects of integration into practice. But, in the nineteenth century, the aggressively secular Third Republic finally began, as the historian Eugen Weber has put it, to make "peasants into Frenchmen." Local dialects and traditions were turned into harmless folklore, while battalions of earnest schoolmasters instructed their charges in proper speech and in the history and customs of the nation as a whole. Aided by powerful social changes that brought country people into the cities—while extending railroads into the countryside—the projects arguably succeeded. Today, despite earnest efforts by regional militants, most of France's traditional regional languages are moribund.

At the same time, French republicans were expanding their assimilationist ambitions beyond the borders of France itself. In the colonial empire that, by 1900, stretched from Indochina to the Caribbean and covered one-third of the African continent, French administrators, for a time, practiced relatively inclusive policies, providing extensive primary education and even offering citizenship on a limited basis, in keeping with the idea of a French "civilizing mission." Certain parts of the empire were fully annexed to France itself, becoming legally as indistinguishable from the metropole as Hawaii is from the continental United States. These policies consolidated French power over the colonies while also affirming France's position as a center of worldwide culture and civilization. It was a point of pride that so much of the world, in effect, seemed to want to become French.

In the late nineteenth century, therefore, immigrants began arriving in large numbers in a country that already had a century's experience of assimilating people different from the French cultural norm into the "national mass." To be sure, even immigrants from neighboring Catholic countries like Italy experienced considerable resistance at first—but probably no more than their equivalents in the United States. And, eventually, resistance and prejudice gave way to widespread acceptance, as long as the immigrant groups themselves willingly accepted a new "French" identity and abandoned their old national one. The Third Republic did see moments of vicious hostility to the Jews (notably in the Dreyfus Affair), but it also saw impressive opposition to anti-Semitism, a broad willingness to accept fully "integrated" Jews into French society, and the selection of a Jew, Léon Blum, as prime minister. All in all, the metaphor of the melting pot actually fits France better than the United States, for ethnic identities melted away far more thoroughly in France than on this side of the Atlantic.

However, just as large-scale immigration from Muslim ex-colonies began in the 1960s, this model of integration started to break down. Muslims were not the cause of this collapse. Rather, several developments challenged the republican model at once. First, industrialization and urbanization finally brought about the end of the peasantry, depriving French educators of the traditional objects of their missionary efforts. As late as the 1930s, half the population lived in rural settings, where schoolteachers enjoyed considerable status as agents of urban civilization. With mass migration into the cities, the status of the educational system itself, and its role as a force for integration, diminished noticeably.

Second, decolonization brought the French empire to an end, and it delivered a terrific shock to France's self-image in the process. Large parts of the world, it now appeared, did not want to be French—indeed, they were willing to fight not to be French. Those who fought hardest, employing terrorist violence against French civilians, were Algerian revolutionaries (against whom the French state, in turn, employed torture and murder). It was the achievement of Algerian independence in 1962 that marked the symbolic repudiation of France's "civilizing mission" by its intended beneficiaries, and bitter memories of the war stoked racism against North Africans in France itself. (Jean-Marie Le Pen, leader of the far right National Front, served in Algeria as a paratrooper.)

In addition, at precisely this sensitive moment came the massive student unrest, widespread rioting, and paralyzing strikes of May 1968. This episode had many dimensions, but the most important was arguably the revolt against the famed French educational system. Students had led earlier French rebellions, but not against their own teachers. One ramification of the revolt was the near-destruction of the magisterial authority formerly enjoyed by French educators and their overweening confidence that they could, and should, squeeze students into national molds of their own devising.

It was into this changed and diminished France—stripped of its empire, unnerved by the wars of decolonization, deprived of its traditional peasantry, and shaken in its cultural authority—that the new immigrants from Africa arrived as cheap labor. Even had they come at an earlier time, their integration would have proved far more difficult than that of Italians, Portuguese, or Jews. The cultural differences were greater, as was the sheer extent of the racial and religious prejudice against them. But in the context of the 1960s, they had hardly any chance. The French state simply no longer had the will to apply the older model of integration fully. Instead, for a time, the state held fast to the fiction that the newcomers were mere "guest workers" who would eventually return home. When it became obvious that large numbers of Arabs, Berbers, and black Africans were in France to stay, the state shunted them into bleak suburban housing projects, effectively segregating them far more radically than earlier waves of immigrants.

Two generations have now grown up in these depressing settings, having little connection to their parents' or grandparents' homelands but feeling unwelcome and feared in France. Not only has widespread racism and discrimination persisted—with the new immigrant groups bearing the brunt of France's massive unemployment problem—but the French state has not even done them the compliment of trying particularly hard to assimilate them. Their experience in the schools has not resembled that of earlier immigrants. I have known several French teachers who worked in suburban *lycées* where North African students were the majority. Only one of them saw the assignment as a chance to follow in the footsteps of those teachers who went forth to proselytize for French civilization, and she received precious little institutional support for her beliefs. The others have endured it simply as a purgatory and counted the days until their release.

Those in France now resisting calls for American-style affirmative action claim that to introduce any sort of special treatment for the "immigrants" would be to violate a basic tenet of French republicanism. Everything to them as individuals, nothing to them as ethnic groups, is the familiar message. But the fact is that the republican model has been broken for close to forty years. For it was never, in practice, simply about the principle of making everyone equal within the civic sphere. It was also about genuine missionary fervor—about taking little Gascons and Normans, little colonial subjects, little Italian and Jewish immigrants, and converting them, in the full meaning of the word, into French men and women. The absence of that sort of fervor in places like Clichy-sous-Bois or Saint-Denis, where some of the worst rioting has occurred, has contributed powerfully to the alienation that has expressed itself in the recent wave of arson and destruction. The very use of the word "immigrants" for these second- and third-generation French youths is an insulting reminder of just how little attention official France has given them. Nicolas Sarkozy is more of an immigrant than many of them.

Can the old republican fervor be summoned from the ashes? Probably not. For one thing, since the 1960s, ethnic groups in France have begun to express themselves far more vigorously than in the past. In the Jewish community, for instance, there have been widespread calls for broader assertions of "communal" identity, causing consternation among those (mostly older) Jews who accepted the bargain offered them by the Republic, going so far as to label themselves not "Juifs" but "Israélites," a term they defined as French citizens of the Jewish faith. Attempts to revive the earlier model of integration with regard to young Arabs and black Africans would now call forth charges of cultural arrogance, Eurocentrism, and racism and meet with widespread resistance.

Yet the riots of the past weeks have made it all too clear that, if the French Republic cannot return to its past, it desperately needs to find some way to offer the youths of the suburbs a meaningful form of integration into broader society—even if that involves some variety of American-style affirmative action. Well before the riots, the Institut d'Études Politiques, Paris's elite college for government and diplomacy, had instituted a program for disadvantaged youths that defined disadvantage by geographic location, rather than race. Such measures could easily be generalized to the other *grandes écoles*. The widespread institution of enterprise zones freed from the burdensome French regulatory apparatus that strangles startup businesses could also help. (Ironically, the very weight of regulation in France could make such zones particularly effective there.) Just as important, France's leading politicians need to go to the suburban areas and declare, forthrightly, that the people who live there are just as French as Sarkozy—or, for that matter, as Jacques Chirac. Sarkozy's cynical order to deport noncitizens arrested in the riots has sent precisely the wrong message by further associating the suburbs with "foreigners."

Certainly, law and order needs to be reestablished, and the vandals who, after all, preyed mostly on their own communities need to be punished. But the problems of the suburbs call for more inclusive measures, not only for reasons of elementary justice but also because, in the long run, nihilistic car-burning is hardly the worst threat presented by communities like Clichy-sous-Bois—radical Islamism is. For the moment, Islamist militants have had relatively little success in spreading their own variety of missionary fervor in France. The rioters of the past weeks have shown greater enthusiasm for American "gangsta" rap than for Osama bin Laden. But whether this will remain the case is a different matter. Recent events in the Netherlands—particularly the murder of filmmaker Theo Van Gogh by an Islamist extremist—illustrate how easily Islamist radicalism can gain a foothold in Europe. And it is hard to see better candidates for religious radicalization than the alienated young people of the French suburbs, dismissed as "immigrants" in the land of their own birth.

3

The Peace Paradox: From Paris to Baghdad

THIS ESSAY RETURNS TO THE PARALLELS between the age of revolutions and the present, in this case looking at issues of war and peace. It was written in 2007, when U.S. forces were still fighting in Iraq, and it drew on arguments I developed in my book The First Total War. *That book itself explored the parallels between the age of revolutions and our own day, including in the dilemmas presented to supposedly enlightened superpowers by savage guerrilla resistance in occupied territories. But in this essay I looked more generally at the way dreams of perpetual peace can unexpectedly give way to nightmares of apocalyptic war.*

Historical analogies have always been popular in foreign-policy debates, and the present day is no exception. For liberals, the best description of our current situation is "Vietnam II" (as Maureen Dowd dubbed it in a *Times* column): another ghastly quagmire from which we can do little but walk away. Nonsense, reply conservatives. It's really "World War IV" (the words of Norman Podhoretz, who counts the Cold War as III): another deadly struggle against totalitarianism for which we must mobilize every possible resource. As for the Harvard historian Niall Ferguson, writing in *Vanity Fair*, the best analogy is what could be called Rome II. We are another colossal empire, perched on the brink of decline and fall.

Yet since history never repeats itself so neatly, the most useful historical analogies are not those that promise to predict the future but those that may reveal unexpected things about the present. Consider, for instance, a parallel rarely cited in current debates: the one between the post–Cold War period and the age of the French Revolution. Both began (by coincidence, in years numbered '89 and '90) with moments of extraordinary elation and hope. A powerful and much-loathed regime (the USSR, the French absolute monarchy) not only collapsed unexpectedly but did so with surprisingly little violence. So transformative did the change appear that many advanced thinkers predicted nothing less than an age of democracy in which warfare would have no place. In our own day, Francis Fukuyama famously spoke of "the end of history," by which he meant an end to conflicts over the proper form of society. Two hundred years before, the fall of the French Old Regime led to surprisingly similar visions. In 1790, the new French revolutionary state even renounced aggressive war, in what became known as its "declaration of peace to the world." A French legislator promised giddily that from now on the human race would form "a single society, whose object is the peace and happiness of each and all of its members."

Yet in both cases, disillusion followed with cruel speed. In our own time, of course, there were the wars in the Balkans and the Gulf, followed by the global upheaval triggered by 9/11. In the eighteenth century, less than two years after the declaration of peace, there began a series of wars that would drag in all of Europe's major powers, take millions of lives, and continue, with only small breaks, for more than twenty-three years, until France's final defeat in 1815. They would make possible the career of a man whose name is synonymous with military hubris: Napoleon Bonaparte. In short, the Enlightenment vision of perpetual peace gave way rapidly to a conflict in which states directed every possible political, social, and economic resource toward the utter defeat of the enemy—humankind's first total war.

Is this a coincidence? During the late eighteenth century, the Western world largely took war for granted. The major powers fought one another at regular intervals and devoted the lion's share of their budgets to the purpose. For this very reason, however, they took care to practice a degree of restraint and to treat their adversaries with honor. The French reformer Jean-Paul Rabaut Saint-Étienne was exaggerating when he said that "armies [now] slaughter each other politely...what was once a wild rage is now just a moment's madness." Still, particularly in western Europe, war took less of a human toll in the century before the French Revolution than at almost any time in history.

In fact, advanced thinkers who believed in the new Enlightenment creed of secular human progress came to hope that war might fade away entirely. European philosophers like Baron d'Holbach called it nothing but a "remnant of savage customs," and no less a figure than George Washington agreed, in 1788, that it was time for agriculture and commerce "to supersede the waste of war and the rage of conquest." It was precisely such sentiments that inspired France's declaration of peace two years later.

Yet the idea that warfare might actually end had a paradoxical effect, for it destroyed any rationale for waging war with restraint. Within months of the declaration, one of its liberal proponents was warning that if revolutionary France did nonetheless come to blows with other European powers, it would be "a war to the death which we will fight...so as to destroy and annihilate all who attack us, or to be destroyed ourselves." In 1792, claiming to be acting out of reasons of preventive self-defense, France declared war on the Austrian Empire, and France's leading general declared, "This war will be the last war" (the phrase uncannily foreshadows "the war to end all wars" of 1914). To achieve such an exalted end, any means were justified, and so there followed total war and the birth of new hatreds that made the idea of perpetual peace look more utopian than ever. France and its enemies both declared that the "barbarism" of the enemy made it impossible to respect the ordinary laws of war and proceeded to ravage civilian populations across the continent.

In our own day, the lurch from dreams of peace to nightmares of war has not (yet) translated into destruction on this terrible scale (except, alas, in Iraq). Of course, the enemy has failed to inflict significant damage on us, and even conservatives have not urged the sort of mobilization and sacrifice that we experienced during World War II. What has happened is a growing willingness to abandon traditional restraints on proved and suspected enemies, foreign and American alike. "Among ourselves, we keep the law, but when we are operating in the jungle, we must also use the laws of the jungle," wrote the British diplomat Robert Cooper in an influential 2002 essay. With ideas like this in the air, abuses like those at Abu Ghraib and Haditha become far more difficult to prevent.

Could it be, then, that dreams of an end to war may be as unexpectedly dangerous as they are noble, because they seem to justify almost anything done in their name? What the history of the late eighteenth century shows is that talk of fighting "so as to destroy and annihilate all who attack us, or to be destroyed ourselves" justifies a slide into "the laws of the jungle" that usually contributes more to polarization than to real security. It magnifies the importance of our enemies and swells their ranks. In short, it actually increases the danger of bloodshed on a massive scale. As the French revolutionaries learned to their terrible cost, talk of the apocalypse can easily be self-fulfilling.

4

Why We Can't Rule Out an Egyptian Reign of Terror: From Paris to Cairo

I DO NOT CLAIM ANY EXPERTISE in Middle Eastern politics, any more than I claimed any expertise in Soviet politics when I wrote about perestroika in 1988. But eighteenth-century European history arguably provides some insight into the phenomenon of revolution in general. When the Arab Spring began in 2011, many American commentators—including many certified experts in Middle Eastern politics—hailed it as a marvelous and transformative event and saw developments in Egypt as particularly hopeful. My sense of how revolutions worked, informed above all by my knowledge of the French Revolution, left me doubtful, and I wrote this essay to explain why. In this case, I was somewhat less prescient than in 1988—the radical revolution I warned of as a possibility (although only a possibility) has not yet materialized in Egypt. But my more general pessimism about the course of events there has unfortunately been quite well borne out.

There are many different ways of categorizing historical revolutions. But for the purposes of understanding what is happening in Egypt in 2011— and the challenges it may pose for the United States—one simple, rough

Essay first published in *Foreign Policy* on February 7, 2011.

distinction may be especially useful. This is the distinction between revolutions that look more like 1688 and revolutions that look more like 1789. The first date refers to England's "Glorious Revolution," in which the Catholic would-be absolute monarch James II was overthrown and replaced by the Protestant William and Mary, and the English Parliament claimed powerful and enduring new forms of authority. The second is, of course, the date of the French Revolution, which began as an attempt to create a constitutional monarchy but ultimately led to the execution of King Louis XVI, the proclamation of the First French Republic, and the Reign of Terror.

A key feature of 1688-type revolutions is their relative brevity. They may be preceded by lengthy periods of discontent, agitation, protest, and even violence, but the revolutionary moment itself generally lasts for only a few months (as in 1688 itself), or even weeks or days. A regime reaches a point of crisis and falls. The consolidation of a new regime itself may well involve much more turmoil and bloodshed, and eventually entail considerable political and social change—but these later events are not considered part of the revolution itself, and there is no sense of an ongoing revolutionary process. Men and women do not define themselves as active "revolutionaries." (In 1688, in fact, the English noun and adjective "revolutionary" did not yet exist—it only came into frequent use after 1789.)

Revolutions of the 1789 type are quite different. Their leaders and supporters see regime change as only the beginning of an arduous, ambitious process of political, social, and cultural transformation that may require years, even decades, to complete. For them, the revolution is not a discrete event but an ongoing cause. They eagerly define themselves as "revolutionaries" and even speak of the "permanent revolution." Revolutions of this type generally have much stronger utopian tendencies than the others and more frequently lead to large-scale violence. They also tend to have ambitions that overflow national boundaries— the local revolution comes to be seen as just part of a process of worldwide emancipation. In some cases, revolutions of this type may be driven from the start by a self-consciously revolutionary party, committed to radical upheaval. In other cases (such as 1789 itself), it may seem to start off as a more limited event, only to change its character as particular groups grow frustrated with the results and the opposition they have encountered, and conclude that far broader, deeper forms of change are called for.

Historically, 1688-type revolutions have been much more common: France in 1830, Germany in 1918, China in 1911–1912, and many of the revolutions of 1848 (of which most ended in failure). By contrast, 1789-type revolutions have been relative historical rarities: above all, 1789 itself, Russia in 1917, China in 1949, Cuba in 1959. They are not, however, necessarily revolutions of the left. One could also include in this category the Nazi seizure of power in Germany (which Hitler termed a "National Revolution") and Iran in 1979. The American Revolution, it could be argued, represents something of a hybrid case—closer to 1688, yet with important features of the other type, thanks to the long process of consolidation and contestation that followed independence.

In recent years, it seems as if the 1789 type of revolution has lost its appeal for most of the world. During the greatest series of political upheavals in recent times—the collapse of communism—most leaders of the victorious reform movements rejected the word "revolution" altogether. Germans refer to the events of 1989 as the "Turning," not the "Revolution." It was, above all, in Czechoslovakia that the word "revolution" came to describe what happened in 1989, but paired with the word "velvet" to underscore the differences from the great revolutions of the past.

Of course, revolutions have hardly disappeared since 1989. But the recent wave of them across the world—the Rose Revolution in Georgia, the Orange Revolution in Ukraine, the recent events in Tunisia—all look much more like 1688 than 1789. They have been short, sharp affairs, centered on the fall of a regime. In none of these countries have we seen the development of an extended "revolutionary" process or party. And though some of these revolutions have triggered others, domino-style, as in 1848, they have not themselves been expansionary and proselytizing. As far as I know, there are no Tunisian revolutionaries directing events in Cairo.

The principal exception to the current pattern—the one great contemporary revolution of the second type to remain an ongoing proposition today—is Iran. Although it has been more than thirty years since the fall of the shah, Iran's Islamic Republic is still a revolutionary regime in a way matched by few other states in the world today. Despite its considerable unpopularity with its own people, it has remained committed since 1979 to the enactment of radical, even utopian change, and not just inside its own borders. Organizations such as the Revolutionary Guard retain considerable importance.

Egypt, interestingly enough, experienced a revolution close to the 1789 type in its relatively recent history. The so-called Revolution of 1952 that overthrew the country's monarchy and brought Gamal Abdel Nasser to power ultimately involved a great deal more than regime change. Nasser had broad ambitions both for remaking Egyptian society and for taking his revolutionary movement beyond Egypt's own borders (most strikingly, in the creation of the short-lived United Arab Republic). Ironically, Hosni Mubarak spent much of his military career in the service of Nasser's revolutionary regime. But well before Mubarak came to power, following the assassination of Anwar Sadat in 1981, Egypt's revolutionary energies had largely dissipated.

The fundamental question being discussed by commentators at present is what shape a new Egyptian revolution might take, if Mubarak's regime falls and the military does not intervene. Will it come to a quick end with the establishment of a new government—hopefully a democratic one—or will a much more radical, long-lasting revolutionary process develop? In other words, will things look more like 1688 or 1789? Anxieties focus not on a resurgent Nasserism, of course, but rather on the Muslim Brotherhood and the possibility that Egypt may experience its own Islamic revolution, with unpredictable consequences, not only for the country itself but for the region and the world.

Against these anxieties, many commentators have been pointing to the lack of ingredients, at present, for such a turn of events. Cairo in 2011, they insist, is not Tehran in 1979. They argue that the crowds protesting Mubarak have called above all for democracy and expressed little enthusiasm for an Islamic Republic. They characterize the Muslim Brotherhood, despite its long and radical history, as a relatively ineffective organization that has recently moved in more moderate directions and lacks a charismatic leader like Ayatollah Khomeini. In short, they are effectively arguing, the signs point to 1688, not to 1789.

This analysis may well be accurate. But the history of revolutions suggests that even if it is, the long-term outlook in Egypt is still a highly unstable one. This is not only because the furious events of the last two weeks are hard to predict, but because revolutions of the 1789 type do not always start out as such. Hardly anyone at the start of the French Revolution could have predicted the demise of the French monarchy and the Reign of Terror. There were no Jacobins present at the fall of the Bastille in 1789, only future Jacobins. France's turn to radicalism took place after the Bastille had been taken, within the revolutionary process itself—between 1789 and 1793. Similarly, Russia's February Revolution of 1917 initially looked to most observers like 1688: a short, sharp crisis that led to the fall of a monarch, and the quick foundation of a constitutional regime. While Bolsheviks were already present, few observers foresaw the October Revolution that would bring Lenin to power.

Egypt probably does not face the prospect of an Islamic Revolution in the next few months. But if Mubarak falls and is replaced by a weak, unstable series of governments that cannot restore order or deliver serious social and economic reforms—and thus quickly lose credibility and legitimacy among the population—then a different, far more radical revolutionary movement may yet develop. And despite the current lack of a charismatic leader for such a movement, one could quickly emerge out of the torrent of events. In July 1789, Maximilien Robespierre and Georges Danton were unknown lawyers; Jean-Paul Marat an unknown doctor, known to most of his acquaintances as something of a crackpot. Within four years, they had emerged as leaders of the most radical revolution yet seen in history.

So the crucial point to keep in mind, as events in Egypt unfold, is that even in the best-case scenario—Mubarak falls without further violence and is replaced by a seemingly stable, democratic, secular government—the Egyptian Revolution of 2011 may still just be getting started. Its crucial moments may lie months, or even years, in the future. It is after Mubarak's fall that American support for Egypt's democratic forces will be most important. And the last thing anyone should do, if Egypt appears to complete a revolution this year that looks like 1688, is breathe a sigh of relief. At the end of 2011, Mohamed ElBaradei may well be president of a democratic Egypt. But then, at the end of 1789, Louis XVI was still king of France.

5

Inglorious Revolutions: Why We Expect Too Much

THIS ESSAY FOLLOWS DIRECTLY from the previous one, likewise drawing on the long history of revolutions to comment on recent events. It starts with another historical parallel between the late eighteenth-century age of revolutions and the present, and goes on to suggest that a great deal of commentary on the revolutions of the twenty-first century reflects a deep strain of Western hypocrisy. On the one hand, Western commentators now condemn as criminal the sort of violence and strife Western countries experienced during their own revolutions, and treat regimes that emerge from bloody struggles as illegitimate. On the other hand, Western countries refuse to give the sort of large-scale material support that might induce peoples in the midst of revolutions to eschew violence, and to work toward establishing the rule of law and tolerance of opposition. It is no wonder that nearly all the revolutions that have taken place since 2000 have been labeled failures in the West. Given this background, perhaps the word "revolution" should be retired altogether.

Two and a half years after it began, the revolution was widely considered a quagmire, even a disaster. Rebels had made disappointingly little

---

Essay first published in *The National Interest*, January/February 2014.

headway against the forces of the hated tyrant. The capital and the country's second major city remained under his control. Foreign powers had provided sympathy, but very little real aid. And despite promising to respect human rights, rebel forces were committing widespread abuses, including murder, torture, and destruction of property. In short, the bright hopes of an earlier spring were fading fast.

This may sound like a description of Syria today, but it also describes quite well the situation of another country: the young United States in the winter of 1777–1778. George Washington had taken refuge in the miserable winter encampment of Valley Forge. Philadelphia (then the capital) and New York were both in British hands. France had not yet agreed to help the new republic militarily. And in areas under rebel control, Loyalists were being persecuted—far more than most American school textbooks admit.

There is little reason to think that conditions in Syria will turn around the way they did in the United States between 1778 and 1781, when major hostilities ended with a decisive American victory. But the comparison illuminates a different point. Historically, very few revolutions have been quick successes. They have been messy, bloody, long-drawn-out affairs. Victory has very rarely come without numerous setbacks, and, unfortunately, without abuses carried out by all sides. It has generally taken many years, even decades, for the real gains, if any, to become apparent. Yet today, international public opinion, and international institutions, usually fail to recognize this historical reality. There is an expectation that revolutions, where they occur, must lead within a very short period to the establishment of stable democracy and a full panoply of human rights, or they will be considered failures.

Consider, for instance, the disappointments that followed the Arab Spring and the resulting worldwide handwringing. Thomas Friedman, that great barometer of elite American conventional wisdom, wrote in May 2011 about the young Arabs who had begun to "rise up peacefully to gain the dignity, justice and self-rule that Bin Laden claimed could be obtained only by murderous violence." Less than two years later, he was lamenting that "the term 'Arab Spring' has to be retired," and comparing events in the region to the seventeenth century's massively destructive Thirty Years' War, in which areas of central Europe lost up to a third of their populations. Many other commentators throughout the world now write off the "Arab Spring" as a disaster and failure, pure and simple. But arguably, not the least of the problems bedeviling the Arab revolutionaries of the past two and a half years has been the absurdly inflated expectations they have had to live up to. Put simply, they have been asked to achieve the sort of rapid and complete success that hardly any predecessors, including in the West, ever managed. The same has been true of the "color revolutions" of the past decade in the former Soviet Union, which commentators like Melinda Haring and Michael Cecire, in a *Foreign Policy* article, were quick to label "terribly disappointing."

But think for a moment about the point which some other major revolutions had reached, two years or so after they began. Two years after the first shots of the American Revolution, Washington had not even gotten to Valley Forge, and victory looked very far off indeed. Two years after the beginning of the French Revolution, a huge and dangerous chasm was opening up between revolutionaries and their opponents, and that summer King Louis XVI severely exacerbated the conflict by trying to flee the country and join an enemy invasion force. Many more years of chaos and bloodshed would follow. Two years after the beginning of Latin American revolutions against Spain, the First Venezuelan Republic had already collapsed, with Spain reestablishing its authority. In each of these cases, the revolutionaries themselves also failed, often quite spectacularly, to behave in a manner that modern human rights activists would have approved. Even the West's paradigmatic example of a "good revolution," Britain's "Glorious Revolution" of 1688, was only "bloodless" and "quick" if one equates Britain with England, and fails to consider the extended series of destructive wars and civil wars that convulsed Ireland and Scotland for decades thereafter. The historian Steve Pincus has written that "far from being aristocratic, peaceful, and consensual," the Glorious Revolution was "popular, violent, and extremely divisive."

Why do most observers today seem so oblivious to the historical record of revolutions? What are the consequences of this obliviousness? And what might it actually take, in the way of concerted international action, to help revolutions like the one in Egypt take place in a way that accorded better with observers' ideal script?

In addressing the first of these questions, one place to start is with a rather odd development: current expectations about revolutions in fact represent something of a return to a very old understanding of such events. Up until the mid-eighteenth century, the word "revolution" meant little more than "political upheaval." Revolutions were held to be sudden, largely unpredictable, and largely uncontrollable. History books bore titles like "The Revolutions of England" or "The Revolutions of Persia," which told the story of countries' violent changes of dynasty almost as if they were a series of earthquakes. Revolutions were things that happened to people, not things that people themselves were seen as capable of consciously directing. A typical usage can be seen in the title of a pamphlet by the seventeenth-century English radical Anthony Ascham: *A Discourse: Wherein is examined, What is particularly lawful during the Confusions and Revolutions of Government*. Samuel Johnson's dictionary gave "revolution" as a synonym for "vicissitude." Tellingly, at the beginning of what we now call "the American Revolution," very few people actually described what was taking place as a "revolution." The word does not appear in the Declaration of Independence, or in Thomas Paine's great 1776 pamphlet *Common Sense* (except in reference to 1688 in Britain). In 1777, John Adams could write to his son John Quincy about "the late Revolution in our government," implying that the event was already finished and in the past.

These ideas began to change in the late eighteenth century, with significant consequences for the revolutions that would continue to convulse the Atlantic world for half a century. In America, by 1779, it was becoming clear that the political and social transformations set in motion by the war of independence had yet to run their course. In that year, Richard Henry Lee wrote to Thomas Jefferson about "the progress of our revolution," and Jefferson himself finally began to use the word in reference to American events. By 1780, John Adams was writing to his wife, Abigail, about "the whole Course of this mighty revolution," treating it as something still taking place. Yet even then, he did not present it as a process he himself had a hand in directing but as a great natural upheaval sweeping him along.

It was in France where the most decisive conceptual transformation took place. As the country's "old regime" began to crumble in 1789, observers immediately started to refer to what was going on as a "revolution" in the traditional (1688) fashion. Then, within a matter of months, they began speaking of it less as a sudden and cataclysmic *event* than as an ongoing *process*. But soon they went even further, to present "the" revolution as something that could be controlled and directed. Stanford University's Keith Baker, who has written luminously on this shift, characterizes it as one from revolution as "fact" to revolution as "act." Before this moment, the word "revolutionary" did not exist and would have made little sense to people, referring as it does to people or actions that actively drive revolutions forward. But in September 1790, the radical deputy Bertrand Barère referred to the demolition of the Bastille as "a truly revolutionary act," and soon his colleague Georges Danton was describing himself as an "a steadfast revolutionary." In 1792, Maximilien Robespierre renamed the executive committee of Paris's municipal government the "General Revolutionary Council," making it the first political institution in history to bear such a title.

Baker's colleague Dan Edelstein has added a further fascinating wrinkle to the story, noting that by 1792–1993, "the revolution" seemed to be taking on a life of its own, becoming, in the eyes of its advocates, a quasi-mythic force, and a source of legitimacy. After armed crowds stormed the royal palace in 1792 and overthrew Louis XVI, there were calls to put the king on trial. The radical Louis-Antoine Saint-Just, however, insisted that the people had already delivered a verdict through their revolutionary action. Any procedure that might exonerate the king therefore amounted to "putting the Revolution itself on trial." A year later, with France at war with much of Europe, Saint-Just made a remarkable speech demanding that the ruling National Convention formally suspend the new constitution it had just approved and declare the government "revolutionary" until the end of hostilities. He insisted on a full overhaul of the government's personnel and procedures, arguing that "the laws are revolutionary; those who execute them are not." And he added the following remarkable sentence: "Those who make revolutions in this world, those who wish to do good, should only sleep in the grave."

This new understanding of revolutions partly reflected the simple fact that the French Revolution was indeed a very different sort of event from its predecessors. Instead of its principal political changes coming to an end quickly, culminating in a document such as a declaration of independence, a process of explosive radicalism continued to build, leading to the deadly Reign of Terror of 1793–1794. But the new ways of thinking themselves provided a spur to radicalization, by giving the political actors of the day a way to see "revolutions" as exceptional historical moments in which ordinary practices and principles could be suspended. The leading figure of the Terror, Robespierre, developed an entire political theory on this basis. In a legislative report he wrote in the winter of 1793–1794, he distinguished between ordinary "constitutional" government, whose role was to govern a republic, and "revolutionary" government, whose role was to found the republic. In the latter, he argued, the state needed far greater leeway, both to protect its citizens and ensure that institutions would be given a durable form. "The Revolution," he thundered, "is the war of liberty against its enemies." Several of Robespierre's allies openly urged him to become a "dictator," a title still then associated with the ancient Roman military office of the name, and one they viewed favorably. In theory, the dictatorship would end once the republic had been durably founded and the revolution completed, but given the vastness of the radicals' ambitions, it was not clear when this goal would be reached. "Revolution" was not just becoming a process, but a utopian one that might extend into the future, indefinitely.

This new concept of revolution as what Hegel would call a "world-historical" event helped to justify the French revolutionaries' most outlandish projects. These included a new calendar that started with the birth of the French Republic; the attempt to replace Christianity either with state-sponsored atheism or Robespierre's deistic "Cult of the Supreme Being"; plans for universal education and charity; and, dangerously, the transformation of a war against other European powers into a crusade for universal human liberation. Robespierre and his allies went so far as to characterize "revolutions" as millennial projects that could literally change human nature. "The French people seem to have leapt two thousand years ahead of the rest of the human race," he mused in the spring of 1794. "It is tempting even to see them as a new species."

It is hard to exaggerate the hold this French model of revolution exerted over imaginations throughout the world in the nineteenth and twentieth centuries. In country after country, generations of would-be revolutionaries plotted to take power and instigate upheavals of similar, or even greater, ambition. Starting in the mid-nineteenth century, the model was potently combined with socialist visions of history as a story of class struggle, but the idea of revolution itself as an ongoing, consciously directed process remained much the same. In Russia, China, southeast Asia, Latin America, and the Middle East, self-proclaimed "revolutionary" regimes took power with goals of nothing less than transforming human beings into something new and better. In *Terrorism and Communism*, written at the height of the Russian Civil War, Leon Trotsky (a great admirer of the French revolutionary Terror) expressed sentiments very close to those of Saint-Just and Robespierre: "We were never concerned with ... prattle about the 'sacredness of human life.' We were revolutionaries in opposition, and have remained revolutionaries in power. To make the individual sacred we must destroy the social order which crucifies him. And this problem can only be solved by blood and iron." Mao Zedong, who repeatedly spoke of revolution as a long and arduous road, called its ultimate goal the changing of society and the establishment of a new sort of human freedom. (He also famously remarked that "a revolution is not a dinner party.")

Of course, in country after country these later revolutions produced even greater chaos and bloodshed than in France. In Russia and China and southeast Asia, the number of victims stretched into the millions. And finally, after the Russian Civil War, and Stalin's terror, and the Gulag, and the Chinese Cultural Revolution, and the Cambodian holocaust, the myth of a redemptive, world-transforming revolution lost its allure, as one moment of dreadful disillusionment followed another. By the late twentieth century, when the self-proclaimed revolutionary regimes of the Soviet bloc began to crumble, the dissidents who stepped into the breach generally refused the label of "revolution" altogether. As the Polish Solidarity leader Jacek Kuron informed French readers in a remarkable newspaper column in the summer of 1989—as the Poles were ousting the Communists and the French were marking the bicentennial of 1789—the age of revolution was over, and a good thing too.

In some cases, the exhaustion that has followed on bloody utopian experiments has itself created the conditions under which moderate democratic regimes could take root. In France, for instance, the events of 1789 marked the start of nearly nine decades of astonishing political turmoil. Monarchies, republics, and empires succeeded each other so rapidly that, according to one popular joke, libraries began storing copies of the constitution in the "periodicals" section. But finally, after the fall of Napoleon III during the Franco-Prussian War and one final outburst of radical utopianism in the doomed Paris Commune of 1871, a relatively stable, moderate republic was established, and lasted until the Nazi occupation of 1940. François Furet argued that in one sense the "French Revolution" lasted for nearly a century and only came safely "into port" with the Third Republic in the 1870s. But it is hard to argue that the turmoil and bloodshed was necessary to achieve this relatively limited goal. And, of course, in many other countries—Russia and China, most obviously—similarly long periods of revolutionary disruption have so far failed to produce similarly benign outcomes.

The long process of disillusionment helps explain why, today, revolutions are expected to be so quick and neat. If revolutionary movements no longer come bearing utopian hopes of redemption, then there is less need for them to extend indefinitely into the future. And indeed, most of the revolutions that have taken place since 1990, such as the "color revolutions" in the Soviet bloc and the revolutions of the Arab Spring, have aimed at relatively modest goals, in comparison with their French or Russian or Chinese predecessors: representative democracy, stability, the rule of law, human rights. The great exception to this rule, of course, are the Islamists who hope to impose their vision of Godly order on human societies. The Iranian Revolution was in this sense the last of the great line of utopian revolutions that began in the eighteenth century. Francis Fukuyama has been widely mocked for his 1989 *National Interest* article "The End of History," and his prediction that free-market democracy would become universal throughout the world. But with the exception of the Islamic world, free-market democracy has indeed overwhelmingly become the preferred political *model* in most countries. As Fukuyama himself put it: "At the end of history it is not necessary that all societies become successful liberal societies, merely that they end their ideological pretensions of representing different and higher forms of human society." At the heart of these earlier ideological pretensions was the idea that the means to these "higher forms" was a French-style revolution.

Of course, even where free-market democracy *has* become the preferred model, reality has often failed quite dismally to comply. Back at the time when Fukuyama wrote, nearly all observers woefully underestimated the

sheer difficulty of instituting such systems in countries plagued by poverty, by ethnic and religious differences, and lacking experience in the
rule of law or the toleration of opposition. The goal of a revolution may
be entirely clear: for example, to transform your country into something
resembling Finland. But how can that goal be reached?

This is a question that continues to bedevil political scientists. But the
experience of Europe, first after the end of World War II and then after
the collapse of communism, suggests at least one absolutely crucial condition: a proper structure of incentives for the population in question.
After the defeat of 1945, as recent historical work has stressed, the population of West Germany did not magically lose all attraction to Nazism.
But the population knew the victorious Allies would not tolerate any
serious attempts to revive Hitler's regime. And at the same time, they
quickly learned that moves toward democracy would reap them substantial rewards in the form of Marshall Plan aid, and inclusion in the
new Western military alliance. After 1989, the population of Poland had
relatively little to draw on in the way of democratic tradition. But it understood that free-market democracy would bring the massive rewards
of closer connections to western Europe—culminating in European
Union membership—and the protection of NATO. In both these countries, the incentives to build free market democracy proved more than
sufficient to overcome the natural tendency of factions within a state to
grab what they can for themselves and to do whatever possible to keep
their enemies out of power. In each country, it was generally recognized
that there was far more to gain from establishing democratic, free-market institutions.

In contrast, the populations of countries with recent revolutions have
had far weaker incentives to establish these sorts of institutions. Take
Georgia and Kyrgyzstan, homes of the "Rose" and "Tulip" revolutions
of 2003 and 2005. Observers like Haring and Cecire have had a simple
explanation for why these revolutions "failed" (their blunt verdict):
"Quite simply, the rule of law never took hold." In fact, they chide the
revolutionaries for making what they call "a key mistake: They took the
revolutions themselves as the apogee of democracy rather than focusing
on the hard, grinding work of institution-building." But what incentive
did the populations of Georgia or Kyrgyzstan have for respecting the

rule of law and democratic governance? What incentive have the competing groups in Egypt had since 2011? Has the United States been offering massive economic aid in return for progress toward free-market democracy? Has the European Union been offering a quick timetable for membership? The "hard, grinding work of institution-building" depends on a large degree of popular cooperation. But most people in these countries have not seen any great benefit to be obtained from such cooperation, while seeing all too clearly the dangers of allowing opponents to seize power, or of not taking the chance for their faction to enrich itself while it can.

Many different factors help populations to play by the rules, and to resist temptations to crush traditional enemies, or to treat the state as little more than an instrument of personal enrichment. Engrained habits of rigid social discipline, found in such widely different societies as colonial New England or early twentieth-century Japan, can serve to dampen forms of behavior that damage democratic cooperation. Inspiring, charismatic leaders committed to such cooperation—a Washington, or a Mandela—can play a critical role as well. The role of eloquently formulated revolutionary principles in inspiring loyalty to democratic institutions should not be underestimated. But these factors are rarely enough. Incentives matter hugely. Furthermore, providing a clear incentive structure is arguably just about the only possible way to "jump-start" democratic revolutions and bring them to successful, rapid conclusions, especially in countries that have long traditions of division, corruption, and intolerance.

In short, it is unreasonable, even rather absurd, to expect revolutions to usher in stable, human-rights-respecting representative democracies virtually overnight. It is condescending and cruel to scold countries for their "failure" to reproduce, within a span of a year or two, what took France, the United States, and many other countries decades or even centuries to achieve. We need to recognize that even the establishment of supposedly limited, nonutopian goals may well require a revolutionary process that lasts for many years, or decades, and that may involve a good deal of violence, chaos, and abuse along the way, including abuse by people we would like to think of as the good guys. In fact, just about the only way to avoid this kind of process (which itself may well eventually fail anyway) is to provide a serious external incentive structure, involving long-term commitments to large-scale aid and protection. Clearly, the West is in no position to start massive new aid programs to democratic revolutionaries across the world. But in that case, we have no cause to tout our own superiority over peoples just starting out on the long and difficult road that took us so very long to travel.

CODA: THE FRENCH DILEMMA

SOMETIMES, THE SHADOWS OF THE PAST can be deceptive. In France today, the country's history looms so prominently over the troubled present that it has become all too tempting to interpret every contemporary crisis as the product of specifically French historical patterns. Commentators proved particularly susceptible to this temptation in early 2015, after the horrific terrorist murders of staff members at the satirical magazine *Charlie Hebdo* and of shoppers at a Jewish supermarket. Was France facing a new upsurge of violent anti-Semitism? Surely the reason had to do with the country's long history of anti-Semitism and the troubled history of French Jewry. Has France proved frustratingly incapable of successfully "integrating" immigrant communities imbued with strong religious beliefs? Look for the reason in the long history of the French Republic's conflict with organized religion, going back all the way to the French Revolution, and to the brittle form of official secularism (*laïcité*) that emerged from this history.

As a historian, I can certainly understand this temptation, and have succumbed to similar ones many times. Still, as I reflected on the January 2015 attacks and their aftermath, in the midst of compiling the essays for this book, it was rather the limits of historical interpretation that struck me most forcefully. Perhaps the long history of the French nation-state was not actually the best prism through which to view events that might easily have taken place elsewhere in Europe. Perhaps these events are best seen as part of a broader story of the West's troubled relationship with the global South, and with the Muslim world in particular. If France seems, today, to lie at the center of this troubled relationship, perhaps the reason is above all just the sheer numbers of Muslims and Jews who live there, rather than anything unique to the country's past. Perhaps, indeed, in the midst of very understandable anxieties, French commentators and politicians reach for a historical interpretation because, by setting the challenges the country is facing into a strictly national framework, it makes them seem more limited, more manageable, and more susceptible to purely national solutions.

In short, I wrote this final essay, which offers a rather bleak account of France in 2015, to push back against the temptation to read the present through history and to point to where the shadows of the past do *not* fall.

———— ⚬ ————

The horrific attacks in Paris in January 2015 spurred a torrent of commentary, most of which addressed their specifically French context. Commentators, particularly in France itself, recalled the long traditions of French satirical writing behind the magazine *Charlie Hebdo*, which had published deliberately offensive cartoons of the Prophet Mohammed. They dissected the militant French form of secularism that goes by the name of *laïcité*, and the long history of French anti-Semitism—which seemed particularly relevant to the siege of a kosher market where a gunman killed four hostages after earlier murdering a policewoman. They discussed the legacies of French republicanism, French universalism, French racism, French colonization, French decolonization, French immigration, and French urban planning. Even when speaking of the effective segregation of immigrant communities in miserable public housing estates—a phenomenon common to many European countries—they tended to emphasize the specifically French features of this segregation. In particular, they pointed to the way French "republican" ideology refuses even to acknowledge ethnic and religious difference, hindering attempts to direct social programs toward particular communities.

Essay first published in *Dissent*, Spring 2015.

This emphasis on France and French history, however, has been misguided. Violence by young, alienated Muslims, directed at Westerners deemed to have insulted the Prophet Mohammed, and against Jews, is by no means a singularly French phenomenon. Think, in the first case, of the reaction to Salman Rushdie's *Satanic Verses*, or to the publication of satirical cartoons in Denmark's *Jyllands-Posten*. Terrorist attacks by radical Muslims have taken place across the West, and Muslims from many Western countries have undergone terrorist training in the Middle East. The sheer size of the Muslim community in France, plus the factors discussed by the commentators, may have made an attack there more likely. Nonetheless, what happened in Paris in January 2015 could easily have taken place in many other locations. It could quite conceivably have taken place in Denmark, a country without a history of colonization in the Muslim world, and with very different traditions of satire and secularism, immigration and race relations. (Indeed, scarcely a month after the killings in Paris, twin attacks took place in Copenhagen.)

Ascribing the events to specifically French factors is certainly understandable. Invoking larger, global changes that have swept across France from far parts of the globe can all too easily sound like the "France under siege" rhetoric of Marine Le Pen and her National Front party. Drawing attention to the homegrown causes of terrorism, on the other hand, not only counters this "siege" thesis, but does something that seems more constructive. It suggests that preventing further attacks may depend less on sending soldiers into the streets and increasing surveillance on Muslims than on improving social conditions for the French Muslim population and finding ways of making them feel part of the national community. Many commentators have called for improving life in suburban communities through improved teaching, better policing, special employment agencies, and better health care and transportation, all to fight against what Socialist prime minister Manuel Valls has called "this terrible feeling that there are 'second zone' citizens."

Such programs are woefully needed and long overdue. Valls was not wrong, soon after the attacks, to describe the situation of largely Muslim French suburban ghettos as "territorial, social, and ethnic apartheid." By many measures, notably school performance, French society is rapidly growing more unequal, with Muslim citizens (largely of North African descent) being pushed toward the bottom of the ladder. And, for that matter, many aspects of France's past are ripe for reevaluation, including the still unsettled legacy of French colonialism, and a rigidly secularist republican ideology originally devised in the nineteenth century to reinforce a frail new regime in a country largely inhabited by Catholic peasants.

But these programs and reevaluations should be undertaken for their own sake, not as a means to prevent further terrorism. In fact, they will probably do very little to prevent further terrorism. Linking questions of French social reform to terrorism, natural as it may seem in the wake of the January 2015 attacks, creates a host of confusions, and nowhere more so than on the left.

To be sure, the social misery, alienation, and frustration that fester in the French suburbs are not irrelevant to what happened in January 2015. They have nourished a rage that can easily turn white-hot. They have left many young Muslims dangerously sympathetic to radical Islamist rhetoric, and to a rejection of the values of the broader society. And while isolated, largely Muslim housing projects exist across much of Europe, the long and unhappy relationship between France and its Muslims, both in its former colonies and at home, has arguably stoked rage in ways absent in Denmark or Sweden (although, as noted, the threat of terrorism in these places is by no means negligible). Yet this rage has also been fed by changes that have swept through Islam over the past generation and have little to do with social conditions in France—it is in fact deeply condescending to assume that Muslims do nothing but react to the crimes and mistakes of the West. And rage can express itself in many ways, including simple criminality, self-destructiveness, and the large-scale rioting that convulsed the French suburbs most spectacularly in 2005. Carefully planned, premeditated murder requires much more than simple rage. It includes, very often, things that have little to do with the immediate roots of that rage. It is this crucial distinction that has far too often been ignored in the commentary on the attacks.

The abundant reporting done on the January 2015 terrorists—the brothers Saïd and Chérif Kouachi, who carried out the massacre at *Charlie Hebdo*, and Amedy Coulibaly, who attacked the Jewish market Hyper Cacher—bears out this point. Yes, these were men whom French society had failed on many levels. The Kouachis were mistreated by their parents as small children and ignored by social services, and moved on to bleak orphanages after the parents' early deaths; Coulibaly, meanwhile, grew up in one of the worst public housing projects in France—the isolated, depressing, crime-ridden "Grande Borne" estate fifteen miles south of Paris.

Yet, as left-wing commentators hastened to point out after the attacks, these men were also in no way typical of French Muslims, the vast majority of whom have no connection to Islamic extremism, let alone terrorism. Overall, in fact, French Muslims constitute one of the most unobservant, secularized Muslim communities on earth. Anger at French social conditions does not necessarily breed terrorism, even among those sympathetic to extremist rhetoric. Coulibaly, meanwhile, suffered from psychological illness and had a record of violent crime going back to his teens. Social programs aimed at improving the welfare and integration of large communities can often do very little to save young men with these sorts of problems.

The process that turned the three men from lost souls into terrorist killers depended in very large part on events far removed from France. Chérif Kouachi fell in with radical Islamists when in his early twenties. America's war in Iraq and the revelations of torture at Abu Ghraib fed his outrage and anger, as they did the outrage of young Muslims worldwide. Kouachi even planned to go and fight against the United States in Iraq, but the French authorities arrested him on his way out of the country. In prison, he and Coulibaly fell under the influence of a jihadist who had been radicalized in London. The Kouachi brothers later received military training in Yemen and pledged their loyalty to Al Qaeda in the Arabian Peninsula. Only at the end of this long process of indoctrination and training did they walk into the offices of *Charlie Hebdo*, ready to commit murder. Muslims from other countries have followed similar paths, a large number of them from relatively prosperous backgrounds. Mohamed Atta, the 9/11 terrorist, came from a middle-class Egyptian family and had an architecture degree. Nidal Hasan, who killed thirteen Americans at Fort Hood in 2009, was a psychiatrist and a major in the U.S. army.

In this sense, the January 2015 attacks did not in fact represent a significant break with long-standing patterns of terrorism on French soil. Since the end of the Algerian War of Independence against France in 1954–1962, France has experienced several waves of terrorism. Nearly all of them derived from conflicts centered well away from France's own borders, such as the civil wars in Lebanon in the 1980s and Algeria in the 1990s. Some of these did not involve homegrown fighters at all. Other prominent attacks have mostly had Jewish targets: El Al passengers, synagogues, a Jewish restaurant, a religious school. While taking place on French soil, they stemmed, like much other recent European anti-Semitic violence, principally from anger against Israel. They represented, in the perpetrators' eyes, an extension of the Middle Eastern conflict to France, more than an assault on France itself. (They were also largely unconnected to France's earlier history of anti-Semitism.)

Given this background, much of the commentary after the attacks has seemed sadly beside the point. Will improved education and health care in places like the "Grande Borne" prevent the radicalization of individuals? Even if, miraculously, they do, the next attacks in France might well come from perpetrators raised in Liège, or Malmö, or Cairo, or Algiers, wholly beyond the reach of French social policy.

As is so often the case after spectacular terrorist attacks, what countries don't do matters just as much, if not more, as what they do. Above all, it is crucial to avoid treating the January 2015 attacks as shots in a war waged on France. Despite the links to international terrorism, these seventeen deaths were not part of a war. They were vicious terrorist crimes. It was the murderers who saw themselves as holy warriors, and French society should do everything in its power to deny them this distinction. The government should institute reasonable security measures to protect people from similar crimes in the future. But these measures should stop well short of anything like military mobilization.

Similarly, the French should guard against any curtailment of civil liberties. And if the government does propose new social reforms, it should make clear that these steps are being undertaken for their own, very obvious reasons, and not because of the attacks. It is not as if the attacks were necessary to reveal what was wholly evident long before they took place. And what could serve as a more potent incentive for future terrorism than the thought that a few spectacular murders could turn an entire society on its head?

The example of the United States after 9/11 offers a very large cautionary tale here. As the historian Juan Cole has argued, Norway, which carefully resisted dramatic security measures after the massacres carried out by the disturbed, far-right killer Anders Brevik in 2011, provides a better model. The French Jewish population needs increased security, not simply because of the very real threat it faces from terrorism, but also because of a worrisome increase in less dramatic anti-Semitic violence.

And, for that matter, Muslim places of worship need increased security as well, particularly after Islamophobic attacks occurred in retaliation for what happened in January 2015. But apart from these specific cases, the French state needs to act with restraint.

Unfortunately, given the terrific emotional shock of the January 2015 events, apocalyptic language has been hard to resist. "Yes, France is at war, against terrorism, jihadism and radical Islamism," said Prime Minister Manuel Valls in a much noted speech, while Socialist president François Hollande, in a hugely unfortunate choice of words during a press conference, pledged to undertake a "reconquest" of minority communities. The huge, spontaneous demonstrations by nearly four million people across France on January 11, 2015, while eminently understandable, all too easily fed into the sense that the country was facing an apocalyptic threat, as opposed to a manageable security challenge.

As the shock of the attacks wears off, and the torrent of commentary subsides, the Socialists in particular have faced some very difficult choices. At first, these choices were not easily visible. Despite worries that Marine Le Pen would reap the greatest political benefit from the attacks, she did not. The depth of the shock instead led the French to rally around their elected leaders. The popularity of Hollande and Valls both soared. (Particularly in Hollande's case, it had nowhere to go but up.) But such patterns cannot continue indefinitely. In France, the most serious ideological divide no longer comes between the two major parties but between them on the one hand and those representing the extremes on both sides of the political spectrum on the other. Nicolas Sarkozy's party (descended from the Gaullists and later baptized "The Republicans") and the Socialists are both dominated by well-heeled graduates of the country's elite *grandes écoles*. They both favor policies both of free trade and free movement of peoples and of embedding France firmly in supranational networks and federations—above all the European Union. As the political scientist Sophie Meunier has put it, they are the parties of "ouverture" (opening) toward the world. A French friend of mine cynically refers to them (in English, deliberately) as "neoliberalism, and neoliberalism light." Both parties also remain firmly attached to the republican ideology of *laïcité* and of refusing to give ethnic or religious difference formal acknowledgment in the public sphere.

Those on the political extremes, by contrast—both the National Front and a number of extreme left factions (including Trotskyite groupings and the "Parti de Gauche" of former Socialist minister Jean-Luc Mélenchon)—are the parties of "fermeture" (closing). In very different ways, they fear and distrust globalization, which they blame for shackling French workers to forces and institutions beyond national control. They have no use for the European Union. The National Front has built its support through its hostility—often overtly racist—toward immigrant communities, and more recently toward migrant workers from central and eastern Europe. The far left's protests against global capitalism have proven less electorally effective but still appeal to as much as 15 percent of French voters.

Already in 2002 political radicals on both sides combined to cause an earthquake in French politics. In the first round of presidential voting, the extreme left siphoned enough support from Socialist candidate Lionel Jospin to push him behind Le Pen's father, Jean-Marie, the National Front's founder. In the runoff, the centrists united behind President Jacques Chirac to crush Le Pen Père. But the defeated candidate boasted, quite correctly, that henceforth the major parties would not be able to ignore his issues and his supporters. Indeed, Nicolas Sarkozy, Chirac's successor, built his political success in large part on the harsh stance he took toward rioters in the heavily Muslim suburbs, referring to them as "scum," and saying that the housing projects needed to be cleaned out with a high-pressure hose. On his election in 2007 he made the reinforcement of "national identity" one of his top priorities.

After François Hollande defeated Sarkozy in 2012, the National Front itself rose alarmingly. Marine Le Pen showed herself a considerably smoother operator than her blustering father, who was prone to embarrassing anti-Semitic outbursts. Indeed, she cannily courted French Jewish support, arguing that only the National Front could protect French Jews against anti-Semitism. She also took full advantage of President Hollande's weak leadership and romantic scandals, and France's deep, continuing economic malaise. By late 2014, polls showed her leading in first-round presidential voting, although she was still unable to beat the most likely centrists in runoffs. She also built up her party organization, which was crucial if the Front is to garner more than protest votes and have a presence in the French parliament. In February 2015, a National

Front candidate (who had once boasted of French civilization's superiority to "that of the Huns and the Bantus") barely lost an important by-election, in a seat recently held by a Socialist finance minister.

As the January 2015 events recede, and what Hollande has called the "spirit of January 11" (and its massive demonstrations) wanes, Marine Le Pen could well recover her former momentum. After all, nothing more perfectly brings together everything that her party has warned about in hysterical tones for decades than the specter of French-born Muslims, the descendants of immigrants, carrying out terrorist attacks at the behest of international jihadist organizations. If the Socialist government proves incapable of preventing additional attacks, Le Pen's popularity could soar.

And so, for a considerable time to come, the Socialists in particular will face difficult temptations. Finding their popularity tightly bound to the "spirit of January 11," they will do what they can to keep this spirit alive. One way to do so will be through the rhetoric of "war," and aggressive security measures. The other will be to push social programs, and the school measures aimed at the "integration" of minority communities.

But President Hollande's embarrassing talk of "reconquest" is only the most recent sign that the Socialists have not done much better than Sarkozy's party in paying attention to what most French Muslims actually want. It is difficult to generalize about French Muslims, because they come from many different ethnic, national, and social backgrounds. But by all indications, a sizeable majority of them reacted to the January events with the same horror as other French citizens—certainly, the leaders of the major mainstream Muslim organizations did. Most of them also want to further their communities' integration into French life. They generally have little affection, however, for the ideology of *laïcité*, which they see, correctly, as far less neutral than its advocates pretend. (The French state gives considerably more support to Catholic religious institutions and schools than to Muslim ones.) And in the wake of the attacks, many Muslims bristled at the idea of honoring, in the name of free speech, a magazine that they saw as deliberately offensive toward what they held most sacred. This attitude, it needs to be said, is different from the radical Islamism that appeals only to a small minority of French Muslims. Michel Houellebecq's 2015 novel *Submission*, in which a Muslim political party wins a presidential election and imposes Sharia law on France, is a fantastical satire, nothing more. Many French observers were shocked to find that large numbers of Muslim students refused to participate in the minute of silence for the January victims—it was a worrying sign of just how deep the alienation now runs in some communities. But the wrong sort of reforms can aggravate this alienation rather than alleviate it.

Socialist leaders, however, despite having won the votes of a large majority of French Muslims in 2012, and despite putting Muslims in prominent positions in the party and government, still seem to think that the most effective response to the problem of "integrating" minority communities consists of increased instruction in secularism, along with aggressive measures designed to counter discipline problems in schools (such as having students stand up when teachers enter the room). It is worth recalling that before the January 2015 attacks, the most ambitious "integrative" measures the French state undertook in this century were bans on wearing "prominent religious symbols"— that is, especially, Muslim headscarves—in schools and face coverings in public. Few things, in practice, have done more to provoke anger in Muslim communities and the sense that their members are unwelcome in France. These bans will certainly do nothing to decrease the susceptibility of the most alienated young Muslims to radical rhetoric.

These temptations for the Socialists will be hard to resist. But the best way to resist will be, even while honoring the "spirit of January 11," to keep the attacks themselves in strict perspective. Again, these seventeen murders, horrible as they were, did not constitute the opening salvos of a war. They were not an invasion. They posed no real threat to the "spirit of France," or to "freedom," whatever Prime Minister Valls may have said. They were not flares exposing deep social pathologies that had somehow previously escaped notice. They were not themselves the direct product of those pathologies. They represent a serious security threat, since it is entirely reasonable to assume that the dangerous organizations that sponsored them will try to attack again. But they are not an apocalyptic threat. To treat them as a crisis that calls the very nature of France into question is not simply a misguided, if natural, reaction, but exactly what the perpetrators hoped for.

ACKNOWLEDGMENTS

MY WIFE, DONNA LYNN FARBER, first suggested putting together these essays into a book. It was just one of the many, many good pieces of advice she has given me in the course of our marriage. I am grateful to her for it, and for so much else. I am also, as always, grateful to our children, Elana and Joseph, for their love, their support, and their music. *L'dor va-dor.*

The single greatest debt I incurred in writing these essays is to Leon Wieseltier, the former literary editor of *The New Republic* magazine. Leon commissioned and edited the majority of the essays collected here, and it was a privilege to appear in his pages. Without Leon, American literary journalism would be a much poorer, bleaker place. I am also grateful to the editors who commissioned and edited the other essays, especially at the *London Review of Books*. A particular note of thanks to Dan Edelstein, who read through the book manuscript with a very keen eye.

I owe an enormous amount to my teachers Patrice Higonnet and Robert Darnton, who guided my first ventures into French history. It has been my good fortune to have teachers and colleagues who encouraged my writing for general interest publications, and never saw it as inconsistent with a serious academic career.

My parents, Daniel Bell and Pearl Kazin Bell, were both wonderful writers, and provided examples that I have always tried to live up to, in this as in so many other respects. My mother, who was physically incapable of composing a bad sentence, taught me from very early on to love and respect the English language, and whatever I have managed to achieve as a writer I owe above all to her.

I published my first book with Oxford University Press USA and am delighted to be publishing this most recent one with them as well. My great thanks to its terrific history editors, and especially to Tim Bent, who has enthusiastically supported this project from the start. I was lucky to have the assistance of OUP's Alyssa O'Connell in putting this book together and moving it toward publication.

Paul Lemerle (1927–2010) was a brilliant, kind, generous, enormously decent man who had a long and distinguished career in government, notably in the Commissariat Général du Plan, as deputy secretary-general of the OECD, and at the United Nations. He exemplified everything that is best about France and its *service public*. When I started visiting France regularly, Paul and his wonderful wife, Monique, opened their home to me, treated me as part of their family, and taught me in all sorts of ways about their country. I have counted them and their daughters as great friends, and owe the family more than I can say. This book is dedicated to Paul's memory, and to the Lemerle family, *ma famille française*.

CREDITS

I GRATEFULLY ACKNOWLEDGE THE PUBLICATIONS where these essays originally appeared for permitting me to reprint them here. Some of the essays have been lightly edited to eliminate repetition.

The New Republic

1. "Paristroika," July 11, 1988.
2. "The Never-Ending 'Herstory,'" January 27, 1997.
3. "Paris Blues," September 1, 1997.
4. "Big," April 6, 1998.
5. "The Ordeal of Legitimacy," February 28, 2000.
6. "Words and Tumbrels," November 26, 2001.
7. "Cherchez la Femme," April 15, 2002.
8. "Just Like Us," May 17, 2004.
9. "Brushes with Power," August 22, 2005.
10. "The Shorn Identity," November 28, 2005.
11. "Bicycle History," February 7, 2008.
12. "Becoming France," April 1, 2009.
13. "The Colbert Report," October 7, 2009.
14. "Was Tolstoy Right?" May 12, 2010 (online only).
15. "Pogroms of Words," August 27, 2010.

16. "La Même Chose," July 3, 2011 (online only).
17. "Conspiracy Porn," November 9, 2011.
18. "Where Do We Come From?" February 8, 2012.
19. "The Conductor," April 5, 2012 (online only).
20. "When French Irrationality Was Deadly," May 31, 2014.
21. "The Humanist as Hero," September 26, 2014.

The London Review of Books

1. "Who Mended Pierre's Leg?" November 11, 1999.
2. "When the Barracks Were Bursting with Poets," September 6, 2001.
3. "Enlightenment's Errand Boy," May 23, 2003.
4. "Violets in Their Lapels," June 23, 2005.
5. "Twilight Approaches," May 11, 2006.
6. "One Does It Like This," November 16, 2006.
7. "Un Dret Egal," November 16, 2007.
8. "Handsome, Charming…" October 23, 2009.

The Nation

1. "Profane Illuminations," December 5, 2005.
2. "The Collaborator," December 11, 2006.

The New York Times Sunday Book Review

1. "Bastille Days," April 18, 1999.
2. "Poison Pen," April 30, 2000.
3. Review of Robert Gildea, *Marianne in Chains* (commissioned, but not published).

The New York Times Magazine

"The Peace Paradox," February 4, 2007.

The New York Review of Books

"A Very Different French Revolution," July 10, 2014.

The Guardian

"The President as Narcissist," November 28, 2013.

The National Interest

"Inglorious Revolutions," January/February 2014.

Foreign Policy

"Why We Can't Rule Out an Egyptian Reign of Terror," February 7, 2011 (online only).

Books&Ideas.net

"The Fault Is Not in Our 'Stars,' but in Ourselves," January 8, 2015 (online only).

Oxford University Press and the British Academy

"The Culture of War in Europe, 1750–1815," originally published in *The Crisis of the Absolute Monarchy*, edited by Julian Swann and Joël Félix, Proceedings of the British Academy 184 (Oxford: Oxford University Press, 2013), © The British Academy 2013.

Dissent Magazine

"The French Dilemma," spring 2015.

INDEX

abortion, 322
Abu Ghraib, 389
Académie Française, 92, 231
  literature and, 21
  Pierre Nora on, 21–22
An Account of Corsica (Boswell), 229
Action Française, 305, 329
Adams, John, 284, 398
Adams, John Quincy, 398
Adorno, Theodor, 99, 123
Africa
  France and, 320
  immigrants from, 383
The Age of Conversation (Craveri), 79
"Age of Reason," 63–64
Agoult, Marie d', 278
Alembert, Jean le Rond d', 83, 129
Alexander, Apelles, and Campaspe
  (David), 240
Alexander I of Russia, 245, 253
Alexander the Great, 255
Algeria, 275, 280
  conflict in, 24
  revolutionaries, 383
Algerian War of Independence, 410

Allen, Woody, 283–84, 380
Alsace-Lorraine, 275
The Ambassadors (James), 283
American Civil War, 107
American revolution, 28, 120–21, 307
  beginning of, 397
Americans in Paris: A Literary Anthology
  (Gopnik), 287
Amiens, Peace of, 269
Anabasis (Xenophon), 232
Ancien Régime, 79, 83, 85, 92, 114, 117
Angell, Norman, 197
The Anger of Achilles (David), 239
"anti-fête," 262, 267
Anti-Semitic League, 319
The Anti-Semitic Moment, 319
anti-Semitism, 7–8, 332
  and Raymond Barre, 33
  Catholicism and, 305, 320
  Charlie Hebdo and, 406
  of Louis Darquier, 340–41
  and Denis Diderot, 30
  of Édouard Drumont, 33–34
  in France, 31, 35–36, 318
  in Germany, 33